S0-BZE-342

HEROES AND HEROINES

BARNES
&NOBLE
BOOKS
NEW YORK

Copyright © 1970, 1979, 1989 by The University Society, Inc.
This edition copyrighted 1994 by Barnes & Noble, Inc.
All rights reserved.

This edition published by Barnes & Noble, Inc.,
by arrangement with David C. Beasley, Sr.

1994 Barnes & Noble Books

ISBN 1-56619-577-2
Printed and bound in the United States of America
M 9 8 7 6 5 4 3 2

ACKNOWLEDGEMENTS

Grateful acknowledgement and thanks are extended to the following publishers, authors, periodicals, and individuals for permission to reprint copyrighted material:

Appleton-Century-Crofts, Inc.—"A Great Life-Saver" from *More Than Conquerors*, by Ariadne Gilbert. Copyright, 1914, The Century Company. Condensed by permission of the publishers, Appleton-Century-Crofts, Inc.

American Junior Red Cross News—"Jacob Riis—American Citizen," and "Charles Steinmetz—American Scientist," by Catherine Cate Coblentz. "The Insects' Homer," by Eleanor Doorly. "Albert Schweitzer, Man of Peace," by Charlie May Simon.

Beckley-Cardy Company—"The Man Who Created New Plants," by Olive W. Burt. "Champion of Homeless Boys," by Elma Martens, and "Conquerors of the Air," by Carrie Esther Hammil, from *Builders for Progress*, copyright, 1950, by Beckley-Cardy Company. Reprinted with their permission.

Bobbs-Merrill Company, Inc.—"The Explorer Who First Sailed Around the World," from *A Book of Heroes*, by Dorothy Heiderstadt, copyright 1954. Used by special permission of the publishers, The Bobbs-Merrill Company, Inc.

Cambridge University Press—"Brother to All the World," "The Maid Who Saved France," and "He Was Disgraced for Telling the Truth," from *Great People of the Past*, by Rhoda Power, published by The Cambridge University Press in England in 1942, and reprinted by their special permission.

Children's Activities—"How a Little Boy Entertained Company," by Carrie Esther Hammil, and "Sacajawea, the Indian Girl Who Guided Lewis and Clark," by Marion Gridley.

W. W. Coblentz—For permission to reprint "Jacob Riis—American Citizen," and "Charles Steinmetz—American Scientist," by Catherine Cate Coblentz.

Marion Gridley—"Sacajawea, the Indian Girl Who Guided Lewis and Clark."

Carrie Esther Hammil—"How a Little Boy Entertained Company."

Hart Publishing Company—"Votes for Women" by Joanna Strong and Tom B. Leonard from *A Treasury of the World's Great Heroines*, copyright 1951, by Hart Publishing Company. "The Four Chaplains," by Joanna Strong and Tom B. Leonard, from *A Treasury of Hero Stories*, copyright 1949, by Hart Publishing Company and used with their permission.

Highlights for Children, Columbus, Ohio—"He Grew Riches from Peanuts—George Washington Carver," by Mabelle E. Martin.

Alfred A. Knopf, Inc.—"Round the World to China," "The Spaniards Hunt for Gold," and "The Frenchmen Trade for Furs," reprinted from *And There Was America* by Roger Duvoisin, copyright 1938 by Alfred A. Knopf, Inc. "Marco Polo Tells About China," reprinted from *They Put Out to Sea* by Roger Duvoisin, copyright 1944, by Alfred A. Knopf, Inc.

J. B. Lippincott Company—"The Boy Who Loved Birds," and "The Boy Who Liked Puppets," by Carolyn Sherwin Bailey. Reprinted by permission of the publisher, J. B. Lippincott Company, from *Tell Me a Birthday Story* by Carolyn Sherwin Bailey. Copyright 1931, 1932, 1933, 1934, 1935 by J. B. Lippincott Company.

Mabelle E. Martin—"He Grew Riches from Peanuts—George Washington Carver."

Random House, Inc. "The Father of His Country," abridged from *George Washington*, by Bella Koral. Reprinted by permission of Random House, Inc. Copyright 1954, by Random House, Inc. "Of the People, by the People, and for the People," abridged from *Abraham Lincoln*, by Bella Koral. Reprinted by permission of Random House, Inc. Copyright 1952, by Random House, Inc.

Row, Peterson and Company—Illustrations by Robert Lawson for "He Chained the Lightning," from *Real People: Benjamin Franklin*. Copyright 1950, by Row, Peterson and Company and used with their permission.

Charlie May Simon—"Albert Schweitzer, Man of Peace."

A Word to Parents about this Volume

HEROES AND HEROINES

THE STORIES in this volume—all true—spotlight great historical events and characterize the men and women who have made outstanding contributions to history, science, invention, literature, religion, or humanity itself.

Most are Americans, but other nations are represented too. The editors have aimed at making young Americans prouder of their country for knowing more about it, but aware, too, that other nations are equally proud of their heroes and that the greatest of all heroes have risen above nationalism for the benefit of people everywhere.

The book begins with some of our earliest "Explorers and Pathfinders"— daring adventurers from the old world who suffered incredible hardships to discover a new one: the Vikings, Marco Polo, Christopher Columbus, and many others.

Next are the men and women who settled the continent we now call North America and those who helped to make it a "Sweet Land of Liberty." This section takes our readers from the landing of the Pilgrims on American soil all the way up to the present era.

"Lives of Kindness and Courage" is devoted to humanitarians who have benefited all mankind. They range from that early brother to all the world, St. Francis of Assisi, to the modern man of peace, medicine, and music, deemed by many also to be a saint, Albert Schweitzer.

"Great Names from Foreign Lands" includes a sampling of heroes and heroines from Europe, Asia, and South America: Joan of Arc, Simon Bolivar, Giuseppe Garibaldi, Sun Yat-Sen, Mohandas Gandhi, Winston Churchill.

Under "Dreamers and Doers in Science and Invention," we find a variety of scientists who have made our lives richer and happier. These come up through the ages from Gutenberg, the inventor of printing, to Einstein who ushered in the Atomic Age.

Finally, under "Writers of Stories Children Love," we tell the stories of a few whose lives we believe would interest children: Charles Dickens, Hans Christian Andersen, Mark Twain, Robert Louis Stevenson.

Illustrators of this Volume

LAWRENCE DRESSER, *The Quaker Who Founded Pennsylvania; Two Explorers of the Great Northwest; The Boston Tea Party; "I Only Regret That I Have But One Life to Lose for My Country;" The Gold Rush; He Conquered Polio and Became President of the United States; Because of Him the Blind Can Read; Newspaper Wonder; The Man Who Could Make Anything; How We came to Have Telephones; Conquerors of the Air*

ELTON FAX, *The Fabulous Adventures of an Old-World Traveler; Danger Was His World; The Indian Girl Who Guided Lewis and Clark; He Made His Peace with God; "Give Me Liberty or Give Me Death;" He Made Freedom His Job; Hero of Texas; Man of Peace, and Medicine, and Music; He Grew Riches From Peanuts*

E. HARPER JOHNSON, *Around the World to China; The Black-Robed Priest and the Algonquins; "Of the People, by the People, and for the People;" His Children Thought He Was Fun; "Duty, Honor, Country;" The Lady with the Lamp; Champion of Homeless Boys; Deaf, Dumb, and Blind, She Spoke to the World; The Narrow Escapes of a Chinese Patriot; India's Hero of Non-Violence; But He* DID *Take All the Prizes; He was Disgraced for Telling the Truth; A Great Life-Saver; In Insects He Saw a World of Beauty and Truth; The Man Who Created New Plants; Miracle Man of Electricity; They Discovered Radium for Humanity; Scientific*

Genius of the Atomic Age; The Boy Who Liked Puppets; Barefoot Boy; He Had to Go to Bed by Day; They Helped to Free the Slaves

ROBERT LAWSON, *He Chained the Lightning*

VIRGINIA RUPP, *He Had a Dream—a Wonderful Dream, "Ask Not What Your Country Can Do For You—Ask What You Can Do For Your Country."*

HARVE STEIN, *The Story of the Vikings; The Spaniards Hunt for Gold; The Explorer Who First Sailed Around the World; The Frenchmen Trade for Furs; Indians and Pioneers; The Pilgrims and the First Thanksgiving; He Went to Jail Rather than Lie; Paul Revere's Ride; The Father of His Country; President for All the People; Old Hickory; The President Who Loved Adventure; He Sent Food to the Hungry; Brother to All the World; Parks and Homes in Place of Slums; His Life Was a Field of Honor; The Maid Who Saved France; Hero of South America; He Fought to Set Italy Free; Thanks to Him, We All Have Books; How a Little Boy Entertained Company; The Boy Who Wanted to Know; He Wrote Great Stories That Make Us Laugh and Cry*

GEORGE WOODBRIDGE, *He Discovered a Great American River; The Long Hard Trail to Oregon; Fighters for Freedom; A French Nobleman to Our Rescue; The Boy Who Loved Horses; Fighting Hero of the South; Pioneer American Battlefield Nurse; The Boy Who Loved Birds*

Table of Contents

In this volume, since the subjects in each *group heading* appear in approximately *historical* order, we have listed them in the same order in the Table of Contents.

ALPHABETICAL INDEX *of the contents of all 9 volumes will be found at the end of this volume.*

"Sweet Land of Liberty"

Writers of Stories Children Love

Lives of great men all remind us
  We can make our lives sublime,
And departing, leave behind us
  Footprints on the sands of time,

Footprints that perhaps another,
  Sailing o'er life's solemn main,
A forlorn and shipwrecked brother,
  Seeing, shall take heart again.

Let us then be up and doing
  With a heart for any fate;
Still achieving, still pursuing,
  Learn to labor and to wait.

— from A PSALM OF LIFE
By Henry Wadsworth Longfellow

Early Explorers and Pathfinders

The Story of the Vikings

By Bella Koral

A THOUSAND years ago, as we know from the Norse sagas, the bold Vikings of the North roamed the seas for adventure, plunder or trade. There lived then, in Norway, a man named Eric the Red. Eric was brave and strong. He could drive a nail into a plank with his bare fists. He got his name from the color of his beard—and he had a temper to match it.

After a violent feud he was exiled from Norway and sailed with his family to Iceland. He lived there peacefully for a while but it was not long before another quarrel forced him to flee Iceland, too.

Eric had heard rumors of westward-lying lands—so he called on his ancient Norse gods, Odin and Thor, to favor his journey, and, with a few hardy companions, he sailed west into unknown seas.

The Vikings were the best shipbuilders of their time. Their boats were called dragon-boats. They were long and shallow and had the head of a dragon carved at the bow while the tail of a dragon lifted above the water at the stern. The dragon-boat had a single square sail, striped red and yellow, that was raised and lowered by ropes made of walrus hide. The shields of the Viking sailors, about sixteen to each side, over-lapped one another along the vessel's sides.

The ship carried a set of thirty oars that could be run through holes in its side. The oars were used when the ship needed to make headway against strong winds or to coast along the shore. When the oars were not in use, the holes in the side of the ship were closed by shutters. For steering the dragon ship, a long oar was fastened to the right side near the stern.

Though the Vikings had no maps, compasses, or other instruments to help them guide their ships, they were the greatest sailors who had ever braved the Atlantic. The Viking pilots kept their vessels on their course by watching the sun and stars and by following the flights of birds.

Eric sailed toward the setting sun and at last found a great island. Snow and ice covered most of the land but the banks of the fjords, or bays, were green with grass and there was plenty of wild game.

Eric sailed back to Iceland for his wife and family. He and his companions told their friends of the seals, walruses, reindeer, and polar bears they had seen. "The land is much like Iceland, with plenty of green grass for our cattle and horses, so I call it Greenland," Eric said.

LEIF ERICSON. Icelandic explorer. Son of Eric the Red, discoverer of Greenland. Leif sailed West in about the year 1000 and discovered a country he called Vineland, (perhaps Labrador or Newfoundland). Introduced Christianity into Greenland and settled it with Norwegians. Date of his death is unknown.

He believed such a promising name would attract others to follow him, and so it did. More and more people who heard of the new land wanted to settle there.

Eric had three sons. One was called Thorsten, the second Thorwald, and the third Leif. Leif was a sturdy boy with keen, icy-blue eyes. He was born with an intense love for the sea and had learned to sail almost before he could walk. When Leif heard his father's tales about Greenland, he could hardly wait to go there. He helped make Eric's ship ready for the trip. The dragon's head was varnished and polished like new. It seemed to nod as it bobbed up and down in the water.

On a spring day of the year 986, twenty-five ships set sail from two of Iceland's western fjords for Greenland. People and animals were closely crowded. Each family with its thralls, or bondservants, carried its most precious possessions, along with food and supplies for the long journey.

Leif stood in the prow of his father's ship. He loved the feel of the cold wind whipping at his hair and the sting of salt spray on his cheeks.

One day they were caught in a heavy fog. They could see only a few feet ahead. "Watch out for icebergs!" Eric shouted to the men in the ship nearest him. The warning was repeated from ship to ship.

"You, Leif, keep a sharp watch," he called to his son, standing at the dragon's-head prow. "Your eyes are the best!"

Leif, proud of his responsibility, peered ahead through the curtain of fog. Suddenly a ghostly figure appeared.

"Ice!" Leif screamed the warning. Eric swung the ship aside. It almost crashed into the one behind. Mountainous waves rushed toward the ships. Icebergs crashed into each other with a dreadful din while the winds howled. Women screamed; children cried. Sheep bleated pitifully and cattle bellowed in terror.

Often Leif saw the great icy shapes just in time to give warning. They were not always able to escape without scraping against the icebergs. All day the boats tossed about in the rough waters and fog.

Eric never moved from the rudder. He steered his ship safely through all the danger. But many of the other ships sank or gave up and returned to Iceland. When the fog lifted and the icebergs drifted away, Eric found that only thirteen ships besides his own remained of the twenty-five that had started the voyage.

The red-bearded Viking steered into a quiet fjord. Grass and flowers bloomed along its banks. The travelers and their animals could hardly wait to get their feet on firm ground again. "Here we shall build," said Eric. Some of the other chieftains sailed to other fjords and took land for themselves.

Eric called his place Brattahlid. Here he settled with his wife, children, kinsmen, friends and thralls, and built barns and a stone house about a hundred feet long. Stones and sod were used for building for neither Greenland nor Iceland had any trees to supply timber.

More and more colonists came to settle in Greenland. They brought their flocks to graze in the pasture lands. Many became fishermen and hunters.

Young Leif grew strong and skillful: He could throw a spear and swing an axe like a man, and he fished, swam, and rode a horse with the best of them. He caught a polar bear and taught it to dance on its hind legs

when he sang to it. Every time the bear did a trick Leif slipped it a silver herring.

But Leif's greatest pleasure was to sail in the dragon ships and to talk to sailors and merchantmen who came from Iceland and Norway. These men, as well as his father, taught the boy the tricks of navigating, the ways of winds and ocean currents off the Iceland and Greenland coasts, and the dangers of calms, storms, and icebergs.

Once a sailor named Bjarni told how storm and fog had blown him off his course on his voyage to Greenland and how he had sighted lands, sandy beaches, flat rocks and even forest lands far to the south and west.

"Didn't you land anywhere at all?" asked Leif in amazement.

"No," replied Bjarni. "It was too late in the winter. I wanted to hurry to Greenland before ice formed in the fjords. I didn't want to risk my ship."

"To think of coming to a strange, new land men have never heard of—and not even to set foot on it!" thought Leif. Bjarni, the incurious, became something of a laughing-stock among the Vikings. Leif never forgot his story.

During the long winter evenings Eric gave great feasts in his halls and there beside the fire, Leif listened to tales told by the skalds. They were the minstrels and news gatherers of those times. They told sagas of heroes, of battles, and great voyages on stormy seas. The stories filled young Leif with a restless desire to see new places.

The Greenland colony prospered. By the time Leif had become a young man, it seemed to him that it was time for him to set out upon his adventures. He went to Eric, his father, and asked for a ship.

"Where do you want to go?" asked Eric.

"West," said Leif. "West, where Bjarni went."

Leif hoisted sail and steered straight for the West. After they had been at sea for several days a great storm arose. The striped sail bellied and thundered in the Atlantic gale. The waves tossed the dragon ship about as if it were a nutshell. Black clouds hid the sky all day and the stars at night, and the hissing spray drenched the men in the open vessel. When the wind died down, a heavy fog lay over them for days.

Leif sailed on. His men trusted him. They knew he was a fine navigator.

One day the fog lifted and Leif saw a beach of shining sand with a great forest of splendid trees down to the very shore. A great cheer rang out from prow to stern of the dragon ship. Leif and his men cast anchor and went ashore. They had been at sea for forty days and when they touched the dew upon the grass and then put their hands to their mouths, it seemed as if they had never tasted anything as sweet. It was indeed a New World.

Leif divided his men into two parties who took turns exploring and staying in camp to guard their ship and supplies.

The exploring parties came back with glowing tales. "What a cargo of logs we'll take back to Greenland in the autumn!" they said. They found salmon leaping in the streams, bigger than they had ever seen, and rabbits and deer scurrying through the woods. All summer Leif and his men lived in great plenty enjoying the bounty of the land. But not once did they ever see another human being.

One day, one of Leif's men came into camp shouting, "I have found vines and grapes!" Because of these vines and grapes Leif called the land he had found, Vineland-the-Good. Today scholars believe Leif's Vineland was the coast of Nova Scotia or New England.

When fall came, the Vikings gathered the grapes which they dried into raisins, cut vines, and felled timber to make a great cargo for their ship. They sailed out to sea and had fair weather until Greenland was sighted once again. Then Leif suddenly changed his course. One of his men asked him, "Why do you head the ship so much into the wind?"

"I see something ahead," answered Leif. As the dragon ship came closer, the Vikings found a reef with some fifteen shipwrecked people. Leif saved them all. From then on his men called him "Leif the Lucky."

He sailed on to Brattahlid and received a royal welcome from Eric the Red. Far and wide were spread the tales of Leif's adventures and the news of Vineland, the paradise to the west.

In the year 1003 there came to Greenland from Iceland a man called Thorfinn Karlsefni, a name that means "he's quite a man." He was indeed a merchantman of great enterprise and daring. He married Gudrid, Leif's sister-in-law, and they decided to make their home in Vineland.

Two ships heavily loaded with seafarers, household goods and cattle, carried all the things necessary to start a colony. The seafarers numbered about one hundred and sixty men, women, and children—the first European immigrants to sail for America.

They sailed south and west till they came to a land of mighty forests and deep fjords. They called it "Markland" (Forestland). Then they came to an island so covered with birds and eggs that they could hardly walk without stepping on eggs. Karlsefni's party wintered near this place. There, in a cabin, was born Snurri, the son of Gudrid and Thorfinn Karlsefni, the first white child born on American soil.

One day when the Norsemen were peacefully going about their tasks, they saw a fleet of canoes coming up the bay paddled by a band of swarthy Indians they called Skraellings. The Skraellings stared at the fair-haired Norsemen who held out their shields toward them as a sign of friendship, and then paddled away.

Not till the next spring did the dark men return. Then they offered fine furs in exchange for the cream, cheese, and butter the Norsemen gave them. They had never tasted such food before and they licked their fingers in delight. The Skraellings pointed to some red cloth. Thorfinn cut it up into narrow strips and traded it for furs. The Skraellings tied the strips around their heads and strutted about proudly.

Now Thorfinn had a large bull that was grazing out of sight in the woods. Suddenly with a furious bellow he charged at the Skraellings who had, of course, never seen such an animal. The terrified savages took to their canoes.

But three weeks later the Skraellings came back, howling their war yells. The Norsemen went to meet them. A flight of arrows came toward them from the canoes. But the Skraellings had an even more terrible weapon—a huge rock wrapped in leather that they catapulted through the air. It landed among the Norsemen with a terrible crash. A bloody battle followed—and a great fear came over the Vikings. The Norsemen no longer felt safe in Vineland. They were too greatly outnumbered by the Skraellings.

When spring came, they loaded their dragon ships with timber, furs, and grapes, and sailed homeward. Karlsefni led his wife and their son Snurri back in triumph to Brattahlid.

Eric the Red had died, full of years and daring deeds. Leif now sat at the head of the table there. And as long as he lived and long after his death, Leif the Lucky, the first white man who set foot on American soil, was honored and remembered.

But Vineland, where the Skraellings were still to enjoy their land for many many years in peace, was waiting to be discovered again as America.

The Fabulous Adventures of an Old-World Traveler

MARCO POLO

By Roger Duvoisin

IN the year 1260, two merchant brothers of Venice named Maffeo and Nicolo Polo sailed from the city of Constantinople to trade in the land of the Tartars. They carried with them a great many beautiful jewels which they hoped to exchange for a chestful of gold.

They traveled far beyond the Black Sea, until they finally came to the great city of Bokhara, in Asia.

"I do not think any European merchant has ever come so far into this unknown land," said Nicolo.

"Certainly not," replied Maffeo.

One day, there came into Bokhara a very important looking gentleman, dressed in a long silk robe embroidered with gold. One hundred horsemen rode behind him, their lances held straight up, like the pickets of a fence. This stranger was an ambassador from Persia on his way to Peking, in China. Of course, Nicolo and Maffeo could not help noticing him and before long they became such good friends that he said to them:

"Why don't you come with me to Peking where the new Khan of the Tartars has built his new Palace? The Khan will be pleased to see you. He will give you lots of presents and you will do some good trading in his capital."

"Thank you very much," answered Nicolo. "It is a good idea."

Thus it came about that Nicolo and Maffeo, instead of going home, went in quite the opposite direction.

The great new Khan, whose name was Kublai, was truly glad to see the merchants from Venice. After their long journey, he received and feasted them like princes.

As Europe was as mysterious to Kublai Khan as China was to Nicolo and Maffeo, he asked them to tell all they could about their homeland.

Nicolo and Maffeo answered so well that the Khan, judging them to be very clever men, asked them to go back as his ambassadors to the Pope.

And so Nicolo and Maffeo, who had come to China as traders, now left it as ambassadors.

During their journey homeward, the heat in the desert, the ice and snow in the mountains, and the flooded rivers in the valleys, brought them so much hardship that years elapsed before they got back among their countrymen.

There they were told that the Pope had just died and so they had no one to whom to give the Khan's letter.

Nicolo's wife also had died. But the merchant's grief was made less by the sight of the fine looking son, Marco, who had been born during his absence.

Marco was already fifteen years old, so

MARCO POLO. Traveler and explorer. Born in Venice, Italy, 1254(?). Traveled with father and uncle to China and entered service of the Kublai Khan (Emperor of China), 1275. Left China, 1292. Returned to Venice, 1295. Wrote the story of his adventures in Genoese prison 1298. Died 1324.

long had Nicolo's trading trip lasted.

Nicolo and Maffeo were very impatient to return to China. But for two years they waited until at last a new Pope was elected. He was called Gregory.

"Nicolo and Maffeo," said the new Pope, "I will give you two beautiful crystal vases, and my benediction for the Khan."

The merchants set out for China with some oil from the lamp that hung over the Holy Sepulchre, and the crystal vases. And they took with them Marco, Nicolo's son.

Marco was now seventeen years old and a very bright boy who enjoyed looking at people and things about him.

During the trip through Asia he kept his eyes wide open so he wouldn't miss the wonders of the lands he passed through: strange costumes and ways of the people; animals and trees unlike anything he had ever seen or heard of; palaces and cities more marvelous than those in dreams.

Because he observed so well, and even took notes of what he saw, he was able, later, to write a book about China which reads like the most beautiful fairy tale.

In traveling across Persia, now on horseback, now on camels, now astride donkeys, Marco, who liked animals, did not forget to write about the strong Persian ox which had a lump on his back and kneeled down like the camel to let himself be loaded; about the big sheep, as big as donkeys, whose tails were so thick and fat that they seemed to have two heads, one in front and one behind; and about the wild asses which browsed among groves of date trees.

Since he wanted to be a merchant like his father, Marco was much interested in the beautiful things the Persian craftsmen made in their open shops.

But as Marco, Nicolo, and Maffeo were traveling through this region a great band of robbers attacked them. They killed many men or captured them and carried them off to sell into slavery. But the three Venetians were lucky enough to escape.

Beyond Persia, they climbed up into the mountains of Afghanistan where many towns had been torn down by Alexander's soldiers, and destroyed again later by Genghis Khan's horsemen. The Venetians rested for a year in a cool mountain spot for the hard trip through the hot plains of Persia had made Marco ill.

This was as far east as Alexander had come with his tired army. For Marco, his father, and his uncle, it was just half of their journey. Ahead of them lay a land which had never before been heard of by Europeans; a treeless country of mountains and plains, which is called the "Roof of the World."

"The mountains are so high," wrote Marco, "that no birds fly near their summits; on their sides live big sheep with horns four feet long. Out of these horns the shepherds make ladles, and vessels to hold their food, and even fences to keep wolves from getting at their sheep and goats."

After many months of travel over dangerous mountains and deserts, Marco, Nicolo, and Maffeo finally came into China.

It was summertime when they arrived at the city of Shangto where the Khan waited for them in his marble palace. He received them surrounded by his officers and guards all dressed in green, purple, red, yellow, and blue silk robes.

"Rise up, my friends," said the Khan, as Nicolo, Maffeo and Marco kneeled before him, "and tell me about your travels."

Nicolo recounted their adventures and gave Kublai Khan the vases and the oil from the Holy Sepulchre.

"And who is this young man who is with you?" asked the Khan.

"He is your servant, and my son," answered Nicolo.

"He is welcome. Because he pleases me I shall give him a place among my officers."

Then Kublai Khan ordered a great feast and there was much rejoicing in honor of Nicolo, Maffeo, and Marco.

Marco now put aside his Italian dress of wool and his tight-fitting trousers, for the long silk robe of the Tartar officers. He also learned to speak and write the Tartar language and four others besides.

"This young stranger is very wise," thought the Khan one morning. "Tomorrow I shall send him to my distant city of Karazan to see how my people are behaving."

In setting out for Karazan the next day, followed by one hundred horsemen, Marco remembered that Kublai Khan liked to hear stories about his faraway peoples and kingdoms.

"I shall put down in my notes the strange and amusing things I have observed on my way," said Marco to himself, "how people dress and talk; the new animals and trees and flowers. The Khan will be happy to hear my stories."

And truly, the Khan took so much delight in listening to Marco upon his return

from Karazan that he sent him again and again on long journeys to the far corners of his empire.

Thus Marco learned all about many of the unknown countries which had never been drawn on any map.

"How polite the Chinese are!" he thought. "They seldom quarrel among themselves. And how honest! Why, one can leave one's door open without fear that thieves will come in and rob one. And they know so many things that we don't know anything about in Europe."

The Chinese knew how to dig coal and burn it to keep warm. Marco had never even seen coal. He was astonished that black "stones" could burn like wood.

In Europe, when a man had written a book, it was copied by hand so that a few more people could read it. But long before that time, the Chinese had already learned how to print their books; and millions of people could read them. The Chinese also printed paper money which was easier to carry than heavy gold and silver coins.

How rich this China was! The Khan's palace was built of marble, decorated inside and out with sculptures and paintings of dragons, birds, beasts, and flowers. The roof was painted in green, red, blue, and violet, and glistened like crystal. The palace grounds with their parks and gardens were so large that it took a horseman all day to ride around them. Musk deer, goats, and stags browsed in the flowery meadows, while fish of all kinds filled the ponds.

The Khan loved to hunt with falcons, and since it was also a good occasion to show how great an Emperor he was, he did not walk to the hunt, nor ride a horse, nor even an elephant. He rode four elephants at once. A little house carved in wood and painted with gold was put on the back of the four elephants, for him to ride in. He could even lie down if he cared to!

He took with him ten thousand men, dressed in blue robes, to carry the falcons; and ten thousand dressed in red robes to catch the falcons after the hunt.

During all the years he spent in Asia, traveling for his friend the Khan, Marco never forgot to write about the marvelous things he saw or heard: the gold and silver towers of Burma which had bells on the top of them to make music when the wind blew; the dog sleds and the big white bears of Siberia; the men of the North who rode reindeer instead of horses; the fierce tigers of Tibet; the Island of Java where grew pepper, ginger, and cinnamon; and many, many, other wonders.

While Marco traveled, his father Nicolo and his uncle Maffeo who continued to trade in Peking, had become very rich. But their black beards had turned white, and they now began to think of their homeland more and more often.

So one day when the great Khan seemed very cheerful, Nicolo told him of their desire to go home.

"It is now seventeen years since we came to visit Your Majesty," he said. "We have been honored and made happy beyond our dreams by your kindness and generosity. But we are old men now and we long to see our homeland before we die."

The great Khan frowned at hearing this.

With Marco, Nicolo, and Maffeo gone, who would tell him the amusing and interesting stories about foreign countries, which he liked so much? Very grumblingly he finally consented.

After bidding goodbye to the old Khan, Nicolo, Maffeo, and Marco at last set sail from China.

On the way home the Venetians sailed along many new coasts of which even the names were unknown in Europe. They saw Indo-China whose king sent twenty elephants each year to Kublai Khan; and Java and Sumatra, where Marco found nuts big as a man's head—coconuts—and rhinoceroses bathing in mud pools.

In Sumatra the ships waited five months for the west-blowing monsoon. Since the wild men of Sumatra like to eat strangers, Marco gave the order to build trenches around the beach to keep the savages away.

After passing many new islands, the ships came to Ceylon, and then to India which was as full of jewels and kings as when Alexander dreamed of conquering it. India still sold pepper, ginger, cinnamon, and other spices, and jewels and silks to foreign merchants.

As the Chinese ships sailed along the Indian coast, the Arab sailors told Marco about many strange lands—the island of Madagascar, far away to the west, where lived giant birds which carried elephants into the clouds, and the islands of Zanzibar and Socotra. Marco was the first European to hear of these places.

At the end of two years, the ships sailed into a Persian port. It had been a long, hard trip.

Marco, his father, and his uncle finally arrived in Venice, twenty-four years after they had left it. It was the year 1295. They easily found their old home, but the servant who answered their knock at the door would not let them in. Their ragged, dirty, foreign clothes, their sunburned, tired faces, and their bushy hair and beards made them look like tramps.

"You, Nicolo, Maffeo, and Marco? No, no, that cannot be," exclaimed the servant. "They have died many years ago. God knows where. Their house now belongs to a cousin of theirs. You are robbers, go on your way!"

"Let's force our way in," said Marco, and he pushed the door open, carrying his bundle after him.

But they had to tell of their trip many times before their cousin would believe them.

A great feast was held at Nicolo's house, to reunite their old friends and relatives.

During the meal Nicolo, Maffeo, and Marco went into another room and reappeared in robes of crimson velvet. But imagine the surprise of the guests when, after the meal, they brought in the old tattered clothes in which they had come home, and when they ripped them apart, streams of rubies, diamonds, sapphires, emeralds, pearls, and jade poured out onto the table!

No one doubted now. They *were* Nicolo, Maffeo, and Marco, and they must indeed have had wonderful adventures!

Some time later, when Marco showed his book which described all the things he had seen, people did not believe he told the truth.

"Who can believe that black stones can burn like wood?" they said, "or that nuts can be as large as a man's head? Imagine shopkeepers taking paper instead of money for their good wares! What a tale teller that Marco Polo is!" And they called him "Marco of the Millions" because he said that there was so much of everything in China.

But in truth, no traveler before him had ever seen so many new birds, and animals; new people, and cities; and no one had added, all at once, so many countries to the map.

Even though people went on believing that the earth was flat and that Marco had invented his stories, a new map was drawn according to his book. On it the shape of Asia was shown a little more accurately.

Around the World to China

CHRISTOPHER COLUMBUS

By Roger Duvoisin

I wish I knew a safe way for my ships to go to China," said the King of Portugal nearly five hundred years ago. "There are so many things I could get there. I could get silks, jade, and turquoises; silver, gold, and many kinds of spice."

The King sent a ship down the coast of Africa to see if it could go around that land and sail east to China. But the sailors were afraid. They went only a little way and returned to Portugal. Another ship tried. Then a third, and a fourth. Each went a little farther than the ship before. But still there seemed to be no end to Africa.

"There is a sailor named Christopher Columbus who has come to see me," said the King to some wise old men. "He says that the world is round. He says he can go to China by sailing west around the world. What do you think?"

The wise old men shook their heads and their long white beards.

"No," said the one. "That cannot be done."

"No," said another. "He will sail forever and he will come nowhere."

"No," said a third. "The world is not round. It is flat. He will fall off the edge."

Then the King forgot about Columbus and tried again to sail east around Africa.

Columbus went to see the King and Queen of Spain.

"If you will give me a ship," he said, "I will sail round the world to China. I will fill my ship with gold and precious stones and spices and silk. These I will bring back to you."

"This is interesting," said the King, "but I am too busy with my armies. Come back some other time."

Columbus went to see the King of England.

"Your idea might be good," said the King, "but I have no ships to spare."

Columbus was discouraged. He thought about seeing the King of France. "Go to see the King of Spain again," a friend said. "He is no longer busy with his armies."

So Columbus went.

"What will you do for me if I give you some ships?" the King of Spain asked Columbus this time.

"I will bring you all the precious things of the East," answered Columbus. "I will find new lands of which you will be King. I will also teach the people of China the stories in the Bible."

"And what do you want for yourself?" asked the Queen.

"I want to be Admiral," said Columbus.

CHRISTOPHER COLUMBUS. Italian map-maker and explorer. Born in Genoa, 1451 or 1446, date uncertain. Became a sailor at the age of fourteen. Made several voyages to England and probably Iceland, 1476–77. Commissioned by Ferdinand and Isabella of Spain, 1492, to head an expedition to the West to discover a route to China. Landed on island he named San Salvador, October 12, 1492. Second voyage, 1493, discovered Dominica and Jamaica. Third voyage, 1498, discovered Trinidad and the Orinoco River. Fourth voyage, 1502, discovered Honduras and Panama. Still believing he had found the coast of Asia, he died in Spain, 1506.

"I want to be Governor of all the lands I find. Besides I want a part of all the things that I bring back."

"Oh, no! That's too much," exclaimed the King and the Queen together. "We won't give you any ships. That's too much."

The tax-gatherer heard all this. He said to the Queen, "You are making a mistake. What Columbus asks won't cost you much, and if he finds a way to China you will be very rich."

"That is right," the Queen decided. "We will give him the ships."

So the King and Queen of Spain arranged for Columbus to have three ships: a large one named the *Santa Maria*, a medium-sized one named the *Pinta*, and a small one named the *Niña*. And Columbus, very happy, sailed away.

For days and days the three ships sailed.

"You will see that we will get nowhere," said a sailor with gold rings in his ears. "We shall fall off the edge of the world and be lost."

"Before that happens," said another, "some big sea serpent will have swallowed us up, ship, masts and all."

They sailed on and on. They could see nothing ahead but the neat line where the blue sea ends and the blue sky begins. Once the man in the crow's-nest cried, "Land! Land!" But he had cried too soon. It was only a cloud. When it had vanished nothing but the sky and the sea could be seen.

The sailors began to be afraid.

"This sea has no end," they said. "We shall sail like this forever. We shall never see Spain again. We must go back. We *will* go back!"

"Have courage," Columbus replied. "We shall soon arrive in China. Think how rich you will be after that."

"We don't care about China. Go there alone if you want to," answered the sailors.

Then Columbus grew stern. "We will not turn back," he said. "And I will put in irons, in the dark jail of the *Santa Maria*, the first one who complains." So they sailed on.

One day a bird flew by. Then a sailor found a stick. It was not a plain stick. It had been carved by somebody. That was a sign that land was near. The sailors cheered up. Soon they saw a log, and a branch with berries. Then more birds flew by.

Then one evening Columbus thought he saw a light ahead. The next morning everyone cried, "Land! Land!"

This time it was not a mistake. "Look!" cried the sailors. "An island! It is all covered with palm trees. There are people on the shore."

Columbus took the banner of the King of Spain in one hand and his sword in the other and he landed on the beach.

"From this day on," he said, "this land belongs to the King and Queen of Spain."

"It's strange," said a sailor. "The people of this island don't have yellow skins as Chinese should have. They have red skins. And they don't wear silk robes such as I have heard that the Chinese wear."

It was true. In fact these people did not wear anything at all. Instead they painted themselves with bright colors. Some had their faces blue, or their bodies red. Some had just painted their noses yellow.

Columbus gave these people red caps to put on their coarse black hair, and strings of glass beads for their arms and necks. The painted people were pleased and they brought presents, too: green parrots, balls of cotton, fruits, and arrows. "Now let's

go look for the King of China," said Columbus.

But he never found the King of China, for this was not China at all. Instead Columbus had discovered America. But he didn't know it. He went right on looking for China's cities. He found many beautiful islands. He saw new kinds of flowers and fruit, new trees with birds of all colors in them, and straw houses where the Indians of these islands lived. But he saw nothing that looked like Chinese cities.

"Let's go back and tell the King and Queen of Spain what we have found," said Columbus. "Then we can come again and look some more."

So Columbus went back to Spain. How happy the people were when they saw him back! They led Columbus to the King and Queen at the head of a noisy parade. The King and Queen made Columbus sit next to them. They made him tell his adventures again and again. They marveled at the green parrots, the balls of cotton, the new plants, the strange beasts, and the painted Indians he had brought back.

Columbus went to America three more times. He still hoped to find the rich cities and to visit the great King of China. He never knew he had found a great new land which no one in Europe had known since Leif Ericson's day five hundred years before.

The Spaniards Hunt for Gold

PONCE DE LEON AND DE SOTO

By Roger Duvoisin

AMONG green palm trees and red Indians, on an island which Columbus had discovered, lived a Spaniard named Ponce de Leon. He was sad.

"I have sailed with Columbus," he said. "I have conquered new lands for Spain. I am governor of an island. But I have not found China's golden cities. And now my beard is gray. My face is wrinkled. I am old."

Ponce de Leon shook his head, and the blue feather in his tall hat fluttered.

"There is a Fountain of Youth," an Indian said, "off there in a land where the trees grow greener and the flowers brighter. Its waters make old men young."

"I shall seek this fountain," said Ponce de Leon. "Then I shall be stronger again and I can sail new seas till I find the cities of China."

Ponce de Leon hung his sword by his side. He put his feathered helmet on his head and he sailed out to sea in his wooden ship.

The ship came to a new land where trees really were taller and greener, where flowers were larger and very bright.

"This must be the place," said Ponce de Leon.

He went ashore. He planted the flag of Spain in the ground. "I shall call this land Florida," he said, "and it now belongs to the King of Spain."

Then Ponce de Leon explored the woods and streams of his new-found land. He bathed in every river. He drank from every spring. Alas, when he returned to his island his beard was still gray. His face was still wrinkled. "I have not found the Fountain of Youth," he sighed, "nor the cities of China. But anyway I have discovered Florida."

In Spain a few years later a man came to the King.

"There is ever and ever so much gold in Florida," he said. "I know. I have been there."

Fernando de Soto, a Spanish Captain, heard this. He said, "I want to get some of this gold. I will sell my houses and my orchard of olive trees and my vineyards. I shall buy a ship and go to Florida."

"We will help you find gold," cried many soldiers. "We will sell our houses too and go with you."

So a good many Spaniards got ready to sail to America to look for gold. They buckled on their steel armor. The horsemen took their horses. The foot-soldiers took their cross-bows and muskets and lances.

JUAN PONCE DE LEON. Early explorer of America. Born in Leon, Spain, about 1460. Sailed to America with Columbus on second voyage. Made Governor of Puerto Rico, 1510. Founded San Juan, 1511. Discovered Florida, 1513. Wounded by natives on attempting to settle there. Died on voyage back to Cuba, 1521.

HERNANDO DE SOTO. Soldier and explorer in America. Born in Spain about 1500. Sent by King Charles I of Spain on expedition to conquer Florida, 1537. Landed in Florida, 1539. Pushed north and west in search of gold. Crossed Mississippi River, 1541. Died on banks of Mississippi, 1541.

"We will take pigs along for food," they said, and they crossed the sea to Florida—men, horses, pigs, and all.

On the Florida beach the horsemen in red, blue, and yellow breeches climbed onto their horses. The foot-soldiers, in polished armor, took their guns and bows and lances. The pigs squealed. The army stood ready behind the red and yellow flag of Spain. How gay it was!

"Forward, march!" said De Soto, and the army followed him into the woods. They followed him through muddy swamps and across rivers.

"Go north," the Indians said. "There

men wear hats of gold when they go to war."

North they went, for days upon days. "We don't see any gold," they complained.

Near a yellow stream among the pines there was a little village of brown log huts with roofs of leaves. Indians were gathering corn in a field.

"Where can we find gold?" the Spaniards asked.

"Where the sun rises," replied the Indians, "in a young Queen's country."

The soldiers helped themselves to the Indians' corn and took it with them and marched toward the sunrise. For weeks upon weeks they marched.

The young Queen lived in another village of log huts among pines. She wore a blue dress of deerskins and a crown of yellow feathers in her black hair.

"My wish is to serve you, great Prince," she said to De Soto. And she gave him a necklace of beads. "My land, my people, all that I have belongs to you."

"I find no gold," said De Soto.

"Go twelve days toward where the sun sets," said the Queen.

The soldiers took some of the Indians and put iron chains on their necks and made them go along to carry the food. Toward the sunset they went, for months upon months. But still they found no gold.

"We are weary," said the soldiers. "Our armor has grown rusty. Our clothes are ragged. Our horses are thin. And see how many of us have been killed by Indians."

"Forward," said De Soto. "The gold country is ahead."

Three frightened Indians stood wrapped in red blankets. "The gold country is beyond a great river farther away," they said.

The Spaniards went on. They came to the great river. It was so wide that the tall trees on the other side looked no higher than bushes. Its water was yellow and muddy. In it floated big logs and dead trees, going down to the sea. It was the Mississippi.

"We will build boats and cross the great river," said De Soto. They built four. The ragged hungry soldiers and their starving horses crossed the big river. But still there was no gold.

Now De Soto, too, was weary and discouraged. He fell ill. He called his officers and said, "I am very sick. I know I am going to die. I have led you through deserts and swamps. We have fought Indians together. You have suffered much and we have found nothing. I ask you to forgive me."

So De Soto died. His soldiers buried him in the great yellow river, the Mississippi, which he had discovered.

Then the soldiers built a ship. "We are hungry and tired and weak," they sighed. "We are a dusty, rusty, rickety army. We have found no gold, and De Soto is dead."

And they sailed back to Spain.

Years afterward the King of Spain sent people to Florida to keep the King of France from taking it. They built St. Augustine, the first town for white men in what we call the United States.

The Explorer Who First Sailed Around the World

FERDINAND MAGELLAN

By Dorothy Heiderstadt

THE short, sturdy, Portuguese boy stood on the pier at Lisbon. He was just one of a wildly cheering crowd. He was shouting with the best of them and waving his cap. His heart beat fast, his black eyes shone.

A battered ship was coming slowly into harbor. It was a wooden ship with tattered sails, the *San Gabriel*, last of the fleet with which Captain Vasco da Gama had sailed to India. Now the great captain was coming home. All his ships were lost but this one, and most of his crew was lost. But he had discovered a sea route to India, and this one weather-beaten ship was laden with sandal-wood, spices and gold!

Those were great days for boys like young Ferdinand Magellan who stood cheering on the Lisbon pier. Explorer after explorer sailed for the fabulous Indies, for China, for the Spice Islands. When the ships came home, what wonderful stories the sailors could tell of far countries and strange sights! And what eager listeners the young Portuguese boys made! Each one of them dreamed of being a sailor and setting out for the Indies on his own some day.

It was only a few years before that the Genoese captain, Columbus, had sailed away to the west, bound for a new passage to the Indies. He had discovered a land no man of his world had heard of. Later Balboa had explored that land and found on the other side of it a new ocean. Amerigo Vespucci had given his name to the new continent—America.

"Someday," thought young Magellan, "I'll be the captain of a ship. Perhaps I shall discover a new part of the world myself."

It was a number of years before Ferdinand Magellan's dream came true. But he never lost sight of it. He became a sailor in the Portuguese Navy, and studied geography and navigation. He sailed over all the seas of Asia, and when at last he returned home, he was the captain of his own ship.

The world was round, everyone knew.

"Suppose," thought Magellan, "a man should sail west instead of east to reach the Spice Islands. Since the world is a globe, some day he would reach the Islands. Then, if he continued and came on home, he would have sailed around the world!"

Magellan went to the King of Portugal, for he needed money and ships in order to carry out his great plan of trying to sail around the world. He promised the king that he would bring home a fortune in spices. Spices were very important—they

FERDINAND MAGELLAN. First navigator to travel around the word. Born in Portugal, 1480. Made several voyages to India in service of King of Portugal, 1495–1511. Sailed east for the Molucca Islands, 1511; west, 1519. Sighted South America, Cape Pernambuco, 1519. Coasted south and through straits now known as Straits of Magellan, 1520. Named the Pacific Ocean. Reached Philippines 1521. After almost completing westerly voyage to Moluccas, killed in fight with the Islanders, 1521.

were used for preserving meat to keep it from spoiling. Spices made the meat taste better, too. They came from lands far away to the east and were as valuable as gold.

The King of Portugal would have liked to have a fortune in spices. But how was he to be sure that Magellan would return from such an odd voyage since he was planning to sail in the wrong direction at the very beginning? The king would have nothing to do with Magellan's wild scheme.

Undaunted, Magellan went to the King of Spain, who was young and venturesome. The king listened to the plan and gave Magellan the money he needed.

On September 20, 1519, a fleet of five small, battered, wooden ships sailed southwestward from Seville. They were the *San Antonio*, the *Conception*, the *Santiago*, the *Victoria* and the *Trinidad*. The ships and sails were old and had been patched often. Their captain was Ferdinand Magellan.

Magellan stood on the deck of the flagship, *Trinidad*, and watched the shores of Spain slowly fading away. His dream was coming true. He was on his way to discover a passage around the world.

Far to the west lay the great continent of South America. Somewhere at the southernmost tip of that continent there must be a strait leading from the Atlantic Ocean to the China seas, he thought. He was sure that China lay just on the other side of South America. He was determined to find that strait.

A torch was kept burning on the high deck of the *Trinidad*, so the other ships would always be able to keep it in sight.

For a time there was fine weather. Then storms began to batter the small wooden ships. The sailors muttered angrily against the voyage and the low pay and the food, which was neither very good nor very plentiful. Magellan refused to be discouraged.

In November the fleet reached the coast of Brazil. The taste of sweet pineapples which the natives brought to the ships cheered the sailors. They began to trade with the natives—a knife for several fowls, a comb for a basket full of fish, a little bell for a basket full of sweet potatoes.

There had been no rain along the Brazilian coast for some months. Now that Magellan's ships had come, the rains came too. The simple natives thought that the white strangers had brought the cooling rains with them. And more to be wondered at were all these things the strangers had brought: knives, bells, looking glasses and bolts of bright-red cloth.

Magellan liked the friendly natives and wished to convert them to Christianity. The Christmas season seemed an excellent time to do it. The natives were taught to fold their hands, kneel and pray. They did so with great reverence.

Magellan sailed on and came to the mouth of a river. He believed that this must be the strait he was looking for—the one which led to the Chinese seas. The five ships sailed confidently into the river. But after two days they had to turn back, for the water was fresh. They knew that fresh water could come only from inland. They must find salt water.

Storm after storm hammered the ships as they sailed along. Magellan had to find a harbor where the ships could spend the winter. When they were in harbor he put the crew on scanty rations. Again the men began to grumble and wanted to return to Spain. A mutiny broke out, but Magellan quelled it. He was determined not to give up and go home.

One day a giant came down to the shore. He capered about and sang. He was so tall that Magellan's tallest men came only to his waist. The giant was good-natured and friendly. His face was painted red and yellow. He brought his friends—other giants like himself—down to the shore to look at the big ships with the little men aboard. Because these giants had such big feet, the sailors called them "Patagons." *Patagoas* means big feet in Portuguese. The giants' country near the southern tip of South America is still called Patagonia.

When spring came the fleet sailed out of the harbor and to the south. Soon Magellan saw a deep channel. He sent two ships to explore it. They found the water to be salt. Magellan felt sure that he had at last found the passage he was looking for—the passage leading to the Chinese seas.

For five weeks the ships sailed through a maze of channels at the southern tip of South America. Later these were to be named the Straits of Magellan. The sailors were angry and discontented. They clamored continually to return to Spain. One ship was wrecked. Another ship deserted and headed back the way they had come. But Magellan went on with the rest.

Then at last they sailed out into a wide expanse of water. Magellan was happy, for any day now he expected to see the coast of China. But day after day passed, and there was only the wide, calm sea.

"How big the world is!" thought Magellan. "Here is an ocean we never knew of. It must be a new ocean. I will call it Pacific because it is so peaceful."

It was tiresome, sailing on and on over that vast sea. Now and then, a desert island was sighted. But there were no natives ashore to bring fresh fruit to trade with the sailors. When at last they landed in a group of islands they found that the natives were thieves, so Magellan named the islands the Ladrones—Thieves' Islands.

Fresh food from these islands made the sailors more cheerful, however, so the ships moved on. After sailing on the new ocean for ninety-eight days, Magellan came to the islands later to be known as the Philippines. The natives were friendly and gentle. They brought oranges, bananas and coconuts to the sailors.

It was a pleasant life on the islands, after the long, hungry sea voyage. Magellan lingered there, converting the natives to Christianity and collecting tribute for the King of Spain. He made friends with some of the native kings.

One king who was Magellan's special friend complained that he was having trouble with another native king. Magellan said that he would fight the enemy king and subdue him.

Magellan and his men met thousands of determined natives armed with bows, arrows and spears. In the battle which followed, Magellan was killed.

Another man became captain of the fleet and sailed on to the Spice Islands. One by one the little ships had been lost. In 1521 the little *Victoria* sailed alone slowly into Seville harbor. She was laden with spices, ginger, sandalwood and birds of paradise. She had sailed completely around the world. But her great captain, who had fought for so long to make the dream come true, was dead.

Only eighteen men survived the long voy-

age around the world. The new captain received great honors and riches.

But it had been Magellan's courage and determination that made the long voyage possible. To Ferdinand Magellan goes the honor of having first dreamed of sailing around the world and of leading that first tremendous voyage almost to its end.

The Frenchmen Trade for Furs

CARTIER, CHAMPLAIN, AND LA SALLE

By Roger Duvoisin

"OH! REALLY," the King of France was saying to his Admiral. "Really, the King of Spain thinks the whole world is his. He is setting up his flag all over these new lands which Columbus has found."

"True," his Admiral answered. "Soon there won't be a big enough space left for you to put up the flag of France. Why don't you send Jacques Cartier over there? He is a fine French Captain. He knows the sea near these new lands. He has been fishing for cod there."

"That is a good idea, Admiral! Tell him to find these mysterious cities of China. And tell him to bring back gold, too."

Soon Jacques Cartier was sailing west. When he got to land he planted a wooden cross with these words carved on it: "Long live the King of France."

"That will stand longer than a flag," said Cartier. "But I don't see any gold or any city around here. There are only green woods and dancing Indians. I will look about some more."

But Cartier found no cities. When he sailed back to France the best thing he had discovered was a beautiful river, the St. Lawrence, in a land which he called Canada.

"Let's forget about this land," exclaimed the King of France. "It has no gold. It is not China. I hear people call it America."

"Call it China or call it America or call it Canada," said the French fishermen, "we shall keep on going there every year to fish."

"But fishing is dangerous and we are paid little," said a fisherman whose face was rough from the salty sea winds. "I am tired of smelling fish. We would get more money if we got furs from the Indians and sold them in Europe. We only have to give the Indians axes and knives and beads and they will bring us beautiful fox and beaver and bear skins."

"You are right," said the other fishermen as they wound up their lines. "Let us become fur traders."

So they began to trade with the Indians for furs. They filled their ships with bear, wolf, fox and beaver skins. And they grew rich enough to live in castles.

Now, after the fishermen and the fur traders, another Frenchman came to Canada. His name was Samuel de Champlain. With his workmen he cut down trees, plowed fields and built the first town in Canada. He called it Quebec.

"It is a very small town," said Champlain,

JACQUES CARTIER. Sailor and explorer. Born in St. Malo, France, 1491. Sailed three times to Canada. Explored St. Lawrence River, 1541–42. Died 1557.

SAMUEL DE CHAMPLAIN. Explorer in America. Born near Rochefort, France, about 1567. Sailed to West Indies, Mexico, Cartagena, Panama, 1599–1601. Sent by King Henry IV of France on fur-trading expedition to St. Lawrence River, Canada, 1603. Founded Quebec, 1608. Explored Great Lakes, 1613–15. Governor of French Canada, 1633–35. Died 1635.

ROBERT CAVELIER LA SALLE. Explorer in America. Born in France, 1643. Sent by King Louis XIV to Canada to trade and establish French Settlement, 1666. Sailed down Mississippi River to Gulf of Mexico, 1682. Founded Louisiana. Shot by his men in a mutiny at the mouth of the Mississippi, 1687.

"with only four houses and a log wall. But it will grow. And we shall show our countrymen that Canada is better than just a place for fur trading. And then, too, we will teach the Algonquin Indians in Canada to like our God."

Just then the Algonquins were sitting around their campfire in the woods talking about other things. "We must ask this great white chief Champlain to help us in our war," said the Algonquin chief. So they sent a messenger to Champlain.

"Ugh! Ugh!" said the Indian warriors to Champlain. "Iroquois Indians are bad Indians. Help us fight them, Great White Chief."

"I will help you," replied Champlain, "and wherever we go I will make maps of the land." So Champlain and two French-

men put on their armor. They took their muskets and went with the Algonquins in their birchbark canoes. They swarmed up the river like bees. They sang and yelled. Birds on the shore flew up in fright.

Up the St. Lawrence River they paddled, then up another clear river to the south. After a while they came to a great blue lake with green mountains around it.

"Careful!" said the Algonquin chief. "We are in the Iroquois country now. We must hide in the woods by day and paddle by night."

Then suddenly one evening the canoes of the Iroquois appeared in the dark. "Here they are," cried the Algonquins.

"Here they come," shouted the Iroquois. "Let's land and build barricades in the woods."

Next morning the Iroquois saw Champlain and his men. "What are those pale-faced men with shining things on their heads?" they asked. "They must have come down from the sky. What are those queer sticks in their hands?"

Then Champlain raised his gun and fired.

"Run, run!" the Iroquois shouted. "It is a stick that throws lightning." They tumbled over one another in their hurry to flee.

The Algonquins danced for joy until they could stand up no longer. The war was ended.

"Well!" said Champlain. "I have discovered a new river and a new lake to draw on my map." And he drew the shape of Lake Champlain.

"I will make other trips with my Indian friends and I will see what else I can find."

He found other great lakes and drew them in their places.

"Perhaps," said Champlain one day, "I spend too much time exploring and drawing maps. I must do something about my town of Quebec. It does not grow fast enough. All the people I bring from France trade with the Indians for furs instead of building houses and plowing fields."

"But Governor Champlain, why should we make our homes in this cold country?" the Frenchmen asked. "We want to become rich as fast as we can by selling furs. Then we can go back to France, our homeland."

"I love New France, this country we have come to," answered Champlain. "I'll work until I am old to make you love it too as your homeland."

But most of the Frenchmen still wanted to trade for furs instead of building homes.

One day in Quebec René La Salle stood on the bank of the St. Lawrence and dreamed of a giant river farther west where trees on the other bank looked no taller than bushes.

"I want to do something better than working on my farm or trading for furs," he said. "I want to find out where the Mississippi goes. I will build a sailboat and sail clear down it. I will take along soldiers and workmen and tools so I can build towns and forts along the banks. Then the flag of France will fly over America all the way from north to south."

For all this René La Salle needed money, so he borrowed, because he was not rich. With his soldiers he went west. Near the Mississippi River he put up a fort. Then he built a sailboat and was ready.

"I hear that the tools and the workmen I wanted have come from France," he said to his sailors. "I am going back to Quebec to bring them."

On the St. Lawrence River as he was going back to Quebec La Salle met someone who said, "The ship that was bringing your tools has sunk. Your workmen have gone back to France."

"Then," answered La Salle, "I will sell my farm and buy other tools and hire other workmen."

"Oh, but the people who lent you money have sold your farm."

"Then I still have many furs that the Indians are bringing me in their canoes."

"But don't you know? Your furs are at the bottom of the river. Those canoes have sunk."

Just then two men, with ragged and muddy deerskin coats, came running up to La Salle. "We come from the fort that you built near the Mississippi," they said. "Your soldiers have pulled it down. They have left your ship to rot in the woods."

"Things are very hard for me," said La Salle. "But never mind. We will go down the Mississippi in canoes. And I will build towns and forts later."

Then La Salle turned west again. Back across the Great Lakes he went, and on through the long woods. Finally one cold winter day, with a few soldiers, some Indians, and a priest, he came to the Mississippi. They all got into canoes. Down the great river they paddled, past the black leafless trees on the banks, which looked like giant whisk brooms turned up toward the gray sky; past buffalo and deer, drinking at the edge of the water; past Indian villages from which there sometimes came the rumble of war drums. The Mississippi grew broader and broader. The weather grew warmer.

"The trees have leaves and even flowers on them here," said the priest.

"The sun is warm enough now to make flowers bloom," answered a soldier, "but it also makes paddling harder."

"Look!" cried an Indian. "There is a sleepy alligator. He looks as dead as an old log."

And they paddled on and on, in the rushing current.

"We must be near the sea," said La Salle one morning. "Taste the water; it is salty."

And indeed, the sea was not far away. Suddenly, around the last bend, there it was, all blue in the sun. The shining ripples looked like thousands of jumping fish.

"It is the Gulf of Mexico, where the Spaniards sail!" cried La Salle. And his soldiers shouted for joy at the sight of the sea. "It seems as good as when the sailors with Columbus first saw land," they said.

By the river's mouth La Salle planted the flag of France and a cross on which they carved: "Louis, King of France."

La Salle pulled out his sword and said, "All the country where the Mississippi flows belongs to King Louis of France. I name it after him, *Louisiana*."

They stood for a while looking at the sea, and talking of the new land that now belonged to their King.

"Now we must paddle up the Mississippi, back to Quebec," said La Salle. "Then I will go to France to ask the King to help me bring French people to Louisiana."

When the King of France received La Salle in his fine palace he said, "I am pleased with what you have done. I will give you four ships with soldiers and farmers and tools. You shall sail south to where the Mississippi meets the sea, and you shall build towns and forts there."

La Salle bowed before the king. He was happy. "Now my dreams come true," he thought. "Now I will begin the making of a great New France in a warmer country than Quebec."

But some months later on a deserted beach of the Gulf of Mexico a few hungry, sick men were all La Salle had left of his dream. "Here I am," said he sadly. "My best fine French ship was taken by the Spaniards. Two of my ships have sunk. Now the fourth has deserted me and gone back to France. Most of my men have died, and here I am, sick on an empty shore."

Then some of La Salle's men turned against him. They hid behind some trees, and they shot him. And so ended La Salle's sad story and all his beautiful dreams.

Danger Was His World

JOHN SMITH

By Helen Woodward

WELL now, Captain Newport, what are we going to do with that prisoner on the ship?"

The young man spoke in a well-bred voice, but he looked rough. His long black beard was scraggly, and his clothes were rumpled and stained.

Newport looked rough and weatherworn too. The two men were standing on the bank of a lonely river. All they could see landward was a swampy dark forest where, they thought, Indians might be hiding. Nervously they turned their backs on the woods and looked at the three small boats anchored offshore. On these boats they had come from England, a miserable journey of ten long weeks. This was an April day in the year 1607. The place was Virginia on the unexplored continent of North America.

"That prisoner?" Newport repeated. "Smith is safe enough, chained to that beam in the hold. And that's where he's going to stay till I get him back to England."

"Good," said the young man. "He's a nuisance always wanting things for that rabble on board the ship, always siding with those worthless wretched men against gentlemen like us. Like himself for that matter."

Newport waved away this talk and said, "We've better things to do." He pointed down to a box that lay between them on the ground, a heavy box made of oak and bound around with iron bands. "Those are the sealed orders they gave me in England. Now we'll have to read them."

He broke the seals, and took out a roll of parchment all covered with curly dark writing. "These are the laws to govern this colony for His Majesty, King James," he said. "And here are the names of the local council to rule—"

He broke off short and his sunburned face grew dark.

"Listen to this," he shouted. "That prisoner—that Captain John Smith—he's named here to join you and three others who are to rule this Colony."

"No, no!" The young man tried to grab the sheet of parchment.

"Yes, I tell you," Newport insisted. "You've got to obey these orders."

In a hoarse voice the Captain shouted out to the crew on the ships, "Release the prisoner, Smith! Send him ashore."

From the boats came faint cheers as the chains were knocked off. John Smith was popular. Chaining a prisoner in those days wasn't just cruelty. There was no place on board to shut up a prisoner. Between decks was the hold, and it was only one big open space with a rough chimney in the corner where the men cooked their meals when the weather wasn't too bad. There were a few

JOHN SMITH. Explorer, colonist, and writer. Born in England, 1580. Came to America, 1606. Captured by Indians. Said to have been rescued by Pocahontas, Indian Chief's daughter. Contributed to success of Jamestown Settlement in Virginia. Author of many books on American Colonies. Died 1631.

rough sheds on deck for the officers.

Captain John Smith leaped ashore, leading the other passengers. These men, ragged, wind-burned, tired, and sick from spoiled food, were glad to follow Captain Smith and to do what he suggested. Most men *liked* to obey him, because they trusted him.

These men coming off the boats were a mixed lot. Some were gentlemen who'd had bad luck. Some were despairing workmen out of jobs, some were criminals exiled for their crimes. But a man could be exiled in those days for things no one would consider a crime today.

Nearly all of them were brave. They had to be to think of going to America at all. It was a desperate adventure in those days, as a trip to the moon would seem today.

But Captain John Smith was more than brave. He was a man who hated to be safe. Danger was a kind of game to him. He had had all sorts of adventures as a soldier, a pirate, and a slave to the Turks. Yet, when he landed that day in Virginia, he was still only twenty-eight years old.

No sooner were the men gathered on the river-bank than a flight of arrows came at them from the woods. They had loaded their guns on board ship, and now each swiftly fired off his gun toward the forest. They couldn't see anything but trees, so the shots went wild. No one on either side was hurt.

While they were reloading, John Smith laid down his gun and walked forward with his empty hands spread wide to show he had no weapon. It was a friendly gesture, as though to say welcome. Out of the woods stepped an Indian chief, also holding his arms wide. The English Colonists looked on open-mouthed, too surprised at the courage of John Smith and of the Indian chief to finish loading their guns.

Then, in dumb show, the Chief made them understand that he was being wary because some time ago another boat had come in here and someone kidnaped two Indians.

Smith shook his head and pointed to himself questioningly. Plainly, with the motions, he was saying "Look at me. Do I look like the man who did that?"

The Indian Chief then shook his head too, and he and his band of Indians came out from under the trees. But this time instead of arrows, they brought berries and popcorn and tobacco for their new friends.

For a while, the Colonists had a hard time. Most of the men were lazy; some were sick; some were foolish. All of them were disappointed. They had come to America expecting to find gold and jewels. They would stroll about with their eyes on the ground hoping to see the shine of gold. They would save stones that glittered, but they all turned out to be a kind of iron, never gold. Some wandered off into the forest and looked about. Maybe they thought, like a child in a fairy tale, that rubies and diamonds grew on trees. Sometimes a man wandered off alone and an unfriendly Indian caught him and killed him.

They got sick from drinking unclean river water, but they wouldn't bother to dig a well. They wouldn't even gather firewood for the winter ahead. They were too lazy to plant crops.

There were plenty of wild turkeys and other game and the river was full of fish. But they wouldn't hunt or fish. They said they weren't used to that sort of work. And many of them had malaria from the mosquitoes. They didn't know what made them

27

sick. It was hundreds of years before doctors found out that malaria came from the bite of a certain kind of mosquito.

At last Captain John Smith got tired of all this shilly-shally and foolishness. He said to his men, "You work or you don't eat." They looked at him astonished. But he merely repeated, "No work, no food."

He made them dig a well. He made them hunt and kill wolves. He sent them into the woods to gather the fruit that grew there: wild grapes and cherries and crab apples and persimmons. They found little watermelons too. Most of these they had never seen before. They also gathered oysters and crabs from the beach. They caught sand dabs and other fish. From the Indians they learned how to plant corn and how to make popcorn. Popcorn was not a playtime food for

them. There was no ice and corn had to be dried or "popped" to keep for the winter.

From the Indians they learned how to smoke tobacco. Tobacco was so new that when an Englishman, Sir Walter Raleigh, smoked his first pipeful, his servant thought he was on fire and threw a bucket of water over him. The settlers enjoyed the tobacco; but they could not know that as the years went by, tobacco was going to make Virginia rich.

But even in early Jamestown, it counted for a lot. The Colonists used tobacco like money. A man paid so many pounds of tobacco for a shirt, so much for a pair of moccasins. One man paid three hundred and seventy-eight pounds of tobacco for a suit of clothes.

When the Indians felt friendly, they

brought things to eat. But they often didn't have enough to eat themselves and they weren't always friendly. Once Captain John Smith went off to make some kind of deal with them. Years later he wrote a book and in it he said that the Indians took him prisoner. Their Chief, Powhatan, he wrote, had him tied to a post and was going to kill him, but the Chief's daughter, a little girl, threw herself on him and begged her father to save him.

That little girl was named Pocahontas and she became a famous girl in our history. She used to come often to visit the colony and was a favorite with the men. When she was older she married a Colonist named John Rolfe. They had a son and went to England to live.

Pocahontas was popular in England, where they called her Lady Rebekah. King James liked her very much and thought she was a great Princess. At first the King said to John Rolfe, "You are not a noble; you had no right to marry a King's daughter like the Lady Rebekah." King James didn't know much about Indians and he thought an Indian Chief like the father of Pocahontas would be as powerful as a King in England. They had to tell him that an Indian Chief was just a simple, wild man heading a small tribe. He was not a powerful ruler like King James himself.

Some people today are not sure how much of the story of Pocahontas' saving John Smith is true, but we know that she was a fine woman. And we know that Captain John Smith went to see Powhatan and took him a present of a grindstone. The Indians thought it was a wonderful gift, the best way to sharpen their tomahawks that they had ever seen.

Slowly the Colony found its way and grew. One day, two years later, Captain Smith was rowing a boat when a barrel of gunpowder exploded. He was badly burned and there was no doctor in Jamestown good enough to heal him. So he went back to England to be cured.

He never came back to Virginia. But he made two voyages to the coast of Maine, hoping to found another Colony there. But he had no luck. After that he had a busy life fighting pirates and other enemies of England.

The men he left in Jamestown had hard times ahead. They were hungry and sick and some were lost at sea. Powhatan became an enemy. John Smith knew how to make friends of the Indians. The other Colonists often did not know how.

Captain Smith had given the Colony a good start, so it pulled through, and it was the beginning of the great state of Virginia.

Without Captain John Smith we might today belong to Spain. Spain was founding Colonies all the way from Florida to South America. England had tried several times to plant a Colony in America and had always failed. Captain John Smith made Jamestown the first successful English Colony in America. Later, he showed the Dutch how to settle in New York. His success in Jamestown gave courage to the Pilgrims who went to Massachusetts thirteen years after he landed in Jamestown, Virginia.

From Virginia came many of our most famous men: George Washington, Thomas Jefferson, James Madison, Patrick Henry, Woodrow Wilson. And it was Captain John Smith, by his strength, his common sense, and his last-stand courage, who turned the little group of tired men into a solid Colony.

He Discovered a Great American River

HENRY HUDSON

By Helen Woodward

JOHN HUDSON, who was twelve years old, looked with adoring eyes at his father, Captain Henry Hudson. That was in the city of London in England more than three hundred years ago. As any boy would, John Hudson loved his father's adventurous spirit and was proud to be the son of the great sea Captain. John had two brothers and a sister, but when Captain Hudson set out on his dangerous voyages and made the discoveries that mean so much to us today, John was the one who always went along.

He sat quietly in the back of the room while his father spoke to the bigwigs of England.

"Consider this," Captain Hudson was saying to them. "For centuries your ships have sailed all around Africa to Cathay, or China, as you may call it, to find the pepper for your meat and the silk for your ladies' gowns. Christopher Columbus tried to go another way. He sailed West and thought he had found Japan. But we know now that he had not. We know that a vast land lies to the West between us and Cathay. Each time our ships have sailed to the West they have bumped into a continent. Now," continued Captain Hudson, "I believe that we should sail *north*, that we should try to reach the North Pole."

"But Captain," said the men he was trying to persuade, "that is all ice and snow."

"Ice and snow first, to be sure," answered the Captain. "But we will get beyond these and when we are through to the North Pole, we will find that it is warm again."

To people today this seems a most foolish notion because we have had first-hand reports and we know that both the North Pole and the South Pole are freezing cold. But Captain Hudson was not ignorant. His friends were the great scholars of the time who were making maps of the world as they thought it was. Now he told the men before him why explorers and scholars thought the North Pole was warm.

He said, "Here we have a few hot days, a few sunny days; then we have rain and then cold for a little while. Now we know that as we go north we find the sun shining for six months of the year and then it's dark for six months. And if we get there during the six months when the sun shines, the ice will be melted and it will be warm."

Now we can be wise today because we know that in the far North the sun, though it shines for six months, is a weak, watery sun and has little effect on the ice. But the scholars and explorers of that day all believed as Hudson did. And so the leaders of England gave him a ship and a crew. He set sail and his son John went along. Half the crew were fine men, including a distinguished surgeon. The rest were rough sea-

HENRY HUDSON. Navigator and explorer. Born in England about 1575. Navigated coasts of Iceland and Greenland trying to find Northwest passage to China for England. Explored Hudson River for the Netherlands, 1607. Sailed up Hudson's Bay, 1610. Abandoned by crew. Died in Hudson's Bay, 1611.

men, far rougher than sailors of today.

John was well provided with warm wool-lens that his mother had woven. On their first trip, in 1606, they set off from England. And they made a second journey a year later. They did not try to reach the conti-nent of America at all. They thought they could sail around the north of Europe and north of Russia, and reach Cathay that way. The ruler of the Russians, Czar Ivan, was known as Ivan the Terrible because of his murderous cruelty. He pretended to be friendly, for a while, to the explorers be-cause he hoped to use that northern passage for his own purposes. But later he turned against them. They soon found out that they could not trust him. So Captain Hud-son wanted to keep as far away as he could from Russia.

But he could not get through by going north of Russia or any other way. He reached Iceland and Greenland and the far North in Norway. And the boy, John Hud-son, saw many new and wonderful things.

He saw great whales and he watched the men who caught them. He had heard of whales but he had no idea how huge they were. John thought that they were fish and was astonished to learn that they were mam-mals and that they gave their babies milk. And none of Captain Hudson's men knew how whales were caught. They were all grateful for the oil that came from the great beasts. They rubbed it on their chapped skins and found it was wonderful for sooth-ing the rough sore places. The sailors were busy learning to use it to make lights and to keep warm.

John learned that sick whales gave off a kind of wax called ambergris. It was found to be worth a great deal of money for it could be used to manufacture, of all things, perfume. How strange, they thought, that such lovely scents could come from this nasty ill-smelling ambergris! And a substance from the teeth of the whales, called whale-bone, was used in making ladies' corsets.

These discoveries led to the great whaling industry that later became so profitable in Europe and America.

Young John was delighted, too, with the white Polar bears. There were many of them and John had a baby one for a pet. He was sad to see the grown-ups kill the full-sized bears for their skins. But the crewmen said, "These grown bears are not playthings. They will kill you if you get in their way."

They caught beavers and foxes. When they got home they brought a rich cargo of whale-oil and skins, but the people who had sent Captain Hudson on the expedition were angry and disappointed because he had not brought back what they had sent him to get: silks and spices and gold and silver. They would not let him go again.

John watched his father's downcast face, but it was not downcast for long. Henry Hudson was no ordinary sea captain beg-ging for a boat or a job. He cared little for money. His mind and his heart were set on one thing—to find a way to Cathay or China by a northern passage. He knew now that he could not do it by going north of Europe. But his gloom vanished when he got a letter from an old friend.

That old friend was the famous Captain John Smith, who had helped to found the English colony of Jamestown in Virginia, the first English colony in America. John Smith said the Indians in Virginia had told him there was a way to go by water across the American continent and if Henry Hudson could find that way he could sail right through the American continent to the Pacific Ocean.

Either the Indians made a mistake or John Smith did not understand them, for the Indians were talking about the Great Lakes. A ship could sail through the St. Lawrence River in what is now Canada and go on through the five Great Lakes, but it would be stopped at what is now Minnesota. And the plains and the mountains would still be between the ship and the Pacific Ocean. But no white man knew that then.

The English would not take another chance with Captain Hudson. But there was another great sea-going nation in Europe. That was Holland, and her people were called the Dutch. They had for centuries been fighting other people in Europe for their independence and for the right to trade. And they had just won the fight. Now they were eager to find the northern way to Cathay. They sent for Captain Hudson. Young John went along and looked with wonder and delight at their canals and their cities.

Captain Hudson read the letter from John Smith to a company of Dutch officials and they thought he must be right. They gave Hudson a ship and he got his crew together. The name Henry in Dutch is Hendrik, and that is why to this day Captain Hudson is sometimes called Henry and sometimes Hendrik. But again Captain Hudson showed how little he cared about money. All the Dutch paid him for the journey he was about to make was $325. And they sent his wife in London $90. The boy John, as a sort of junior member of the crew, got only something like $5.

The ship had a nice name, the *Half Moon*. This time Captain Hudson sailed farther south and he sailed up and down the coast of what is now the United States. He thought of going in to Virginia and seeing Captain Smith, but Captain Smith's colony was English and Hudson was sailing for the Dutch. He was afraid he might have had to give up his ship if the English found out about it.

So Captain Hudson and his men sailed north again. Here and there they ran the ship into sheltered coves and caught lobsters and fish.

The Indians there, who were glad to see the strangers, smoked green tobacco. They offered Hudson their tobacco or anything they had if he would give them some bright red robes he had on board. No one knows now what the robes were for, but Captain Hudson gave them to the Indians and got furs and tobacco and pipes and fresh fish in exchange.

Then as they sailed farther south they discovered a place which came to mean a great deal in American history.

The night had been dark with neither moon nor stars, and they could see nothing. But with the coming of the dawn, they saw a lovely low land, and they sailed into an opening that led into a beautiful, empty, silent bay. The opening is what we now call the Narrows and the bay is New York Harbor.

Captain Hudson was thrilled to see that a wide river opened out from the bay. The *Half Moon* sailed up the river like a bird with white wings. At the right lay a long narrow island, which was to be called Manhattan and is now a part of the gigantic

city of New York. The river, of course, was named the Hudson.

Captain Hudson was really not the first to find the Hudson River. An Italian, Verrazzano, had discovered it much earlier. But he didn't do anything about it.

Captain Hudson sailed up the river almost to where Albany is now and he told what a wonderful land he had found. "It is a pleasant place to see," he wrote. And he added that it was the finest land for farming that he had ever seen.

The Indians were friendly. They came out to the ship with hands full of blueberries which were new to these white men. And the Indians brought them fine fresh oysters. Hudson went ashore with the Indian chiefs and when he told them he could not stay long, they thought he was afraid to trust them while they had their bows and arrows. So they broke their arrows in pieces and threw them into the fire to show their friendliness.

When Hudson got back to Holland the Dutch were pleased with the news about the good new land he had found for them. Hudson wanted to go again and try to find the northern Arctic way to Cathay. But the Dutch saw no sense in that. Several years later they sent some of their own people from Holland to live on the banks of the Hudson River. And they built a tiny village on the island at the south of that river. They called the village New Amsterdam after their fine city of Amsterdam at home. And they called the island Manhattan which was an Indian name.

The Dutch did not come to America for freedom. They had fought for and won their freedom at home in Holland. They came to America to do business. The little village they built grew into a big village, and the big village grew into a town, and the town grew into a city, and the city grew into the tall and mighty metropolis that is now New York.

But in all this Captain Hudson had no part at all. He did not want to stay with the colony on the Hudson River. He was still set on finding the Northwest Passage to the Pacific Ocean. He would sail north, he said, along the American continent and then northwest.

Henry Hudson was right. There *was* a way to get through in the far North, though it was by way of the North Pole. But no man in Hudson's time could have found it or made the journey. More than three hundred years passed before a Canadian canoe laid out the route. It was in the year 1954 that a United States Navy ice-breaker and a Coast Guard ice-breaker broke through the passage. Even at this late day, with all the inventions of modern navigation to help them, they found it a terrible journey. They had power-driven ships while Hudson had to battle blizzards with mere sailing sloops. He had no ice-breaker, and he had no way of keeping food fresh for his men, none of our modern conveniences.

When the Dutch refused to send him on any more journeys, Hudson went back home to England. Once more, because of Captain John Smith's letter, the English gave him a ship and a crew. Once more he set sail. His son John, now in his teens, went too.

This time he sailed north again and then he sailed west and in Canada he reached the vast ice-cluttered bay which was named for him, Hudson Bay.

The voyage had been fearfully cold. The sails froze, the ropes froze. When they tried to drink water it froze before they could carry it to their lips. Once a look-out yelled, "White swans ahead!" The "swans" turned out to be ice floes rushing toward the ship and the men spent a whole day pushing them off with long poles.

At Hudson Bay they made a camp and built a rough shelter. They were weary and cold. Here they joined the Eskimos in catching whales and extracting oil from their fat or blubber. The oil and the ambergris smelled so bad they called their place Blubbertown.

They learned how to catch walrus, and found that the tusks of a walrus are like ivory and worth a lot of money. They were tired and they wanted to go home with their oil and tusks and bearskins. Worse than that, they had lost faith in Captain Hudson. So when he said, "We must go on. We must find the Northwest Passage; it cannot be far," they thought he was crazy. And they refused to go farther. "If we take these things home with us," they said, "we will be rich." But Hudson answered them, "You will be richer if we go on."

They would not. There were good men in the crew. As it turned out, there were eight such men. But the rest were tramps and criminals as many of the sailors of that time were. People said that Hudson, who was a kind man, was too good to the ruffians in his crews. This crew, greedy for loot, defied their Captain and there was ugly fighting on board. It was a mutiny. But not all the men had any clear idea of what was going on because there was so much yelling and confusion. The better men stood by their Captain.

When the ruffians won, they put Hudson and his son John and the surgeon and one or two others into a shallop, which is a weak little boat. When they were in the frail little shallop, some of Hudson's other loyal sailors, seeing what was being done, jumped in after them. One man, the ship's carpenter,

34

a God-fearing Englishman from Surrey, cried, "My place is with the Captain!' And he went overside into the little boat. But first he had the good sense to gather his carpentering tools and take them with him.

The ship sailed off and Captain Hudson and his friends were left adrift in the freezing waters of Hudson Bay. They were never heard from again. This was in 1611.

The ruffians of the crew, it is good to know, had an awful time. They did not know how to find their way home. The native Eskimos fought them and they nearly starved. But at last those of them who survived reached England.

"Where is Captain Hudson?" asked the English at home.

The men lied. They said that Captain Hudson had found the Northwest Passage to Cathay and had stayed there. But some of the crew let the truth leak out. The men were arrested and seven years after Hudson was set adrift, the leaders of the mutiny were hanged.

What became of Hudson and his loyal friends no one knows. Most people think they were drowned with their little boat. But some explorers say that twenty years later, they found traces of a house. They could see that it had been built by a skilled carpenter. There was none such except the man who had joined Hudson in the boat. So perhaps they fared better than we feared. Perhaps their bones are buried on Canadian soil. At any rate, the name of Henry Hudson lives in glory in America's history.

The Black-Robed Priest and the Algonquins

PÈRE MARQUETTE

By Jason Robbins

Yᴏᴜ fool! Why did you let Black Robe have your gun?" The Indian who spoke had colored stripes on his face and hands. He had them on his shaved head and on his body too, but heavy furs hid them. He was an Algonquin Indian and a medicine man. He was supposed to cure the sick by magic.

The other Indian wore the red feather of a warrior Chief. Both of them, trying to get warm in the icy weather, stood close to a camp fire on the border between Canada and what is now the United States. At that time, in the year 1666, it was only a group of small British colonies along the Atlantic coast.

The camp was freezing cold. The snow had stopped, and it lay hard-packed on the ground. Icicles hung from the trees and from the ridge-poles of the tents. Other Indians sat huddled around a great fire, the only bright thing on that frozen spot. They hardly lifted their faces to listen to the medicine man. All that day and the day before they had had nothing to eat. They were sick and weary with hunger. The men sat close to the fire, the women and children in a ring behind them.

Again the medicine man asked the Chief, "Why did you let Black Robe have your gun?"

The Chief looked back at him with a troubled face. "Black Robe has more than my gun. He has my son too. The man you call Black Robe is Père Jacques Marquette, a French priest. His Manitou is more powerful than yours." Manitou is the word the Algonquin Indians used for the Great Spirit, or God.

"When I was sick," the Chief went on to the medicine man, "you made all your magic sounds. You made them as loud as you could. But your Manitou did not listen. I did not get better. Then Black Robe came. He talked to his Manitou in a low voice. His Manitou heard. And I came out of my sickness and was well."

The truth was that Père Marquette was not only a priest but a doctor and a surgeon too. "We Algonquins have been the enemies of his French people," the Chief continued. "Black Robe could have killed me."

The Indian medicine man hated all white men, but especially he hated Père Marquette, the French Jesuit priest. He knew that if the Indians turned to the white man's Manitou, his own power would be gone forever. He growled, "Only a coward saves the life of an enemy. He will put a curse on your son. You will see."

But the Chief had turned away and was facing the woods. The pines stood straight and tall, their tops snow-capped. The Chief put out his arm and pointed to an aisle between the trees. "Look," he said. "Here comes Black Robe—Père Marquette."

PÈRE MARQUETTE. Jesuit missionary and explorer in America. Born in France, 1637. Mission to Ottawa Indians, 1668. Voyaged with Joliet down Mississippi River to mouth of Arkansas River and back by Illinois River. Died 1675.

Through the forest aisles, a tall man was striding toward them. From head to foot his long black robe was caked with snow and ice. In his arms he carried a snowy bundle.

"There! I told you," said the medicine man to the Chief. "Your son is sick. The priest has to carry him."

But suddenly the bundle began to wriggle, and in a moment a small Indian boy, also snowy white from head to foot, jumped out of the priest's arms and came running toward the Chief, letting out a full-grown war whoop as he came.

"It is my son, my Little Big Mouth!" exclaimed the Chief happily. "See, he is not sick at all."

"Oh, Father," shouted the boy running toward the Chief, "we have killed a moose, a big moose. There is meat." The boy poured out the words in his excitement. "My arrow . . . Black Robe's gun . . ." The boy's breath gave out.

The medicine man hated to give up. He

advanced angrily toward Père Marquette. "How could you find a moose when we could not?" he yelled.

Some of the campers crowded around the priest. They paid no attention to the medicine man. All they wanted was to bring the moose into the camp. Père Marquette pointed back and said, "We left the moose because the boy's short legs could not keep up with mine."

The Chief then repeated the medicine man's question, but in a quiet voice, "How is it, Père Marquette, that you were able to find meat when skilled Indian hunters, who looked for two days, could find none?"

Père Marquette raised his eyes to heaven. "It was with the help of God," he answered.

"His Manitou," murmured one of the Indians with respect.

Père Marquette looked into the eyes of the Chief. "It was the voice of God that told you to let your son go with me too," he went on. "Without him I would not have had the moose. He is the one who found the way."

Before the priest could say more, a group of the men came out of the woods, dragging the moose. The men shouted with joy. There would be enough meat for days. Everything else was forgotten as some of the Indians cut the great animal apart and threw the pieces to the squaws to cook, while others cleared away the flaming logs, leaving only the glowing embers. The squaws filled great iron pots with snow and when the snow bubbled and boiled over the hot ashes, they threw in the hunks of moose.

The children put small pieces on sticks and held them to the fire. The men took no part in this. Even a starving Indian would not do the squaw's work of cooking.

The medicine man made a last effort to defeat the priest. "This is evil meat," he groaned. "It will poison you." But the good smell of the roasting meat was too much even for him. Soon he was gobbling down great hunks with all the others.

Père Marquette ate too, slowly though, and not much. And not until he had lifted his crucifix, now coated with ice, and thanked the Lord for His guidance and help. He wanted the Indians to save some of the meat for another hungry time, but he knew they wouldn't do it. He managed to put away a little for himself and the boy. At last, when their first hunger was satisfied, the braves asked the priest once more how he had found the moose. The boy was bursting to tell the story, but he kept silent, waiting for his father's permission. Père Marquette said quietly to the Chief, "Let the boy tell you."

Little Big Mouth stepped into the ring of the braves. It was a strange sight in an Indian camp to see grown men listening to a boy.

"We walked a long way," said Little Big Mouth. "We listened for the sound of a snapped twig, for the call of a bird. But we heard nothing. I was glad to be with Père Marquette because I would have been terribly lonely in all that silence. Everywhere we looked for berries or nuts. There was not even one." The boy pointed to his left. "Along one side there was deep underbrush. We thought there might be game there. But we could not go into it without noise that would scare the birds and the deer. At last I caught sight of a little tunnel in the thicket. I asked Black Robe if I could crawl into the tunnel. It was much too low for a grown man, but I could manage to get through. I crept in, very slow, a little at a time. I found a few nuts. But I found much more. When I got to the end of the little tunnel, I could see through the branches into a hollow. Down in it stood this moose. There was no snow there. I fitted an arrow into my bow and the arrow flew true. But I did not kill him. The buck leaped out of the thicket right into the open. Black Robe saw him and fired his gun. The white man's Manitou made that tunnel. The white man's Manitou sent me with Père Marquette."

Père Marquette patted Little Big Mouth on the head. "Well done, my boy," he said.

All this talk in the Indian camp was in the Algonquin language. Only a short time before Père Marquette had come to Canada from France. He did not know a word of any Indian language. Most of the French settlers spoke Iroquois, because the Iroquois were their friends. But Père Marquette felt that he must go to the Algonquins, who were his enemies, and make them friends. The first thing he did was to learn the Algonquin language.

The region of North America, then ruled by the French, to which Père Marquette came, was full of lakes and rivers. The mighty St. Lawrence River flowed out to the sea. The Great Lakes spread like giant fingers across the land. Traveling on these waterways was much quicker than going through forests on land. So the French learned from the Indians how to make canoes and how to paddle them.

These canoes were harder to handle than a modern canoe. Their ribs were of cedar covered with birch bark. A hasty movement and there was a hole in the thin birch bark. The paddles had to move in rhythm like the oars of a modern racing shell. In these eggshell boats men fought rapids and windswept eddies and the stormy distances of the Great Lakes.

The French Canadians became much better boatmen than the Indians who taught them. They were small, rough, strong men. They were called *voyageurs*, a French word that means travelers. At first the *voyageurs* smiled as they watched Père Marquette trying to keep his balance in their canoes, trying to learn how to handle a paddle. Still, when they came to a rough place they carried him on their shoulders. But Père Marquette was also a strong man and soon he was as good as they were at the paddles of the canoe.

The *voyageurs* amused themselves by shooting with bows and arrows. But their real weapons, which came from France, were heavy clumsy guns called blunderbusses. They couldn't be aimed as well as a modern gun but they spattered shot over a wider space. They took a long time to load. The *voyageurs* were skillful with these blunderbusses. Père Marquette was a good shot, and it was with one of these that he had shot the moose for the Indian camp.

So Père Marquette learned to live in the wilderness, learned the languages of many Indian tribes, brought many of them into his Church.

But he had long had a secret dream. He was a priest and a surgeon, but he was also an explorer. He longed to explore more deeply into the American continent. Although the first French explorers had come to America a hundred years before Marquette, there were still not many in Marquette's time. There were many more British. And there was keen rivalry among

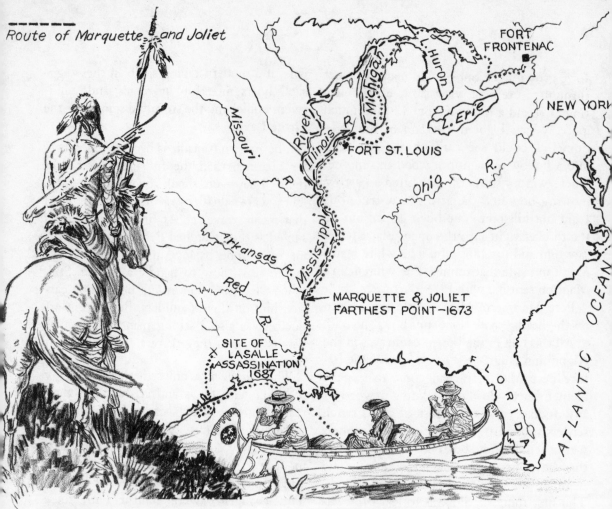

Route of Marquette and Joliet

FORT FRONTENAC

L. Huron

L. Michigan

L. Erie

NEW YORK

Missouri R.

River Illinois R.

FORT ST. LOUIS

Ohio R.

Mississippi R.

Arkansas R.

Red R.

MARQUETTE & JOLIET FARTHEST POINT—1673

SITE OF LASALLE ASSASSINATION 1687

FLORIDA

ATLANTIC OCEAN

the settlers of both nations for the American continent. But they all thought the continent was just a narrow strip of land and that if they went just a little way west, they would reach the Pacific Ocean. Neither the French nor the British had any idea of the vast width of North America.

Many times, rumors had come to Père Marquette that there was a mightier river even than the St. Lawrence. Some said it was to the west and some said it was to the south. He longed to explore but he felt his first duty was to the church. So he worked and waited patiently.

At last, one day, as he stood on the shore of Lake Huron, he watched a large canoe coming in fast. As it came closer, he saw that it had a crew of *voyageurs*. And he saw that the man in command was his dearly loved friend, Louis Joliet. Joliet was neither a noble nor a priest. He was the son of a poor wagon-maker. But he turned out to be one of the greatest explorers in history. Now he jumped out of the boat, a gay smile on his daredevil face, his deerskin clothes dyed in bright colors, his fur hat on the side of his head. No one had gone farther or knew more of the country than Joliet. And he brought wonderful news from the government in Quebec. Père Marquette and he were to be allowed to explore the unknown country.

Some of the Indians had a pretty good idea of where the great river lay. But they were afraid of it with a deep superstitious fear. They said that there were demons and evil forces in the river which swallowed whole boatfuls of men. And they said that the shores were lined with fierce fighting tribes.

For this reason the two French explorers wanted no Indians in their crews. But that was all right since no Indians wanted to go. Of course, neither Marquette nor Joliet believed the stories about demons. But they thought it likely that the tribes were savage. They built themselves two large canoes with one of them in command of each. Their crews were *voyageurs*.

The journey was long and hard. There were rivers and lakes and in between portages where they had to carry the canoes on their shoulders, walking single file. And wherever they stopped, there was word of the mighty river farther on.

And at last they saw the broad sweep of the Mississippi, the longest river on the American continent. Where their canoes swept into it, the river was a mile wide, and Louis Joliet gave a wild Indian war whoop as the canoes breasted the mighty waters.

All along there were Indians, but not one fought the explorers. High up on the river they had met the tribe of the Illinois. The Illinois were friendly and smoked the calumet, the pipe of peace, with the explorers. And after that when the canoes approached a new shore of the river, Marquette stood up and held the calumet high, with his hands widespread, to show he came in peace. This was a wonderful thing about Père Marquette. At a time and in a land where white men and Indians fought so much, he never fought Indians at all. His was the way of peace.

Long they journeyed down the river. At first they thought it might empty into the Pacific or the Atlantic. But they found that it emptied into the Gulf of Mexico. This great river, then, the Mississippi, was a highway from Canada to the Gulf, a swift way to travel from North to South, a swift way to ship furs and lumber and, later, iron ore and grain. It became the great highway for the entire United States later on, and helped to make it rich and powerful.

On the way back from his great journey, Père Marquette fell sick. He was only thirty-eight years old when he died in the year 1675. He died on the lonely prairie on the east shore of Lake Michigan. Nothing was there then, not even a fort. Today a city, Ludington, stands there. Marquette had been in America for only nine years, but in those years he had crowded more adventure than most men do in a long lifetime. Louis Joliet tended him to the last and went on sadly and alone.

Today if you should go to the states of Wisconsin or Michigan you would find many monuments to Père Marquette and Joliet. These states now cover much of the land over which the two great Frenchmen traveled. There are villages and cities named for Marquette, and in Milwaukee, there is a university bearing his name. In Chicago there are plaques honoring Joliet, and in Illinois the city of Joliet is named for him.

Strangers in a strange land, Marquette and Joliet opened a path for the great countries that came after them. The history of Canada followed the lakes and rivers they explored. A great part of the history of the United States marched along the Mississippi.

The Quaker Who Founded Pennsylvania

WILLIAM PENN

By Toby Bell

I SHOULD like to call the new American colony *Sylvania*," said Mr. William Penn to King Charles of England.

The King smiled. "We prefer to call it Pennsylvania."

"But it would be vanity on my part to name the colony for myself," said William Penn with characteristic modesty.

"We will keep it Pennsylvania," said the King, "but not on your account. We will keep the name in honor of the Admiral, your father."

This was strange, because William Penn, who had become a Quaker, was founding a colony to help the cause of peace among men. And Charles II, the King of England, was naming it for Penn's father who was a fierce and fighting Admiral. But William Penn loved his father even though they had different ways of thinking and living. So he said no more.

In England Quakers were put in prison for their religion. How did it happen, then, that the King of England was turning over to William Penn a vast stretch of land in the American colonies where the Quakers could live and work? It was, for Penn, a final victory in the struggle which he had begun many years ago.

When William Penn was eighteen years old, he strode into his father's house one day, keeping his hat on his head. The Admiral, Sir William, coming into the great hall, stopped short and stared at his son in amazement for such a show of seeming disrespect. They were both upstanding men and they both had keen blue eyes, but beyond that no one would have guessed that they belonged to the same family.

The Admiral wore the silks and lace ruffles of a gentleman of his time. His gold buttons caught the light. He was smoking a pipe with a long stem, an expensive luxury in that day. It nearly fell from his hand as he faced his son.

William stood straight and defiant in his suit of plain woollen cloth, with not a gold button, not a bit of lace, no decoration of any kind. His gray cloth hat with its wide straight brim stayed on his head. Aristocrats like the Penns did not wear plain clothes like that. Workers and farmers wore long-lasting leather or, sad to say, rags and patches. Even the servants in a house like Admiral Penn's wore fancy uniforms.

At last the Admiral found his voice. "What are you doing here in the middle of your term? Why are you not at Oxford?" he demanded.

"I was expelled from the college," said William in a steady voice.

"Expelled! Why? And why don't you take off your hat to greet me?"

William held up his head proudly. "I take off my hat only to God, not to men," he replied. "I was expelled because I am a

WILLIAM PENN. Quaker champion of religious freedom. Born in London, 1644. Studied law. Joined Society of Friends, 1666. Framed Charter of Pennsylvania, 1677. Made peace treaties with Indians. Founded Colony of Pennsylvania (later to become a state in the Union), 1681. Presented plan to England for Union of the Colonies, 1697. Died in England, 1718.

Quaker. We wear these clothes because we believe that men today use too many ornaments in their clothes and their homes and their churches. We are trying to get back to the simple ways of the early Christians. I hope this will not displease thee."

"Do not say 'thee' to me! Quaker! You are one of those who refuse to kill. You shake or quake or whatever you call it."

"Nay, father, we do not shake nor do we quake. People can call us any names they wish. That does not matter. We are not afraid. But we will not kill. We will not murder."

"You dare to say that to me who have fought in the King's Navy, who have fought the enemies of England to keep England strong and the King on his throne!"

The young man's blue eyes blazed as full of fire as his father's. "England has fought her enemies. But more Englishmen have fought and killed each other. Thee thyself hast called on the Lord of Peace to help thee kill our own people. We Quakers believe that if we talk to men in peace, they will listen."

The Admiral laughed scornfully. "As Admiral of the Royal Fleet I have won a war against the Dutch," he said. "What do you think would have happened if, in the middle of our battle with the enemy fleet, you had gone up to them in a little boat, and preached to them? You would have been dead before you could so much as speak."

"The Dutch are men of sense," said William. "We would have talked with them before there could be a battle."

"Never mind all that," said his father. "You are traitors to the King. That is enough for me."

"Traitors! Go to London, Father, and look about you. Look at the sailors on your ships whom you kidnap from their homes."

"Their homes! They are mud huts. The sailors are glad to get away from them." Then he saw how his son's face grew red, and in a quieter tone he said, "You look as disturbed now as any sailor of the King's Navy. You too are an angry man."

That indeed was true. William Penn was angry because men were not allowed to choose their own religion, because poor men had no chance to live decently in England.

But the Admiral could not understand any of this. He really believed that a family like his was made of finer stuff than a farmer's or a workingman's. So he was worried about his son. Perhaps William would be put in prison; perhaps he might even be killed. The Admiral thought that perhaps if William got away from England he might amuse himself like the other young men at the King's Court. So he sent him to Paris, where young men often went to see the world.

But William did not care for Paris. His mind was on the troubles of the Quakers. He wanted to do something to help them. When he came back he said so to his father.

This time the Admiral gave in. "Very well, my son," he said. "You are a Quaker. You believe that you will win with prayer and words. But listen to me. You will get nowhere by being rude and defiant as you were to me when you came back from Oxford."

William started to speak, but his father held up his hand. "You were not only rude, William. You were foolish. You will not get people to believe in you by insulting them. You shake your head? Never mind, you will

learn some time. But one thing I must warn you about. Do not *thee* and *thou* the King. And take off your hat to him."

The Admiral stalked off. He felt he had wasted his breath.

One day the very next week, when William was walking in the park, he saw the King there. King Charles did not walk alone as other men did. He walked with elegant courtiers and a train of ladies beautifully dressed. There were Dukes and Princes, and each of them held his hat in his hand. Only the King wore a hat, or, as they said then, only the King remained covered. William could have hurried off down a side road, but he would not. He walked toward the King. He bowed but he did not take off his hat. He could hear the gasp of horror of those around the King. In that day this was not only a rude thing that William did; it was held to be treason and men were executed for it. So each Lord and Lady waited breathless to see what the King would do.

Charles II was not a serious man. He was good-natured and he was clever. So, with a flourish, he swept his own plumed hat off his head.

Other men called Charles "Your Majesty," but not William Penn. He called him "Friend Charles," which was the way the Quakers spoke to everyone. He asked "Why remove thy hat, Friend Charles?"

"Because," said the King, "wherever I am, only one man may remain covered."

William got the point of this rebuke, and as he grew older, he learned that he could make more friends for the Quakers by not hurting people's feelings. He even became known, in time, for his kindly manners. But he remained firm in his great purpose, to find freedom for the Quakers.

In 1672, when Admiral Penn died, William learned that the King owed the Penn family a good deal of money. William knew the King lived so extravagantly that he could not pay back the debt. And here William saw his chance to carry out the great purpose he had held in his heart and his mind for so long. Here was a chance to get a place for the Quakers. He asked the King to settle the debt by giving him a stretch of land in the American Colonies. The King agreed, and to that vast territory went William and a large company of other Quakers. And that was how the State of Pennsylvania was founded.

In Pennsylvania, the Quakers could live as their religion told them to. They could dress plainly and work hard. They could be all plain people together, no aristocrats and no slaves. And there they would let other ill-treated people come too, and each would be free to live by his own religion and his own ideas, just so they lived decent lives.

From the beginning the colony of Pennsylvania was a success. The colonists did not have to go through the wars and hunger and sickness that plagued the other colonies. Because they lived so simply, they saved a good deal of money and became rich. They were thought to be good business men. Pennsylvania grew into one of the most powerful states in the United States.

Not many Quakers still say "thee" instead of you. And most of them dress like everyone else. But some still stick to these ways. All their meeting-houses and services are plain and simple as they were in the time of William Penn.

William Penn believed with all his soul that war is wrong. He wrote a great essay outlining a plan for a congress of nations where all disputes could be settled without fighting.

This peace-loving man is remembered by Americans for his peaceful settlement of Pennsylvania. All the colonies except Penn's waged war with the Indians. Only the Quakers, under Penn, met them without weapons. They signed their famous treaty, known as Penn's Treaty, under an elm tree on the river bank above Philadelphia. It was a treaty made in good faith and never broken. No Quaker ever killed an Indian, and no Indian shed a drop of Quaker blood. This is an extraordinary tribute to the faith of a great man named William Penn.

Indians and Pioneers

DANIEL BOONE

By Jason Robbins

WHEN Daniel Boone was eleven years old he lived on the wilderness edge of the colony of Pennsylvania. Only a narrow strip of land along the Atlantic Ocean then had houses and farms. The rest was wild forests where Indians hunted or lonely prairies where buffalo thundered in mighty herds. In that vast space there was hardly a white man.

Daniel's father, Squire Boone, was a farmer. He was a small man with a quick temper. Daniel's mother was kind and patient, as she needed to be, for Daniel had two brothers and five sisters, and they kept her busy. They were a lively family and they had good times together.

What Daniel liked best was to play with his Indian friends, the Delawares, who were the Boones' nearest neighbors. The Delawares were peaceful and they taught Daniel their wilderness ways. His special friend was a young Indian whose name, in English, was Longsight.

"Look at those crows!" said Daniel to Longsight one day when they were in the woods together. "It means someone is walking by—doesn't it? Maybe it's an enemy."

"You have learned well what I have told you," replied Longsight. "It is true that when birds fly suddenly, it is time to watch out. Crows are our best alarms in the woods. But wait; while you were listening to the crows, you left your footprints on that soft ground." Quickly he covered Daniel's footprints with leaves. "And now come into this brook and walk as far in it as you can. That will hide your trail best."

Daniel listened to all his friend taught him and never forgot. But there was still much for him to learn.

One day Longsight stopped him suddenly and asked, "What is that you have dropped?"

Daniel was eating cherries. Longsight bent over and picked a cherry pit from the ground. "That one cherry pit could cost you your life if an enemy was chasing you," he warned. "It would show which way you had gone. And there *are* Indian enemies beyond those western mountains."

"I want to go beyond those mountains," said Daniel. "I want to see new places. But why are Indians our enemies?"

Longsight told him that the Indians had been the first people to live in that land. They thought the country was theirs and that only they had the right to shoot and fish there.

"But," said Daniel, "there are so many buffaloes and bears and deer, what does it matter if our people shoot some too?"

"If too many people hunt over the ground, the animals will run away and then we Indians will starve. And you have heard, Daniel, of cruel white men who raid our Indian camps and steal our deer and other

DANIEL BOONE. American frontiersman, Indian fighter. Born near Reading, Pa., 1734. Established first settlement in Kentucky, 1773. Died 1820.

skins and kill us. Your father is one white man who has been fair with us. For that reason I am willing to teach you." And then Longsight paid Daniel his highest compliment. "You should have been an Indian," he said.

Daniel soon learned that though the Indians were clever in many ways, they did not learn white men's skills. One day Daniel came upon Longsight sitting gloomily on a log, holding his gun in his arms like a baby that was sick. When Daniel asked what was wrong, Longsight held out the gun to him. There was a break where the barrel joined the stock and Longsight was puzzled. Like all Indians of his day, he never asked how a gun was made and had no idea what to do

about it if it broke.

Daniel knew how guns were made and he knew how to repair this one. He tried to show Longsight; but the Indian, who was so clever in forest ways, just looked bothered and could not learn. Daniel made the simple repair himself at the forge on the farm. When he brought the gun back, Longsight danced with joy. But in a moment he stopped and again looked glum. "I have no gunpowder," he said.

It was against the law to sell gunpowder to Indians but Daniel had often wondered why they did not make it themselves. He knew it was easy to make, but no Indian tried it. Daniel wondered, too, why they kept tilling the ground with a stick instead of using the white man's plow and why squaws carried things on their backs instead of using wagons with wheels. And he asked Longsight why the squaws did not spin wool as Daniel's mother did, or weave cloth like Daniel's brother.

Longsight just shook his head and answered, "We wear deerskin." He pointed to Daniel's soft deerskin jacket and breeches. "I made those you have on. And I will teach you to make your own moccasins. Deerskin is good to hide in woods. Deerskin is warm, deer are plenty and deerskin lasts a long time."

Daniel was proud of his deerskin outfit, and he liked the leather belt Longsight had made for him. From it he hung his hunting knife and a powder horn. But the powder horn was empty. Daniel's father would not let him have a gun while he was so young.

One thing puzzled Daniel more than anything else. He could not understand why the Indians had no domestic animals except dogs. They had no pigs or cows or goats or chickens, though some Indians did have horses and they became the finest riders in America. Longsight explained that Indians did not stay in one place long enough to have many animals or crops to feed them.

When Daniel was twelve, his father gave him the gun he wanted so much, and taught him to fire it. In those days people depended so much on hunting for their food that boys were taught how to use guns much earlier than they are today.

When Daniel was sixteen a few other settlers moved into the part of the country where the Boones lived. "It's getting too crowded here," said Daniel's father. So Squire Boone bought some covered wagons and with his family and his horses and

cows, he started off to look for a new place to live. Daniel was a young man now and he walked with the other men, while his mother and sisters rode in the wagons. They took their time looking for a good place to settle down. There was so much untouched land in the American Colonies then that they could choose carefully. Sometimes they camped in one place for a week.

They decided at last on a small settlement called Yadkin in North Carolina. It took them two long years to reach Yadkin.

Daniel married in Yadkin, worked his farm, and had children of his own. Once in a while Daniel went off by himself to the wilds and hunted. On a tree in deep woods he cut the words "D.Boon cilled a Bar." He never had learned to spell because he had been so busy learning to be a backwoodsman. He did study arithmetic when he found that he could use it in measuring land and selling skins and crops. If he had known how many millions of people in later days would come to read that sign he cut on the tree, he would surely have learned to spell.

All through his ten years at Yadkin Daniel Boone longed to find an untouched place in the wilderness where he could start a new settlement. Friendly Catawba Indians said there was a wonderful place called Kaintuck. "It is hard to reach," they told him. "To get there you will have to cross to beyond those Great Smoky Mountains. On top of those mountains, there are always clouds and in the winter heavy snows. You will have to find a way through."

"I have found many hidden paths," said Daniel. "I will try this."

"You will do it too, we know," said the Catawbas. "But there is worse. Kaintuck lies between two Indian tribes. The Cherokees are on the South and the Shawnees are on the North. These two tribes fight each other all the time for the rich Kaintuck land. You may be able to deal with the Cherokees. But the Shawnees are a fierce tribe. You will have to fight them."

These were dangers that Daniel understood and was ready to face. He was a strong muscular man who always won at wrestling, at high jumps, and in foot races. He was not tall but he had wide shoulders and a deep chest. He wore his black hair in two braids. His blond eyebrows looked odd against the dark hair. His nose was bold, as though trying to get to new places even faster than his swift body could go.

Daniel set out to find Kaintuck. He picked five men to go with him, his wife's brother Bryan and four others. They loaded pack animals with food, blankets, powder and shot, and they dyed their deerskins black so they would not show in the dark. After long weeks they got through the trail in the Great Smokies. At the top of the mountains they stood, and when the clouds cleared away for an hour, they could look down to where the rich land of Kaintuck lay spread before them.

On the other side of the mountains, the danger from the Shawnees was greater. Daniel and his small band were wary. They never hunted near their own camps, for if they had, the buzzards would come and fly around the food, and that would tell the Indians where they were. Even so, the Shawnees captured Daniel and Bryan twice. They did not torture them, but they warned them, "Longknives not hunt here." Longknives was an Indian word for white people.

Once the Shawnees tied a bell around Daniel's neck and made him run around like a horse. They thought this great fun and they laughed and laughed. And while they were laughing, Daniel and Bryan escaped. The four white settlers with them said they had had enough and they went back home.

Later Bryan went back too, for fresh supplies. Then Daniel was left all alone in the vast stretch of this wild and dangerous country. He had to use every bit of the backwoods training he had learned as a boy. Once he escaped by walking through a river. And once the Indians almost got him. He was running fast, and suddenly there was no more path ahead of him, only a deep gorge. Daniel had not so much as a second to find out if it was possible to climb down the steep sides of the gorge. Instantly, then, he *leaped* over and landed down fifty feet into the top of a tree. The Indians were so filled with amazement at this feat that they didn't go after him.

At last, after many such dangerous adventures, Daniel came upon just the land he wanted. He went back to Yadkin where he and thirty other men started to build a wide road leading from there to the new land he had found.

But Daniel knew that first they would have to do something about the Indians. He and his men got together fifty thousand dollars and paid it to the Cherokees. The Cherokees then said Boone could have the land of Kaintuck and that if the Shawnees attacked, they, the Cherokees, would help the white men fight them off.

The wide road that Daniel started was finished at last. He called it the Wilderness Road, and in the year 1773 Daniel Boone led his wife and his seven children, as well as the other settlers who wanted to go along, into Kaintuck. By then they were

calling it Kentucky, which is its name today. In the place Daniel had found they built the first white settlement in that region, and they called it Boonesborough.

Boonesborough was not a town but a large fort. It was about two hundred and fifty feet long and almost that wide. For greater strength they had placed the logs it was made of standing up instead of lying down. Inside the fort there were thirty cabins, and there were a few outside too, between the fort and a river. Daniel and his family lived in one of these.

For a long time the Indians caused no trouble and some of the young people in the settlement grew careless. On a sunny warm afternoon in June, Daniel Boone's oldest daughter, who was then about fifteen, said to two other girls, "Come on, let's take out that canoe and paddle up the river."

One of the girls was afraid, but the other said, "Oh, come on. The Indians aren't around here any more. Let's have some fun." So the three girls got into the canoe and they were paddling along and laughing when, to their horror, five Indians leaped off the opposite bank, grabbed the canoe, pulled the girls out, and ran off with them. Nobody saw it happen. No one knew the girls were gone. But late in the afternoon when they did not come back to milk the cows, there was an alarm all through the camp, and Daniel and a party of other settlers started out to look for them.

The searchers found the empty canoe and a few Indian moccasin prints. But these clues soon gave out. The girls, however, had been brought up in the backwoods, and scared though they were, they kept their heads. Every little while they secretly broke a twig or dragged their heels in the mud to leave a trail. But night fell soon and it became so dark that it was hard to see anything. The angry settlers could do nothing but worry.

But in the morning Daniel said to the other men, "Let us not waste time in anger. It must have been the Shawnees who did this thing. They will try to take the girls to their village and make them slaves. There are three young men among us who wish to marry the girls. Love will make them run faster. So they and I will go ahead. And you will come on after us."

Luckily the Indians, thinking they had shaken off the white men, were gleeful and careless. They even left a freshly killed buffalo on the trail.

"They are eating," said Daniel. "They must be very near. But if we all go toward them at once, it will make too much noise. Let me go ahead alone, and as soon as you hear my gun, you hurry up."

Daniel crept up and soon saw the Indians eating around their fire. The three girls were tied to a tree, their heads up proudly, but their faces were smeared with tears. Daniel fired. An Indian fell. The three young men rushed up. Another Indian fell. The rest of the Indians ran off. The girls were saved. But they never tried such an adventure again.

All the settlers knew that what the Shawnees wanted most was to capture Daniel Boone himself. And one day, while he was hunting in a snowstorm, they caught him.

Daniel knew, from their red and black paint, that they were on the warpath. Now if ever, Daniel would have to think fast. He turned to them and pretended to be glad to see them.

"Welcome," he said and added, "I am tired of farming and doing women's work. I have come to join you."

They took him to their Chief, Blackfish. To Blackfish Daniel said, "If you wait until spring when the paths begin to open, I will go back to the settlement and bring its people out to you."

The Shawnees, though they were his enemies, admired Daniel Boone. They said that he was almost as skilled as an Indian, that he could hunt and follow a trail as well as they could. So Blackfish set out to adopt him and make him into an Indian. They pulled out the hairs of his head one by one, all but a patch on top for a scalp lock. They painted his body and hung beads on his neck and arms and gave him red feathers for his head. The squaws scrubbed him hard, for they thought scrubbing would wash his white blood away.

Daniel let them think he had become a son of the Shawnees, and Blackfish called him Big Turtle. For four months Daniel kept up the masquerade, always watching for a chance to escape. Then one day when the Indians were all looking up to aim at a flock of wild turkeys, Daniel leaped on a horse and galloped away. He rode and swam and walked four days till he reached Boonesborough. When he got there he was in rags and exhausted.

He saw then that there were only a few people left in Boonesborough. They told him his wife and children, thinking he must be dead, had gone back to North Carolina. He planned to go at once to get them, but before he had a chance to set out, Blackfish and his Shawnees attacked the fort. Most Indian attacks lasted a few hours or a day. But Blackfish was so furious that this attack

kept on day after day. The few white settlers defending the fort were worn out
when, on the fourth day, the Indians threw
in flaming arrows and the logs caught fire.
A boy put the fire out with his hands. But
the flaming arrows came again and the men
were desperate until, on the seventh day, a
great rain came from the skies and put out
the fire.

Then the Indians tried to dig a tunnel
into the fort. They were almost inside when
the long rain wet the earth through, and
the tunnel fell in. The Indians gave up.
When they went away, Daniel traveled to
North Carolina to find his family and bring
them back.

There was one more great battle with
the Indians. It lasted only fifteen minutes,
but in it Daniel's son was killed.

Soon after that, the Indians were utterly
defeated and there was no serious trouble
between these Indians and the white men
for nearly a hundred years. And settlers
poured into Kentucky thick and fast.

Through the Wilderness Road, Daniel
Boone had opened the way into the great
American West. Thousands and even mil-
lions of men came through. And so Daniel
Boone became one of the makers of the
United States of America, a hero to all
explorers and to all who admired boldness
and courage.

Two Explorers of the Great Northwest

SIR ALEXANDER MACKENZIE AND CAPTAIN JAMES COOK

By Rosemary Nicolais

A FIFTEEN-YEAR-OLD boy, Alexander Mackenzie, was strolling alongside the docks in Montreal, Canada, on a spring afternoon in 1779. He was a refugee from the Revolutionary War in America. During the three months since his arrival in Canada Alex had spent a good many hours at the docks. They fascinated him.

A shipment of furs was being loaded for England—mink, marten, muskrat, fox, raccoon, and beaver. Alex knew the names of all the animal skins by now.

Farther along the harbor he stopped to look at the colorful picture made by the fur-traders' men, French and British, as they piled their canoes high with guns and supplies and gifts for Indian trappers. In Canada these men were called *voyageurs,* the French word for travelers.

A *voyageur's* life must be the most thrilling in all the world, he thought to himself. He would love to go sailing along the rivers and lakes, exploring the unknown, buying skins from the Indians.

The excuse he gave his friends for his long absences at the harbor was that he had to find out when the boat would arrive from America that was to bring his Aunt Syb and Aunt Muriel. But he didn't bother to ask any more. Some sailor, sea-captain, or shipping-clerk would let him know. He had talked to everyone around the harbor about those two aunts.

They had taken the place of his mother who had died in Scotland so many years ago that he could hardly remember her. They had come to America to keep house for his father, but now his father was dead too. He had been killed fighting against the American Revolutionary Army. It seemed to Alex that the three who were left, he and his aunts, ought to stay together, but the aunts thought otherwise. New York State, where they were living, was no place just now, they said, for the son of a British officer. The best place for Alex was across the border. And off he had gone as soon as a responsible person was found to take charge of him. Aunt Syb promised they would follow as soon as possible. When Alex objected to leaving them behind she put on her severe expression.

"Are you in charge of us or we of you? Now you be off before I take a cane to your legs," she said.

That was three months ago. Now Alex, waking from his daydream on the docks, turned abruptly in the direction of home. Accidentally he stepped on the toes of a tall, proud man behind him.

ALEXANDER MACKENZIE. Explorer in Canada. Born in Scotland, 1763. Explored the river flowing into Arctic Ocean later named after him. First white man to cross the Rocky Mountains and reach the Pacific. Knighted by King George III of England, 1802. Died in Scotland, 1820.

JAMES COOK. Mariner and explorer, known as Captain Cook. Born in England, 1728. Surveyed St. Lawrence Channel, Newfoundland and Labrador Coasts. Explored Pacific in search of an undiscovered new Continent. Skirted Antarctic. Rediscovered Sandwich (now Hawaiian) Islands. Charted Pacific Coast of North America as far as Behring Straits. Killed by natives in Hawaii, 1779.

"You young scoundrel!" the man cried angrily. "Have you no manners? Why don't you look where you're going?"

"I'm sorry I trod on your toes," Alex began, apologizing, but then he threw back his dark curly head in resentment. The man had raised his whip and was striking him over the shoulders with it, shouting at him.

"Don't give me any of your back-talk, young fellow."

"I said I was sorry," Alex shouted back. "And I'm no scoundrel." He seized the whip, threw it on the ground, and ran as fast as his legs would carry him.

If Alex Mackenzie had kept on running, his great chance might never have come to him. But he didn't. He stopped in a doorway and peeped to see if he was being followed. He was, but not by the man who had beaten him. A shorter, less important-looking man, who wore the clothes of a workingman, called out to him to stop.

"Hey! You're Alexander Mackenzie, aren't you? I want to talk to you."

The boy's dark shining eyes met the man's with defiance. He was prepared to stick up for himself if he was going to be attacked again. But this man's eyes had a kindly twinkle in them.

"I'm John Gregory," he said. "My boy, I've never before seen anyone, man or boy, stand up to Simon McTavish the way you did. Walk along with me. I have something particular to say to you."

Now Simon McTavish was the richest and most powerful fur-trader in all Canada. He was greedy and wanted to keep all the fur-trade to himself. And that meant ruin for the small traders. John Gregory was one of these small traders.

"I could do with a young clerk like you in my office," Gregory told Alex after a while. The boy's heart beat fast as he agreed to be in the office of this new friend the next morning. It was a proud and happy day for him when his two beloved aunts arrived and he was able to tell them he was earning his own living.

As time went on Alex learned more and more about the business of fur-trading. But he never ceased to dream of the adventurous life of a *voyageur*. That was the life for him. He didn't want to work in an office all his life.

Again something happened to give him the very chance he wished for. One wintry evening as he sat at supper with his aunts, a message was brought to him.

"Meet me at the tavern at eight o'clock tonight," it read, "and tell no one." It was signed "Charles Ducette."

"Who's it from?" Aunt Syb asked, suspiciously.

"Oh, a friend."

"That's no answer."

"Just one of the *voyageurs*," Alex explained, airily. "I've got to meet him tonight. He's going up river pretty soon and I suppose he wants to talk to me about provisions."

"Huh!" Aunt Syb snorted. But Aunt Muriel grew pink with pride because the boy sounded so manly.

The Charles Ducette who had signed the note was a humble man, but because he was a real *voyageur* Alex felt flattered by having this secret rendezvous with him. When he reached the tavern he tried to behave like a man. He wasn't going to be scared by the bright lights, the scurry of waiters carrying trays, and the clamor of loud talk and laughter and tinkling glasses. All the same it was quite a relief to see Ducette beckoning him into a quiet corner.

"Is it always so noisy?" he asked.

"Well, perhaps tonight's a bit special," Ducette replied. He lowered his voice to call Alex's attention to some gentlemen who had just entered. "Those three the landlord's bowing to as if they were great lords."

"Why, that tall one's McTavish," Alex exclaimed.

"S-sh! Yes, and his two new partners. They're going upstairs."

"Too good to dine with us common people?"

"Not that. They're plotting something and don't want any big ears taking it all in." Ducette chuckled and went on, "They're too late, though. I know all about their scheming. And Mr. Gregory ought to know. That's why I asked you to meet me—so that I can tell you and you can tell him. He trusts you."

Alex listened with bated breath while Ducette outlined McTavish's plan of action. Upstairs the old Scotsman and his companions were signing papers that named them partners in the Northwest Company. This new Company was going to decide who could trade in furs and who could not, and all small traders were to be kept out, by fair means or foul. Already hundreds of *voyageurs* were preparing to start for the interior, and more were to follow. Supplies were being ordered on a scale unheard of in the history of the trade.

Such news could not wait. Alex ran all the way to John Gregory's little cabin and knocked on the door. The trader woke up and came shivering in his nightclothes to see who could be wanting him at such an hour.

Alex poured out his story and then asked, breathlessly, "What are we going to do about it?"

"Nothing tonight," John Gregory replied, smiling at his young clerk's enthusiasm. "I'm going back to bed. We'll talk about all this tomorrow. Good night."

Next morning Gregory told him, "We will form our own Company. I'll get some of my friends among the small traders to come in with me. It's going to mean a fight, a long fight. And, to deal with the Indians, I want a man I can trust beyond the shadow of a doubt. I can think of no better man for that job than you, Alex Mackenzie."

Alex didn't hear the rest of what his employer was saying. "I shall be a *voyageur!*" he kept saying to himself, and his heart sang for joy. He felt he ought to say something so he asked "What are you going to call your new Company, sir?"

"Call it Anything you like. The XY Company, perhaps. But start immediately for Detroit. Take all the canoes you can load, and all the beads and blankets and knives and trinkets you can get hold of for the Indians. Take clerks, paddlers, guides, but start at once."

Detroit, of course, belonged to the United States by this time, because the American Revolutionists had won the war. But the United States government had not had time to claim it, and Canadians could still move in and act as if they owned it and all the surrounding country.

The new XY Company ran into many difficulties, but Alex knew how to handle them. He was happier than he had ever been in his life. He learned to understand and love the Indians. A few weeks after he had established camp in Detroit, the Indians sold him his first six huge bales of furs, and from then on the trade of the new Company increased rapidly. His men told stories of how he won the confidence of the Indians. One of them was about an old Indian Chief who was very ill with fever.

"I have some white powder that will make him better," said one of the clerks.

"No, no!" screamed the Indian. "I will not take your powder."

The white man smiled. "You think I am offering you poison. See! I myself will take some to prove it is harmless." He swallowed a dose of the powder. Still the Indian refused to touch it.

Alex had been watching, close by. He drew near, sat down by the sick man's couch, and stroked the long black hair from his forehead.

"We are your friends," he said in a gentle voice. "We are unhappy to see you sick. You will be doing us great honor if you take this powder we are offering you."

To the astonishment of the other white men, the old Chief swallowed the powder at once.

"To honor you," he said, solemnly, "I will take the magic powder if it kills me."

John Gregory thought so well of Alex's work in and around Detroit that he made him a partner at the end of his first year. He had heard how, time after time, the young

man had foiled the Northwest Company's attempt to bribe his men and turn the Indians against him. The bitter war between the two Companies continued for many years, and McTavish's men and Alex's often came to blows.

Much of his time had to be spent in the frozen Northwest. No white man had penetrated farther into Canada at that time than to the shores of Lake Athabasca and the Great Slave Lake, a little more than halfway across the continent. Beyond that was the wilderness. And it was on the shores of Lake Athabasca that Alex spent his next long, hard winter. There was little to do until the ice broke up and the Indians could come down the rivers with their furs to the trading settlements. Meantime Alex had time to dream and to listen to Indian tales of

the Rocky Mountains and what they called "the great stinking water" beyond them. That must be the Pacific, he thought, and the great rivers of Canada must flow west into it. A man with strength and endurance could follow the rivers to see where they came out. And he read all the books he could get that told how great explorers had devoted their lives to discovering new lands.

One night he closed a book he had been reading by the fire, got up and began walking restlessly up and down the hut he shared with some of his men.

"Amazing!" he exclaimed. "One of the greatest navigators the world has ever known!"

"Who? Columbus?" asked a man in the corner, sleepily.

"No. I was thinking of Captain Cook,"

replied Alex. "Do you know, he ran away to sea at fourteen. Had no education but what he taught himself. Worked for nothing for four years. Became an able seaman. Then, just when he got to be first mate he gave it all up to join the Royal Navy, because his country was at war and needed him. At the end of the war he started all over again at the bottom of the ladder . . ."

"Not so fast," Roderick Mackenzie interrupted. He was Alex's cousin and a clerk in the XY Company. "You forget that while he was in the Royal Navy he was Master of the King's Ship-of-the-Line *Pembroke* . . ."

"You tell it then, Rory, if you know so much about it."

". . . and the *Pembroke* took part in the Battle of Quebec in 1759. Master James Cook played quite a part in winning the battle. You're right. He was a fine navigator. He made it possible for the troops to land because he charted a passage through that dangerous channel below Quebec."

"Then he lost his job," Alex said, with some bitterness.

"Oh, a man like Cook is never out of a job long," Rory went on. "Every nation that has any ships today is sending them out to explore strange waters and discover new lands, and it was the same when Cook was a young man, twenty or thirty years ago. He was needed right enough, and soon after the war he was sailing the Southern seas in search of a new continent between Australia and the Americas."

"And it didn't exist."

"That's right. It was useful to know, anyway. He grazed polar ice many a time searching for it."

"And he found New Zealand and Australia," said Alex, "or, rather, re-discovered

them. I believe some Dutch navigator or other was the first to land in Australia a few centuries ago."

"Yes, but Cook made maps of the coasts and charted the seas wherever he went. Then, of course, he was really the first white man to discover the Sandwich Islands (Hawaii), Tierra del Fuego, the Friendly Islands . . ."

"And America . . ." Alex got no further for the peals of laughter that greeted this remark. When he could be heard again he went on to explain that he meant the west coast of America. "His job was to find a passage across the North American continent. We know he landed and saw great forests and an unbroken chain of high mountains. But he sailed on right around the northwest tip of the continent without finding a way through."

"For a good reason," smiled Rory. "There is none."

Alex stared into the fire and shook his head thoughtfully. "I wonder!"

There was a moment's silence, then a young clerk who had been trying to get up courage to ask a question, suddenly blurted it out. "Is it true the Hawaiians made a god of this Captain Cook, then killed him?"

"I wouldn't put it like that exactly," replied Rory. "A quarrel broke out between the natives and the sailors about some knives that were stolen from the ship. A couple of shots were fired, and this scared the natives. Poor Cook got stabbed in the back during the excitement. The Chief was quite unhappy about it. He gave his friend a magnificent funeral service and sent his body to the ship with great ceremony."

Not long after this talk about Captain Cook, Alex persuaded John Gregory to give him a few months leave so that he could explore the Peace River that flowed out of the Great Slave Lake. Gregory did not stand in his way and in June 1789, Alex took four canoes and started up the river.

One hundred and two days later he was back telling Rory all about it.

"So much for my wonderful Peace River," he said, gloomily. "I found an ocean all right, but it turned out to be—not the Pacific, but the Arctic!"

"You think the expedition amounted to nothing, then?" Rory asked with a laugh. "Why, Alex, think what you have done! You have gained three thousand miles from the wilderness, and no serious accident. Isn't that a kind of record? You explored the whole of the Peace River, next in size to the Mississippi. Instead of calling it the River of Disappointment, I'd call it the Mackenzie River."

Rory was the only encouraging friend Alex had. McTavish, of course, thought exploring a waste of time. But even John Gregory discouraged any further effort to find a way to the Pacific, and that hurt Alex.

He decided to go to England and study navigation and astronomy and anything else that would give him more knowledge to help him conquer the wilderness. He spent a good part of the year 1792 studying in England. When he returned to Canada he found that Rory had built a new Fort on the mighty Peace River and made friends with the local Indians. That was a great help, for he was able to spend the winter there preparing for his new expedition. Another Scot, Alexander McKay, went with him, and the faithful Ducette and several others.

The twenty-five foot canoe containing ten young men and Alex's dog, Eskimo, who had refused to be left behind, was launched from the fort on May 9, 1793. Whenever they came to a place where the river forked, Alex had to guess or consult Indians who lived there about which fork to take. His own Indian guides often disagreed with the strange Indians. They called Alex Kitchi Okema, which means He-who-travels-fast, and they said "Kitchi Okema is leading us to the land of the evil spirit, the Matchi Manitou" when he insisted upon taking the advice he thought wisest. Sometimes the fork he took led the little party into swift, rocky streams, full of cataracts, and the boat had to be unloaded, carried over the cataracts, then re-loaded many times. But, though navigation was difficult and though the canoe had to be patched up every other day, the route Alex took proved to be the right one. On the afternoon of May 17 he thought he could make out a white line against the sky and called to the others to look. "The Rocky Mountains!" they all cried, dancing with joy. "Soon we shall cross them!" Only the Indians didn't want to cross the Rockies. They said, "We have seen the great mountains. Now the good kind Kitchi Okema will let us turn back and go home." They had had enough.

Alex had to be patient. "We now have a chance of really finding the big water," he told them. "That is what we went through so much danger and endured so many hardships for, isn't it?" And gradually he persuaded them to go on.

During the next two months and more they met with even worse mishaps. Storms and rushing waters swept all their supplies away. Unfriendly Indians threatened them. Starvation faced them at the last. Yet the

Indian guides and paddlers never complained again. They remained loyal and went doggedly on.

It was on a warm sunny morning—the 20th of July, 1793—that the sturdy but battered canoe at last came out into a little bay of the Pacific Ocean.

The Indians they met near the coast treated them with great friendliness. One day a Chief showed Alex a blue cloth coat with brass buttons and some European cooking-pans.

"These," he explained, "were gifts ten winters ago from a white man like you."

Captain Cook! Alex could hardly speak, he was so overcome by this proof that the great navigator had really landed on the west coast of America, and had actually stood on the same spot he was standing on, ten years before.

The full story of Alexander Mackenzie's expeditions was written by himself a few years after his return to civilization. The book brought him great fame, and the King of England made him a Knight. From being a poor, fifteen-year-old clerk in John Gregory's office, the boy Alex, while still in the prime of life, had become Sir Alexander Mackenzie, the famous Canadian discoverer of the road to the Pacific.

The Indian Girl Who Guided Lewis and Clark

SACAJAWEA

By Marion E. Gridley

"THE buffalo move! Get ready! Get ready!" came the cry. Far out on the prairie two scouts circled about on horseback and tossed their robes into the air, signaling the news to the Shoshone village some distance away. The plains-dwelling tribes were so dependent upon the huge, shaggy beasts that they had no choice but to follow where they led. From the buffalo came both meat for food and skins for clothing.

"Come, my little bird," Sacajawea's mother said.

She picked up the cradle board, padded with soft leather and bright with quill embroidery, and hung it from the saddle of her horse. A skin pouch, attached to the board, held the tiny baby snugly. Sacajawea's eyes sparkled, and she crowed with glee. She looked like a baby bird swinging in its nest.

The men had rounded up the ponies. The women had taken down the light skin tepees, each wrapped around a cone-like framework of poles, widely rounding at the base. The strong poles were lashed together over a horse to form a crude drag that carried the family possessions. Sacajawea's brother, Cameahwait, sat there.

At the head of the column rode Sacajawea's father. Into a buffalo horn he had packed a few coals in moist, rotten wood. He had to go first so that a fire could be kindled at the next camp to start the lodge fires anew. No one knew where or how far the buffalo would lead them, whether they would stay upon the flat table-land, or whether coming into enemy country, they would seek the mountains, a purple shimmer in the distance, and hunt only as they could.

This was Sacajawea's life. The sweeping winds, the mountain heights, the sudden moves, days of feasting or days of hunger, and constant work. Skins must be cleaned, tanned, and made into clothes. Meat must be cut, pounded, and dried to keep. Berries and wild roots must be picked or dug. There was no time for settled ways, for the buffalo were never still.

When she had reached the age of ten, Sacajawea had long had a horse of her own. When she rode along the high trails, she saw the vast country rolling before her. Most of it she knew.

"I wish I were really a bird," she would say to Cameahwait. "Then I could see it all. What lies on the other side of the mountains? Where do the rivers go? How far does the prairie reach?"

One day the Shoshones were in the midst of preparing buffalo meat after a hunt.

"Run! Run!" Cameahwait cried as he leaped upon his horse.

Loud war whoops drowned out his words. Many of the Shoshones fell in the surprise attack. Others fled back to the mountains. Sacajawea was seized by her long

SACAJAWEA. American Indian woman interpreter. Born a Shoshone in 1787(?). Captured and sold to Canadian trapper, Toussaint Charbonneau. Married him. Acted as guide, with her husband, in Lewis and Clark Expedition, 1805. Died 1884.

black hair and lifted to a warrior's horse. As she was carried away, she saw her brother in the midst of the fighting.

This was the last she was to know or hear of her people for many years.

When the Minnetarees came to their own village, they gave Sacajawea to the women.

"Take her, she is yours," they said. "Put her to work."

But though she had to work hard, she was not treated unkindly.

The women showed her how to plant fields of corn, beans, and squash. Sacajawea had to hoe the ground with a buffalo shoulder blade. She dug the soil with a pointed stick, pushed in the seeds, and later helped with the harvest. The Minnetarees were surprised at her wonder over the planting.

"My people could pick only the wild plants," Sacajawea said.

She thought of the endless drifting of her tribe, of the skin houses that traveled with them. The Minnetaree houses were not made of skin, but of earth. They were great circular rooms with hard-packed floors and dome-shaped roofs. The houses were clustered on a bend of a river and walled off from attack by a high, strong fence.

Sacajawea found the new way of life a happy change from the fear and danger of the old day-to-day one.

One day a French trader named Toussaint Charbonneau came to the village. Sacajawea was now seventeen. She was pleasing to see, young and strong; and Charbonneau made her his wife.

Soon afterward he told her a strange thing. "Many white people live to the far east," he said. "Two of them, Captain Lewis and Captain Clark, have come to explore the land between the Missouri River and the great west. They will winter at the Indian village and start out in the spring. They will claim the land for the United States."

Although Sacajawea knew about white men, she could not understand all her husband told her. But her heart pounded at his next remark.

"Can you still speak your own language?" he asked her.

"Yes, oh, yes!" Sacajawea replied. "I have never forgotten it!"

"Do you still know your old country?" Charbonneau asked next.

"Yes, oh, yes!" Sacajawea answered. "Just as I see the clouds and the stars in the sky, I can close my eyes and see the mountains and the valleys and the old trails that we followed!"

"Good! Good!" Charbonneau said, smiling. "Then we will go with the white men, for they need help through the mountains. They will pay me well."

Sacajawea trembled with excitement. It was she, the only woman with the expedition, who would guide the white men, for only she knew the way. She would see her own people at last! She would see what lay on the other side of the mountain spires!

In February a son, Baptiste, was born to Sacajawea and Charbonneau. By April the river ice had broken, and the expedition started out. This was in the year 1804. Sacajawea swung her baby to her back and took her place in the first boat. Behind this came another boat, and six canoes. Baptiste was carried on his mother's shoulders, held close and tight in her blanket shawl for the whole of that journey of many hundreds of miles.

The days stretched far ahead. At first the

travelers had enough food, for there was plenty of game; but the river and the winds fought them desperately. The boats, heavily loaded with food, clothing, ammunition, and gifts for the Indians along the way, moved upstream slowly. They were often grounded in the sand and gravel of shallow water.

Janey was Captain Clark's name for Sacajawea. It was easier to say than her Indian one.

"Janey," he would say when they camped for the night, "tell us about the country."

So in sign language and in halting French or English Sacajawea would tell of Indian trails and camps. She would warn of bad water and of poisonous plants and of fierce animals. Her gentle manner and her young child softened the rough men and gave them heart to keep on as the way grew more difficult. Somehow she sensed that this was a matter of the utmost importance to them all, though she did not understand why.

Once the wind and water overturned a boat filled with instruments and valuable papers that could never be replaced. Into the icy stream plunged a figure, swimming about until everything had been saved.

"It is Sacajawea!" the men shouted. "It is Janey, with Baptiste still on her back!"

They pulled her into the boat and made for shore and a roaring fire.

At last the travelers came to where the river divided into three separate channels. Sacajawea knew this was near her homeland. The two captains were worried, for no white men had passed to the west of Sacajawea's people. Would the Shoshones recognize the long-lost girl? Would they listen to her? Would she really remember her language? The party was in need of help. They must have horses in order to cross the Great Divide.

As the expedition reached the crest of a hill, Sacajawea suddenly gave a cry of joy. She saw a Shoshone camp. A band of Indians waited the approach of the strangers, the chief at their head. Sacajawea rushed forward and threw her blanket about the shoulders of the chief.

"We are of the same blanket!" she cried in her native tongue. "Oh, Cameahwait, my brother! Do you not remember Sacajawea?"

The Indians looked at her in wonder.

"This is the 'Lost One'!" they cried. "She is of our people!"

There was great rejoicing, and a council was held. Sacajawea spoke to her people in behalf of the Captains Lewis and Clark. The Indians listened to her with close attention, even though a council circle was no place for a woman and this was an unheard-of thing.

"My sister's friends are my brothers," Cameahwait said when she had finished. "Ask of us what you will. You may have horses and guides to help you over the mountains."

"Janey has saved the day!" Lewis said. "We owe her not only our instruments but our very lives! If we get through to the coast, she will deserve most of the credit!"

The Lewis and Clark Expedition did not get away from the Shoshone village until the end of August, and now they came to the hardest part of the journey. In the mountains the winter storms began to swirl, and snow and sleet bit at their faces and hands. Horses and men were exhausted from the steep trails. It seemed sometimes as though they could not stand up against the

hardships. But somehow they kept on.

Then, one clear November day, the explorers stood in silence as they saw Old Glory float to the top of a tall tree. There, in sight of the ocean, Captain Lewis spoke slowly and firmly.

"I claim this land in the name of the United States of America," he said.

Sacajawea held Baptiste up to see the breakers as they roared and pounded on the beach. She was the first woman to cross the great mountains. She was Sacajawea, the Bird Woman.

Captain Clark tried to thank her for all she had done.

"Without you, Janey," he said, "perhaps all this might never have been!"

Sacajawea smiled at him. She did not understand his words, but she wanted to share with him something of her own deep feeling. She pointed to the breaking waves.

"I see!" she said. "I see!"

The Long Hard Oregon Trail

NARCISSA AND MARCUS WHITMAN

By Jason Robbins

THERE was a wedding a long time ago, on a cold, snowy February day of the year 1836. The bride was as beautiful as any moving-picture star of our own time. Her name was Narcissa and she was as lovely as the flower she was named after. The groom was a hero and looked like one. He was young Dr. Marcus Whitman, big, powerful, with keen blue eyes in a sunburned face. But this was no movie wedding. Narcissa wore no white gown, no veil over her golden hair. Instead she stood in a plain black dress before the altar of a little church in Angelica, New York.

Some old friends stood aside to hide their worried faces. Mrs. Prentiss, Narcissa's aunt, wiped tears from her eyes. She was saying, "It is a shame for Narcissa to go off on this dark and dangerous journey. That Western trail is hard enough for a strong young man like Marcus, but Narcissa is such a young and lovely girl. How will she stand it?"

Nearby two guests were listening. They were two Indian boys. Dr. Whitman had brought them back with him from a journey a year ago. Because their Indian names were hard to say, he called them Richard and John.

Now John felt he had to speak. "Ma'am," he said to Mrs. Prentiss, "we will watch over Mrs. Whitman. We are going to Oregon with them. And Dr. Whitman has made this journey once before. He knows the way and he is a wonderful pioneer in the wilderness. He can cut a trail where none has been before. No Indian can do it better. But he can do much more. He can also save a sick horse. And he can cure a sick man."

"I am sure of that," said a man standing near by. "But because Marcus Whitman is a great doctor, we need him here at home."

"Sir," said John timidly, "you have other doctors. We have none except the old magicians. They know little and they will not learn. Our people need Dr. Whitman more than you do. And we have other needs for him too. He is a preacher as well as a doctor. We need him to bring us God, your God, the God of the white people."

"Still," said Mrs. Prentiss, "I do not see why Narcissa has to go too. No white woman has ever been in that wild Oregon region."

"She is a teacher, Ma'am," protested Richard. "She has taught many children. And what good would your Book of Heaven be —your Bible—if our people did not learn to read it?"

Narcissa had come up then and heard them. "Dry your tears, Aunt," she said. "You know how long I have wanted to be a missionary to the Indians. As an unmarried woman I could not go. Now I am happy to go."

To all of them there at the wedding that day, the Oregon region seemed far away

MARCUS WHITMAN. Physician and preacher. Born in Rushville, N.Y., 1802. Married Narcissa Prentiss, a teacher, of Plattsburg, N.Y., 1836. Set out with her for Oregon Territory same year. Suffered incredible hardships on journey. Secured Oregon Territory to the U.S. by treaty, 1846. Both he and his wife Narcissa killed by Indians, 1847.

indeed. Its mountains reached snow-capped into the sky, its great stretches of grassland were unused, its mighty forests were wilderness. Indians were there and a few fur trappers, no one else. Today that vast space covers the states of Oregon and Washington and part of Idaho. And it was for this wild pathless land that Narcissa and Marcus set out. It was a strange wedding trip.

Two other people set out with them, newlyweds too, Henry and Eliza Spalding. These two had been married on the same day as the Whitmans. Eliza was not as beautiful or as lively as Narcissa, but she had a cool calm courage. She was to need every bit of it.

There was, of course, no railroad, no quick way to go. As far as Independence, Missouri, there were wagon roads and a few scattered towns. From there on, the way was trackless.

The two young couples set out with two covered wagons. They took along sixteen cows, horses for riding, and mules to pull the wagons. They carried seeds and simple tools. Above all else in their precious care were their Bibles, their school books, and their medicines. Narcissa had a little trunk and a few small treasures. At first, the men rode the horses while the two girls rode in the wagons. Dr. Whitman said that they must take these wagons all the way to Oregon.

The Oregon region did not seem to belong to anyone except a few scattered Indians. The only white men in that western part of the continent were fur trappers, and Dr. Whitman saw that there would some day be settlers bringing up their families there. If the settlers were mostly Americans, Oregon would belong to the United States.

If they were mostly English, then the land would belong to England. It was to help American settlers that the Whitmans and the Spaldings were opening the way.

Not everybody wanted what Dr. Whitman wanted. Many of the trappers were dishonest. They got furs cheap from the Indians by cheating them. If the Whitmans were going to teach these Indians the ways of the white men, perhaps they would learn to hold their own against the traders too. When Dr. Whitman had made his first journey the year before, the trappers had thrown mud at him and threatened him with rifles. Then cholera had broken out among them and they had begged him to save them.

Dr. Whitman defeated the cholera, and the trappers became his friends. So this time, when he came back with Narcissa and the Spaldings, the trappers welcomed all of them. They even joined them. Some peaceful Nez Percé Indians also went along so that they became a good-sized caravan as they moved to the west.

The journey was hard and bitter. There were great streams to cross, deep woods. One wagon broke down; they had to leave it behind. The women then rode horses. Eliza Spalding was very ill. She could not digest the rough food. "Go on and leave me," she said. "I only hold you back."

Of course, they would not do that. Weak and shaky Eliza got on her horse and rode on. Then the mules died. Then the wheels on the other wagon broke. For a while they tugged it along like a sleigh. But in the end they had to leave it. It just wouldn't go. Then the horses began to die. Then they came to the end of their food supplies.

Up to now Narcissa had kept the little trunk she had brought from home. In it

were small gifts from her friends; a white collar for her neck, a brooch her mother had pinned to her dress. At last, she had to throw the trunk away because the going was so hard they kept only what they had to have.

As she dropped it sadly into the wild rapids of the Snake River, she whispered to it, "Poor little trunk, I am sorry to leave thee. This shall be thy place of rest. Farewell, little trunk. I thank thee. I have been cheered by thy presence so long."

But even when things were bad, Marcus could make Narcissa laugh. It is hard to believe, but at times they actually had fun!

One other thing was good. For long distances they did not have to chop down trees or cut trails through woods. They rode over the prairies, with nothing to see but the long grass waving in the wind. At last, off in the distance they saw a dark cloud, then more clouds. Soon the clouds seemed to mount into the sky. These were the Rocky Mountains—their tops all covered with snow. The Whitmans found a pass at last and went

through. And on the other side they looked down on a rich land.

All along the way they were uneasy about strange Indians. Once an Indian followed them day after day, too far behind for them to talk to him. When they slowed up he stopped. And when they hurried he hurried too. Was this a scout ready to set a tribe on them? At last John, the Indian boy, said "I will go and ask him." And without giving them time to stop him, he rode his horse back to where the Indian was.

The Whitmans watched as John talked to the Indian, mostly by signs. They were not of the same tribe, and there were many Indian dialects. In a few minutes the Indian turned his horse and rode off. And when John came back to join them, he was laughing so hard he had to hold on to his horse's mane. "He says he wanted to marry Mrs. Whitman," reported John. "He says she is so beautiful he wants her for his squaw. I told him she was your wife, Doctor, and he rode off."

At last they came to the turbulent Green River. No wagon and no white woman had ever gone beyond that river. Narcissa and Eliza had to force their horses into the wildly running stream. Some of the horses were drowned. The two women came out dripping wet and exhausted. On the other side was a trading post, called Rendezvous, where trappers and Indians met. But as the two women got off their horses on the other bank, Indian women rushed to kiss them and hug them.

On September first they reached Fort Walla Walla, a British trading post. They had been on the way for six months, half a year of rough going.

In this region there were two tribes of Indians. One, the Nez Percés, were friendly and happy to see the Whitman party. The other tribe were the Cayuse, fierce and warlike. Eliza and her husband decided to start a settlement among the friendly Nez Percé Indians. But Dr. Whitman said that he and Narcissa would start their settlement on the Walla Walla River among the Cayuse. The Nez Percés argued with Dr. Whitman. They said, "The Cayuse are dangerous. They may smile to you, but behind their smiles, they hide frowns of hate. They do not want you."

Dr. Whitman shook his head. "They are warlike because they do not understand what we can do for them," he said. "They know that Indians are not strong or as healthy as white men. They do not live as long. They asked me to come and make them stronger. They wanted me to set their broken bones and to fight the smallpox which kills so many of them."

"Yes, but they did not know you would bring a woman. They will not like that."

"They will come to love her," said Marcus. He looked down at Narcissa standing smiling beside him. He knew that in a few months she would be a mother.

There were no stubborn woods to be cleared off where they were settling; the land was rich. This was a place for cattle and for crops.

Soon the Whitmans had a great farm flourishing. A few of the cows had lived through the journey. And now they gave milk. The seeds which the Whitmans had often held high above streams to keep them dry now went into the ground. Soon there were vegetables growing in the rich Oregon soil. The hogs flourished. The Whitmans had even brought apples and apple seeds. Oregon, now famous as a place of fine fruit, had no apples or pears then.

When their baby came, they named her Alice Clarissa. She was the first white baby born in Oregon, and she brought great joy to her mother and father. But when she was only two years old, the Whitmans lost her. She fell into the river and was drowned.

For a time the Whitmans were numb with grief. But the doctor had to do his work, and Narcissa continued bravely with her teaching. They soon adopted a neglected little Indian boy. Narcissa cleaned him, healed him, loved him, and brought him up

as one of the family.

Settlers began to follow along the paths the Whitmans laid out. Narcissa and the doctor built a hotel, mills, a school. They built a hospital and an orphanage.

At the hospital Dr. Whitman worked with a sure touch to cure. At the school Narcissa taught all who wanted to come. Fifty children boarded in the settlement, children whose parents were dead or who had gone on to find a place for their families to settle. When a baby was born or a woman was sick, Narcissa helped at the hospital. Because of her golden hair, her beautiful face, and her goodness, the settlers and the Indians soon began to call her the "Angel of Oregon." She welcomed and took care of all newcomers. Dr. Whitman answered every call of the sick, sometimes riding endless miles to save an Indian. He taught the Indians how to plant and gather the harvest.

The Whitmans called the settlement Waiilatpu. This is an Indian name so hard to say that it would be best just to wail it softly. At Waiilatpu the settlers from the East, who now came in great numbers, stayed to bathe and rest and eat before they went on to seek the farms they wanted for themselves. All the land was free.

As the years went by the settlements needed more people, more supplies, and more money. They decided that Dr. Whitman should go to Washington and get the help of the American government. When he left it was the middle of winter and freezing cold. One by one his Indian guides gave up until he was all alone. Wherever he went, people thought he was a ghost because he was covered with snow and ice from head to foot.

When he rode into Washington at last, he was a terrible sight. His coat of buffalo skins was torn to rags. His hat was in shreds. His beard was long and shaggy and gray. To Congress and the President he said, "The British want that territory of Oregon. They are helping to get their settlers in first. If you do nothing for our American settlers, we will lose all that vast territory."

One Congressman answered him, "Why should we bother about your Oregon territory? It takes six months to get there. Let the British take it and welcome."

Dr. Whitman's eyes blazed, but he kept his voice quiet as he said, "Oregon is one of the richest regions in the world. Everything grows there. Fruit is bigger. Cattle are fat. Horses grow stronger. It has harbors on the Pacific Ocean. There are a thousand Americans there now. Would you desert them?"

Among those who heard him was a great newspaper man, Horace Greeley of New York. In his paper, the *New York Tribune*, he told his readers the fabulous story of what the Whitmans, the golden-haired bride and her stalwart husband, had done.

Money and help poured in to Marcus Whitman. This was Marcus Whitman's third journey to Oregon. On the first he went alone to feel the way. On the second he took his bride and the Spaldings. This third time he led a huge caravan of wagons and settlers.

While Marcus was gone the Cayuse Indians had behaved well. They sang hymns and smiled. But Narcissa began to fear that this was all make-believe. She said that when they thought no one was looking at them, they gave her black looks. They had never liked Narcissa because they thought that women should be slaves who obeyed men. The sight of this lovely blond woman equal in authority with her husband enraged them. They were afraid their own squaws would follow her ways and take the reins away from the men.

As for the doctor, they were glad enough to have him set their broken bones and get rid of smallpox and their other sicknesses. But in spite of the doctor's best efforts, some of them died. Now the Indians had had an old code: If one of their people died, they killed the medicine man who had treated him. In their hearts they blamed Dr. Whitman for every death.

When they saw the great caravan which he was now bringing with him, they were afraid. They thought the white people would drive them out.

Over and over again the Nez Percés warned the settlers. But like all pioneers, the Whitmans felt they had to take the risk.

Then one day, the Cayuse sent word that measles had broken out in their camp. One of them came in with the message. As Dr. Whitman reached out to greet him, the Indian shot the doctor down. Narcissa caught the children to her, but the Indians poured in and shot her too. That day the Cayuse killed fourteen men and boys and captured eight women and forty-five children.

And then United States troops moved in and rescued all those still alive. It was the end for the Cayuse.

Today there is a college near by that is named for Narcissa and Marcus Whitman. The Oregon they settled is now a rich and fruitful land. And it is proud indeed of this wonderful couple who gave all they had, even their lives, so that other people might live in peace and prosper.

The Pilgrims and the First Thanksgiving

By Bella Koral

ONE August day more than three hundred years ago, in the harbor town of Southampton, England, two children, Giles and Constance Hopkins, were waiting with their parents below decks on a three-masted sailing ship called the *Mayflower*. With another ship, the *Speedwell*, it was being loaded with food and water and the many other things needed by families going to a new land across the ocean.

For days the *Mayflower*'s sailors had been carrying furniture, utensils, and tools into the hold of the ship. Giles and Constance laughed now as the men hoisted up squealing pigs and struggling goats. The squawking of chickens and barking of dogs added to the noise.

On the passenger list were Brewsters, Winslows, Carvers, and Bradfords—names that were to become famous in America's history. And their children were called by names that seem strange to us today: Love and Wrestling Brewster, Remember Allerton, Resolved White, and Humility Cooper.

Most of them were Pilgrims—people who traveled to distant countries seeking freedom to worship God in their own way. They were leaving England because their King was forcing everyone to go to the same church and pray to God exactly the way he ordered them to. If they refused, they were driven from their homes and sometimes thrown into prison.

Their religion meant more than anything else in the world to the Pilgrims. Some years before this they had gone to Holland, a country where people could worship as they pleased. They had found peace and security there for a while. But as their children began to grow up, they seemed to be losing their English ways and customs.

The Pilgrims were disturbed by this. "We cannot let our children become strangers to us," they said. So they had returned from Holland to sail to America.

The rattling of chains was heard as the anchor was heaved up. The *Mayflower* and the *Speedwell* put out to sea. Giles and Constance were on deck some hours later when they saw signal flags go up from the *Speedwell*. She had sprung a leak! Both ships sailed back to England. Some of the *Speedwell*'s passengers remained behind, but others joined those on the *Mayflower* which was now more crowded than ever. Besides a crew of fifty, she carried one hundred and two passengers. This time the *Mayflower* sailed from Plymouth harbor.

The small craft tossed in the rough waters of the Atlantic, the seasick passengers huddled in their narrow bunks. Many were also ill of scurvy because they had no fresh fruit or vegetables. Usually their meals consisted of hard biscuit and salted or dried

meat. But sometimes they made a charcoal fire on sand placed in an iron box and cooked a nourishing porridge or stew.

Many days passed. The crowded ship grew more uncomfortable. There was no place for the passengers to bathe or wash their clothes. Food rations had to be reduced.

Then came a great storm. The ship rolled and pitched in the huge waves. Everything in the cabins was upset. Some of the smaller children had to be tied to their bunks.

They were all afraid they might have to return to England. But at last the sea became calm and the Pilgrims gave thanks to God.

When they saw the sun again, Constance and Giles laughed with joy. And their happiness was all the greater when their baby brother was born aboard the *Mayflower*.

"What will you call him, Mother?"

"We'll call him Oceanus, for he was born on the ocean," she said.

The *Mayflower* sailed on. More and more people became ill. Everyone was afraid the supplies would not hold out.

"We've been on this boat for sixty-three days now," said Constance one afternoon. She and Giles were leaning against the railing watching the water. Suddenly Giles cried, "I see a dead tree branch out there!"

"It means land!" shouted the sailors. Never were more welcome words heard. Sick and weary men and women thronged the deck. Children clambered up the rigging.

Their fathers and mothers talked of Virginia, the part of America where they were expecting to land. The climate would be mild, and other English settlers who had founded the Jamestown Colony there would help them in the new land.

As the *Mayflower* neared shore, the passengers saw evergreens and pines growing down to the beaches. This was not the sunshine and flowers they expected in Virginia. Indeed it was not Virginia. Atlantic storms had driven the *Mayflower* far off its course, and the land that lay before these Pilgrims was Cape Cod. There would be no English friends here to welcome them or houses to shelter them. Instead, there might be only Indians and wild beasts. And it was winter, bleak and cold.

But the Pilgrims were grateful that their long and dangerous voyage was over and they knelt to thank God for their safe arrival in the new land.

Before they anchored, the Pilgrim fathers named John Carver as their Governor and they signed a document, later called the *Mayflower Compact*, one of the most important papers in American history. In it they agreed to make just and equal laws for all in their colony.

On November 11, 1620, the *Mayflower* anchored off what is now Provincetown Bay. High hopes filled the hearts of the Pilgrims as before them stretched the shores of this new land.

But first a landing party of sixteen men had to explore inland to find a safe place to build homes. They had heard much about the danger of Indians; so they put off in their rowboats wearing helmets and breastplates and carrying muskets.

Their leader was a soldier, Captain Myles Standish. He had been training some of the men in the use of arms. Constance's and Giles' father was in the expedition.

The children stood on the *Mayflower's* deck watching the rowboats take off. They watched anxiously as the men waded through the shallow icy water and pulled the boat up on the beach.

Throughout the long cold day they waited for their father and the others to return. It was almost dark when the men came back cold, wet, and tired. They brought back juniper branches for firewood.

As they dried their clothes about the fire the men reported on their trip. They had seen no Indians at all and the only animals they had met were some squirrels and a rabbit. "The soil is too marshy and sandy for us to settle here, though. We could not grow enough food," said Mr. Hopkins.

As soon as they could, some of the women and children went ashore and had a much-needed washday. They scrubbed the clothes in water they got from a fresh-water pond they found nearby. And what fun the children had racing on the beach after all those days on the ship!

A few days later Captain Standish led another party ashore. The Pilgrims had heard about corn and wanted to trade with the Indians for it. For if the grain seeds they had brought from England would not grow here, they were afraid they would starve.

This time the men stayed ashore for three days. At last they saw some stubbled fields that the Indians had planted. At first the men found no corn. But then they saw some strange sand mounds. They dug them up and found fine Indian baskets filled with yellow, red, and blue corn—baskets so heavy it took two men to lift them! Now they would have plenty of corn seed for the spring planting. Some day, they hoped, they would find the Indians who had left the corn there so they could pay for it.

Another larger expedition set out again,

going farther inland. The men were camping for the night by an open fire when they were startled at dawn by a horrendous yell from the nearby woods.

"Indians!" cried Captain Standish. "Arm yourselves!" A shower of arrows whizzed past them. The Captain and another man sent blasts from their muskets towards the woods. Again savage yells rose about them.

As dawn grew brighter, the Captain saw a strapping young brave leaning behind a tree, aiming an arrow at him. Whang! the arrow flew, but the Captain ducked in time. He pointed his musket at the Indian. There was a fiery flash. The bullet splintered the bark of the tree. Three times the Captain fired and each shot hit the tree. Bark and wood splinters fell all about.

"After this barrage, the Indians had enough," Mr. Hopkins told his family afterwards. "They ran into the woods shrieking. We followed them, firing a few shots, so the Indians would see we weren't afraid of them."

A few days later the Pilgrims sailed across the bay. Again they sent out an expedition from the *Mayflower* to find a good harbor and a place to settle. Eighteen men guided by Captain Standish, William Bradford, and John Carver, came to the shores of what we now call Plymouth in Massachusetts. They named it after the English town the *Mayflower* had sailed from.

On a cold, sunny December day they landed. Plymouth would be a good place to build homes, the Pilgrims thought, for they found cornfields that the Indians had left long ago. There were lots of fish, and many rivers and brooks to give them fresh water.

The women and children lived on the *Mayflower* while the men cleared land for a settlement. A few days before Christmas, a new baby, Peregrine White was born, the first English child born in New England.

On Christmas day, the wilderness quiet was broken by the noise of swinging axes, crashing trees, and shouts of the Pilgrim fathers. First they put up a Common House to serve as meeting place, church, and storehouse. Then they built seven small homes, one for the Hopkins family.

But during that hard winter, the Pilgrims were cold and hungry most of the time. Their food stores grew smaller every day. Wintry storms howled about their flimsy houses, and many of the settlers became ill. By the time spring came, nearly half the people who had come over in the *Mayflower* had died.

Then the sun began to shine. Trees burst into bud and songs of birds rang through the woods. Spring had come at last and soon it would be seed planting time. Constance and Giles were happy to explore the beaches and woods about the village, and to bring home varieties of plants and flowers unknown in England.

One day while some of the Pilgrim children were down at the beach gathering clams, Constance was startled to see an Indian walking towards the Common House! Every settler well enough to stand on his feet came to see the visitor. He was tall and wore a leather girdle about his waist, and he carried a bow and two arrows.

To the amazement of the Pilgrims, Samoset, as the Indian called himself, spoke some English. He had learned it from fishermen who had come to the Maine coast where he lived.

The Pilgrims realized that it wouldn't do

to let the Indians know how low their supplies were. So they gave Samoset a good meal of roast duck, cheese, and pudding, which he ate with relish.

Samoset enjoyed himself so much, in fact, that he would not leave. Finally it was decided that he spend the night at the Hopkins' while the womenfolks slept at a neighbor's. So it was that Giles slept under the same roof with an Indian. Captain Myles Standish stood guard, not yet quite sure Samoset could be trusted.

When he left, next morning, to return to his people, he carried with him a ring, a knife, and a bracelet that the Pilgrims gave him as gifts.

Later he came back with another Indian named Squanto. Squanto and Samoset reported that the great Indian Chief of the district, Massasoit, would visit the white men. Soon the Chief, bringing sixty braves with him, was camping on a hill outside the settlement. Now there were only thirty men left among the Pilgrims. They were afraid of what might happen.

Squanto brought a message from the Chief. "Send a man to Massasoit to say you are friends," he told Governor Carver. Edward Winslow came forward. "I will go," he said. He walked toward the hill carrying biscuits, butter, knives, and a copper chain for the Chief.

While Winslow was held as a hostage to insure the Indians' safety, Massasoit, with many of his braves, came down the hill. The Indians wore deerskin leggings and their faces were brightly painted.

Captain Standish and his men marched forward to meet them, firing their muskets in the air as a salute. Then they all marched to the Meeting House where rugs and cushions were spread on the ground for Massasoit to sit on. Governor Carver, wearing a red sash and a feather in his hat, welcomed them. A drummer beat a tattoo, and a trumpeter blared forth a few notes on a trumpet. The Indians were familiar with drums, but the trumpet astonished them. Massasoit tried blowing it, but couldn't make a sound!

After this the settlers offered the Indians food and then Englishmen and Indians made a treaty promising not to injure but to help one another if trouble came. And they kept this treaty for fifty years.

Squanto stayed on with the Pilgrims and became one of the best friends they had. Indeed, they might not have survived at all if it had not been for him. Squanto spoke much better English than Samoset because he had been taken to Europe by an English captain and had lived in England for several years. He had lived in Plymouth before the Pilgrims came there and when he came back from England he had found his tribe gone—wiped out by a plague. He had been too long with white men, however, to be happy with Samoset's people. "Squanto is your friend, and will stay with you," he told the settlers.

One day in April Squanto approached some men who were digging in the fields. "Time to plant corn—oak tree leaves now big as squirrel's ear," he said. They would use the corn seed they had found in the Indian mounds on their first trip inland.

Giles watched as Squanto showed them the Indian way of planting corn. First he made little mounds of earth a foot apart. Then he dug a small hole in each mound and put into the soft earth three dead herrings and three corn kernels. He covered all

this with earth again. The fish, which at this time of year filled the brooks around Plymouth, had started their run. They fertilized the soil and helped the corn grow well. It was back-breaking work to carry the baskets loaded with fish up the steep hills to the planting fields and then to plant the corn. And now there were only twenty men and six boys to do it. But they did it.

Soon it was time for the *Mayflower*, which had been anchored in the bay all winter, to go back to England. Everyone knew hard times still lay ahead. It might be many months before another ship arrived. But when the Captain asked, "Does anyone want to return with us to England?" not one of the Pilgrims wanted to go back, though many of the men looked sad and stern and the women had tears in their eyes.

But no one could be unhappy for very long after the *Mayflower* left. There was too much to do. When autumn came, the Pilgrims, with Squanto's help, had raised a good crop of corn as well as wheat and barley. Now they would have plenty of food for the coming winter.

After the harvest had been gathered, Governor Bradford called a meeting of the settlers. He had been chosen their leader after John Carver died of sunstroke while working in the fields. Bradford, a good and able man, was to guide the colony for thirty-six years.

"We have much for which to give thanks," the Governor said. "Our houses are snug and ready for winter. None shall go hungry or cold. We have made friends of our neighbors, the Indians. Let us set a special day to thank God for all He has given us." The day for the Thanksgiving feast was set. The Pilgrims decided to invite Massasoit with some of his braves to share in their rejoicing. The Chief sent five deer as his gift toward the feast. The Pilgrim fathers went hunting and brought back wild ducks, geese, and turkeys.

The women and girls cooked, baked, and roasted while Giles and the other boys kept the fires going with logs from the forest. Tempting smells of stews and puddings, of roast venison and turkey, must have drifted over to the Indians' camp, for Massasoit

came with ninety men!

Dressed in deerskin leggings and shirts, they had feathers in their hair and painted stripes on their faces. Massasoit wore the copper chain the Pilgrims had given him on his first visit.

Tables were set up outdoors and the Governor and Massasoit sat together. Elder Brewster, the minister, said a prayer, giving thanks to God for their shelter, food, and safety in the new world. Giles noticed how seriously the Indians listened, though they could not understand the words. Their people, too, had Thanksgiving prayers of their own.

Heaping platters of venison, turkey, fish, and geese were set on the tables. The Indians all ate as if they were hollow to the knees. Giles chuckled when he saw a brave pick up a whole turkey and gnaw away at it till it was nothing but bones. The Pilgrims ate heartily too.

After all had eaten till they could eat no more, there were games of quoits. The boys ran races and the men held wrestling matches. Captain Standish paraded and drilled his soldiers to the beat of drums as the Indians watched. The Indians showed their skill at shooting with bows and arrows. Bonfires were lighted as evening came and Massasoit's men gathered in a circle and sang, danced, and whooped around them.

At the end of the dance, they tossed handfuls of corn on the hot stones near the fire. The kernels leaped in the air, popping open like white snowflakes. Constance picked up a piece and put it in her mouth. It was her first taste of popcorn.

The Indians must have enjoyed the Thanksgiving feast, for they stayed for three days!

The Pilgrims did not forget the sad times they had been through and they knew there would be more hard times to come. But they had much to be thankful for. And they were free in this new land. They were free to work and to worship God in any way they chose. Because they were brave and held fast to what they believed was right, the Pilgrims will be remembered as long as our nation lasts.

The Landing of the Pilgrim Fathers

By Felicia Dorothea Hemans

The breaking waves dashed high
  On a stern and rock-bound coast,
And the woods against a stormy sky
  Their giant branches tossed.

And the heavy night hung dark
  The hills and waters o'er,
When a band of exiles moored their bark
  On the wild New England shore.

Not as the conqueror comes,
  They, the true-hearted, came,
Not with the roll of stirring drums,
  And the trumpet that sings of fame;

Not as the flying come,
  In silence and in fear,
They shook the depths of the desert's gloom
  With their hymns of lofty cheer.

Amidst the storm they sang,
  And the stars heard and the sea!
And the sounding aisles of the dim wood
    rang
  To the anthems of the free!

The ocean-eagle soared
  From his nest by the wild waves' foam,
And the rocking pines of the forest roared—
  This was their welcome home!

There were men with hoary hair
  Amidst that pilgrim-band;
Why had they come to wither there,
  Away from their childhood's land?

There was woman's fearless eye,
  Lit by her deep love's truth;
There was manhood's brow serenely high,
  And the fiery heart of youth.

What sought they thus afar?
  Bright jewels of the mine?
The wealth of seas, the spoils of war?
  They sought a faith's pure shrine!

Ay, call it holy ground,
  The soil where first they trod!
They have left unstained what there they
      found—
  Freedom to worship God!

78

He Went to Jail Rather than Lie

JOHN PETER ZENGER

By Jason Robbins

WE ARE all used to our big newspapers filled with lively news and pictures.

In New York in 1730, they were smaller. Let us tear out one page of a large-size newspaper. Now let us fold it in quarters. That one page of a big paper today is all people got in a newspaper in those days. And they got it once a week and not every day.

John Peter Zenger put out a little newspaper like that in New York. He called it the *New York Weekly Journal*. But even this little paper was hard to get out. Nowadays newspapers have large machines called linotypes to put the words into printed letters, and they have gigantic machines to print them. Most boys and girls today have seen little toy printing presses in which they can arrange letters to make words and sentences for printing. Peter Zenger "set type," as we call it, the same way. He would put the flat plate of type on a machine just about like a toy printing machine of today. Of course he didn't think of it as a toy. It was the only kind of printing machine there was at that time, and it was very expensive. Sometimes a man like Peter Zenger, to save money, would make his own printing machine in a blacksmith shop.

Only one copy of a newspaper could be printed at a time, and often the newspaper owner would have to deliver the papers himself. Peter Zenger was lucky to have a good helper, a young man named Jan, who did the delivering for him and helped get out the paper. Peter's wife helped him with it too.

But Peter Zenger did most of the work himself. He wrote the little paper, he edited it, he "set it in type," and he printed it, with Jan's help. There were no pictures; it takes modern machinery to print pictures.

But all that work didn't bother Peter Zenger a bit. He had a good time with it. There *was* something, though, that bothered him a good deal. In those days there was no United States. There were just the American colonies and they belonged to England. The English gave orders to the American colonies. They said you *can* do this and you *can't* do that. They tried to boss the little newspapers in the colonies. All they wanted them to print was tiresome news about when ships sailed and things like that, some poor little ads, and a lot of letters that no one wanted to read.

New York colony was ruled at that time by Governor Cosby who had been sent over by England. Governor Cosby didn't care about most of the people in the colony. He had a few friends and he wanted everything done for them. He liked people just to stand around and say how wonderful he was. But John Peter Zenger wanted to tell people how things really were and how Governor Cosby was taking money and land away from them and giving them to his friends.

JOHN PETER ZENGER. American champion of freedom of the press. Born in Germany, 1697. Arrived in America, 1710. Editor *New York Weekly Journal*, founded 1733. Unjustly tried for seditious libel. Acquitted. Established freedom of press in America. Died in New York, 1746.

There was no radio, of course. Instead, people stood on street corners and listened to men making speeches. And some men belonged to clubs or went to taverns where they could hear the real news too. But not everyone had time for that. So Peter Zenger wanted to tell them the truth in his paper.

He knew it was a dangerous thing to do. In Connecticut Benjamin Franklin's brother had been arrested for trying it. But Zenger went ahead anyway. He had come from Germany when he was only a boy and he loved the kind of life he found in America. He loved the people of New York colony too, and he was a man who would fight for what he loved. He went right ahead and let his newspaper tell the truth about what was going on. So, sure enough, the English came to his shop and arrested him. But even while he was in jail he kept right on publishing his *New York Weekly Journal*. Each week, when it was time to get out the paper, Jan, his young helper, would go to visit Zenger in the jail. Jan was sixteen years old, a bright young man who was devoted to both his work and his boss.

One day when Jan was at the jail, he was sitting on the floor outside a cell. There was a narrow slit in the cell door and from inside came a strong indignant voice. A stone crock of ink stood on the floor beside Jan and he was writing with a goose-quill pen. Jan wore a leather jerkin, short trousers, and thick home-knitted wool stockings, the regular clothes working-men wore in those days. He was breathing hard as he tried to catch the angry words coming through that narrow opening in the door.

"Jan," boomed the voice through the slit, "are you getting all I've said?"

"Yes, Mr. Zenger," said Jan.

"Better read it back to me to make sure," came the voice again.

Jan began to read back what he had taken down: "We say once more—and we will say it as long as we have breath—Governor William Cosby of the colony of New York is trampling on our rights. He gives our money to his friends. He throws honest judges out of our courts if they do not obey his smallest wish. We ask that England send us a Governor who will work with the citizens of our colony and not against us."

"Enough," Zenger called out from the cell. "You have it exactly right. And for honest words like these the British overlords have kept me in this jail for nearly a year! Will they keep me here all my life?"

"The people are for you," said Jan. "Every day they grow angrier. They want to fight for you."

"Listen to me, Jan. Whatever happens, tell the people I want no disorder. The people will win. I am sure of it, no matter what happens to me. I thank you, Jan, for your help. And now take what I have dictated to my wife. She will print the paper."

Jan hurried away, clutching the paper and the crock of ink. Outside on the street friends came to meet him and to guard him from the Governor's men who might try to stop him.

A small crowd gathered to hear if there were news.

"No," the young man said, "nothing new."

Now a stranger came up to him, a dignified gentleman from out of town. "What is this?" he asked. "What's wrong?"

Jan's friends all began to speak at once. But the man clapped his hands over his ears to shut out the babble of voices. So they

kept quiet and let Jan do the talking.

"Sir," said Jan, "they have put Mr. Zenger in jail for telling the truth in his newspaper. They charge him with libel."

A workman from the edge of the crowd now spoke up. "What is this libel, anyway?"

One of the older men spoke then. "Libel is what they call it when someone publishes something that can hurt a person's reputation. Zenger has never said a word about anyone that was not true. It has just made the Governor unpopular."

"But," asked the workman, "if it's true, why can't he say it?"

"In England," said the older man, "if someone publishes anything against a man, true or not, it's libel. And libel is a crime. England wants to hold us down the same way here."

"It's not fair!" cried the crowd. "Tomorrow Mr. Zenger is to be brought into court to be tried. And we will see that the right will win."

Jan shook his head. "But how can we win when the Governor will not even let Zenger have a lawyer to speak for him?"

The crowd growled and shook fists. "That is tyranny!" declared the man from out of town.

"Tyranny," they all agreed. "We know it. But Mr. Zenger says there must be no disorder."

Next day the courtroom was crowded. There was a sort of narrow box without a top where a prisoner like Peter Zenger had to stand. Zenger's head was up and his eyes flashed. But the judge would not let him speak.

Nearly everybody in the courtroom wore a wig, as gentlemen did in those days. The wigs were almost all white. The three judges and the lawyers had on long black silk gowns, and they wore wigs too. But their wigs, to show their importance, were bigger than those of the other men.

So there was Peter Zenger against all those men who wanted to please the Governor. Things looked black for him. Suddenly, at the back of the court, a tall stooped man rose and strolled forward.

"Your Honors," he said to the judges, "I am Andrew Hamilton of Philadelphia."

Everyone except the judges stood up and stared because Andrew Hamilton was the most famous lawyer in America. There wasn't a sound as he said, "I wish to defend this man."

Governor Cosby's men were furious, but they did not dare to order Hamilton out or to shut him up. The old man was over eighty and he had made a long hard journey to reach the court. He was gaunt and bent, but his voice rang out like a bell. He made a wonderful speech. He said that tyrants mistreat people and then arrest them if they complain about it. "This is not only the cause of a poor printer. No! It is the best cause: It is the cause of liberty."

The verdict for Peter Zenger was "Not Guilty."

The people in the court shouted with joy, and outside, in Wall Street, other crowds roared "Zenger is free! Hurrah for Zenger! Hurrah for Lawyer Hamilton!" And they carried Andrew Hamilton and Peter Zenger on their shoulders through the city.

It was a great victory, the first one in America for the right to speak out and tell the truth in a newspaper. After that the people of the colonies could read what was wrong with their British government because Zenger's victory gave other men the courage to speak and to write the truth too.

Today every newspaper is grateful to Peter Zenger. There were many who came after him who also fought for the right to speak out. But it was he who started the fight and who won it. So today if a man runs for public office, any newspaper that wants to can tell the truth about him. We all have John Peter Zenger to thank for that.

He Made His Peace with God

JAMES OGLETHORPE

By Toby Bell

IN THE year 1672 a man named George Brown sat in prison in London. He had done nothing that we would think wrong today. He was a farmer and the year before there had been heavy rains that drowned out the grass for his sheep. He himself was ill from going out in the cold wet rain to try to save what he could of his farm. But no matter how he tried, he could not save enough to pay the rent.

At that time in England if a man could not pay a bill or his rent, he was put in prison. And that is what happened to George Brown. It was a silly law because while a man was in prison he could never earn the money to pay what he owed.

George Brown was a proud man; yet here he was, lying on a pile of straw in prison. Prisons then did not give prisoners cots to sleep on. The only time a prisoner could get enough to eat or anything else he needed was when some friend or member of his family came to visit him.

George Brown's wife and his young son and daughter came to see him often and they were usually downhearted. But today, as the prisoner lay on the straw, holding his aching head and wondering what he could do, he heard them laughing happily. He sat up slowly and looked at them with wonder. His wife was smiling but when she started to speak, she choked up. "You are free,

Father!" called the children. "You are free!" And they jumped up and down with delight.

"But how?" asked Farmer Brown not daring to believe the news. "You know I cannot go free unless someone pays the money I owe for rent on the farm. Who will pay it?"

"A gentleman you have never seen or heard of," answered his wife between sobs of joy. "His name is James Oglethorpe."

"A stranger? Why should he do such a thing? What does he want?"

"He wants nothing. He will even give us a home," Mrs. Brown assured her husband.

By this time other prisoners had crowded around, eager to hear.

"Now, wife," said George Brown, "tell me what this means."

"This gentleman," said Mrs. Brown, "this great rich gentleman, Mr. Oglethorpe, has asked King Charles for a certain piece of land across the ocean in the Colonies of America. He is picking Englishmen who are in prison for owing money, and sending them to that land in America. He chooses only men who are respectable and hard working, as you are, my husband. He will pay what you owe. More, he will get a ship and send you and us to America. Once there, he will give each one a piece of land for a farm."

JAMES OGLETHORPE. Philanthropist and reformer. Born in London, 1696. Member of British Parliament, 1722–54. Interested in prison reform. Took unemployed men freed from debtors' prisons to America and got them jobs. Founded Colony of Georgia (later to become a state in the Union), 1733. Died in England, 1785.

Farmer Brown looked more astonished than ever. "But why should he do such a thing? Why?"

"I do not understand, myself," said his wife. "I thought at first that in America we would have to work for him. But he says he does not want to make any money from the colony. We would work only for ourselves."

Some of the other prisoners were now wild with excitement. "Could I go too?" begged one after another.

"He will choose the people from among you. I pray that you will all be chosen," said Mrs. Brown.

Not all wanted to go. Several said, "Not I. I don't want to go to America where there are bears and other wild animals, and no theaters; nothing but hard work."

One prisoner told the Browns, "You will be three months on the ocean. Pirates will chase you. The boat will sink. I would rather stay here in prison than face such danger."

But Farmer Brown knelt in prayer and thanked God for His goodness.

A man, a little better dressed than the rest, now came up. "What is this?" he asked. They told him that a gentleman named James Oglethorpe was about to pay for the freedom of Farmer Brown and was going to send him and his family to America, and all for nothing but kindness on his part.

"This news is passing strange," said the gentleman. "I used to know Mr. James Oglethorpe. He was a bold young man. He served with me at Flanders in the army of the Duke of Marlborough."

"In the wars against the Dutch that we won?" asked one of the prisoners.

"Yes," said the gentleman. "And one day a strange thing happened. After we won the war, the Duke gave a fine dinner to celebrate our victory. One of the guests was a German Prince. We did not like this Prince, but he had fought on our side and we were polite to him. He considered himself better than anyone else. And he thought the way to prove his importance was to insult someone. He did not dare to insult the Duke, but as he looked around the long table, he saw, right across from him, a very young Englishman who was only a Lieutenant. That was James Oglethorpe, who, the Prince thought, would not dare to answer back.

"Soon the Prince's questions grew insulting. Oglethorpe kept his temper and answered as quietly as he could. The rest at the table sat listening. At last the Prince laughed nastily and said, 'And what would you do in a case like this?' He lifted his wineglass from the table. A few drops were left in the bottom. He threw these in Oglethorpe's face. James did not wipe away the liquid. He let it drip, but his own glass was full. 'This is what I would do,' he said in the same quiet polite voice he had used all along. And he threw his whole glassful of wine in the Prince's face.

"Like all bullies, the Prince was furious when someone defied him. 'Punish this insolent puppy! Arrest him,' he yelled.

"But the English Duke of Marlborough looked at the German Prince with a little smile and said only, 'It served you right.'"

The prisoners all laughed. Farmer Brown was more surprised than ever and said, "If he was nobody then, how did he become so wealthy that he can send us to America?"

The gentleman explained that a good deal of Oglethorpe's money came from capturing Negroes in Africa and selling them as slaves.

"They do say," he added, "that now he is ashamed of it and wants to do something to make up for having practiced that trade."

"Perhaps to make his peace with God," said Mrs. Brown.

And so it must have been, for when Farmer Brown and the others arrived in America, they learned there was to be no Negro slavery in Oglethorpe's Colony. This was astonishing because in that day most people believed in slavery. But as long as Oglethorpe remained in command, he would not permit slavery in his Colony, and it was the only one in America where it was not allowed.

This Colony where Farmer Brown and his family went was at first part of North Carolina, but later it broke off and became Georgia. And Georgia it is today. Georgia was the last Colony settled that later became one of the United States. Everyone there could have any religion he wished. That, too, was a big step ahead for freedom. This was truly a Colony of the people.

The Boston Tea Party

By Helen Woodward

CHRISTMAS was only nine days away. Yet the two boys, slipping along an unlit street, were not talking about a tree or stockings bulging with good things. It was 1773 and these boys lived in Boston where people thought that celebrating Christmas in any but a religious way was sinful.

Just the same the two boys were excited. Their mothers thought they were in bed, but they had slipped out in secret. The tall thin one was Bartholomew. He was edgy and kept cracking his knuckles. Daniel was the little roly-poly with red curly hair. He was trying to walk quietly, but he couldn't. He went hopping along and peeping around turns in the narrow twisting street.

"This is a queer night in Boston Town," whispered Bart. "All those wagons full of men coming down the road from Concord Town. Ay, and those horses tied in front of the taverns."

"Listen, Bart," Daniel whispered back. "My Uncle Jabez came home this morning from New York. First thing he said, before he even pulled off his coat, was 'I'm glad I got here in time. I would not miss this day in Boston.' He was all tuckered out too. He came all the way from New York on the fast stagecoach. It took him only a week. I asked him why he was in such a hurry."

"I wonder why too," said Bart.

"He paid me no mind," Dan went on. "I heard something else . . . funny it was. . . . He said, 'I brought you a package of tea. You'll be needing it.' "

"That was queer," said Bart. "Everybody always has a plenty of tea. It must have something to do with the tax."

"My mother was cross with him. She said 'Such a to-do! Tea and taxes! Tea and taxes! That's all I hear these days!' "

"What did your uncle bring you, Dan?" asked Bart.

"Oh, some blue wool for mittens. I told him I was sorry it wasn't red like the British soldiers' coats. His face got all red too when I said that. He said, 'Don't talk about those British coats. We've had enough of them.' But then he said, 'Never mind, boy, you'll see. Here's something good.' And he gave me one of those bananas, that new fruit he got from a Spanish sailor in New York."

"Save me a piece," said Bart. "I've heard of bananas but I've never seen one."

Then suddenly he pulled Daniel to the side of the road and hissed, "Sh! Someone's coming."

The man wore a leather jerkin, and they knew he must be a workman or a servant. It had been the law that workmen must not wear fine clothes. That law was going out of fashion, but leather clothes were cheap at that time and they wore well. As he came up the man lifted a deer's-horn lantern in their faces.

"Why, it's Aaron!" both boys exclaimed.

"Aaron it is," the man said, looking down at them. "And what are you two rascals doing out of your beds this late of the night?"

"Aaron, don't tell on us. Please don't." The boys teased him until he gave in.

"But it's an ill night for boys to be out. Be careful."

"Why is it an ill night? I wonder why Uncle Jabez said to keep away from the British soldiers! And why does everybody look so darkly whenever anybody says anything about tea? I wonder where my father is."

Aaron only shook his head and croaked, "Here comes someone else. Maybe he'll tell you."

But the boys were already behind a bush. Peeping out they saw that the man approaching had ruffles at his sleeves, and so he must be a gentleman. Aaron touched his forelock as the man strode by without a word.

"That," said Aaron respectfully, "is Mr. John Adams. He is a great lawyer. He defends the patriots when they are in trouble with the British."

What Aaron did not tell them, because he could not foresee the future, was that Mr. Adams was to become the second President of the United States.

"But," said Dan, "I thought it was Mr. Samuel Adams who was the patriot. The orator, I mean. Are they brothers?"

"Nay, they're cousins," replied Aaron with the air of one who knows all. "Mr. Samuel Adams' mind is all on fighting King George of England. He talks only of setting this colony free. He's a man of fire. Now, Mr. John, he's a cool head. They do say it is Mr. Samuel who thought of this thing tonight. He's in the middle of it right now, I'll wager."

"Oh," said Bart, "I guess it's got something to do with the Sons of Liberty."

"Be careful, boy, how you say that name," said Aaron. "They do not like to be talked of, not even by friends."

"Then tell us what's going on," said both boys together.

"Ha! Wait and see. Tomorrow you'll have salt in your tea."

"Salt? You mean sugar, Aaron."

"No, I don't," declared Aaron. "Salt is what you'll get in your tea. How would you like some good cold salty tea? Maybe no tea at all . . . never any more? Maybe you'll have to drink coffee."

"Ugh!" said Dan, "I would not drink coffee."

"Well then," laughed Aaron, "it will be milk for your supper. Or cider. Mr. John Adams drinks a great beaker of cider every day for his breakfast. If it's good enough for him . . ."

But the boys ran off. They raced each other to the South Church, winding up in a tie. Out of breath they dropped onto its steps.

"Let's play 'Hull, hull, handful, how many?'" said Dan. He took a handful of corn kernels out of his pocket.

"No," said Bart. "We can't count the kernels in the dark. Let's go home." He hugged himself against the wind. "We'll never know which way to go."

At that moment a wild sound came out of the cold dark. The boys jumped up scared.

"What was that?" quavered Dan.

"Indian war whoops!"

Never before in their lives had they seen or heard Indians on the warpath. Around Boston at that time Indian fighting was a thing long past. It couldn't really be Indians.

87

Still, fear and panic caught the boys.

"Which way did it come?" asked Dan.

Bart, the cooler of the two boys, said, "They will not attack. The Indians are friendly here."

When the fearful sound rang out again the boys whirled around the corner of the church. And then they saw the harbor a few squares away. Only it did not look calm as it usually did. At the wharf they made out a ship and the shadowy figures of men. The boys began to run down to the wharf. But soon they pulled up short.

"They *are* Indians. See the feathers!" gasped Bart.

They crept down the street and when at last they reached the wharf they hid behind boxes or barrels or whatever they could find. Bart tripped over something and all but fell. He picked up the thing that had tripped him. "Dan," he called. "Look! This is our own fire-bucket. I carried it myself to the fire in the barn yesterday." He held up the leather bucket. "See? It has our name on it."

Bart turned a somersault with joy at this discovery. "These aren't Indians at all! They must be the Sons of Liberty."

The Sons of Liberty were a group of colonists who met in secret and plotted, in all kinds of ways, to get rid of the British. They objected to many of the taxes the British imposed on the American Colonists. But they were especially indignant at the tax on tea, the beverage everyone drank at that time, rich and poor alike. Every boy in the colony waited impatiently to be old enough to join the Sons of Liberty. Sometimes these patriots would blacken their faces, sometimes they put on masks, and sometimes they wore Indian disguises as they were doing now.

No wonder the boys found them a dread sight, these mixed-up figures of masquerading men and heavy moving black shadows half lighted by smoking torches.

"I see men with pistols on the wharf," exclaimed Bart. "They are standing guard."

"They are throwing things overboard," whispered Dan. "Look! They are slashing bundles and emptying them into the Bay."

Two men came striding down the wharf and the boys hid once more behind a barrel, pulling the leather fire-bucket with them. One of the two men was dressed in skins like an Indian, with tall feathers on his head. The other man was in plain clothes but he wore a powdered wig and a fine coat. The man in Indian masquerade was banging a fist against his own left hand.

"What would you do, my good sir?" he rasped. "Let the King of England put taxes on us and say no word? Mr. James Otis has made a fine watchword for us: 'Taxation without representation is tyranny.'"

"But can't we do this thing decently, like gentlemen?" the other man burst out, waving his hand toward the hullaballoo on the water.

"We've tried doing it like gentlemen, and now comes this tea," retorted the Indian masquerader. "This is a trick of the East India Company. They promise us cheaper tea, and then they send us tea with taxes on it so high that we cannot afford to buy any. Come on! Help us to throw this tea into the Bay."

"Did you hear that, Bart? They're throwing tea into the Bay! In the salt water. Come on, let's join in!"

No one noticed the boys as they jumped aboard the ship. With their strong young arms they lifted a bale of tea and held it while a man cut a deep gash in the bundle and emptied the spicy-smelling leaves into the harbor. "Whee! Whoo!" yelled the boys, having a wonderful time.

But after a while one of the men, seeing them in a good light, took an arm of each and said, "Dan! Bart! What are you boys doing here? Go home at once!"

"Please, Father," said Dan, "let us stay. We can help."

"Your mother will be searching for you. Home, I say, home! You have already seen more than you should. You must, on your honor, keep secret whom you have seen here tonight. This could mean death or prison to some of these gentlemen. Your promise now."

In deeply solemn voices the boys promised, more excited than they had ever been in their lives.

Happy in sharing this grown-up secret they started for home. As they left they heard a cheer on board. "Hurrah!" the men called out. "Hurrah for the Boston Tea Party!"

Neither Dan nor Bart could guess that by their small act of lifting a few bundles of the three hundred and forty-two chests of tea that were dumped overboard that night, they had helped to make American history.

In the morning, as they gulped their bread and milk, they heard that all along the coast the tides were bringing in drifts of wet tea leaves.

King George III of England heard of it in London a few weeks later, for there were no fast ships, nor, of course, any telegraph or cable or radio to send news. King George shook his head and wondered at these people across the Atlantic who did not want to remain under his rule. He did not dream that the Boston Tea Party was one of the first skirmishes in what was to become the American Revolutionary War.

Paul Revere's Ride

By Henry Wadsworth Longfellow

LISTEN, my children, and you shall hear
Of the midnight ride of Paul Revere,
On the eighteenth of April, in Seventy-five;
Hardly a man is now alive
Who remembers that famous day and year.

He said to his friend: "If the British march
By land or sea from the town to-night,
Hang a lantern aloft in the belfry arch
Of the North Church tower as a signal
    light—
One if by land, and two if by sea;
And I on the opposite shore will be
Ready to ride and spread the alarm
Through every Middlesex village and farm
For the country folk to be up and to arm."

Then he said: "Good-night," and with
    muffled oar
Silently row'd to the Charlestown shore
Just as the moon rose over the Bay
Where swinging wide at her moorings lay
The *Somerset*, British man-of-war,
A phantom ship with each mast and spar
Across the moon like a prison bar,
And a huge black hulk that was magnified
By its own reflection in the tide.

Meanwhile his friend, through alley and
    street,
Wanders and watches with eager ears;
Till in the silence around him he hears
The muster of men at the barrack door,
The sound of arms and the tramp of feet,
And the measured tread of the grenadiers
Marching down to their boats on the shore.

Then he climbed the tower of the old
    North Church
By the wooden stairs, with stealthy tread,
To the belfry chamber overhead;
And startled the pigeons from their perch
On the somber rafters, that round him made
Masses of moving shapes of shade—
By the trembling ladder, steep and tall,
To the highest window in the wall,
Where he paused to listen and look down
A moment on the roofs of the town
And the moonlight flowing over all.

Beneath, in the churchyard, lay the dead
In their night-encampment on the hill,
Wrapped in silence so deep and still
That he could hear, like a sentinel's tread,
The watchful night-wind, as it went

Creeping along from tent to tent,
And seeming to whisper: "All is well!"
A moment only he feels the spell
Of the place and the hour, and the secret
  dread
Of the lonely belfry and the dead;
For suddenly all his thoughts are bent
On a shadowy something far away,
Where the river widens to meet the Bay—
A line of black that bends, and floats
On the rising tide like a bridge of boats.

Meanwhile, impatient to mount and ride,
Booted and spurred, with a heavy stride
On the opposite shore walked Paul Revere.
Now he patted his horse's side,
Now gazed at the landscape far and near;
Then, impetuous, stamped the earth,
And turned and tightened his saddle-girth;
But mostly he watched with eager search
The belfry-tower of the old North Church
As it rose above the graves on the hill,
Lonely and spectral and somber and still.
And lo! as he looks on the belfry's height,
A glimmer and then a gleam of light!
He springs to the saddle, the bridle he turns,
But lingers and gazes, till full on his sight
A second light in the belfry burns!

A hurry of hoofs in a village street,
A shape in the moonlight, a bulk in the dark,
And beneath, from the pebbles, in passing,
  a spark

Struck out by a steed that flies fearless and
  fleet:
That was all! And yet, through the gloom
  and the light,
The fate of a nation was riding that night;
And the spark struck out by that steed in his
  flight
Kindled the land into flame with its heat.

He has left the village and mounted the
  steep,
And beneath him, tranquil and broad and
  deep,
Is the Mystic, meeting the ocean tides,
And under the alders that skirt its edge,
Now soft on the sand, now loud on the
  ledge,
Is heard the tramp of his steed as he rides.

It was twelve by the village clock
When he crossed the bridge into Medford
  town.
He heard the crowing of the cock,
And the barking of the farmer's dog,
And felt the damp of the river fog
That rises after the sun goes down.

It was one by the village clock
When he galloped into Lexington.
He saw the gilded weathercock
Swim in the moonlight as he passed
And the meeting-house windows, blank and
  bare,

Gaze at him with a spectral glare,
As if they already stood aghast
At the bloody work they would look upon.

It was two by the village clock
When he came to the bridge in Concord
town.
He heard the bleating of the flock,
And the twitter of birds among the trees,
And felt the breath of the morning breeze
Blowing over the meadows brown.
And one was safe and asleep in his bed
Who at the bridge would be first to fall,
Who that day would be lying dead,
Pierced by a British musket-ball.

You know the rest. In the books you have
read,
How the British Regulars fired and fled—
How the farmers gave them ball for ball
From behind each fence and farmyard wall,
Chasing the Red-coats down the lane,
Then crossing the fields to emerge again
Under the trees at the turn of the road,
And only pausing to fire and load.

So through the night rode Paul Revere;
And so through the night went his cry of
alarm
To every Middlesex village and farm—
A cry of defiance and not of fear,
A voice in the darkness, a knock at the door,
And a word that shall echo evermore!
For, borne on the night-wind of the past,
Through all our history, to the last,
In the hour of darkness and peril and need
The people will waken and listen to hear
The hurrying hoof-beats of that steed
And the midnight message of Paul Revere.

He Chained the Lightning

BENJAMIN FRANKLIN

By Will Lane

Two men were standing under an open shed. They were a father and a grown-up son. The son was holding a bundle of sticks. The father pulled a silk handkerchief out of his pocket, and together they set to work making a big kite. This was in a lonely field outside the city of Philadelphia, a long time ago, in the year 1752.

Now several things were queer about this. There was no boy around; so what were these two grown men doing playing with a kite?

The next odd thing is that it was not a nice clear day when a person might like to fly a kite. No, a storm was coming up, the sky was dark with heavy clouds, lightning flared far off, and distant thunder rumbled.

It could not be fun to be out in such a storm. Indeed it would be dangerous. Father and son knew they were in danger. They knew they might even be killed by the lightning.

The two men were serious and careful about the kite. At first they did not talk at all, until the father said, "We are nearly ready, William. Look around and make sure no one sees us."

William went out and looked about the lonely field. The only motion he saw was the long grass bending before the wind.

When he came back he reported, "There's not a soul in sight."

"Good," said his father. "Now no one will laugh at us if we fail."

William could not keep a shiver of fear out of his voice. "They would wonder what the great Mr. Franklin was doing here with this toy. Or maybe they would think, of course Mr. Franklin is a wise man, but he also likes a joke. Maybe they'd think this was a game or a joke."

But it was not a game and it was not a joke. It was an experiment of top importance to the whole world. Today everyone knows that lightning and electricity are the same thing. But in that day no one knew it. And on this dark and stormy day, Benjamin Franklin was risking death to find out.

To make his kite, Franklin used a large silk handkerchief. A kite made of paper would be ruined in the rain and it would not be able to fly to any great height. Over a cross made with two light strong strips of cedar wood, he stretched the handkerchief. Then he tied the corners of the handkerchief to the four ends of the wooden cross. To the top of the upright stick he fastened a sharp pointed wire rising about a foot above the wood.

The kite had a tail, loop, and string just

BENJAMIN FRANKLIN. Statesman, philosopher, inventor, scientist, printer, writer. Born in Boston, Mass., 1706. Laid foundations for public library in Philadelphia. Invented Franklin stove for better heating. Improved street lighting. Discovered electricity in lightning, 1752. Published *Poor Richard's Almanac* for 25 years. Worked in England for U.S., 1757–75. U.S. Minister to France 1776–85. Helped write Declaration of Independence and Constitution of U.S. Author of famous *Autobiography*. Died 1790.

like other kites. The string was of cotton twine except for a short piece of ribbon at the lower end, which was of silk. This piece of silk ribbon Franklin planned to hold in his hand. He attached an iron door-key to the twine at the point where it was tied to the silk ribbon.

Franklin believed the pointed wire at the top of the kite would draw electricity from the clouds when the lightning flashed. He thought, too, that the electricity would run down to the iron key as soon as the kite and the cotton string were wet. If he was right, he would get a strong and maybe even a dangerous shock on touching the iron key. For that reason the silk ribbon had to be kept dry all the time. And that was why he had to stand under the shed, protected from the rain.

Franklin was risking his life, but he was determined to see his experiment through.

Now the kite was ready. They set it flying to the sky releasing the string as far into the air as it would go. Franklin and his son waited to see what would happen. The black clouds were right over the kite. If it was to happen, it must happen as soon as the lightning streaked across the sky and the rain fell.

But now their spirits sank for the distant lightning had stopped. The clouds were still black, though, and they waited. While they kept looking up anxiously, William asked, "Father, how did you happen to think of using a kite for this experiment?"

"I've always loved kites and I found out what a help they could be one day when I went swimming."

"Everybody knows you are a champion swimmer and diver. But what's that got to do with a kite?"

Before he answered, Mr. Franklin took a hasty look at the distant sky. "The lightning has begun again. It is coming closer." He turned to his son and saw that William was nervous. So, to keep him from worrying, he went on, "Oh, about the day I went swimming with a kite. It was when I was a boy in Boston. Our house was small and those twelve brothers and sisters of mine took up a lot of room. I was the youngest and all the rest were busy. So I got out whenever I could, especially when the swimming was good. One day it was very windy, but not stormy like today. Even then I was always trying something new. That day I got a notion. I took a kite into the water with me, holding it so it wouldn't get wet. When I began to swim, I set off the kite, and at once the kite started to pull me along. It was a wonderful feeling." For a moment Mr. Franklin's usual twinkle came back into his blue eyes. "But, my son, I do not want my grandchildren to know about this. You remember that I wrote once,

'Vessels large may venture more,
But little boats should keep near shore.' "

Mr. Franklin grew silent and watched the skies closely. A bolt of lightning flashed across the heavens and thunder rolled. Then the rain poured down! But there was no effect of electricity on the kite. If those storm clouds held electricity, as Franklin thought they did, the fibres of the cotton string should move in a moment and stand on end.

The storm clouds were coming closer. Lightning flashed again. The rain pelted down on the roof of the shed and in through the doorway. Franklin held the silk ribbon carefully, keeping it dry. Suddenly he

noticed that the loose fibres of the cotton string, now wet with rain, were beginning to stir. When he moved his fingers up and down near the string, though not touching it, the fibres slowly rose and fell with the motion of his hand.

William broke out excitedly. "Look, the threads on the string are standing up!"

"Watch out, son," said Franklin quietly. "This is a point of danger now."

The young man's heart pounded when Franklin touched his knuckles to the iron key. Fiery sparks came flying to his hand. He felt a distinct electric shock go through his body! But he did not care. His face was full of joy. Again and again, his eyes shining with pride, Franklin touched his finger to the iron key, and each time he saw the fiery sparks and felt the electric shock.

Those sparks were electricity!

"We have proved it," shouted William.

"Yes," said his father. "Electricity is lightning and lightning is electricity. I believe this is the most useful thing I have ever done."

They walked home through the fields, and now that the strain was over, William asked the question that had been bothering him. "I do wonder, Father, why all those great scientists in Europe haven't tried an experiment like this."

"They have been trying to find out about electricity for centuries," said Mr. Franklin. "Without their work I would not have thought of this today. They are learned men, and they have tried to find out what electricity *is*. I went to school for only two years but I am a practical man. I want to find out what electricity can *do*. You see, my son, in one way I have the best of it. These scholars won't work with their hands. When they need a new kind of tool or machine for an experiment, they have to hire men to make it. Sometimes the machine is not made right and they don't even know it. But I have spent many years working with my hands. I helped my father to make candles. I have been a printer. I know carpentry. So I have always been able to make the tools I needed for my experiments. If I made a mistake I knew it. And from each tool I made I learned something. I needed the knowledge those learned men gathered and they needed my skill."

"And your good sense," said his son.

When the European scientists learned about how Franklin had brought the lightning from the sky, they were amazed and delighted. But one person was not excited at all. And that was Benjamin Franklin himself. "That's all very fine," he said to himself. "But now what can we use it for?"

The first thing he did then was to invent the lightning-rod so that houses should not be struck and destroyed by the power of the electricity in the skies. He made a thin iron pole that led from the roof of a house down to the ground. The pole caught the lightning before it could hit the house, and carried it down into the ground where it could do no harm. That is called "grounding" the lightning.

Benjamin Franklin made no profit from his lightning-rod. He gave it to the world free. It was a generous present, but Franklin was just as generous with all his inventions. There were many of them and he never tried to make money from any. In his day, the only way to heat a house was by burning wood in an open fireplace. A fire like that may look cosy but your face burns from it while your back is cold. And an open fire scatters ashes and dust. Franklin made a stove that burned logs of wood and looked cheerful too, but it spread the heat more evenly than an open fireplace and it held back the ashes. This kind of stove is called the Franklin stove and many people in country places still use it.

He also invented bifocal lenses which are a great help to people who are both far-sighted and near-sighted and used to have to wear two pairs of glasses.

Franklin loved gadgets. In his house he had a huge library with shelves that ran from floor to ceiling. So he invented a mechanical arm that would reach out and take a book from the top shelves.

When disaster hit him, he did not complain but turned it to use. Once, when a terrible wave of smallpox hit Philadelphia,

Franklin caught it and nearly died. As soon as he was able to get about again, he helped to found the first hospital in Philadelphia.

He remembered how hard he had had to work to buy a book when he was young and he founded the first public library in Philadelphia. And he started the first insurance company in America. He improved Philadelphia's police and fire departments and many of the roads. He started a club among his friends to think up inventions and methods that might help the world. Its ideas were so practical that it was nicknamed the Leather Apron Club because of the leather aprons that workingmen wore in those days.

All this would be a full life's work for any man. But Benjamin Franklin's mind never rested. When he was seventeen years old, he walked clear across what is now the state of New Jersey to reach Philadelphia. When he got there, he was covered with mud and dust. All he owned in the world was in his pockets. They bulged with socks and shirts. Under each arm he carried a loaf of bread and he was biting into a third loaf. He looked so absurd that a girl named Deborah Read stood in a doorway and laughed at him. It was just like Franklin, though, that this was the very girl he made up his mind to marry and did marry. Deborah was not brilliant like her husband, but she was a devoted wife. And she had plenty of courage. Once when he was away, a mob of enemies attacked their house. With some of her relatives, she sat up all night holding a shotgun ready and drove them off.

But before he married Deborah, Ben Franklin got a job as a printer. Later, he set up his own printing shop. He made money, built a house for himself and his wife, began to publish *Poor Richard's Almanac*, which was the first American magazine. It was full of facts and jokes and wise articles, also many sayings which have become famous, like "Early to bed and early to rise makes a man healthy, wealthy, and wise." People everywhere read it and they gave Franklin the name of "Poor Richard."

It was Franklin's talent for making friends that led to the greatest part of his career. When he first came to Philadelphia from Boston, Pennsylvania was still a colony and belonged to England. As years went by, the American Colonies grew bigger and they felt they knew better what they needed than England did. After all, it took months to reach England in a ship and by the time the ship got back to America, there were new troubles to be settled. The Colonies thought that if an able man could go to England and be their agent there, things would go better. They felt that no one could do a better job of smoothing things over than Franklin. So, in 1757, when Franklin was fifty-one years old, he went to England, to represent the United States. And he was there, on and off, for eighteen years.

In London Mr. Franklin made friends quickly. They were important friends in high places. They had heard about his work with electricity. And they admired his simple ways. He got Tom Paine to come to America and give us the benefit of his valuable services. But he could do little about getting England and the Americans together. The English would not budge and after awhile the Americans got angry and violent. That made things worse. Franklin reached America in March 1775. In the end

the Americans started the Revolutionary War.

After he came home, Franklin helped to write the Declaration of Independence. He was a member of the Continental Congress and was ready to do anything he could to help. But the Congress made up its mind that the biggest thing Franklin could do would be to go back to Europe once more, this time to France. And it was in France that Benjamin Franklin did his greatest service for his country.

The American Colonies were weak and

poor, and they were fighting England which was strong and rich. So the Colonies sent Franklin to France to borrow money. This he did, and more too. He got the French Government to join with the Americans in sending ships and troops and arms. This French help turned the tables on the British and won the Revolutionary War for the Americans.

When Franklin went to France in 1776, he was so sad at the thought of leaving his family that he took two of his grandchildren with him. He was seventy years old, a time when most men sit back and take life easy. But he had no such idea.

With many people and in many places Franklin was popular, but never more so than in France. He had taught himself French, and that helped him too.

France was then the most fashionable country in the world. People went there to imitate its ways so that they too could be fashionable. But even in Paris, where the French King led in extravagance of fashion, Franklin wore an old pioneer's fur hat and homely brown clothes. The French gentlemen all carried swords; Franklin carried only a cane. But the nobles liked his independence. France also had many people of great learning and these especially admired Franklin. He was so popular that they put his picture everywhere, on walls and windows, even on handkerchiefs. He wrote his daughter that in France he was as well-known as the man in the moon. Franklin loved a joke and so did the French. To this day, the French think that Franklin was the greatest American who ever lived.

One day he was walking with a group of nobles in a garden. They came to a little pond whose water was ruffled by the wind.

"You have been talking of miracles," said Mr. Franklin to the nobles. "Very well, watch and I'll show you one." They all laughed, but he stood at the edge of the pool, muttered some mysterious sounds, and waved his cane over the water. In a moment the ripples died away and the pond was like glass. They stood speechless with surprise, while Mr. Franklin walked off arm in arm with an Abbé who was a friend of his. After awhile the Abbé asked Franklin how he had calmed the waters. "I know perfectly well that it was no miracle," he said.

Franklin smiled. "Look at my cane. It is hollowed out inside. I had filled it with oil. When I waved it over the rough water of the pond, the oil came out and smoothed the water." That's what we mean by "pouring oil on troubled waters." Franklin and the Abbé both laughed heartily, as did everyone else when they heard the little joke.

When Franklin was young, the American colonies were scattered and weak. When he came home from France, they were united in one country. Benjamin Franklin had a great part in making them so.

Of course, he was not perfect. He had failures like other men. One came when Pennsylvania made him a judge. He was not a good judge. He always wanted to take sides, and that is something a judge must not do.

If Benjamin Franklin were alive today, he would not seem old-fashioned to us at all. He would fit in easily. He was a practical American to his fingertips. He said he hoped the time would come when a wise man "could go anywhere in the world and say 'This is my country.'" He wished that all nations would be friendly so that people could feel at home anywhere in the world.

The Father of His Country

GEORGE WASHINGTON

By Bella Koral

WHEN George Washington was born in a comfortable plantation farmhouse in Virginia, most of this land was still a wilderness. Virginia was one of thirteen colonies belonging to England. There was no such thing as the United States.

By the time George was six, he had three younger brothers and a sister, and his family lived at another of their plantations called Ferry Farm.

George loved to swim and fish in the Rappahannock River that ran close to Ferry Farm. When he played at pitching horseshoes, his arm was sure, and when he wrestled he could easily down any boy his size. He was a fine rider, and was proud of his pony, Hero.

The sexton of a nearby church taught George to spell and write, for schools in Virginia were few. He acquired a beautiful

GEORGE WASHINGTON. First President of the United States. Born in Wakefield, Va., Feb. 22, 1732. Colonel of Militia, 1758. Helped take Fort Duquesne from French. Commander-in-Chief of American Forces, 1775. President of U.S., 1789-97. His name heads the list in the American Hall of Fame. Died in Mt. Vernon, Va., 1799.

handwriting, but never did learn to spell really well. Another teacher taught him arithmetic. George was very good at that.

Young George and his companions loved to watch sailboats and trading ships from Boston and New York pass by the plantation on the river. Sometimes they landed at the Washingtons' wharf. The boy would watch eagerly as the sailors unloaded their cargoes and reloaded the boats with tobacco and other crops to take back to England. George dreamed that he, too, might one day wear a captain's uniform and sail to foreign lands!

One day when George was about ten, an English ship brought his two older half-brothers, Lawrence and Austin. They were returning from England to help their father manage his plantations. Lawrence, fourteen years older than George, became the young boy's hero.

When George was eleven, their father died. Mrs. Washington now had to care for her five young children and manage the Ferry Farm plantation. As was the custom then, Mr. Washington had left most of his other property to his eldest son, Lawrence. This was the plantation on the Potomac River where the family had lived before coming to Ferry Farm.

Lawrence soon married and rebuilt the house he had inherited. He named it Mount Vernon.

George was going to a new school where his teacher gave him a book called *The Rules of Civility*. It contained one hundred and ten maxims for good conduct that George copied out in his fine handwriting. Some, such as "Cleanse not your teeth with the tablecloth," seem humorous to us today. But the maxim George took closest to his heart was, "Labor to keep alive in your breast that little spark of celestial fire called conscience."

George was delighted when one day he came upon some surveyors' instruments his father had used to measure land. George had always liked arithmetic and numbers. Now he decided to study surveying. He became expert at it.

By the time he was sixteen, George was spending most of his time at Mount Vernon. A neighbor, an Englishman named Lord Fairfax, who had been a soldier and had seen a great deal of the world, owned vast, unmeasured tracts of land in Virginia. He liked the way George rode a horse and they often went fox-hunting together.

Soon they became fast friends. Lord Fairfax saw how brave George was and how careful and exact in everything he did. So, before long, he asked George to be one of a party of surveyors he was sending out to measure his property. He hoped that after the land was surveyed and divided into farms, more settlers would go there to live.

The surveyors could travel only a small distance each day, for the forests were dense. Sometimes they had to swim their horses across streams.

At nights, wrapped in a blanket, George slept before a campfire or in a hut. Once, when his straw bed caught fire, he was nearly burned to death. Another time a band of Indian braves wearing war-paint and feathers slipped into camp. They were the first warrior Indians George had ever seen but they were quite friendly to the surveyors who gave them gifts and asked them to perform their war-dance. George thought their dance was very comical and wrote about it in his copybook.

Lord Fairfax was so pleased with George's work that he arranged to have him chosen surveyor for the county. George bought land with the money he earned, and for the next three years the young surveyor made many long journeys into the Virginia wilderness.

There he learned the ways of Indians and backwoodsmen. He learned how to face danger and be prepared for anything. And he learned how to be a leader of men. From his brother Lawrence and Lord Fairfax he gained enough knowledge of military tactics to become a Major in the Virginia militia.

Now came a sad time for George. Lawrence became very ill. George went with him to the West Indies, hoping the climate might help. This was the only time George was ever to leave his native land.

But Lawrence did not get better. After his death, when his estate was settled, George became master of Mount Vernon.

Now trouble had been brewing for some time in the Colonies. Frenchmen were coming down from Canada claiming land the English said belonged to their King. They were building forts and, with the help of Indians friendly to them, were driving out Virginia backwoodsmen who had built settlements in the wilderness.

The Governor of Virginia decided to send a message to the French Commander ordering him to stop building forts and to allow the settlers to live in peace. For this mission the Governor needed a brave, determined man who knew the wilderness well. He chose George Washington.

With some Indians, hunters, and a guide named Gist, Washington started on the dangerous journey. He won over to his side an Indian chieftain who helped him and his companions reach the French fort.

The French Commander there replied to the Virginia Governor that he had been ordered to hold that fort and there he would stay!

By the time Washington and his guide started back it was December. The ground was covered with snow and they could not use horses. They planned to cross the Allegheny River by walking over the ice, but now they found it was only partly frozen. Great cakes of ice floated through the open waters. The two men began cutting down trees for a raft, but it was slow work for they had only a single hatchet. While steering their raft between cakes of ice, George was pitched into the water. Almost drowned, he struggled back on board, his clothes frozen stiff. The two men spent that bitterly cold night on an island. By morning the ice on the river was firm and they were able to walk across to shelter.

After many such adventures, Washington delivered the French Commander's reply to the Governor, together with his own report of what he had found out. Everywhere people in the Colony praised Washington's skill and courage. Soon the Governor appointed him a Lieutenant-Colonel of Virginia troops.

The next winter the English sent a strong force of British troops to America under General Braddock to drive the French out of the Ohio Valley, and to teach the Indians a lesson.

Braddock had heard of the fearless young Washington who knew the western wilderness so well; so he invited him to be his aide.

What a handsome sight Braddock's Army

made in their bright red coats as they marched in perfect order! The Colonial soldiers under Washington did not even wear uniforms. Like the Indians, they wore buckskin shirts and fringed leggings. The English called them "Buckskins."

Braddock and his soldiers had never fought in the wilderness. They were to attack a French fort near where Pittsburgh now stands. Washington, who knew how the Indians and the French fought from behind rocks and trees, tried to warn Braddock. But the General replied proudly, "It would be too bad if British troops could not meet a handful of naked Indians."

In their proud scarlet coats, Braddock's fine Army marched through a narrow road in the forest not far from the French fort they planned to attack. Suddenly shots rang out from behind rocks and trees. The woods echoed with Indian war yells. But no one was seen.

The English troops, confused by this strange fighting, huddled together like sheep, their scarlet coats fine targets for the Indians. The Buckskins, of course, knew how to meet the Indians. They took cover behind trees, too, and returned the fire.

Through all the confusion it was Washington who prevented the English from being entirely wiped out. Bullets riddled his hat and uniform. Two horses were shot from under him and he jumped on the back of a third. It was a miracle he escaped unharmed.

Braddock was not so lucky. Not until he was wounded did he order a retreat. He died four days later, grateful that his aide, Washington, was at his side.

Braddock's defeat grieved the people, but they were proud of Washington who had upheld the honor of the Buckskins. He was made Commander-in-Chief of the Virginia troops and became renowned throughout the Colonies.

For three years after this Washington commanded troops in the West. The French were finally driven back to Canada by fresh armies from England and by Colonial troops in the North.

When Washington was twenty-seven, he married Mrs. Martha Custis, a widow with two small children. He took them to live with him at Mount Vernon. He came to love Martha's children as if they were his own, and they loved him dearly, too.

Soon after his marriage, Washington was elected a member of the Virginia House of Burgesses to represent the people of his county and to help make some of the laws of the Colony.

At Mount Vernon Washington lived the life of a gentleman farmer planning crops, and raising cattle and horses. Fifteen happy, peaceful years followed and Washington would have liked nothing better than to spend the rest of his life in this way.

But storm clouds were gathering.

The Colonists had always considered England their mother country. But when the new King, George III, came to the throne, he decided to make them pay the huge costs of the French and Indian War. He made unwise laws forcing the Colonies to trade only with England. Then extra harsh taxes were laid on almost everything the Colonists used. They could not drink even a cup of tea without paying England a tax on it.

In Boston, fifty patriots dumped a shipload of tea into the harbor rather than pay the tax. To punish them, the King ordered

Boston harbor closed. This meant hunger and suffering for the people. And the King sent troops to arrest or shoot anyone disobeying his commands.

The Colonies, aroused at this, decided to act together. They sent delegates, Washington among them, to a Congress at Philadelphia. They sent the King a petition begging him not to enforce his unjust laws. No answer came back. The Colonists began drilling and arming their soldiers.

Washington was asked to train the men of his county. He loved peace, but he said, "No man should hesitate to use arms in defense of freedom."

Then in April, 1775, came the dreaded news. A company of British soldiers started secretly toward Concord, near Boston, to seize arms and gunpowder the Colonists had hidden. News of their plans was spread by swift riders during the night. Quickly farmers and townsmen took up their muskets and gathered at Lexington to stop them.

Shots were fired by both sides and many men were killed. This, the Battle of Lexington, began the long Revolutionary War.

Again a Congress was called in Philadelphia. Washington appeared there in the uniform of a Virginia Colonel. It was his way of saying, "The time for fighting has come and I am ready."

The delegates voted to make this Congress the Government of the thirteen Colonies. They appointed Washington Commander-in-Chief of their armies. No other man was so well fitted to command. He refused pay for his services.

At Cambridge, near Boston, Washington took command of his Army. It was an odd Army—the men poorly armed and trained, and dressed just as they happened to come from their shops or farms. But they were brave and would defend their country with all their might. It was the first *American* army.

In a few months Washington had trained these men so well that the British, knowing they could not hold out, sailed away from Boston.

But Washington knew the British would attack New York, so he moved his Army there. And then came wonderful news from Philadelphia. On the Fourth of July, 1776, the Colonies declared themselves *free* from England. The British, however, did not accept this, and the war continued. Until that time the Colonies had been fighting for the right to make their own laws and raise their own taxes even if they were subjects of the King. But with the Declaration of Independence, they had made themselves a free and independent nation. King George would never again rule over them.

Washington had the Declaration read to his troops. Its ringing words would make them fight on till every British soldier had left America. Washington often had to retreat, but he held on through long bitter years. Even when others thought all was lost, he had faith.

By the winter of 1776, Washington's Army had managed to reach Pennsylvania, across the Delaware River. The British were in Trenton, on the New Jersey side of the Delaware, waiting for the river to freeze over solid. Then they would be able to march across and destroy Washington's Army.

But Washington had a daring plan. He would turn the tables on the British and their hired troops, the Hessians, who were preparing to celebrate Christmas while wait-

ing for the Delaware to freeze.

In the wind and sleet of that stormy night, Washington's men rowed across the river, pushing their boats through great cakes of floating ice. Some of them were barefoot, shivering in their ragged clothes. The path they took to the river was marked by their bloody footprints in the snow. Yet somehow they managed to get themselves, their horses and their cannon across the icy Delaware to Trenton.

The Hessians and their British officers were sleeping soundly. At dawn they woke to the thunder of American guns—and could hardly believe what was happening. After a short battle they surrendered.

Washington's victory at Trenton was a Christmas gift that brought joy and fresh courage to the new nation.

But more hardships were in store. The next winter Washington's Army camped in nearby Valley Forge. Deep snow lay on the ground. The men had no shoes and their feet were wrapped in rags. The wind blew through their tattered clothes. And there was not enough to eat. Many died of hunger and disease. Some left camp unable to suffer any longer.

Washington stayed in a hut close to his men, sharing their hardships. Martha, his wife, came to spend the winter with her husband and went from hut to hut to comfort the sick. Washington's heart was heavy with suffering for his men. It seemed that terrible winter would never end. He kept begging Congress to send supplies.

But before the winter was over, a young French nobleman, Lafayette, arrived at Valley Forge. He had heard of Washington and America's struggle for freedom and had come to help. A warm friendship sprang up between Washington and young Lafayette, who soon became the General's aide. This young man contributed nobly to the American cause.

When spring came, food and supplies began rolling into camp. The men were cheered and Washington's hopes rose. Then came the wonderful news that France was joining America in the war.

Yet even with French help, there were to be three more years of bloody battles. But Washington's faith was like a rock to his men.

In October, 1781, a large British Army under General Cornwallis was trapped at Yorktown, Virginia. American guns had been firing at the British forts for ten days. French ships had blockaded the Redcoats from the sea. The British had to give up. They sent out a messenger with a white flag of truce.

Washington rode with his officers to the meadow where the British were to surrender. He sat on his horse watching from a slight distance as man after man laid down his musket. Then the British General handed his sword to an American officer. It was his act of surrender.

Finally King George III had to admit that his thirteen Colonies were now the United States of America, and a peace treaty was signed.

When the last British soldiers sailed from New York, Washington felt his task was done. There, at Fraunces Tavern, he bade farewell to his officers, urging them to preserve the nation they had fought so hard to build.

At last, after eight years, Washington came back to Mount Vernon. Here he planned to spend the rest of his life peacefully as a farmer. But Mount Vernon was always filled with company. Important people kept coming to pay their respects. They brought troubling news that the thirteen states had begun to quarrel with one another and were not *really* united.

Wise men saw something must be done to save the country. So a great Convention was held in Philadelphia to make a set of rules—a Constitution—to govern the whole country.

This Convention chose Washington to preside over it. There were many stormy arguments by the delegates, but his calm wisdom was always there to guide them. The Convention brought forth a great and wonderful work, the Constitution, by which the United States has been governed ever since.

According to this Constitution, the people were to elect a President for the new Government. They chose a man they trusted and honored above all others—George Washington.

Though he had hoped to spend his remaining years at Mount Vernon, Washington could not refuse when called to serve. So, in April, 1789, he left Mount Vernon for New York. It was to be the first Capital of the United States.

All along the way there were parades and celebrations in his honor. He crossed the Hudson on a barge decked with flags. Bells rang as he reached New York. Crowds cheered and cannon roared. Houses were bright with flags.

Washington stood on the balcony of Federal Hall looking down into the faces of the people. The wild cheers hushed as he stepped forward and laid his hand on the Bible. Slowly and clearly, he repeated the oath every President has taken since then:

"I do solemnly swear that I will faithfully execute the office of President of the United States and will to the best of my ability preserve, protect, and defend the Constitution of the United States."

"Long live our President!" cried the people. They loved and trusted him, for he was wise, fearless, and strong.

To them he was indeed, "first in war, first in peace, and first in the hearts of his countrymen." And to all Americans ever since he has remained the Father of his Country.

Inscription at Mount Vernon

WASHINGTON, the brave, the wise, the good,
Supreme in war, in council, and in peace,
Valiant without ambition, discreet without
    fear,
Confident without presumption,
In disaster, calm; in success, moderate; in
    all, himself.

The hero, the patriot, the Christian.
The father of nations, the friend of mankind,
Who, when he had won all, renounced all,
And sought in the bosom of his family and
    of nature, retirement,
And in the hope of religion, immortality.

"Give Me Liberty or Give Me Death!"

PATRICK HENRY

By Will Lane

WHEN Patrick Henry was a boy in old Virginia, he wanted to be an orator. But when he tried to speak he ran his words together and swallowed the ends of them, like saying *goin'* instead of *going*. He set out to correct this, but he knew the other boys would make fun of him if they ever heard him practising. So he would slip away to the woods and make speeches to the trees.

He had read about Demosthenes, a statesman who lived in Greece long long ago. Demosthenes too had made up his mind to

be an orator. But his trouble was that he stuttered. To try to cure himself the little Greek boy would go down to a lonely beach where he would put three or four pebbles in his mouth and orate to the waves and the sand. He was careful to put the pebbles in front of his teeth; otherwise the practice wouldn't have cured the stutter. After awhile he could throw away the pebbles and speak like anybody else. And he grew up to be one of the greatest orators who ever lived.

So the boy, Patrick Henry, said to him-

PATRICK HENRY. American Revolutionary leader. Born in Hanover County, Va., 1736. Opposed Stamp Act. Member Continental Congress, 1774–76. Speech urging defense of Colonies contained the famous words, "Give me liberty or give me death." Governor of Virginia, 1776–79 and 1784–86. Largely responsible for adoption of first ten Amendments to U.S. Constitution. Died 1799.

108

self, "If Demosthenes could learn to be an orator when he had a stutter, why can't I learn to be one too?"

There wasn't any beach handy where Patrick lived, but there were plenty of big wild woods, and the trees were always there to hear him. Sometimes a beaver would stop by and often a woodchuck would sit up on a stone and listen too.

Patrick knew that an orator must not be afraid to face a lot of people; but he was used to doing that because he often played the music at neighborhood dances. He was an awkward lad and didn't dance well, but he played lively tunes on his fiddle and his flute. Like the good neighbor he was, he played for nothing while others danced.

Patrick was good at sports too, but he was not good at making money. One time his father bought a store for him and his brother to run. But the two boys trusted everyone and gave goods to people who were too poor to pay, and soon there was no store left.

When he was only seventeen years old, Patrick married a farmer's daughter, Sarah Shelton. They were both poor. They did have plenty to eat because food was cheap. But clothes were expensive. Fashionable people, in those days, ordered their fine clothes sent all the way from London. Sarah spun and wove cotton and wool and she and Patrick wore the plain clothes she made. They didn't mind that, but what bothered them both was that no matter how hard he tried, Patrick never got any nearer to his great dream of becoming an orator.

Patrick used to gather with the other men in the town square. There they would read the papers and argue about politics.

At that time Virginia was still one of the American colonies and belonged to England. But trouble between the colonies and England was bubbling up in a lot of places. In America people had more freedom than they had in England. In the American colonies a plain man could get ahead. In England he had to be an aristocrat to reach a high place in the world. There was a great deal of misunderstanding between the two countries. Besides, England was far away from America and it took a long time for messages to go back and forth. If the colonists sent a message to London in April, they had to wait till Christmas before an answer came back in the slow boats of the time. That left plenty of time for people on both sides to get angry.

In the town square in Virginia the men began to get very angry indeed. One man walked up and down shaking his fist. He was a tobacco farmer and he snapped out, "How long does King George think I can run my farm at the price I get for my tobacco? Why must I sell my tobacco first in London and then let London sell it back here? Why can't I sell right to the man who wants it? I'd save time and money that way."

Another man tried to quiet things. "That's not King George's fault," he cut in. "He wouldn't stand for anything like that. It's the people under him."

That wasn't true, but this man was one of the few Americans who thought King George was all right. It was too bad that such a situation had come to pass. But the British people really meant well. They just didn't understand and they were too far away to talk things over.

The angry farmer turned to one man in

the crowd and went on, "Jamie, you own the store down there. Suppose I wanted to buy a bag of sugar—sugar that you raise right here. You wouldn't be allowed to let me buy it from you. First you would have to go to Richmond and sell it to somebody there and then he would have to bring it back and sell it to me. What happens to our tobacco is worse. Our tobacco has to go all the way to England and then back here. It doesn't make sense. Never mind whether it's the King or the people, it's the same bad business for us."

A dignified older man, who had been sitting silent, now rose and spoke in a sober tone. "It isn't respectful to talk about the King as though he were a simple man like us. You should say, 'His Majesty the King.' Anyway, be careful. The British soldiers may hear you and then you would go to prison." He walked away, shaking his head.

A young man with a woollen cap on his head called after him, "We're as good as anybody over there. I have no use for the British. One of their soldiers made fun of my cap."

Now this was a small thing, but when people are angry small things count as much as big ones. It was the custom for everyone from the King of England to a small errand boy to wear a wig. Some of the wigs were powdered white and had curls at the side; some were arranged with a sort of club in back tied with a leather strip or a ribbon. But in Virginia, where it was hot, some men wore caps because they were cooler than wigs. The man who said the English had made fun of his cap went on, "That English soldier said only colonials wear caps. The airs those English give themselves! Think

they're better than anyone else."

That day Patrick Henry listened and for once took no part in the talk. He went home very sad and said to his wife, "I knew what to say, and the men wanted to hear me talk too. But I'm only a country man like them. Now, if I was a lawyer . . ."

His wife answered quickly, "Patrick, why don't you study to be a lawyer? Then you'd have a chance to speak out."

Patrick was only twenty-four. But he said he was too old.

Sarah laughed at that. "Twenty-four is young," she said.

"But," said Patrick, "I haven't the money to go to college to study law."

"You won't need it," said Sarah. "You can study right here at home. Other lawyers here will help you."

That is how Patrick Henry became a lawyer. His first clients were a group of farmers. When he walked into the court for the first time, to plead their case, he was a homely man, tall and lank, with red hair and shabby clothes. He looked so poor next to the aristocratic lawyers on the other side that even the judges were sorry for him. He rose and turned to the jury. He began to speak, and all of them stopped being sorry for him right there. He proved he was a good orator and a good lawyer too. He won the case for his farmers.

At last he was doing the work he loved, and he got ahead fast. Soon he was elected to the Legislature of Virginia. They called it the House of Burgesses, which really means House of Citizens.

That was the year 1764. Patrick Henry was still young and he was a new member of the House of Burgesses. He was supposed

110

to sit silent and listen to his elders for a year or two. But he was burning with the fire of independence. He knew that the older members wanted to talk gently to England. But he had been elected to the House of Burgesses by men who expected him to speak against British tyranny.

Patrick Henry *did* speak, and his words rang out. Again he proved he was a great orator. His fiery speech in the House of Burgesses was printed and sent over all the colonies. Patrick Henry's name became known throughout the land.

Ten years went by. The quarrel between the colonies and England grew worse. Patrick Henry went to Philadelphia. There, for the first time, the colonies got together in the Continental Congress and joined in the fight against England. But Virginia had not joined. In the year 1775 Patrick Henry came home to Virginia to show his people that they could not stand alone, that they must join the other colonies.

Once again Patrick Henry talked to the House of Burgesses. By this time he was so famous that every corner of the hall was filled. Many could not get in; they stood outside and tried to hear, but they could not make out the words. At last one man climbed onto a window-sill where he could hear what went on inside. From his narrow perch he called down to the others what Patrick Henry was saying inside. He couldn't quite keep up with the swift talk of the great orator. But he did the best he could.

"Mr. Henry says," the man on the window-sill called out, "that the British use kind words but they send over warships and armies. He says the British promise us a lot but do mighty little. He says we've been arguing with them for years and what happens? Nothing! He says shall we go to them and beg? No! He says we must fight."

By this time the man on the window-sill was hoarse from shouting, and he stopped to rest. But Patrick Henry had trained himself for long speaking, and now he raised his voice suddenly and it came through the window clear as a bell.

The excited crowd outside heard him shout, "Gentlemen may cry Peace! Peace! But there is no peace. The war is begun. Our brethren are already in the field." Then he spoke again in a lower tone and those outside could no longer hear him.

By this time the man on the window-sill had got back his breath and he called out, "He says we must fight. Hurray for Patrick Henry!"

"Hurray!" yelled the crowd.

"Mr. Henry says the British think *we* are weak and *they* are strong. He says if we wait they will be stronger. Shall we grow stronger by lying on our backs while they tie us hand and foot? He says they will have us in chains!"

"I can hear the chains clanking now," called a man from the crowd.

"Boo!" yelled the others.

The man in the window motioned for silence. "Quiet! Mr. Henry says they will put a soldier in every house, in your house and my house."

And then before he could go on, in a sudden quiet, the crowd heard Patrick Henry as he flung out these heroic words: "Is life so dear, or peace so sweet, as to be purchased at the price of chains and slavery? Forbid it, Almighty God! I know not what course others may take, but as for me, give me liberty or give me death!"

Inside the council chamber, there was a second of stunned silence, then a roar. His fiery speech urging the colony to arm aroused Virginia. The Burgesses voted with Patrick Henry by an overwhelming majority.

Once more he had won. And Virginia joined the rest of the colonies to fight England, and to form the United States of America.

Patrick Henry was Governor of Virginia four times, and he helped to write many of the laws of the United States. But for more than anything else he is remembered by those ringing words which mean so much to every American, "Give me liberty or give me death!"

Fighter for Freedom

THOMAS PAINE

By Jason Robbins

A WILD crowd was screaming and cursing in a square before the Tuileries Palace in Paris one hot day in July. Across the ocean George Washington was the new President of the United States. The square was huge, the palace was grand, but there was no pavement and the crowd shuffled around in mud and dust. They were yelling "Down with the King! Down with the Queen! Long live the Republic!"

The French people were tired of their kings and queens and were determined to be rid of them. What they wanted was a republic like ours in America.

Many of these people were in rags, but each one wore a jaunty cockade of red, white and blue. The cockade was a fashion of the time, but they had copied the red, white and blue colors from our American flag. Some men wore the cockades in their hats. Most of them, though, had no real hats. The men wore paper or knitted caps with tassels hanging over one ear. Today we'd call them stocking caps. The cockade meant that the person who wore one was for the people and against the king.

Squeezed into the crowd was a short man with fine blue eyes. His neat gray suit was beginning to be spattered with mud and he looked lost. Suddenly the crowd turned on him in a new burst of fury. "Look," they yelled. "He has no cockade! Hang him! Kill him! He's a King's man!"

This was not true. The man was a friend of the people. He was an American who understood no French, and he did not know what they were saying about him.

But at this tight moment another man rose over the heads of the crowd. He was standing on the shoulders of two husky friends. In a voice of command he called out, "Citizens! Stop! This man is our friend, Thomas Paine, the great American who helped to win their Revolution over there. He has come to France to help us! He is the friend of Lafayette! He is the friend of Washington, of Franklin! Citizens, hear me! He fought for America! Now he fights for us! Long live Thomas Paine!"

As he jumped down he whispered to Paine, "Have you forgotten your cockade?"

Paine remembered, took the red, white and blue cockade out of his pocket and stuck it in his hat. At once the excited crowd changed around and began to cheer. They pulled off their caps and made an aisle for Thomas Paine to march through. He was deeply moved.

This was at the beginning of the French Revolution and France loved Paine. Three years went by. The King and Queen were beheaded by the revolutionists, and the government of French liberty became the government of French blood. This period has

THOMAS PAINE. Political leader and author. Born Thetford, England, 1737. Came to America, 1774. Wrote *Common Sense*, a long pamphlet urging Americans to declare their independence, 1776. Went to France, 1787. Wrote *The Rights of Man*, defending French revolutionary measures. Wrote also *The Crisis, The Age of Reason*. Died in New York City, 1809.

come to be known as the Reign of Terror. The tyrants who now ruled France did not want freedom for anyone but themselves. They hated people like Paine who believed in freedom for everyone.

One night Tom Paine was sitting in his room in Paris, writing a book by the flickering light of a candle. Tom's pen flew across the page for he was hurrying to write the last few words of a book he was putting his whole soul into. His title for it was *The Age of Reason*. Actually it wasn't a pen he was using. He wrote with the sharp end of a goose feather dipped in ink he had made himself, just as everyone else did then. Each time he came to the end of a page, he reached into a bowl of sand and sprinkled some over it to blot the wet ink. There wasn't a sound in the room except the scratching of the quill pen and the crackle of a log falling in the fireplace.

It was three o'clock in the morning when Paine heard a soft tap on his door. He hurried over and opened it about an inch, because he thought this might be an enemy. But the man standing out there in the dark was a friend. He slipped in and spoke fast. "Bad news, Tom! Tomorrow they are coming to arrest you."

"But my book," exclaimed Paine, pointing to the sheets on the table. "I can't let them have that!"

"No so loud," whispered the friend. "Tell no one that I came. And hurry."

He turned to rush out, but Paine caught him by the arm. "Wait! Take my book with you."

"No time . . . I cannot . . . hurry . . . escape now." And the friend was gone.

Paine stood looking down at the scattered pages he had written. Slowly he piled them together and thoughtfully looked at the title, *The Age of Reason*.

Many people believed wrongly that Paine had no religion. Here in this book he was answering them. He was telling of his belief in God. These pages must be saved from his enemies. The tyrants who were then in power did not believe in God. They made all religion a crime. Some spy had told them about Paine's book and they wanted to get hold of it so that it could not be used against them.

Tom Paine was not afraid for himself. He was a man of cool courage and would not run away. But he was afraid for his book, afraid that it would be torn and destroyed. He had no copy; there was no such thing as carbon paper and any copy would have to be made by hand, and there was no time for that now.

So, instead of trying to save himself, Tom Paine went out, late as it was, to search for an American friend. His name was Joel Barlow and Paine knew he could be trusted. Tom wanted to leave the book with him.

All the rest of that night, through daybreak and the morning of the next day, Paine hurried about Paris. But he could not find Joel Barlow. Several times he went to a hotel called the Philadelphia House where Americans used to gather. There the police finally found Paine. They were polite to him but they searched his room from top to bottom. They were looking for anything that would show Paine believed in God and in freedom.

The pages of *The Age of Reason* were lying right there, but Paine had scattered them about and the guards thought them just scraps of paper. The guards could not read English, and besides they did not know

what a book looked like before it was printed. At last they found Joel Barlow, and right before their eyes Paine handed the loose pages to his friend as though they were nothing. Barlow understood and tossed the sheets on a table any-old-how. The police were fooled. Tom Paine's book was saved. It is, to this day, one of the world's best sellers and people all over the world read it in countless languages.

But that afternoon, when the book was still only some handwritten pages, the police took Paine to the Luxembourg Prison. They needed no trials or evidence then to put a man in prison. They could do it for any reason, real or imagined.

The Luxembourg was not in the least like a prison of today. The building was old and made of heavy gray stones. People were frightened just to look at it. Tom's cell was cold and it was damp. There was no way to take exercise. Prisoners without money starved. Hot fevers and cold chills ran through the cells, and if there was a doctor it was because he was a prisoner too and on his way to be killed. But Paine did not complain. He really did not care much about comfort or what he ate or what his surroundings were. He lived in his own thoughts.

Still, the Luxembourg was not as strict as most prisons are today. For one thing, Paine and the other prisoners were allowed to sit in each other's cells and talk if they wanted to. Jailers could be bribed for special favors.

Hardly one of these unhappy people was a real criminal. Mostly they were men and women who had fought against tyranny. Children were there too, some with their parents. Most of them knew that one night the guards would bang in and push hundreds of the prisoners onto open carts. The carts would run over rough cobbles and crowds would jeer. The prisoners would reach an open square. There they would be beheaded, while the crowds looked on and laughed.

Tom Paine made new friends among the prisoners. One of these was General O'Hara, a jolly Irishman. One night General O'Hara came to Tom Paine's cell. His face was sad. In a heavy voice he said, "Mr. Paine, I have been told I am to be released today."

Paine looked puzzled. "But this is wonderful news! Why do you look so unhappy?"

"Not as good as it seems." The General shook his head. "You see, the French tell me that when I get out of here, I must leave this country at once. I should be glad to go back home. But I have no money to pay the fare. The French took all my money when they arrested me. So I must stay in Paris, and then they will arrest me again and you will see me here once more."

Paine's eyes grew bright. He told the General not to worry. "I will give you the money," he said smiling.

The General looked at him in amazement. "But, my dear sir," he said. "You are a poor man. Everyone knows you give away all the money you earn from your books. It must have been a good deal of money because everyone who can read has read your books. And I have seen crowds of people who could not read, listening while one man read them aloud. Anyway, you can have no money here. The guards would have taken it from you long ago."

Paine kept on smiling. He said, "I have the money and I will give it to you. But first let us close this cell door tight. Now I will show you my secret. I have two hundred pounds hidden away in this cell." Paine pointed to the lock on the inside of the door. Locks were very roomy in those days and keys were so large and heavy that they were often used as weapons.

"Watch," said Paine. He put a finger inside a hidden opening in the lock. Slowly and carefully he drew out a crumpled roll of paper money. He smoothed out the bills. "All this money has been hidden here for months," he said. And with no further fuss he handed all of it to the astonished General.

The General was free, but Paine was still kept in the prison. Each day Paine watched as hundreds of men and women were led off to be killed. Each day new prisoners came in and brought news that the governors of France were becoming ever more tyrannical. They said the new tyrants called themselves "patriots," but they were more like the gangsters we have today. Each day, as his friends left the prison, Tom Paine thought, "When will my turn come to be led off and murdered? Maybe I'll be next."

At last that day came. The police tramped through the dark corridors. This time the papers they carried bore the name of Thomas Paine as one of those to be beheaded.

The way it was done was this: The police would stride through the prison and when they reached the cell of a man who was to

be beheaded, they put an indelible white mark on his door. Tom's cell was on the ground floor. It was one of a row on a dark corridor. It happened, on that day when his name was on the list of the condemned, that Paine's cell door was open. When it was open, it stood flat against the outer wall. There were one hundred and sixty-eight people on the death list that day. The guards were in a hurry to be through with this job. The light wasn't good. They had no electricity those days and no gas. They didn't even have oil lamps. The police carried flares that flickered in the drafts and the cells had only weak candles. These threw dark shadows. So, in the uncertain light the police put their mark on what was really the inside of Paine's door.

That was in the morning. Later, in the middle of the night, the police came again, this time to take away the condemned prisoners—that is, those with white marks on their doors. But Tom Paine's door was now closed and of course there was no mark for the police to see. So they passed him by.

Tom stayed in the prison for months and his name did not come up again. He became ill. He was weak and gaunt when the new American ambassador to France, James Monroe, arrived in Paris. Monroe quickly got Paine out. Paine was a free man again.

It is just possible that those guards who marked Tom's door did not really make a mistake. Many in France were still grateful to Paine. No one will ever know whether a friendly guard put the death mark on the wrong side of the door on purpose.

"I Only Regret that I Have But One Life to Lose for My Country"

NATHAN HALE

By Jason Robbins

"CAPTAIN NATE," said the soldier, "I'm quitting this war. I'm going home. That way I'll be back in time for spring planting. Some of the other men are going along with me."

Captain Nathan Hale looked sadly at the young man's ragged uniform and torn shoes. He was wondering what he could say. Hale's own uniform was shabby and the Army hat on his golden head was full of holes. The men were half-heartedly kicking a ball around.

The young soldier went on, "You know, Captain, we haven't had any pay for months. We just can't stand it any more."

"I know," said Captain Hale. "We're all fighting for our liberty against King George of England. But our American government is new and it is poor." He thought a moment. Then he said, "How would this be? I've some of my pay left and a little money besides. If you boys will stay on, we'll divide that money among those who need it most."

"All right, Captain. If you can stand it, we can. We'll stay. Most of us are farm boys and used to a rough life. You were brought up to be a preacher, and you've been a teacher. It must be harder for you than for us."

But Captain Hale had grown up on a farm too. When he was fourteen he got on his horse and rode the fifty-five miles to Yale College in New Haven. It took him two days. He was a good student and he graduated when he was eighteen. But he was also an athlete and he set a record for the broad jump. He didn't like to say all this because he thought it might sound like showing off. But he knew he had to show the men that he could do as well as they did. He laughed and said, "Let me have that ball you've been kicking around."

Then, while they looked on wide-eyed, he kicked the ball over the top of a tree. The men crowded around while he did it again and again, and with ease.

Of course, they already knew how brave he was. They had watched him in many a tight spot. At Bunker Hill they had seen him promoted for bravery on the field of battle.

But Captain Hale was worried by the suffering of his men. This was during the American Revolution. The British troops in their fine red uniforms were camped on Long Island and in downtown New York. The Americans in their shabby hit-or-miss uniforms were camped on Harlem Heights.

Between the two ran the East River with currents too dangerous for swimming. "If we could only get some of those British supplies," thought Nathan.

NATHAN HALE. American Revolutionary officer. Born in Coventry, Conn., 1755. Commissioned in Continental Army, 1775. Caught behind British lines and hanged as a spy, 1776.

118

Things got worse for his men. They had almost nothing to eat, hardly any tents, and no decent clothes. And then, one day, up the East River they saw the sails of a British sloop. They knew it was packed with things the Americans needed badly. But close by her side lay the British warship, *Asia*.

Nathan Hale thought up a plan. It was risky and he had to have the help of a few men. He asked for volunteers. That night there was no moon. As the distant church bells rang out twelve times for midnight, Nathan and his few men stepped into a whaleboat. He hoped the British sentries would be careless and think no one would dare attack them under the guns of the *Asia*.

"Now," said Nathan to his men, "each of you knows what he has to do. Not a word, not a whisper from any of you."

They muffled the oars of the boat with rags, and without a sound they rowed out into the river. Swiftly they climbed aboard the sloop. In a silence that seemed almost queer, they knocked out the sentries on the sloop and put them into their whaleboat as prisoners. Then, still in silence, they got aboard the sloop and sailed away to their own camp. Cheers broke out as they landed, and the men went wild with joy when the food, tents, clothes, and blankets were unloaded.

Later that same year—1776 it was—General George Washington was much bothered because he was not getting all the information he needed about what the British were doing. The Americans had secret agents in lower Manhattan, but recently one of the best of them, Haym Salomon, had been arrested. General Washington said to General William Heath, "We must know more about what the British are doing. We

are working in the dark. We need a man who will slip across the British lines and bring back information."

General Heath called a meeting of his officers and reported what General Washington had said. He looked around the group of worried men and went on, "I should like to have an officer for this because he would have to make maps and charts. But whoever does go will be in danger every minute of his stay. So he must volunteer."

Nathan Hale said quietly, "I should like to try it, sir." General Heath looked sternly at the young man.

"You know what this venture means?" asked the General. "You know that if you are caught, you will be hanged. You will not be shot, as an honorable soldier would, but you will meet a disgraceful death. You will go through the pain and misery of hanging. I do not say all this to you to discourage you. But it is only fair for you to know all you are risking. Besides, you are just up out of a sickbed. You are not yet strong."

One of the other officers spoke up. "General," he said, "this will not need strength. It will need daring and brains. And Captain Hale has both in plenty."

Captain Hale spoke in a low voice, "Sir, I will do my best."

So Captain Hale set out. He was careful, of course. He dressed in a brown coat and trousers, as this seemed the color hardest to pick out in the night. And it was a color which most plain men wore in those days. Under a broad-brimmed hat he hid his bright blond hair. He wanted to look and act like a schoolmaster. He left his papers with his friend Sergeant Stephen Hempstead. He kept only his diploma from Yale because that would prove that he could teach. And he pretended to be looking for work as a teacher. That gave him an excuse to go about freely in forbidden places.

For a short part of the way, his friend, Sergeant Hempstead, and his devoted servant, Ansel Wright, went with him. They arranged that Ansel was to be at Norwalk, Connecticut, on the twentieth of September. He was to have a boat ready and pick up Nathan early in the morning.

After his two friends left, Nathan Hale went on alone. His handsome face, his quiet manner, and his plain dark clothes smoothed things for him at first. He got through the British lines without trouble. In a back room belonging to the secret agent, Haym Salomon, he made drawings, on the thinnest paper, of the British fortifications. He also got hold of a complete plan of the British campaign. This he translated into Latin and put on the same kind of thin paper. Then he put the papers between the layers of the heavy soles of his shoes. He spent a week among the British at the tip of Manhattan Island, which the British had just captured.

His work was done. He was ready to go back and everything seemed to be going well. On the nineteenth of the month, a day before Ansel was to meet him, Nathan was at Norwalk. He spent the night at a farm house. Next morning early he ate his breakfast at a little inn called *The Cedars*. While he was eating, a man came into the room, stared at Nathan hard, and walked out. Captain Hale wondered whether the man recognized him. But he threw off the worry and hurried to the beach. A boat was coming in. Captain Hale thought his friend Ansel would be in it. Too late he saw that the men in the boat were British soldiers. He turned to escape. But a voice from the boat yelled, "Surrender or die." The British leaped out, grabbed him, and took him aboard.

Next day he stood before General William Howe, who was in command of the British troops in New York.

It was a warm day, but damp, and in the handsome sitting room of the house a fire was burning. General Howe sat in front of the fire and looked up at the slim young man. Howe was a poor General. It is said that he felt ashamed of what he was about to do. But he had made so many failures as a commander that now, when there was no danger, he was going to be stern and hard. Even so, he shrank from giving the final dreadful order. He left that to a brutal officer named Cunningham.

Since Nathan Hale had been captured in civilian clothes, he was considered a spy. According to the rules of war, he would be hanged. But there was no need for the dreadful cruelty that Cunningham then inflicted on him.

Hale was held under strong guard in the greenhouse of Howe's headquarters overnight. Next morning he was led to the place of execution. He asked for permission to write letters to his mother and to the girl to whom he was engaged. Cunningham said he could. And then, when the letters were written, Cunningham tore them up before Nathan's eyes. Hale asked for a minister and a Bible. Cunningham refused both. The other British officers were angry and ashamed of Cunningham's brutality, and later asked him why he had torn up the letters. Cunningham said he did not want the Americans to know they had a man who could die so bravely!

One of these British officers, Captain Montresor, did all he could to make up for

Cunningham's cruelty. It was Captain Montresor who told how proudly Nathan Hale faced his end and who reported the patriot's famous last words.

It was early on a Sunday morning, on September 22, 1776, when Nathan Hale met his courageous death. The spot where he was hanged is near the grounds of what is now the United Nations.

In the end he stood straight, his golden hair shining in the early light. Many of those who saw him, even hardened soldiers, sobbed aloud when they heard his last words: "I only regret that I have but one life to lose for my country."

He Made Freedom His Job

HAYM SALOMON

By Will Lane

HAYM SALOMON had an exciting time during the American Revolution. It was not an easy time, nor a quiet time. But it was a time filled with the doing of great things. Haym Salomon was a thin man who had left Poland because he was Jewish and Jews had no liberty there.

But in New York he had found freedom. His general store was popular and doing well. He had a pretty wife and nice children. He could have just sat back and made money and become a rich man. But to Haym Salomon freedom meant more than money.

And then the British Government began to interfere with the freedom of the American colonies. And so the American colonists who had loved England turned against her. In each colony young men joined in chapters of a secret patriotic society called the Sons of Liberty. They were active in starting the Revolution against England. In New York Haym Salomon joined them.

When the Revolution began, they met quietly in Haym's shop. At the first meeting he showed them the musket he had bought. Soldiers in our American Army bought their own muskets because our government was small and had very little money. Haym wanted to be a soldier.

At that meeting the other young men said, "No. You are not as strong as the rest of us, but you have a fine brain. There is more important work for you to do. You are to stay here and if the British capture any of our men, you can help them to escape. And when we have to come in secret to New York, we can use your shop. Then you can gather news for our army. You will also be able to watch the British and report to us on what they do."

And that's the way it was. The British troops took New York. They were suspicious of all Americans left in the city, but Salomon's shop did business as usual. One day a fearful fire broke out and burned down five hundred houses. The British needed those to house their troops and they were furious. They did not know who had set the fire—so they arrested men right and left. They arrested Haym Salomon too although of course he had not set the fire. That was on the very same day that they caught Nathan Hale, the patriot and American spy. If Haym had not been arrested, he might have helped Nathan Hale to escape as he had helped many others. But he had to sit in a prison cell and there he heard the news that Nathan Hale had been hanged.

The British could find out nothing from Haym except that in Europe he had learned to speak ten languages. So they let him go but ordered him to be an interpreter for their Hessian troops. These Hessians were Germans, mostly poor men, subjects of the

HAYM SALOMON. American merchant and financier. Born in Lissa, Poland, 1740. Arrived in America, 1772. Condemned to death by British as spy, but escaped (1778). Helped finance America in Revolutionary War against Britain. Died in Philadelphia, Pa., 1785.

Prince of Hesse who had sold their services as soldiers to the British. They were homesick and they hated this foreign war. So they were delighted with Haym Salomon who could speak their particular kind of German. And Haym was delighted because here was a wonderful chance to get these Hessians to desert from the British. He helped many of them to come over to the American Army. This turned out to be a good thing for our country because after the war many of these Hessians settled as farmers in Pennsylvania. Today their descendants, sometimes called the Pennsylvania Dutch, have prosperous farms there with great stone barns.

After dark Haym Salomon's shop, with the curtains closed, became a busy place. Men slipped in with news and orders from Washington's army. Prisoners hid there until Haym could find money for them. But the British arrested him again. This time they were going to hang him as they had Nathan Hale. But now his friends, the Hessians, helped *him* to escape.

At last he joined the American Army in Valley Forge and was sick at heart when he saw his friends, ragged, sick, and hungry. It was winter and there was snow everywhere,

but many of the American soldiers were barefoot because their shoes had worn out long ago.

The American colonies had no money left now. Many who had helped them thought the war was lost and would no longer sell the Army anything. They got better prices, they said, from the British.

But Haym Salomon was not one of these. His courage was high. He was a sick man himself by this time and his friends told him he ought to rest now and get well, that he had done enough.

He laughed at that and went on making his long hard journeys to his friends, gathering money wherever he could for General Washington's Army. Because of Haym Salomon's efforts, many of the men got shoes and coats and food. Before the Revolution Salomon had been a rich man. Now there was nothing left because he had given all he had to the cause he believed in.

When the war was over and we had won, Haym Salomon planned to go back to his wife and his children. But he had done too much. When he died, his wife was comforted by the knowledge that her husband had given not only his money but his very life for the freedom he loved.

A French Nobleman to Our Rescue

LAFAYETTE

By Helen Woodward

H<small>E WAS</small> a handsome little French boy, and a rich one. His clothes were made of brocaded silks and satins. He wore long silk stockings, fine shoes with big silver buckles on them, and, often, a small sword at his side. He looked like a tiny copy of the grown-up French nobles of his time, two hundred years ago. He was made an officer of the French Army when he was only twelve years old.

No one thought much of the boy. No one dreamed that one day he would shine out as a hero in American history and be honored by cheering crowds. Or that the French castle in Auvergne, where he was born, would become a shrine that Americans would go miles to visit, even today.

He was a lonely little boy. His father was dead and he seldom saw his mother who was a grand lady at the court of Louis XV, King of France. But he loved his mother dearly. He was only thirteen when she died too, and her death left him lonelier than ever.

His name was a long one, Marie Joseph Paul Yves Roche Gilbert du Motier, Marquis de Lafayette. His mother called him Gilbert, but we call him just Lafayette. For Americans he needs no title.

While he was still in his teens as an offi-

GILBERT de LAFAYETTE. General in American Army, diplomat. Born in Auvergne, France, 1757. Officer in French Army. Major-General in American Army, 1777. Lost property in French Revolution, 1793. Revisited America, 1824. Only honorary American citizen. Died in Paris, 1834.

cer in the French Army, he fought against the British. The British treated Lafayette with contempt as a useless young noble. At the court of the King nobody took him seriously.

Many people envied him his high social position and his wealth. But he hated the idle life of the court with its gossip and foolishness. He had grown rather awkward and the Queen made fun of his dancing. But he didn't care about dancing. He preferred fighting, if it was in a good cause. There was fighting in the American Colonies and that's where he wanted to go.

The King said no. Lafayette stood before the King as straight and tall as he could. His gray eyes blazed. He said, "The American Colonies are fighting for their liberty. They are fighting against England. That is where I belong, Sire."

The King smiled. He smiled with good nature, it is true, but he showed plainly that he was thinking to himself, "What a foolish young man you are, Lafayette!"

That was the last straw. The dream that had been in Lafayette's mind from the time he was a boy turned into a purpose. He was tired of having all the great ones look down on him. He would show the King, he would show his own people, he would show the British that he was somebody. He would find a way to get to America and prove himself, to win glory in a good cause.

But that was easier thought than done. For how could he get to America against the King's will?

He was indeed low in his mind when, by chance, he met another man with an ambition like his own. This was the Baron De Kalb, an older man who was a General in the French Army. He too was trying to get to America. And he too was to become a great name in our history.

Now De Kalb and Lafayette began to make plans in secret. They were in a hurry, but they had to be careful.

"There are volunteers who will be glad to go with us," said De Kalb.

Lafayette agreed. "But how about a ship? No captain would take us. They would all be afraid of the King."

"Could you perhaps *buy* a ship, Marquis?" suggested Baron De Kalb.

"So I will!" cried Lafayette eagerly. "What is money good for if it cannot buy a ship?"

But then he had a second thought. "No captain will dare to sail with us to the American Colonies, even if we own our ship."

"That too will be taken care of," replied the Baron. "I know a way."

What they did was this. They sent a friend to Bordeaux to buy a ship and hire a captain and crew. The messenger was not to tell the captain where they were really going. Instead, he was to say that he and his friends were planning to sail for the Spanish island of San Domingo off the American coast.

The ship was called *Victoire*, which is French for Victory.

The Marquis was just nineteen years old when he and De Kalb went aboard. With them went fourteen young French officers. Captain and crew were ready. At last, on a cold night in March 1777, they set sail.

The ship was small. Not even the shortest of the men could stand easily below decks. The air was bad. There was nothing at all to do. It was a long trial to the patience of lively young men.

Fifty-four long days went by. They were

cold, windy, damp and weary days. But one night, in the light of the stars, they made out a low line that meant land. Soon they came upon an opening into a bay. Slowly and carefully they sailed on until they began to fear they might get stuck on a sand bank. When they dropped anchor, they were in the calm of Georgetown Bay, in South Carolina.

Lafayette and De Kalb got into a small boat and sailors rowed them closer in shore. By straining their eyes they could just make out sandy beaches and palmetto trees. The sweet odor of jasmine in full bloom blew across the water. The only sound was the piping of little didappers and the crying of gulls. The only people they saw were Negro slaves who were dredging for oysters from a canoe. The Negroes said they came from Mr. Benjamin Huger's plantation a few miles away, up the Pee Dee River.

Lafayette and his men rowed up the river until they saw a handsome house that gleamed white against black-looking trees. The trees were live oak, thick and solid and hung with long curtains of brown Spanish moss. The moss waved gently in the summer breeze, but otherwise the whole place was still. On this hot July night the Huger family and everyone else lay asleep.

Suddenly there was a great yelling and shouting. From their cabins the servants came running in a panic. All the Hugers, mother and father and even a three-year-old baby, hurried down to the porch. They had good reason to be afraid. They knew that British ships were patrolling the coast and might make a sudden raid any time. They thought this might be one of them.

But in the light of their lanterns, the family saw just a handful of men rowing a boat to their landing. Benjamin Huger, the plantation owner, strode down to the wharf. He was amazed as a slim young man leaped from the boat, raised his right hand and, in French, took an oath to live and die for the American Colonies. He was dressed in clothes fit for a courtier and looked elegant indeed. He came forward, bowing. In stumbling English he said, "I am Lafayette, Marquis of France." He turned graciously to the older man who had followed him from the boat, and said modestly, "M. the Baron De Kalb speaks English better than I do."

But the Baron's English was not needed. Mr. Huger's voice trembled with joy as he said in excellent French, "Monsieur le Marquis, you are doubly welcome. We are Huguenots. The language of this household is French."

It was a wonderful meeting. The young Marquis was amazed and overjoyed that in all this long coast line he had had the luck to stumble on friendly people who spoke French. As for the Hugers, they were glad indeed to see these people who had come all the way from France to help the Colonies.

And then, as always in a Southern household, came a feast. The Hugers knew, without being told, how poor the food must have been on the ship, and how hungry everybody would be by this time.

Preparing a huge meal in the middle of the night for so many people did not bother the servants at all. Instead they were delighted. They were superb cooks, and loved to show their skill to company. Nearly everything they could eat was grown right there on the Huger plantation. Soon the Hugers and their new friends sat down to a huge meal of eggs and ham and fried

chicken, which was a new kind of chicken to the French.

The overseas guests stayed for two days and a great deal of eating was done by all. They had wild turkey, stuffed with pecans. They had shrimps and oysters from the bay. And there were huge cakes which no one could think of baking nowadays because the recipe for them begins "Take a hundred eggs."

Then, rested and refreshed, Lafayette and his friends set out once more on their journey. They were trying to reach Philadelphia.

On the way to Philadelphia Lafayette was shocked by his first sight of American troops. The soldiers were in rags and barefoot. Many of them didn't even have rifles.

The American Army was having a hard time and it had almost no money. Lafayette gave these men arms and complete outfits of clothes out of his own money. That was his first act of kindness for our people.

When they reached Philadelphia, Lafayette and De Kalb met with a disappointment. No one expected them. No one knew who they were. They stood in the street in front of the brick building where the Congress was meeting, the building that is now called Independence Hall. No one paid any attention to them. But even then Lafayette's spirit did not fail him. He wrote a letter to our Continental Congress and told them that all he asked was to be allowed to serve. He wanted no pay.

By this time stories had reached Philadelphia of Lafayette's long hard struggle to get here and of his gifts to our ragged soldiers. The American Congress gratefully accepted Lafayette and his friends and, to the young Marquis's delight, they made him an American Major-General.

George Washington was at that time the General in command of our American troops, and when he heard that Congress had made Lafayette a Major-General, he was indignant. "He is only a boy, and he knows nothing of the kind of fighting we have to do over here," exclaimed General Washington.

But the next thing that happened was that Washington got a letter from Benjamin Franklin who was then in France trying to make friends for the American Colonies.

At that time Benjamin Franklin was considered our greatest American. His letter to Washington said that the Marquis de Lafayette was a great noble and very wealthy and dearly loved by the French. He added that it would please Lafayette's influential friends if we treated him well.

Washington thought he had better meet Lafayette personally.

Their meeting turned out to be the beginning of a deep friendship. Both men had quiet speech, good manners, and courage. They were not time-wasters. They acted while others talked. They liked each other at once.

The day after their meeting, Washington invited Lafayette to review the troops. The young man was again shocked at the misery and poverty of the American army.

As time went on these two men, Washington and Lafayette, grew closer and closer. Washington had no children of his own and he came to look upon the young Marquis as a son. And Lafayette felt that Washington took the place of his own father whom he had never seen. He admired Washington so much that he imitated his gestures, his actions, and his ideas. The two men suffered together through the hard days of our Revolution when it looked as if we might be defeated by the British army. They slept on army blankets in muddy fields. They fought together. Neither of them ever lost courage.

After the hard-won American victory, Lafayette went back to France. But his heart remained here. Years later, the French had a Revolution of their own to get rid of their King. Lafayette tried to pattern that Revolution on our own and to have the French people elect a President like Washington. But his efforts failed. Lafayette lost all his property in France and came near to being beheaded.

He lived to be very old and many years later he came back to visit America. He was modest about his own gallant part in our Revolution. So he expected no special welcome. But once more the American people surprised him. This time, to his delight, he was met with parades and a gift of two hundred thousand dollars from a grateful Congress. He travelled all over the country. He loved our people and was loved by them. And so, at last, his childhood dream of glory came true.

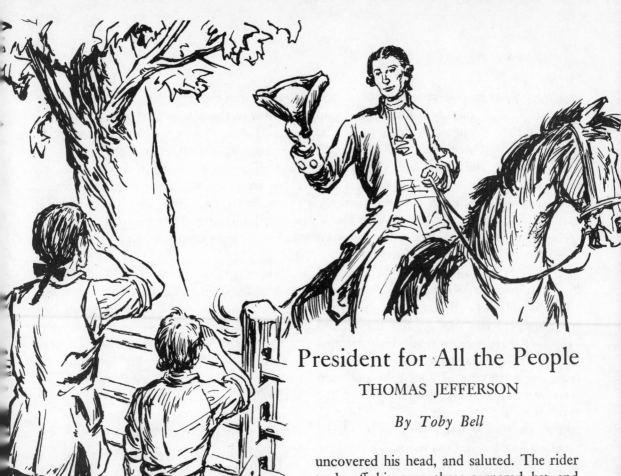

President for All the People

THOMAS JEFFERSON

By Toby Bell

uncovered his head, and saluted. The rider took off his own three-cornered hat and waved it. The two in the field could see his red hair and keen light blue eyes. With a cheerful word, the horseman rode on.

"Who is that, Father? He seems a plain man like us. Why did we salute?"

"Randy, that gentleman is Thomas Jefferson and he is going to Washington to be President of the United States. Look at him, boy, and wonder. You have seen his handsome house at Monticello. But on this important day, he has left all that behind. He is going alone, without escort of soldiers, and in plain dark clothes. Yet he is on his way to take up the highest office in the United States. He wants to show by his

A VIRGINIA farmer and his son Randy were spreading covers over their new tobacco plants to keep them from getting too much sun. Directly, they heard a horse's neigh and saw a tall man riding on a tall horse. Randy started to run toward the road. He wanted to see who it was; passers-by were few in that farm country.

But his father called out, "Take off your cap, Randy. Stand straight and salute as I'm doing." His father stood straight as a soldier,

THOMAS JEFFERSON. Third President of the United States. Born in Albemarle County, Va., 1743. Elected to Virginia House of Burgesses, 1772. Member of Continental Congress, 1775–76. Wrote basic draft of Declaration of Independence, 1776. Minister to France, 1785. Secretary of State, 1790–93. Vice-President of the U.S., 1797–1801. President of the U.S., 1801–09. Died in Monticello, Virginia, 1826.

every act what he believes: that one man is born as good as another. How would you like to go to Washington with me to see Mr. Jefferson inaugurated?"

"But, Father, how can we? We are not aristocrats. We have no velvet coats. How can we go in our farmers' clothes? Even my best coat is only leather."

"Didn't you notice that Mr. Jefferson himself was not wearing velvet?"

In their farm wagon Randy Walker and his father rode to Washington. The capital city was only a small place then. Its streets were unpaved and muddy. But Randy and his father were used to mud. They hitched their mule to a post at the edge of town and took out a package of cold ham and corn pone that Randy's mother had put up for them, with a stone bottle of cider. They ate and drank slowly while they watched the people going by into the town. There were all kinds. Some were farmers like themselves. There were fine gentlemen and ladies in grand carriages and Army officers holding in their frisky horses. And many were plain laborers who had to walk.

One farmer, who was going the other way, stopped for a minute to talk. "I've got to go home, Mr. Walker. Got a new calf coming. Did you hear about Mr. Jefferson? He rode in here just like anybody else yesterday, hitched his horse to a post, and walked into the White House. He is one of us indeed, just a citizen of this country."

Neither Randy nor his father had ever seen the city of Washington before. This was the year 1804, only twelve years since George Washington had picked out the site for the White House. Father and son walked along the half-finished roads and looked at the houses. The little city of Washington

disappointed them, though they did not say so. Most of the houses were cheap and ordinary. There were a few fine public buildings, but all around them were ragged rough fields. The streets mostly had no names and there were swamps right in the center of town. At last they came to a stately bulding with tall columns. They stopped and stared. "That must be the President's palace!" said Mr. Walker.

"What a white house it is!" said Randy. And so, by chance, Randy called the building the name we know it by today. It had just been finished.

That night Mr. Walker and Randy slept in their wagon. Next day they found a pond in what is now Rock Creek Park. The spot was lonely and much too cold for a swim in March. So they took just a quick wash in the icy water. Then they put on clean socks and shirts, brushed off their coats, and put on the hats which at home they wore only for Church.

Next day they set out again, this time for the Capitol Building, where Mr. Jefferson would be inaugurated. They were sorry there were no parades with soldiers and bands and cannon firing. Mr. Jefferson would have nothing like that, they heard. He said if the people wanted to celebrate, each of them could do it as they liked. So men and women and children got into lines any old way, most of them without uniforms. But they all sang and cheered, and church bells rang and bonfires flared. People picnicked and cooked food at the fires. It was all friendly and natural and Mr. Walker and Randy felt entirely at home and welcome in their leather coats.

Of course, there were also high-spirited horses pulling carriages with foreign ministers in them. These were not Church ministers. It was a title Governments gave to their representatives in foreign countries.

Every once in a while Randy and his father saw and heard an orator reading the Declaration of Independence. That was the great cry for freedom that Thomas Jefferson had written. For Thomas Jefferson had been chosen by the delegates to the Continental Congress, in 1776, to draw up the charges of the Colonies against the English King. This famous document, the Declaration of Independence, declared the independence of the Colonies from England. It was really the birth certificate of the United States.

As Randy heard the orators reading the Declaration, he could catch a few words here and there. And the ones he remembered best were these: that "all men are created equal," and that all have the "right to life, liberty and the pursuit of happiness."

At last they stood in front of the Capitol. It was a building of marble with a dome and a high flight of steps. This was where the House of Representatives and the Senate met. Today the Capitol is much larger than it was then, with sweeping wings. But the dome is still there, and visitors still look for it.

Randy and his father got to the front of the crowd right near a wooden platform over the steps. They looked at the important men on the platform. The older men wore breeches and long stockings. The younger ones wore a new style of long trousers. Some of the young men wore such high collars they could not turn their heads. There the Chief Justice of the Supreme Court, in black robes, faced Thomas Jefferson standing six feet two inches tall and very handsome as he took his solemn oath.

The Walkers rode home happy, and as they rode Mr. Walker told Randy that most of the people in the United States were small farmers, and that President Jefferson did not like big cities and big farms and big businesses.

There were few newspapers in that day. But people going by would often stop for a meal or stay the night and bring the news. They all said Mr. Jefferson was doing some odd things at the White House. "What do you think?" said one visitor. "The other day the British minister came to pay his respects. He wore the gold braid and fine uniform he was supposed to wear for such a visit. And you know what the President did? He walked into that reception room dressed in old clothes and slippers run down at the heels."

Randy's mother stopped her work to listen. "I wonder why he does it," she said. "Everybody knows Mr. Jefferson is a real aristocrat."

"Well," said Mr. Walker, "I reckon there's a reason in it."

The visitor said, "That's it. President Jefferson thinks one man is as good as another. He's against Negro slavery too. Negro slavery is no help to us small farmers."

Stories like that piled up. Another neighbor on his way home from Washington, told about the dinner the President had for the foreign ministers. "President Washington's was so stately and elegant, no one will ever forget it," said the visitor. "Or President Adams' state dinner either."

"I've heard about those dinners," said Mrs. Walker. "The most important go first and so on down. There's a card at each place to show where people will sit."

"Not this time," chuckled the visitor. "President Jefferson had no place cards. Everybody rushed in helter-skelter. Some of our roughest politicians grabbed the best seats and pushed important people away."

"What will happen at the President's birthday ball, I'd like to know," said Mrs. Walker.

"There won't be any," answered the visitor. "The President won't even tell the date of his birthday. And he won't accept a present if anyone sends it."

"Good for him," said Mr. Walker. "Lots of people don't understand that one man should have just as good a chance as another. This'll tell them."

Time went on and Jefferson was elected President for the second time. By now he felt that most people had learned the lesson he was trying to teach them, and after awhile affairs at the White House were as polite and formal as they were expected to be.

But in the meantime, the more elegant people in Europe were shocked. They couldn't understand why a President of the United States should want to behave in such an unseemly manner. Not all the leading men of Europe thought that way, though. The scientists and teachers admired and loved Jefferson.

One day a Baron Humboldt, who was both a nobleman from Europe and a scientist too, visited President Jefferson at the White House. On the President's desk he saw a newspaper. He picked it up and glanced through it. He was astonished to see that the paper abused the President and called him names. The Baron asked why the President allowed the paper to say such things. "Why is not its editor imprisoned?"

Jefferson smiled. "Put this paper in your pocket," he said, "and if you should ever hear our freedom of the press questioned, show your people this paper and tell them where you found it."

In little things and big, Jefferson helped the American people. One day a man from South Carolina stopped for a visit at the home of his friends, the Walkers. He handed Mrs. Walker a big bag of rice, and she was delighted with its fine quality.

"We owe that to President Jefferson," said the man from South Carolina. "That was something he did for us when he was our minister to France, before he was President. He saw that good rice growing in Italy. It is much better than ours, and he just stuck a couple of handfuls in his pockets to bring home. It made a great change for us. It is better rice and it grows faster than our own. In South Carolina, you know, we depend on rice."

"He brought back a new way to lay bricks too," said Mr. Walker.

"They say," the visitor went on, "that while he was in Europe, he went around among the French peasants and slept on their straw. They say Jefferson was a great inspiration to them and helped them get rid of their bad King."

But the biggest news about the President came to the Walker farm a few years later, in 1808, when the United States had bought from France what was called the Louisiana Territory. If Jefferson hadn't had the courage to buy that territory, England and France would probably now own all of the United States west of the Appalachian Mountains.

This is how it came about: Up north in the state of Minnesota there is a modest

place on a high hill called Lake Itasca. A little river starts from it. Other rivers join it and after awhile it becomes the Mississippi, the long river that runs through the heart of the United States. Then three more big rivers come in: the Red River, the Arkansas, and, largest of all, the Missouri. Then the Mississippi becomes one of the mightiest rivers in the world and it flows, broad and rich, through state after state, through lands of wheat and corn, of iron and cotton, until it reaches the city of New Orleans and pours into the Gulf of Mexico.

In Jefferson's time Florida and Louisiana and Alabama belonged to France. This land was then nothing but swamps and alligators.

But trappers and farmers took their wares from other states and went down the Mississippi in flatboats. When they got to New Orleans, the French charged them high prices for storage and anchorage and treated them unfairly in other ways too.

So President Jefferson sent James Monroe to see Napoleon, the Emperor of France, to see if the United States could buy New Orleans and a narrow strip of land in Alabama and Florida. Monroe joined Robert Livingston, who was then our minister to France. They offered the Emperor two million dollars.

Now, it so happened that Emperor Napoleon was worried. He was at war with the

British and he felt sure that the British could and would sail into the Mississippi and conquer all the land around it. He didn't have a navy so far from home to fight them off. So when the Americans came along and offered to buy that small strip of land, Napoleon was delighted. He startled them by agreeing to sell them the land they wanted and much more. He offered to sell them all the territory clear west to the Rocky Mountains and north to Canada. It was rich in fertile land for crops and cattle, and under the land lay unforeseen fortunes in iron and nickel and silver and coal.

Monroe and Livingston knew they could not let this chance slip. So they took their courage in their hands and asked how much France wanted for the land.

"Sixty million dollars," said Napoleon. They argued about the price and they knew they ought to ask permission of the government in Washington, but in those days that would take at least six months and Napoleon would not wait.

They finally got the land for fifteen million dollars, and it turned out to be the biggest real-estate bargain in the history of the world. Twenty-three states now occupy that land, and the purchase turned the small United States into a mighty country.

Jefferson was delighted and the whole country was agog. When the news came to the Walker farm, there was a sensation. They talked about it and dreamed about it, until Mr. Walker said what they all were thinking, "We must go to that new land. Here we will always be small farmers. There we will have a place to spread out."

For a year they planned and prepared. And then one day the whole family set forth. They made a long procession winding along the road. First Mr. Walker on a horse, then Randy on a smaller horse, then a covered wagon with Mrs. Walker and several younger children, then colored servants on mules carrying tools for farming and barrels of water and bundles of food, then cows and pigs and chickens. Mr. Walker wore a coonskin cap and so did Randy. They cut their way through forests, forded streams, shot game and caught fish on the way. They came to Tennessee and stayed awhile and at last they reached Alabama where they settled.

In that distant settlement, news from Washington came slowly. They heard that Jefferson had been Governor of Virginia many times and then had gone back to Washington to be a Senator in that same building where they had seen him inaugurated as President.

Randy Walker grew up and had children of his own, and all of them mourned when they heard of Jefferson's death. He was eighty years old and he died on the Fourth of July in 1826. John Adams died the same day, just fifty years after both of them had signed the Declaration of Independence.

Jefferson had been born rich, but he died poor. He kept open house at Monticello and was so generous and open-hearted that people nearly ate him out of his lovely home.

Jefferson believed in rights for small farmers and plain people. He thought it would be dangerous if the government in Washington became too big and powerful. He did more in his life than most other ten men, and he did it all for the good of the people of the United States. It is as the great champion of liberty for all that we remember him and honor him today.

Old Hickory

ANDREW JACKSON

By Will Lane

"Mrs. Jackson," her neighbor observed, "that little redheaded boy of yours starts too many fights."

Elizabeth Jackson stood before her log cabin with her hands on her hips. "He wins them all too; doesn't he?" she said.

The cabin was rough, only one room with a dirt floor, no paint and no windows. This was in South Carolina in the year 1780. The Revolutionary War was not yet over and there were British soldiers all over. The Americans were defiant and angry.

Elizabeth Jackson thought daily of her two sons who had gone off to fight in the war and who now lay dead somewhere far off. As the other woman walked away, Mrs. Jackson stayed in her doorway looking out across the fields, and soon she saw the flaming red hair of her son as it caught the sunshine. He was running fast as a deer, but he just had to stop once or twice to pick up a pine cone and throw it. Not at any target, he just threw it. Her face grew warm and smiling, but as he dashed up to the house, she put on a frown which didn't fool him in the least.

"Andy," she said, "are you always in fights?"

"You know why, Mother." His freckled face grew red, but his clear blue eyes half smiled, the way a natural fighter half smiles when he is very angry. "When the boys make fun of our house or because we don't own any land or they grab my shirt"—he looked down at the ragged clothes he was wearing—"I've just got to fight them."

"Pay those boys no mind," said his mother. "There are plenty of poor people around here. It's no shame on you, with your father and brothers all dead."

She patted his head and went on, "I've got to go up to the big house now and help out." This was the work she did to support them both. "And while I'm gone, try to stay out of trouble. But if you do fight, you keep on winning; you hear me?"

Later in the Revolutionary War, Elizabeth Jackson went to serve as a volunteer nurse for American soldiers. Andrew, eager to take part in the war, ran away. He got together with a company of boyish guerrillas who were pestering the British troops from the rear. The British, trained in the great bat-

ANDREW JACKSON. Seventh President of the United States. Born in New Lancaster Co., S.C., 1767. Self-educated. Major-General U.S. Army, 1814. Defeated British at New Orleans same year. President of U.S. 1829–37. Died 1845.

tles of Europe, never got used to the American day-after-day sharpshooting. Andy and others ran along behind and around the British, always hidden by trees and rocks, and shot the soldiers one by one. Each boy owned a gun because each lived on a lonely frontier and had to shoot game for food.

About this time, when Andrew was fourteen years old, his mother died and he was all alone in the world. He had been a harum-scarum lad, full of tricks and foolishness. But now he had to stand on his own feet with no mother to run to. For the first time, he did some real thinking and planning. There were no schools where he lived, but he wanted to learn. So he began to study by himself while he worked as a farmhand.

But learning this way was too slow, so he tried a new way. Although he could barely read or write, yet in this rough country he actually got a job teaching school, especially as the people liked Andy. As each lesson came along, he would learn it first and then teach it. Of course, from then on, he learned fast. When he was only nineteen years old, he became a lawyer.

He moved to Nashville, Tennessee, and did well with the law although the people who were his clients were not rich and he had a hard time making a living. But, poor as he was, when Andrew fell in love with Rachel Donelson, they got married.

Rachel was the daughter of an important man and was used to living well. But she was glad to go as Andy's wife and live in the simple log cabin he built for them. She was quite satisfied to begin their married life in a small way like nearly everyone else around them. They called their cabin the Hermitage. Andy adored Rachel.

One day he heard that a young man named Dickinson had said something rude about Mrs. Jackson. Jackson demanded an apology. The young man said he was sorry and would not do it again. But Dickinson didn't keep his word. He was a spoiled and scatter-brained young man, and he had a temper. So once again he made a rude remark about Rachel Jackson. She never knew about it, but this time, Jackson challenged Dickinson to a duel. Everybody knew that Dickinson was the best pistol shot in the state of Tennessee. He accepted the challenge with pleasure, and Jackson fully expected to be killed. Dickinson used to pin an ace of spades to a tree, then stand off fifty feet and hit the ace every time. Yet when the two men met on the duelling field, Jackson stood still with his arms at his sides and let Dickinson fire at him. Perhaps it was because Dickinson was nervous, but this time he missed. Jackson won the duel.

That was a terrible fight in a wild, rough part of the country. But most of Jackson's fighting was for great causes. Today, of course, duelling is illegal.

Jackson was so tough and his skin so leathery that men called him "Old Hickory" after one of the strongest trees in the forest. Jackson fought the Seminole Indians in Florida. He defeated the Cherokees in Alabama. Then came the War of 1812 between the United States and England. Now, that war need never have been fought. Both the English and the Americans could have settled all their disagreements and differences without a war. But most people in both countries did not know that. Jackson, now a General in the United States Army, knew only that his country was at war and that his duty was to lead troops to drive out the British. That he did in Florida. Then at the end of the War of 1812, he won a victory so amazing that people still wonder at it.

It happened in New Orleans and the year was 1815. New Orleans lies at the mouth of the Mississippi River. Its entrance is a great Delta, so wide and long that even today fast steamships take hours to sail through the quiet waters of the Delta dotted with islands, with snipe and wild ducks hidden away and with birds flying overhead in vast numbers. When the ship reaches the flat stretch of New Orleans, there isn't a hill or a speck of natural cover for hundreds of miles.

On the day of this battle of New Orleans, the Americans had signed a peace treaty in Europe. But there were, of course, no cables or planes, and no one in America, either British or American, knew that the war was over. So they went on fighting and the British set out to capture New Orleans.

Sir Edward Pakenham commanded the British. He was an old soldier and he had 12,000 men, all veterans. On the American side, Jackson had only 6,000. They were untrained men but they could shoot and they were brave and hard. But they could not take orders. Each man fought like the Indians, from behind a tree or from a ditch. Pakenham didn't know that.

The British sailed up the Delta in their ships and General Pakenham looked over the American side. He could see only some rough crude mud forts and he could hear nothing. Not a movement, not a sound. He could not see the men behind the breastworks, or that they hid behind every bale of cotton that Jackson could find in New Orleans.

General Pakenham gave a signal and the British lined up, spick-and-span in their uniforms. Then they marched on the Americans, in straight rows, their bayonets at the ready. It was like a dress parade. Still there was only a silence behind the cotton bales. And when the British came near enough, the Americans fired and each got his man. The whole first line of the British fell down. Those Englishmen didn't know American ways of fighting, but they were brave. No danger could stop them. They rallied and came on again. It was hopeless. In twenty minutes the whole battle was over. Nearly 2,000 British were killed. General Pakenham lay dead. The Americans lost only thirteen men.

The American nation went wild. Old Hickory had been a hero at home in Tennessee, but now he was a hero throughout the country.

Jackson stayed his plain self. He said he was a common man and he was proud of it. The night after the victory, New Orleans had a celebration ball. And there Andy Jackson and his wife Rachel danced to the tune of "Possum Up a Gum Tree."

In 1828 Old Hickory was elected President of the United States by a huge majority. Up to that time the Presidents had been aristocrats from New England and Virginia. Jackson was the first man of the plain people and the first to come from the frontier.

But he was a sad man when he set out for Washington for his inauguration, for his beloved Rachel would not be there. She had died a few months before. For her he had built a new Hermitage, very fine and handsome. But she never lived in it. Until his last day on earth Jackson stayed loyal to her memory.

Jackson had no use for the showy grand manners of the time. But he had learned, over the years, how to be polite. After his inauguration there was a White House reception as there always was with a new President. But there never was another like Jackson's. He was a man of the people and he would show the country that the people ruled. So he invited not just the usual important officials to the reception. He also invited thousands of backwoodsmen and workingmen, both Negro and white. Many of them had never been in a fine house before and they turned the reception into a wild jubilee. The aristocrats were shocked. But the people loved it.

Jackson was not a man who followed old fashions; he started new things with high courage and he saw them through.

He was not always right. He made many mistakes, but he stands, in United States history, for the right of every man to have a chance. And though he fought hard, he did not fight those who were weaker than he was. He fought for the weak and against the strong.

The Gold Rush

By Helen Woodward

GOLD is a magic word. It makes us think of crowns for Kings and Queens; of watches and wedding rings. It gives us the money we use to buy all kinds of things. But first the gold must be found. And gold lies hidden in the earth, like the Princess whose beauty is disguised by an ugly witch. Men have always hunted for gold.

One day in California a man was going about his daily work of helping Captain Sutter build a mill. He kicked some pebbles out of his way and saw specks shining in the sun. "Why," he said to himself, "it's gold!"

That was in the year 1848. It *was* gold and it worked its magic, for it brought excitement and adventure and wealth to the whole country.

California was a sleepy place then, not even a state, with fewer people in it than a small town there would have today. There were great haciendas, as they called the plantations, owned by Spanish and Mexican grandees. There were also a few United States soldiers and many Indians. There were no movie studios; there was not even any such thing as a movie then. There was no such place as Hollywood.

This was where the man who worked for Captain Sutter found the dusty pieces that turned out to be brand-new gold. He tried to keep the news a secret, but it was too wonderful and it leaked out. Neither telegraph nor railroad reached California in those days; so it took a long time for the word to get around. But when it did, people hurried to California. They came by boat, by mule, by wagon. Farmers walked off their farms, storekeepers locked their doors and set out. There were so many and they arrived in such numbers that this came to be known as the Gold Rush.

Pretty soon the news of the discovery of the gold reached New Orleans. New Orleans even then was a fine rich city. The people there held fancy masked balls and lived in stately houses.

Roger Borden lived in one of these houses. He was a young man of twenty, dressed in black broadcloth, and his white shirt had a froth of ruffles in front. He was arguing with his father.

"But, Father," he was saying, "they have found gold in California."

"I don't believe it," his father said. "It's nonsense!"

Roger waved a newspaper at him. "You see what the paper says? It's the richest find of gold in the whole world. I'm going there to see for myself. I'm tired of this do-nothing life here. I want adventure."

His father gave in at last; but when Roger asked for the money for the journey, his father said, "If you want adventure, you must take some risk."

Roger was discouraged until he heard that a ship shortly to sail for San Francisco needed a barber. Many men wore beards then, and barbers could earn a good living, especially in rough pioneer country. So Roger learned to be a barber.

Roger left his fine shirts behind and set out, wearing a red shirt and a bandana handkerchief and rough trousers tucked into high heavy boots. He packed his shaving tools. But he also had to take much that no one would bother with today when people can buy what they want almost anywhere. He packed needles and thread and pins, pen and ink and papers. He packed simple medicines and coffee and a coffee pot. He packed a pistol and bullets. And with special care he packed matches, as many as he could manage to carry. He would need them to light fires for warmth and for cooking. Matches were expensive and hard to get. He knew he would not find any in the rough places where he was going.

The little steamship sailed from New Orleans, with Roger aboard and others as eager as he was. They ran into a storm that tossed them about like popcorn in a shaker. But at last they reached the city of Colon on the Isthmus of Panama, the narrow waist between North and South America. There their real troubles began.

There was no canal across Panama then as there is now. Roger bought a mule. So did the others. They traveled across Panama in a group because there was danger from strange native Indians. But after a while that became the least of their hardships. For this was a land of solid jungle, with dreadful heat, fleas and mosquitoes, cholera and yellow fever. On the way the men threw away a lot of their gear, but Roger was able to keep all of his. They were tired indeed when they reached the damp hot town of Panama on the Pacific side of the Isthmus. And there was no ship there to take them further. They had to sit and wait. But a ship came at last. The time was New Year's Eve

in 1849. Roger got in just in time so that many years later he could tell his children and grandchildren that he was one of the original Forty-Niners.

No beautiful white city rose before them as San Francisco does today. What they saw was the sweeping blue bay dotted with silent and smokeless ships. Their crews had walked off to join the Gold Rush and the ships lay rotting in the harbor. The city itself was a huddle of buildings at the shore front against the mountains and forests behind.

Roger had no time for the beauty of mountains or bays. He stayed in San Francisco a week and in that time earned a small fortune as a barber. Men were quite willing to pay him five dollars for cutting hair and a beard. At the end of a week Roger was able to buy a horse and a place in a caravan. He set out for the Sacramento Valley where the gold had been discovered.

And so he reached Sacramento which is now the capital of California. The Sacramento that Roger saw was a wild rough place. Everybody was in a hurry. Strangers met, shook hands, and slapped each other on the back.

The few houses were crowded. Roger was glad to pay five dollars to sleep on the floor of a wooden shack. There were tents everywhere and piles of goods in the streets. It was winter and it rained a good deal. A tent was worth more than the gold itself. One day when the rain stopped, Roger joined a half dozen men who were trying to cook over a fire in the street. He lent them his coffee pot and they lent him a frying pan. He had bought a tin of corned beef for a dollar and that was his supper. After supper one man in a ragged shirt played a banjo

140

and they all sang to the tune of Stephen Foster's *Oh, Susannah!*:

> It rained all night the day I left,
> The weather it was dry.
> The sun shone hot, I froze to death.
> Susannah, don't you cry.

Next morning Roger started off for the place where he was going to stake out a claim. First come, first served was the rule. If you were the first on the spot, the gold you found belonged to you. There were many fights over this with both fists and guns. But Roger was a tall strong young man who looked as though he would be dangerous to quarrel with; and he had no trouble.

The place he chose had a brook running through it. He went into the water barefoot, rolling up his trousers and his sleeves. He carried a bucket. In this he scooped up sand and pebbles from the stream. When he was lucky he could see a few gold specks in the bucket. He filled it with water and shook it to left and right. The gold was heavier and sank to the bottom. Then he carefully threw away the sand and water. What was left was gold. He tried out a sort of sieve that he rocked back and forth like a baby's cradle. But Roger found that too much of the gold came through the holes with the sand. So he stopped using the sieve.

Once in a while he found a gold nugget on the ground. This might be as small as a grain of sand or as big as a pea or once in a great while as big as a hickory nut. He took his gold to Sacramento to be weighed. There he spent a good deal of the money he got for his gold. Everything was very expensive. He had to pay a laundress as much for washing a shirt as it would cost to buy the shirt today. There was an old woman there, eighty years old, she said, and as spry as any of them. She knitted socks. Roger had to buy a pair, for his were in rags, but in those days the price of a pair of socks was about what a man would pay for a suit today. The old woman would sit and talk and chew tobacco. She told Roger that she had come across the continent by land with her son.

"It was a long pull," she said. "My son wanted me to stay home, but his wife was going along, and I said what one woman can do I can do too. We come from St. Joseph on the Missouri River. We joined a wagon train there."

"Tell me about it," said Roger.

The old woman laughed. "Wait till I light my pipe. We all traveled by caravan in many wagons. Some of the men were farmers who just walked off and left their crops to die. My son sold his goods at auction. Maybe the farm'll still be there. Good thing we had a little money when we got to St. Joseph. Know what we had to buy? Blankets and cheese and lard and bacon and pots and pans and crackers and salt and coffee and sugar. We women had our sewing things and my son had his knives. But he bought him a gun and some powder. Mighty handy they were killing meat on the way."

"What about a wagon?" asked Roger.

"We were lucky there. We met a man going back from here. He got sick and couldn't get any gold. He sold us his wagon cheap—the kind you see all round here, with a cover over it. And he sold us a couple of mules. When my son heard about all the bad times this poor man had out here, he wanted to go back home too."

The old woman laughed again, put down her pipe, and picked up her knitting needles. "I told him no indeedy. I'm not going back to have the neighbors laugh at us. But if I'd a known how awful it was going to be to cross those Rocky Mountains, I woulda turned back too." She sighed a little. "Well, here we are . . . and here I'll be when you want another pair of socks, young man."

Roger left the noisy cheerfulness of Sacramento and went back to his cold hard work of gold digging.

Of the rough gold prospectors in Sacramento, some got sick and died, some failed and went home. Some, who found no gold, worked as laborers for others and got well paid for it. But the Forty-Niners, bold as they were, just found the gold that was on top of the ground. There was more—far more—under the ground. But to get it expensive and heavy mining machinery was needed.

As for Roger, he made a fortune in gold and he went back to New Orleans to visit his family and friends. But he had grown to love California; so he went back to Sacramento and lived there.

The finding of gold opened the country to many industries. Men began to build railroads clear across the nation so that they could get to California more quickly. And because the land was so vast, the new telegraph system that Samuel Morse had invented, came into wider use.

Today we fly to this land which is golden with oranges. And we look at the mansions that some of the gold millions built. California is rich with many things today, with many treasures worth far more than the gold men sought there in the early days. But no Californian ever forgets the Gold Rush and the adventurous Forty-Niners.

"Of the People, By the People, and For the People"

ABRAHAM LINCOLN

By Bella Koral

THE wind howled down the chimney of the gray log cabin that stood in a small clearing in the Kentucky woods. It made the door rattle on its leather hinges. But inside a great fire blazed in the fireplace, warming the cabin where Thomas Lincoln, his wife Nancy, and their little daughter Sally lived.

Now on this Sunday, the twelfth of February, 1809, there came to this family a new baby boy. Nancy Lincoln lay on her corn-husk mattress covered by a bearskin, with her new baby cuddled in her arm.

"We'll name him Abraham, after your father," she said to her husband. "Abe Lincoln," Nancy whispered to the baby.

Later Dennis Hanks, Nancy's cousin, came running down the wilderness path from the cabin where he lived. Dennis tip-toed to the bed, took a long look at the new baby, and rocked him in his arms. The baby began to cry.

Dennis gave him back quickly to his mother.

"Take him," he said. "He'll never 'mount to much."

Dennis could not have been more wrong —for that little baby, born in a log cabin, was to become one of the greatest men the world has ever had.

Abe's mother was quiet and gentle, loved by everyone who knew her. Nancy was different from most women in the Kentucky settlements then, for she was able to read and write. She knew there was a great world outside where people lived and thought in ways different from those of folks around her. She dreamed that some day her children would see that world "out yonder."

Abe's father was an easy-going man, quiet and brave, too. He was a good carpenter, but he would rather track down a wild turkey for supper than build a cabin. He liked to sit around and tell yarns and crack jokes.

When Abe was three the Lincoln family moved to Knob Creek farm. The new cabin was like the old one—built of rough logs. It had one room, one door, one window, and a floor of packed-down earth. The fireplace of stone and clay was so large that logs the size of a man could be rolled into it for a winter fire. Nancy did all her cooking here. The children slept on corn-husk mattresses on the floor.

Knob Creek was in the wilderness, but it was on a big highway, the Louisville Pike, where many travelers passed. Covered wagons rumbled along carrying people west-

ABRAHAM LINCOLN. 16th President of the United States. Born in Hardin (now Larue) County, Kentucky, Feb. 12, 1809. Little formal education but read books whenever he could. Studied law in spare time. Elected to Congress, 1847. President of U.S., 1861–65. Issued call for volunteer Army, 1861, after attack on Fort Sumter by Southern General Beauregard. Issued Emancipation Proclamation, 1863. Dedicated National Cemetery at Gettysburg, Pa., with famous Gettysburg Address, 1863. Re-elected President, 1864. Shot in Ford's Theater, Washington, by John Wilkes Booth, April 14, 1865, five days after end of Civil War.

ward. Preachers and lawyers sometimes stopped at the Lincoln cabin and Abe always listened as they talked of the world beyond the hills. He would ask questions and remember everything he heard.

Hunters sometimes stopped at the cabin. Abe listened wide-eyed when one of them spoke of a big town named Washington where the President of the United States lived. His eyes opened wider when the hunter told how the President and some of the townspeople in Washington rode in coaches and ate off china plates.

And when Abe heard words like "freedom" and "slavery" he tried to figure out what they meant.

There was plenty of work to do on Knob Creek farm. Mr. Lincoln had some horses, a cow, pigs, and sheep. Abe helped taking care of the animals. Wearing his linsey-woolsey shirt, Abe rode a horse hitched to a "bull-tongue" plow. He helped his father plant corn, beans, and potatoes, and he weeded the corn-patch till his hands were blistered. He ran errands, carried pails of water from the spring, and kept the wood-box filled.

One day, when Abe was seven, Thomas Lincoln brought home exciting news. "Zachariah Riney is opening a school four miles up the pike!" he declared.

"The children will go, Thomas, won't they?" said Nancy, her eyes sparkling.

"Well, I don't know," Tom said. "I can't read nor write more than my name, still I get along."

"But Thomas, I've always wanted Abe and Sally to learn reading. Reading is *good!*" Nancy went on anxiously.

"Well, all right then, Nancy," Tom agreed. "I'll see Zachariah."

In those days there were no public schools in Kentucky, but parents would offer a schoolmaster the use of a deserted log cabin. The settlers had little money. They paid the schoolmaster by giving him meals or lodging or by washing his clothes.

Sally and Abe walked the wilderness path to the school. The only light there was came in through a space where one log had been left out of the wall. It was a "blab" school and it was called that because all the pupils shouted their lessons out loud until it was time to recite. That made the schoolmaster think that the children were working hard. A B C's and arithmetic tables and spelling words were all in the air at one time.

Mr. Riney stood, switch in hand, to see that no one was idle. If a pupil stopped "blabbing," he went after that unlucky one with his switch. Abe was the youngest pupil. Most of the others were big boys and girls who had grown up without ever having seen a book.

That night, after his first day at school, Abe, under his bearskin covers, kept softly reciting "A–B–C, A–B–C."

His mother heard him. "Are you all right, Abe?" she called.

"Yes, Mammy," he answered. "I'm just saying the lesson."

She came over and covered him more snugly. "Learn as hard as you can, Abe, while you have the chance," she whispered. "Learning's real fine."

When the few weeks of school ended, Abe had the best teacher of all—his mother. Books were scarce, but Nancy had a Bible that she loved to read.

He never forgot the stories his mother read to him from her Bible. They became

as much a part of him as the language of the Bible became part of his own speech. Abe's mother taught her children to be honest and kind and friendly.

One autumn evening Abe's father announced, "Kentucky is no place for us any more. Too many folks who own slaves are moving in."

Thomas and Nancy hated slavery. Nancy could not bear to hear of Negro mothers sold as slaves and sent so far away that they never saw their children again.

"My brother Joe's moved to Indiana. It'll be a free state with no slavery allowed. And folks say there's rich corn land there, to be bought cheap," Tom went on. "I reckon we'll move on to Indiana. What do you say, Nancy?"

Early one December morning they piled their belongings on two horses. Sally and Nancy rode on one, and Abe and his father walked, leading the other horse over the rough roads. After about a week they reached Indiana. They had traveled about a hundred miles. Abe worked with his father cutting down trees and shrubs to clear the way. And from now on the ax was scarcely ever out of his hands. At last they reached the little clearing near Pigeon Creek where Tom built his cabin.

By the time Abe was nine, he was so tall he kept growing out of his breeches. He could do almost a man's work with an ax.

Then came a terrible time. A strange illness broke out in the Pigeon Creek neighborhood. It struck at cattle and people, too. Abe's mother nursed some of the sick neighbors and a few days later she became very ill. There was no doctor for many miles around. Her husband and the children did all they could, but Nancy did not get better.

When his mother died, Abe felt as if his whole world had ended. He would wander into the woods and think about the things she had told him. His father, too, was lonely and sad.

A year went by. The cabin became untidy, the children grew thinner and shabbier. Thomas Lincoln decided something must be done. He left for Kentucky. One day the children heard wagon wheels coming near. They ran out and saw a wagon piled high with furniture. Several children were there too, and a woman was sitting on the seat beside Thomas Lincoln.

Thomas had married her. She was a widow, Sarah Johnson, whom he had known as a young girl. Now she was here and had brought her own three children.

"Here's your new Mother," Thomas told Abe and Sally. They looked up at a tall, kind-faced woman who spoke to them in a warm and friendly voice.

The new Mrs. Lincoln's heart went out to these children in their dirty, ragged clothes. She saw in Abe's gray eyes his need for a mother's love. She held out her arms to him, and the boy went to her. From then on his stepmother was, as Abe later said, "the best friend I ever had."

Sarah Lincoln saw that Abe was not like other children. She came to understand his deep thirst for learning, and tried to help him all she could.

When there were enough settlers at Pigeon Creek, a school was started and Mrs. Lincoln saw that Abe went, even though Thomas kept saying it was a waste of time. The school, nine miles away, lasted only a few weeks, but Abe learned to write. He had no pencil, so he used charcoal. He had no paper or slate, so he wrote on a wooden shovel. When he had covered it with writing, he would scrape it off to have a smooth clean place to write again. The Lincolns had no candles, and Abe would lie in front of the fire and study by its light.

When Abe was able to get some paper, later on, he made himself a pen out of a turkey quill. For ink he used the juice of wild berries. With his home-made pen and ink he wrote his first composition, an essay against cruelty to animals.

When Abe was a grown man, he said, "I went to school by littles, and all my school life didn't amount to much more than a year."

Abe would walk miles to borrow a book and would read it far into the night till he knew it by heart. He would read while he rested his horse from ploughing at the end of each furrow.

Once Abe borrowed a book called *The*

Life of George Washington from a farmer named Crawford, and took the book up with him to the loft where he slept. He tucked it between two logs in the wall before he fell asleep. During the night a storm came up and the book was wet through and the covers spoiled. With a heavy heart, he returned the book to Mr. Crawford and explained how the accident had happened.

"Well, Abe," said the farmer, "if you want to make up for it, come and work three days in my cornfield."

So for three days, from sunrise to sunset, Abe gathered fodder in Mr. Crawford's cornfields to pay for the damage to the book. Then Abe had a wonderful surprise. Mr. Crawford *gave* him the book! He walked home, the happiest of boys, for Washington was Abe's great hero.

Besides helping his father on the farm, Abe earned extra money by working as farm hand for the neighbors, and splitting rails for their fences. By the time he was seventeen, he was six feet four inches tall. "Why, that lanky Abe is as strong as three men," said a farmer.

By that time Abe was the best wrestler in several counties. And he was the best runner and jumper too. Still, whenever he could, Abe kept on studying and reading. Sometimes, out in the fields, he would recite from memory speeches he had learned from his books. Other farm boys would come running to hear them. Once, when this happened at the Crawfords' during harvest time, Mrs. Crawford asked him, "What's going to become of you, Abe?"

"Why, ma'am," he answered, half joking and half in earnest, "I'm going to be President—leastways I'll study and get ready."

To earn some money Abe ran the ferry-boat from the Indiana side of the Ohio River. One day, two men who ran the ferry from the Kentucky side, brought Abe to court before a Kentucky judge. "He's from Indiana," they complained, "and has no right ferrying people across the river to Kentucky. It's against the law!"

The judge asked Abe how far out he had taken passengers. Abe answered, "I only ferry them as far as the steamboats in the middle of the river."

"Then," said the judge to the men, "he's not breaking the law."

The judge's words gave Abe a new idea—a new direction in life. Here was something he was going to learn about—the law. From another judge he borrowed a book about Indiana laws. In this book he found the Constitution of the United States and the Declaration of Independence which said that "all men are created equal." Abe thought about what he learned in the law books and talked about these things with people he met.

At about this time Abe had a chance to see something of the world. He was hired by a Mr. Gentry to go with his son Allen down the Mississippi River by flatboat (a kind of raft) to New Orleans. There they were to sell a load of farm products.

New Orleans was the first large city Abe had ever seen. He and Allen wandered through its narrow streets, staring at the houses with their lacy iron balconies. They saw richly dressed people riding in carriages, and sailors from many lands.

But in a big market place white men were selling Negro men, women, and children. Slave buyers from Southern plantations were looking over these Negroes, feeling their muscles and counting their teeth to see if they were strong and healthy.

Slavery was not allowed in the Northern states. In the South, where slave-owning was allowed, plantation owners had bought thousands and thousands of Negroes. Some worked as servants, but most of them were used as field-hands on their masters' great cotton and sugar plantations. Some slave-owners treated their slaves cruelly, though many slaves were given good care by their masters. But no slave knew when he might be sold to a master far away, and be separated from his family forever.

Abe Lincoln was disturbed. The slave market made a deep and lasting impression on him. "If ever I get the chance to hit that," he said, "I'll hit it hard."

When he was twenty-one, Abe felt it was time to strike out for himself. Saying good-by to his parents, he put his arms about his stepmother and held her close. "I'll never forget you, Mother, and all you've done for me," he said.

Soon he met a man named Offut who asked him to be the clerk at his store in the village of New Salem. At Offut's store Abe made many friends who enjoyed his good nature. But it was his honesty that they talked about most.

One day, by mistake, Abe gave a woman less tea than she had paid for. When he discovered this, he walked four miles to give her the tea he owed her. Such deeds earned him the nickname of "Honest Abe," and by that name he was known as long as he lived.

Later Abe opened a store with a man named Berry. Friends, who trusted Honest Abe, lent him money.

Berry was a lazy, wasteful man—and Abe loved books and people too much to be a real business man. Once a family going west in a covered wagon stopped at his store. They asked Abe to buy a barrel of old things they couldn't use. Abe couldn't use the things, either, but the people looked hungry, so he gave them fifty cents for the lot. Later, to his delight, he found in the barrel an important law book he had long wanted. Now he would stretch out on the store counter and read, or lie under a tree outside, studying and thinking.

It was not long before the store failed. Berry died and Abe was left to pay the debt they both owed. Abe felt Berry's debt was his, too. It took him years, but in the end Honest Abe paid back every penny.

Lincoln made friends wherever he went. People enjoyed listening to him talk. "If you want to know anything about politics," they would say, "go and ask Abe."

That fall they elected Abe to be their representative in the legislature at Springfield, the state capital of Illinois.

Lincoln now met a young lady, Mary Todd from Kentucky, who was visiting in Springfield. She was pretty and smart, with a saucy way of talking. Many young men admired her. Of them all, Mary chose to marry lank and awkward Abe.

After his marriage Lincoln spent many months of the year as a traveling lawyer. Jogging over the countryside on "Old Buck," his horse, he became known and loved far and wide. Courts were crowded when he appeared.

The years rolled along and great changes were taking place. Railroads spread over the land and great cities grew up across the country. Yet slavery and the cruel slave trade was still going on. The Northern States did *not* want slavery; the Southern States *did*. A new party, the Republican

party, was formed by men who thought slavery was wicked.

Stephen Douglas, a famous laywer and Senator from Illinois, nicknamed "The Little Giant," traveled through the state telling the people what his plan was. "Let the people of each state decide whether to have slavery or not."

Abraham Lincoln felt strongly that this could not be. "The nation cannot go on forever half slave and half free," he declared.

The Lincoln-Douglas debates made Lincoln's name known throughout the nation. His clear honest words made everyone want to hear more of this man who had been an Indiana backwoods boy.

Before long important men of the Republican party called on Lincoln to tell him he had been chosen to run for President. Douglas and two other men were chosen by other parties. Torchlight parades were held in the cities, night after night. "We want Honest Abe for President," roared the crowds.

When the returns came in showing he had won, Lincoln rushed home. "Mary, we've been elected!" he shouted.

It was a dark and rainy morning when Abe left for Washington, but the station was filled with old friends and neighbors who came to say farewell. Lincoln, wearing a tall silk hat and a fringed shawl about his shoulders, shook hands with his well-wishers.

"Goodby, God bless you, Abe," they called. The train pulled out, slowly gathering speed.

He was going to the great task before him. Years of suffering and sorrow for himself and the nation lay ahead. But Lincoln would keep the country united and preserve the Union. With a ringing Proclamation he would wipe out slavery and prove to the whole world that "government of the people, by the people, and for the people" would not perish from the earth.

—Adapted from *Abraham Lincoln* by Bella Koral

The Gettysburg Address

AT THE DEDICATION OF THE NATIONAL CEMETERY, NOVEMBER 19, 1863

By *Abraham Lincoln*

Fourscore and seven years ago, our fathers brought forth upon this continent a new nation, conceived in liberty and dedicated to the proposition that all men are created equal.

Now we are engaged in a great civil war, testing whether that nation, or any nation so conceived and so dedicated, can long endure. We are met on a great battlefield of that war. We have come to dedicate a portion of that field as a final resting place for those who here gave their lives that that nation might live. It is altogether fitting and proper that we should do this.

But in a larger sense we cannot dedicate, we cannot consecrate, we cannot hallow this ground. The brave men living and dead who struggled here, have consecrated it far above our poor power to add or to detract. The world will little note nor long remember what we say here, but it can never forget what they did here.

It is for us, the living, rather to be dedicated here to the unfinished work which they who fought here have thus far so nobly advanced. It is rather for us to be here dedicated to the great task remaining before us; that from these honored dead we take increased devotion to the cause for which they gave the last full measure of devotion; that we here highly resolve that these dead shall not have died in vain; that this nation, under God, shall have a new birth of freedom; and that government of the people, by the people, and for the people, shall not perish from the earth.

With Malice Toward None

FROM THE SECOND INAUGURAL ADDRESS, MARCH 4, 1865

By *Abraham Lincoln*

With malice toward none;
With charity for all;
With firmness in the right, as God gives us
   to see the right,
Let us strive on to finish the work we are in;
To bind up the nation's wounds;
To care for him who shall have borne the
   battle,
And for his widow, And his orphan—
To do all which may achieve and cherish
   a just and lasting peace among ourselves
And with all nations.

Hero of Texas

SAM HOUSTON

By Helen Woodward

THE first time the Cherokee Indians saw Sam Houston, they were astonished. The Cherokees were friendly and used to white men. But they had never seen one as handsome as this youngster who came walking into their camp like an everyday visitor. Sam was sixteen, but he was already taller than most grown men and straight as a Carolina pine. His chestnut hair caught the sun and his blue eyes shone.

Sam looked sure of himself, but he was not really sure of a welcome; so he did not speak, only held up his hand in greeting.

This Cherokee village on the Tennessee River did not look at all like the Indian camps of rougher tribes. There were no tents or tepees. From the solid log cabins Indian women and children came running out to look at the handsome stranger. The men pushed through, raised their hands in greeting. One young Indian, who seemed to be a leader, spoke up and asked politely, "Who are you? What do you seek here?"

"I am Sam Houston and I come from Tennessee. I have a gift from a Cherokee friend." And Sam held out a knife, with the handle forward. That was a sign of friendship, and the young Indians took him to meet their chief. They led him toward the largest of the cabins, while squawking chickens fluttered out of their way. An Indian squaw leading a cow stopped openmouthed to watch.

Sam thought, "These Cherokees are civilized. I can tell by the way they care for their chickens and cows."

SAM HOUSTON. Soldier and statesman. Born in Rockbridge County, Va., 1793. Adopted by Indians. General in Mexican War. Victor at San Jacinto. Senator from Texas, 1846–59. Governor of Texas, 1859–61. Died 1863.

He asked the name of the Chief. The young Indians spoke English but as though they didn't use it often. "Our Chief is named Oolooteka," they said.

"Oolooteka," repeated Sam. "It is hard to say," he thought, "but you could sing it. Sort of sounds like an owl hooting."

The young men guessed what he was thinking and they said, "In English his name is John Jolly." When Sam told Oolooteka that his own father was dead, the Chief adopted him as a foster son.

"We will now make you a member of our tribe," said the Chief. "Your Indian name will be Colonneh. In English that would be the Raven. We believe that the Raven is sent by God to help men." And all his life long, even after he became famous, both Indians and white men called Sam Houston the Raven.

Sam loved his mother, but in his time there was much unknown territory and boys like Sam often went exploring. And Sam was tall as a man, already six feet of bone and muscle.

Sam fitted into the Indian life as if he had been born to it. He learned to hunt with bow and arrow as well as gun; he learned how to trail game on foot and how to catch fish with his bare hands. He learned to eat meat as the Indians did, by catching a huge hunk in their teeth, then slashing it off with a sharp knife, leaving only a piece like a big bite. The first time Sam tried it he nearly cut off his nose. But he got used to it and found it handy when he couldn't stop to eat any other way.

Sam became a champion at their odd game of ball. They played with a ball of deerskin, the size of a baseball, and stuffed with hair. A Cherokee girl made a racket for him to play the game with, and she also made him a fine shirt beaded in the Indian style. Dressed up in this, he helped win a game against a tribe of the Choctaws.

One day, several months after he came to live with the Cherokees, he was lying on the river bank, reading, when he fell asleep. He was wearing Indian clothes, a buckskin shirt, leather leggings and moccasins. His face was burned an Indian copper color. Into his light sleep crept a whisper of sound. His eyes flashed open. In a moment he caught sight of a canoe with two young men in it. He knew them; they were his older brothers from his home in Tennessee. Sam rose to his tall height. One of the men in the canoe feathered his paddle and the boat turned in to shore. "Jumping Jehosaphat!" he called out. "That's brother Sam. I thought it was an Indian."

Sam shook hands, but he looked pretty cool. "Hello, John. Hello, James," he said. "What are you doing here?"

"Looking for you," answered James. "We've come to take you home."

"I like it here. I'm not going home."

"Mother's worried about you," they pleaded.

"Tell Mother I'm all right," said Sam. "Give her my love and say I'll be coming home to see her soon. But I'm coming by myself. No one's taking me."

The two brothers looked up and down Sam's tall figure and gave in. "Yes, Mother sure doesn't have to worry about you," they agreed.

"What do you like so much about the Indians, Sam?" asked James.

"They think I'm all right," drawled Sam. "At home you all made me feel like I was no good for anything. You called me a lazy loafer. Well, I'm not lazy. You thought I was a loafer because I like to read. I didn't like feeding chickens and such things at home. That's woman's work here. I'm doing a man's work here. Anyway, you don't need me to work the farm; there are so many of you at home."

Sam stayed with the Indians for three years. Then he went home to see his mother. He was nineteen years old and had grown to his full height. He was six feet six inches tall. She was proud as she looked at her handsome son. She saw that even though he had lived the rough Indian life, he had not forgotten the good manners she had taught him.

He dressed carefully in the white man's fashion, though he sometimes put on an Indian blanket when he felt like it. He taught school and earned some money. Then he studied law. Years went by and Sam Houston became an important man. By the time he was thirty-five he was the Governor of Tennessee. Then once more he felt the need of his Indian friends. Everyone was astonished when he resigned as Governor and, all alone, went back to the people who loved him, the Cherokees.

They made a great feast for him of beef and venison and cornbread and fish. They sang and beat their drums and danced. He saw that while a few of the Indians were still dressed as in the old days, in buckskins, most were dressed like any farmers.

After the feast, Sam sat down with his foster father, Chief John Jolly.

"I am troubled," said the Chief. "Your men in the government at Washington are not keeping their word. We were living in Georgia and getting along well. The white men came to settle and the government said that if we would move to Tennessee, they would give us better land and money. The land was not better; it was worse. Then they sent us to Arkansas, where we now are. The same thing is happening again. Now they want us to move farther west. You know the fierce Comanches are there. We fear them as much as you do now. Our young bucks want to fight your white friends. You talk to them."

Sam calmed the young Indians. Then he went to Washington to see the President, who at that time was John Quincy Adams.

In Washington people stared at him, stared at his six feet six, his handsome face, and even more at the Indian blanket which he wore. He won some peace and better treatment for his Indian friends for a while.

President Jackson in Washington was friendly to the Indians too, but Washington was far away. Settlers, who needed land, were blind to the needs of these Indians. This is something in our history of which we Americans are ashamed and we have not done enough to make up for it.

Sam Houston himself could do nothing more for the Cherokees at that time because there were wars going on by then and he was ordered to take his part in them. Sam hated violence; but the Creek Indians, who were a fierce fighting lot, attacked white settlers and had to be stopped. In the Creek war Sam had served under General Andrew Jackson whom he adored. And Cherokee scouts had served with him. That had been a short sharp quick fight. Sam's six feet six had shown his men just where he was every minute as his long legs leaped easily over the log barricades of the Creeks.

But a bullet caught him. He was badly wounded. Even as the blood ran from the wound in his leg, he rose and led another charge. Again he was wounded, this time in the arm, and he almost fainted. Yet he would not give in or leave the battle until, at last, General Jackson ordered him to.

And then came the long trouble with Mexico. The huge territory of Texas did not at that time belong to the United States but to Mexico. American settlers began to move in to take over the unused land. We tried to buy this territory from Mexico, but the Mexican government would not sell it. The United States did not really offer enough money. But the settlers needed the land. In that vast territory there lived 30,000 Americans and only about 300 Mexicans who inhabited a few small otherwise unused places. The Mexicans demanded that the Americans pay them taxes and follow the Mexicans' religion. The Americans, rough tough pioneers, refused. Then Mexico began to seize the settlers' lands. The Texans rebelled and a bitter fight followed.

There were 6,000 Mexicans fighting against a few hundred Americans. Some of the Americans were besieged in an old mission in San Antonio called the Alamo. Those few men in the Alamo fought until every single one of them was killed or wounded. The Mexicans had no mercy on them. The war seemed lost.

In desperation the Texans called for Sam Houston to lead them. He had only 300 men in his army. Settlers were fleeing, leaving their goods behind them.

The young ones who remained were wild to fight the enemy. "Let's go. Let's get them!" they implored their leader.

But Houston said "No, we are not ready. We must wait for cannon."

He meant the two little cannon—all they had—that were to come. But he also meant that these settlers who were such good shots and frontiersmen did not know how to fight in an army. So he trained them.

At last the two little cannon came. Then Houston struck. He encouraged his men with cries of "Remember the Alamo!" They remembered and fought like demons. The bitterest fight was at San Jacinto. It was short and the Texans won.

For ten years Texas was a republic and not part of either Mexico or the United States. The Texans had just one star in their flag and that is why Texas calls itself "The Lone Star State."

Both the United States government and the Texans, wishing Texas to be part of the Union, started the senseless Mexican War of 1846. Later General Ulysses S. Grant branded it "a wicked war." The Mexicans were quickly defeated. In this war Houston played no part.

In the long run the United States did pay some millions of dollars to Mexico, and Texas became a state of the Union. While it was the Lone Star Territory, Houston was its Governor and when it became a state, he was elected Senator from Texas.

Texans liked to try new things. They had a good deal of dry desert-like country, so they said, "Camels do well for the Arabs in *their* deserts. Why not for us?" So they got the camels, but the camels didn't like Texas.

But Texans never wanted anything new in place of Sam Houston. To them Sam Houston *was* Texas. After a while he came back from Washington and they made him Governor again. He was a good Governor and saved the people's money. He worked hard to keep peace with Mexico and with the Indians who idolized him. The legisla-

ture passed a bill to make him a Czar, but to his credit be it said, he would not accept.

Sam Houston had gone many strange ways. When he was a small boy he had traveled in a conestoga, or covered wagon, with his mother. He had walked the wilderness; his white horse had been shot under him in battle. In days gone by people would have called him "lordly," for he was always a leader, never a follower.

He was one of the bravest men who ever lived, but when he was seventy years old, he had to face something that took all his courage.

That was in 1860 when the Southern states broke away from the Northern states and this country nearly split in two. Sam Houston said "No, we are all Americans and we must stick together." But people were wild with anger, because the South wanted slavery and the North did not. Each side was sure it was right.

All Sam's friends and neighbors were against him. The people in Texas sided with the Southerners who wanted to break away and they hated Sam Houston because he would not agree with them. Angry mobs shouted down this man who had been so beloved. "Let's tar and feather him!" they yelled. They shot at him. He traveled all over the state of Texas trying to stop the coming war. But the war did come. Sam Houston, six feet six and straight as a pine, his hair white now but his eyes blue as ever, had lost his fight.

Today in Texas they know he was right and he is their greatest hero.

The Boy Who Loved Horses

ULYSSES S. GRANT

By Helen Woodward

THE circus had come to town. It was a little bit of a place in Ohio in pioneer days. The circus was a big thing full of life. All the boys and girls were wild with excitement. But this time a new wonder was piled on, a trick pony. And the ringmaster announced: "Any boy who can stay on that pony's back will get five dollars."

Every boy crowded around to try. This was before the day of automobiles and almost any country boy could handle and ride a horse. But this pony looked like a hard job. His mane and tail were cut off. There was no saddle or bridle, nothing to hold on to. And his bare back was greased to make it slippery.

Just the same all the boys wanted to try. One after another the boys fell off as the crowd whooped and laughed.

But one boy came forward who had been standing quiet, too busy watching the pony even to smile. This was Lyss Grant, a little fellow with wavy chestnut-colored hair. Now in his turn he ran up and jumped on the slippery back. At once the pony's forefeet rose high in the air, but the boy had his arms around the animal's neck and he stayed on.

The ringmaster cracked his whip around the pony's legs and then the little horse really started acting up. He jumped with all four feet, he bucked, he shied. Lyss hung on. The pony's ears were lying back with rage. But Lyss whispered into those angry ears, "Go on, pony!" He was telling him "You've met your master, pony. Be good now. I won't hurt you."

Lyss could have been a rodeo rider if there had been such a thing as a rodeo then.

Lyss won the five dollars. His freckled face grew red with embarrassment, and all he said was, "Why, that pony is as slick as an apple." But he was proud and pleased.

A farmer standing there said, "That's Lyss Grant. I knew he'd win. I remember when he was a baby just beginning to toddle, I'd see him crawling around the horses' legs. Swinging on their tails too. That little bit of a thing and those big horses!"

Lyss was only eight years old the day he rode that pony. His people were poor; they lived in a house with only two rooms for the whole Grant family—his father, his mother, his three brothers and three sisters. But everyone else in the little midwestern town was poor too. They were new settlers and about all they had was some land and animals to work it. In Lyss's house they cooked on an open fireplace big enough to stand up in, with a swinging crane to hold pots.

Lyss was small for his age, but his body was solid muscle. He was strong enough to drive a team of horses. When he was only eleven he began to do the heavy plowing

ULYSSES SIMPSON GRANT. 18th President of the United States. Born in Point Pleasant, Ohio, 1822. Graduated from West Point, 1843. Captain in Mexican War. General of the U.S. Army, 1866. President of the U.S. 1869-77. Died 1885.

and all the other farm work that was done with horses.

He wasn't very good at school. He was a quiet boy and he seldom played games with the other boys. But he was strong and unafraid.

In that pioneer country every man and boy hunted. But Lyss hated hunting. He hated guns. Once he did go along on a hunt because the family needed food. A flight of wild turkeys swept overhead. Lyss stood and watched them and thought how wonderful they were—and forgot to fire his gun!

The people just couldn't make him out. If you had prophesied that Lyss would some day command great armies with guns, they would have laughed at you. And if you had asked them whether they thought Lyss might ever become President of the United States, they would have hooted because the idea was so ridiculous.

But they knew that when it came to a horse, Lyss did everything just right. One day he was coming home from a long trip along a dusty muddy road. He was in a buggy, driving a wild horse that had never worn a harness before.

The horse was hard to handle and at last he ran away. When Lyss was able to pull him to a stop, the horse's forefeet were right on the edge of a sheer high drop. Lyss knew that a horse would go right over a cliff if he wasn't turned back.

For the moment the horse stood, winded and shivering in a cold sweat. Slowly, making not a sound, one step at a time, Lyss climbed out of the buggy. He remembered that a blind horse would never run away. From his shabby shirt he tore a rag and tied it carefully over the horse's eyes. At once the horse calmed down and Lyss drove him home as peaceful as a tired lamb.

The boy who did these things was never going to be upset by sudden danger. He never lost his head. The more danger, the cooler he would be. When that great peril, the Civil War, came upon us, Lyss Grant met that too and won out.

When Lyss was fourteen, his father asked him, "Would you like to become a tanner like me?"

Lyss thought over what a tanner must do, how he must strip the skin from animals. He loved animals too much for that kind of work. He looked up at the stern man with the gold-rimmed eyeglasses and said, "I would not be a good tanner, Father. What I want most is to get a better education."

His father had no money and he knew the only way to get an education without money was to go to the United States Military Academy at West Point. Lyss didn't want to be a soldier either; but he was willing to learn to be one for the sake of the free education he would get at West Point.

There always was a lot of mix-up about his name. His first name was Hiram, but no one ever called him that. Some people called him Useless. They thought that a funny way of pronouncing Ulysses.

When he was leaving for West Point a kind neighbor marked his little trunk with the correct initials of Lyss's name, Hiram Ulysses Grant, which came out H U G. Lyss said, "That's worse than anything. They'll call me Hug."

"Well, then," said the neighbor, laughing, "what'll I put? What was your mother's maiden name?"

Lyss told him it was Simpson. So the neighbor made these initials with tacks: U. S. G.

"Nobody can make that a nickname," said Lyss. He was wrong. When the cadets saw these initials they wondered what the "U. S." stood for.

One cadet said, "Must be United States Grant."

"That's silly," said another. "Nobody would have a name like that. I tell you what it is. It's Uncle Sam Grant. We're all Uncle Sam's boys here at West Point, aren't we?"

They called him Sam, and Sam was what most people called him all his life. He liked that nickname. But he could not guess that those initials, U. S. G., would one day blaze across the pages of our history.

He got to West Point on May 29, 1839. He was wearing a suit of butternut-colored jeans. Country folk got a homemade dye from butternuts. His shoes were farmers' shoes. His face was covered with freckles. He was still small, only five feet two inches tall. And he was anxious and worried thinking of the tall aristocratic cadets with their high polished shoes.

He had a hard time making an officer of himself. Too much hard work when he was too young had given him a stoop. He had a clodhopper walk, for he was a boy who had hopped over the clods of a farm. And the truth is he was untidy. That is a serious fault at the Military Academy. He got demerits for throwing his clothes about, for not buttoning his uniform, for slouching along as he walked. And he was not quick at his lessons.

Pretty girls would come to West Point to watch the drills and to dance with the boys at their parties. Sam Grant was awkward with girls and kept away from them. While others danced the gay polkas, Sam would shut himself in his room and read novels. All in all, he was no shining light at the Military Academy.

Luckily though, there were horses at West Point. All army officers at that time rode horseback where today they would ride a jeep. The cadets had many riding shows and there Sam Grant shone.

They had steeplechases where two cadets would hold up a pole and the boys jumped over it on their horses. The band played and people talked and hardly anybody looked at the jumpers until the cadets raised the pole so high that people thought no one could jump it.

W. E. Woodward, in his book, *Meet General Grant*, tells what happened then:

"Horse and rider flash out of the stable shadows like a streak of light. The slovenly cadet has become a being of alertness and muscle. Riding with wild Cossack grace, he makes straight for the hurdle. The horse flows through the air with the smoothness of water flowing over a stone. The soldiers raise the pole even higher and Grant and his horse go over it. Ladies split their gloves with applause."

But Sam Grant only bowed as he hurried away. He did not stay to meet the ladies.

After four years like that, the boy who had been Lyss Grant and Useless Grant and Sam Grant, graduated and became Lieutenant Ulysses S. Grant of the United States Army.

Lieutenant Grant made a fine record in our War with Mexico. In a hot hard march, he saved his regiment by knowing what they needed in the way of food and clothes and guns, and getting them. When all that was over, he was Captain Grant and he went

home and married his best friend's sister, Julia Dent.

But Captain Grant was not allowed to stay home. He was ordered off to a wild west army post where there might be trouble with the Indians. But, as it turned out, there was no trouble, no fighting, nothing to see. It was an empty life and Captain Grant resigned and went home. But a hard time began then for him. He tried storekeeping; he tried farming. Nothing worked.

When Captain Grant was thirty-nine years old, he was living in a poor little house with his wife and four children. He was a clerk in his brother's store and he thought he was a failure. So did everyone else.

And then, like a crash of thunder, the terrible struggle that we call the Civil War burst upon this nation. This was not a war with a foreign enemy. It was a war between the North and the South. Americans fought Americans and brother fought brother.

Grant heard the drums of war, and he knew what he had to do. He went back to his home town of Galena, Illinois, and began to train young men for battle. He was the only one there who knew how. He drilled the men, he taught the women how to make bandages and uniforms. But he himself was poor and shabby, and they thought he didn't look fine enough to be made an officer in this new army.

At last the tall strong young men whom Grant had trained marched off to the music of bands. Grant went trailing along behind because he didn't have money for a new uniform. The cheering crowds did not guess that this little man, plodding along behind, would come back in four years a General in

159

command of these same men, that he was to win where other Generals had lost, that only a few years later he was to be the President of the United States.

This day, as he trudged along, he himself had no glimmer of all this. He had set out because he wanted to do his share. He said, "The government has educated me and I feel I owe it to the government to do what I can."

After many disappointments and delays for Grant, a couple of hard jobs turned up. The fine new officers didn't want to tackle them. "Send Grant," they said. "He's a West Pointer."

Grant did every job patiently and thoroughly. He was a man who wouldn't give up. He waited when he had to. But he didn't know how to turn back.

At last his chance came. There was a regiment of men near by so disorderly that they scared the people around. These soldiers hated their own officers and would obey no one.

Grant was a Colonel now; but when he took command of this regiment his coat was torn at the elbows, his hat was almost ragged. The soldiers laughed in his face. The worst of them all, a hard private called "Mexico," stood behind his back and pretended to shadow-box with him. When roll-call sounded in the morning, they laughed louder than ever and did not turn up.

Grant showed no anger. "Very well," he said coolly. "Any day you miss roll-call, you get no breakfast, dinner, or supper." After that they came to roll-call on the dot.

It took him just a week to tame them. They were not bad men, but farm boys, restless and full of nonsense. When he got through with them, they made a first-class regiment. What's more, they liked Colonel Grant.

Grant was on his steady way to the top. But it was a slow way. He kept his men drilled, he saw that they had uniforms, that their food was all right. He had them taught to shoot. He watched out for the horses. Each day he did the many jobs before him.

And then came the actual fighting. Grant won battles where other men had lost because he didn't know how to give up. When the enemy asked for terms he answered "Unconditional Surrender." And again those initials of his, U. S., caught the people's fancy. They said, "U. S. Grant—that means Unconditional Surrender Grant."

He said he was sometimes afraid at first, but he found that the enemy was just as much afraid. "I never forgot that," he said. And he went on to become the General in command of all our armies.

The war ended when General Robert E. Lee surrendered the Southern Armies to General U. S. Grant. General Lee, a great soldier, was handsome in his fine uniform. Grant's uniform was wrinkled and shabby. But he was polite and his voice was low. It is a bright spot in our history that Grant was merciful to the defeated Confederates. Lee's army was hungry and Grant gave them food. He let the men go home as free men and he let them take their horses along so that they could start to farm right away.

Grant was such a hero that in 1869 he was elected President of the United States.

Years later he travelled around the world. And to one of the kings in Europe who gave him a magnificent reception, he said something remarkable. He said, "I never liked war." His message to the world was "Let us have peace."

Fighting Hero of the South

ROBERT E. LEE

By Will Lane

THE boy on the white horse came galloping up to the stable. It looked as though he were going right through the closed door. Just in time he reined sharply and pulled the horse back till it stood almost on its hind legs. The door flew open and a white-haired Negro slave came running out.

"Marse Robert!" exclaimed the old man. "You look out there! Some day you're going to go right through the door."

The boy laughed and the man couldn't help laughing too. He said, "You do look like a real soldier when you sit on that horse. Your father, God rest his soul, he was a great General, and he looked like that too."

Robert was so pleased that he threw his arms around the old man and hugged him.

More than anything else he wanted to be a soldier like his father, "Light-Horse Harry" Lee, General in the Revolutionary Army under George Washington.

Robert marched proudly into the house. In the small parlor he came to a halt before a picture of his father riding a beautiful horse. He wore the blue uniform and the bright gold braid of General Washington's officers. The portrait had been painted for the big house, Stratford Hall, where the Lees used to live. The portrait was really too big and fine for this modest parlor in Alexandria. But Robert didn't think so. He made himself as tall and straight as he could and gave a snappy military salute. "At your command, sir," he whispered to the picture.

ROBERT E. LEE. General in Command, Army of Confederacy. Born in Stratford, Va., 1807. Graduated from West Point, 1829. Officer U.S. Army in Mexican War, 1847. Headed Army of Confederacy, 1861. Surrendered to General Grant, 1865. President of Washington and Lee University. Died in Lexington, Va., 1870.

Robert could not remember how the General had looked, for he had never again seen his father after he had left for the West Indies in a vain effort to regain his health. Robert had been only six at the time. In his mind he mixed him up a little with the Commander-in-Chief, General George Washington. And he patterned his life on Washington's. As well as he could, he walked like him and thought like him. In his daydreams he saw himself doing all the things his father and Washington had done.

He was happy because one of his playmates, Mary Custis, was the daughter of George Washington's adopted son, George Washington Custis. Mary lived with her father and mother in Arlington, in a mansion that was full of things that had belonged to George Washington. Little Robert went there often to play.

He was a fast runner, a fine swimmer, and a natural fighter, although it was seldom that he had to fight. His look was enough because even when he was a boy his eyes would blaze when he was angry, and the other boys would shy away.

But this boy, though in his heart he loved to fight, learned to control himself. This he did to please his mother. Mrs. Lee had a hard time bringing up her family of children without their father, and with almost no money. They understood and did all they could to help. But Robert looked on himself as his mother's special knight, like a knight in chivalry protecting a lady. When Robert was fifteen, the older boys were away at school, and Robert stood by, the man of the family. All his life through he held to this love and admiration for his mother.

Robert E. Lee grew up and went to West Point and became an officer in the United States Army. When he was twenty-two years old, he married his childhood playmate, Mary Custis. Rain came down hard on the day of their marriage. But they didn't care about that. Bad weather was shut out and Robert and Mary had a lovely wedding in Mary's home, the stately house that Mary's father had built. Pretty bridesmaids in gay silks, army officers in gold-trimmed uniforms, and hundreds of lighted candles, made this one of the finest weddings in Virginia.

Later Robert E. Lee and Mary, his wife, went to live in that house. It stands high on a hill, across the Potomac River from Washington, and many visitors to Washington go to see it.

The Lees had four children. They named the oldest George Washington Custis Lee after Mary's father. But that was too big a name for a small boy, so he was called Boo.

But Robert Lee could not stay at home long with his wife and children. He was sent on many engineering jobs for the Army. And then he was sent by the Government to fight in our war with Mexico. There for the first time he showed himself to be a brilliant commander. And there too he fought side by side with a young Lieutenant named Ulysses S. Grant. Neither of these two young men could guess that they were to be fighting on opposite sides in later years.

Then the Civil War broke out. That was the terrible war in our own country between the South and the North. The South had slaves; the North wanted no slavery. They might have talked things over and made friends again, but instead, both sides shouted and called names. The South said they didn't want to belong to the United States any more and they started firing on the North. The South put on gray uniforms and the North put on blue ones. And the Blue and the Gray fought each other bitterly.

That was in 1861. Abraham Lincoln was our President then and he asked Lee to command our armies. But Lee was from Virginia which is part of the South. He thought slavery was evil and he had set his own slaves free. But he fought on the side of slavery because he was a Virginian and a Southerner and he thought his duty lay with his own people.

He became Commander-in-Chief of the Armies of the South. He was a great General. He loved war and when his men saw him on his white horse, Traveller, looking over the field of battle, their courage burned high. He was a religious man and he prayed often for the help of God. Like all good officers he thought much about the men under him. Sometimes his aides complained because the food at his headquarters was so poor. The privates had boiled cabbage, sweet potatoes, and corn bread. But Lee thought that was good enough for himself and his aides too.

"He is a great gentleman," said one of the Colonels on his staff to a friend.

"I am sure he is," said the other man. "One thing worries me, though. They say he's so gentle butter wouldn't melt in his mouth."

"Don't you believe it," said the Colonel, laughing. "People who make that mistake are mighty sorry before they get through. He's a man's man all the way. He's a fighter first and last. Why, I've seen him get red in the face and shake his fist at the enemy."

The Civil War went on for four years. At last Lee's Confederate Gray lost and the Union Blue won. And in April 1865, General Lee rode up on Traveller and surrendered to General Ulysses S. Grant at Appomattox Court House.

Grant and Lee shook hands. They had known each other a long time. The other officers looked on and wondered at the difference between the two Generals. Grant was a small man. General Lee towered over him. Grant was dusty with battle and careless of his clothes as always. Lee was splendid in his gray uniform. Grant looked as though he had lost the war and Lee as though he had won.

Grant was generous. He said he would take no prisoners. If the men in gray would promise not to fight any more, they could go home.

Lee asked if his cavalrymen could take their own horses home with them; they would need them to work their farms. Grant said yes and Lee was grateful. General Grant sent food to the hungry beaten Southern Army.

General Lee rode away and Union soldiers saluted him in admiration as he passed by. His head was high but his eyes were sad when he met General Meade of the Union Army. Lee said, "Meade, how did you happen to get all that gray in your beard?" General Meade shook his head. "I'm afraid you're the cause of most of it," he said.

It was after this terrible defeat that General Lee became a much greater man than he had ever been before. He was a poor man now. He had lost everything. His cause had been defeated. He could have hung his head and complained. But he didn't. Instead he used the great lesson he had learned as a boy

from General George Washington. As Washington had often been, Lee was strong and firm in defeat. He told his men to be loyal to the United States.

He never was a soldier again or fought in any other war. He became a private citizen.

took a modest job as president of a small college, and did it well.

Today our whole people, North and South, honor the memory of Robert E. Lee not only because he was a good General, but even more, because he was a good loser.

"Votes for Women!"

SUSAN B. ANTHONY

By Joanna Strong and Tom B. Leonard

W HAT the blazes are you doing here?" shouted the man at the big desk. "You women go home about your business. Go home and wash the dishes. And if you don't clear out of here fast, I'll get the cops to put you out!"

Everybody in the store stopped and listened. Some of the men just turned around and sneered. Others looked mockingly at the fifteen women and guffawed. One man piped, "Beat it, youse dames. Your kids are dirty." And at that, every man in the place bellowed with laughter.

But this banter didn't faze Susan Anthony, the tall, dignified woman who stood with a piece of paper in her hand at the head of the fourteen other ladies. She didn't budge an inch.

"I've come here to vote for the President of the United States," she said. "He will be my President as well as yours. We are the women who bear the children who will defend this country. We are the women who make your homes, who cook your meals, who rear your sons and daughters. We women are citizens of this country just as much as you are, and we insist on voting for the man who is to be our leader."

Her words rang out with the clearness of a bell, and they struck to the heart. The big man at the desk who had threatened her was turned to stone. And then, in silence and dignity, Susan B. Anthony strode up to the ballot box and dropped into it the paper bearing her vote. Each of the other fourteen women did the same, while every man in the room stood silent and watched.

It was the year 1872. Too long now had women been denied the rights that should be theirs. Too long had they endured the injustice of an unfair law—a law that denied them the simplest rights of citizenship.

In 1872, women could earn money, but they were not allowed to own it. If a woman was married and went to work, every penny she earned became the property of her husband. A man was considered complete master of the household. His wife was supposed to be incapable of managing her own affairs. She was considered a nitwit unable to think clearly, and therefore the law mercifully protected her by appointing a guardian—a male guardian, of course—over any property she was lucky enough to possess.

Women like Susan Anthony were furious at this injustice. Susan saw no reason why women should be treated that way. "Why should only men make the laws?" she cried. "Why should men forge the chains that bind us down? No!" she exclaimed. "It is up to us, the women, to fight for our rights." And she vowed that she would carry on an everlasting battle, as long as the Lord gave her strength, to see that women were made the equals of men in the sight of the law.

Fight she did. Susan B. Anthony was America's greatest champion of women's rights. She traveled unceasingly, from one end of the country to the other. She made thousands of speeches, pleading with men, and trying to arouse women to fight for their rights. She wrote hundreds of pamphlets and letters of protest. It was a bitter

SUSAN B. ANTHONY. Woman-suffrage advocate. Born in Adams, Mass., 1820. Organized National Woman-Suffrage Association, 1869. President National American Woman-suffrage Association, 1892–1900. Died 1906.

and difficult struggle that she entered upon, for the people who opposed her did not hesitate to say all kinds of ugly and untrue things about her and her followers: "No decent woman would talk like that. No refined lady would force her way before judges and men's associations and insist on talking. She is vulgar!"

Many women who knew that Susan Anthony was a fine, intelligent, courageous lady were afraid to say so. They were afraid that *they* would be looked down on. But in time, they grew to love her for trying so valiantly to help them.

After a while, many housewives took courage from her example. Then, in great meetings, they joined her by the thousands. Many a man began to change his notions when his wife, inspired by Susan B. Anthony, made him feel ashamed of how unfairly men treated women.

On that important day in 1872, Susan B. Anthony and her faithful followers cast their first ballots for President of the United States. But though the men in the polling place were impressed, their minds were not yet opened. In a few days they had Susan arrested and brought before a judge. She was accused of having illegally entered a voting booth.

"How do you plead?" asked the judge.

"Guilty!" cried Susan. "Guilty of trying to uproot the slavery in which you men have placed us women! Guilty of trying to make you see that mothers are as important to this country as fathers!"

And then, before the judge had time to reply, she added, "But, Your Honor, *not* guilty of acting against the Constitution of the United States, which says that no person is to be deprived of equal rights under the law."

She went on, "How can it be said that we women have equal rights, when you men take upon yourselves the right to make the laws, the right to choose your representatives, the right to send only sons to higher education? You, you blind men, have become slaveholders of your own mothers and wives."

The judge was taken aback. Never before had he heard these ideas expressed to him in such a forceful manner. However, the law was the law! The judge spoke quietly, and without much conviction. "I am forced to fine you one hundred dollars," he said.

"I will not pay it!" said Susan Anthony. "Mark my words, the law will be changed!" and with that, she strode from the court.

"Shall I follow her and bring her back?" said the court clerk to the judge.

"No, let her go," answered the elderly judge. "I am afraid she is right, and that the law will soon be changed."

And Susan did go on, on to further crusades, on across the vast stretches of the United States, proclaiming in every town and village her plea for the rights of women.

Today we take it for granted that women have as much right to vote as men have. Women may keep what they earn. Whether married or single, they may own property. It is taken for granted that a woman may go to a college and work in any business or profession she may choose. But these rights, enjoyed by the women of today, were secured through the valiant effort of many fighters for women's freedom, and first of all by the great Susan B. Anthony.

The President Who Loved Adventure

THEODORE ROOSEVELT

By Will Lane

Two cowboys were galloping across the wide and empty prairie of Dakota. Suddenly they heard a wild war whoop behind them. The cowboys whirled their horses around, snatched the guns from across their saddle bars, and held them ready. In one second they changed from peaceful easy-going riders to fighting men on the alert. Their horses caught the feeling and grew nervous and tight. Then the men saw a single rider galloping across the open prairie, standing up in his stirrups, yelling and laughing.

"Aw, it's only Tex," said Blackie, who was tall, thin, and dark. They calmed down their horses and waited for Tex to come up.

"Got news for you, boys," he yelled as soon as he was near enough for them to hear the words. "Things have been happening here while you were taking the herd down to the railroad."

Blackie reached out to punch him, but Tex backed off. He knew the boys would rough him up for scaring them with that war whoop, so he spoke fast. "Bad news," he said. "Joe Ferris sold the ranch while you were away. That's right, he's gone and sold the whole ranch and the horses and steers—everything. And you know what? He sold

THEODORE ROOSEVELT. 26th President of the United States. Born in New York City, 1858. Organized volunteer Cavalry regiment for Cuba and served as its Colonel, 1898. Governor of New York State, 1898–1900. Vice-President of the U.S., 1901. Became President on the death of President McKinley, 1901. Elected President 1904, and served 1905–09. Received Nobel Prize for Peace, 1906. Headed big game expedition to East Africa, 1909–10. Organized National Progressive Party ("Bull Moose"), 1912. Author of many books on politics, hunting, exploration. Died at Oyster Bay, N.Y., 1919.

'em to a dude, a dude from New York City."

Blackie groaned. "What's got into Joe? If this territory of Dakota is going to get crowded up with a lot of Eastern dudes, I'll be moving on." The nearest neighbor was a day's ride away but to these ranchmen who always sought new country, that was too near.

This was the year 1874 and Dakota, that is now two states, was then a vast territory with hardly any people, just wide ranges for cattle and horses. Before the coming of the white settlers, the buffalo and the Indians had the ranges to themselves. Now the Indians were beaten and the buffalo were fleeing into the woods.

"Better wait a while before you move on," Tex said. "Joe's bringing in that tenderfoot now. Ought to be here any minute."

The third cowboy now spoke up. He had light hair, so the others called him Whitey. "Might as well wait and see the fun. Of course I wouldn't want that New York fellow to *hurt* himself, but I would like to see him take a tumble from one of those ponies. Just want him to look silly, that's all."

By this time the three had come up to the ranch-house. It was only a shack of logs. A rough fireplace was used for cooking. There were no chairs but homemade benches and some kegs turned on end. On the beds were mattresses stuffed with dried grass. The roof was packed dirt resting on poles. Here and there a little grass had sprouted in the roof.

The three cowboys fed and watered their horses and turned them loose in the corral near by. Then they went inside the house to the cook-stove and came out with great dishes of fried chicken and bread. They flopped down against the wall of the house slack as though there wasn't a bone in their bodies.

"What'd you say his name is? Roosevelt?" asked Blackie.

"That's right," said Tex, "Theodore Roosevelt. And he comes from a high-toned family. Rich people. He's a Harvard man." He said these last words as though he thought they were a joke. Today many a cowboy goes to college and many a college boy works on a ranch. But in those days the two were far apart and seldom met.

"Expect he'll want us to call him *Mr.* Roosevelt," said Whitey in disgust. "I see myself doing that." He laughed at the idea of calling anyone *Mister*. "Where did Joe find him? What's he out here for anyway?"

"Joe says it's for his health," said Tex. "Seems he was a sickly little boy, had something they call asthma, makes it hard for a guy to breathe. So he's been trying to toughen up. Chinned himself on bars and skipped rope to make his legs strong. Expect it helped him too. When Joe took him on a buffalo hunt he kept saying he never saw a tenderfoot like this Roosevelt before."

Whitey cut in, "Hey, here they come now. Look! There's one of 'em out ahead. I guess that's Joe."

The three cowboys jumped to their feet and strolled forward. Their clothes were rough and comfortable and ready for work. Each of them wore a red bandanna around his neck and a big cowboy hat. Both the bandannas and the hats were to keep off sun in summer and wind and snow in winter. Otherwise their clothes had none of the trimmings people expect nowadays on a cowboy.

Tex, Blackie, and Whitey lounged against the corral gate and waited. All three were smiling. Suddenly Blackie stood up straight and peered forward. "Wipe off those grins, boys. That's not Joe in the lead. That's our new boss. Look at him ride! You're not going to see *him* fall off any horse."

Then, seeing him closer, Blackie said, "Oh, oh! He's got spectacles. Four-eyes."

They saw the tenderfoot dash up and leap off his horse. He was a short man about five feet seven with broad shoulders. His face was pale, not yet red with wind and sun as the others' were. He came forward with a broad grin that showed all his teeth. Teeth and spectacles caught the sun. No one would have guessed then that one day that grin and those teeth and spectacles would be famous all over the world.

"Dee-lighted!" he said heartily and the next moment he was clapping Blackie on the back so hard that that husky young man nearly toppled over.

"Good old Blackie!" said the new boss. "Joe tells me you know all there is to know about this ranch. Glad to know you. Shake."

Their old boss, Joe Ferris, threw his horse's reins over his head and let him find his own way to the corral. "This is Mr. Roosevelt, boys," he said with city politeness.

"Call me Teddy," called out the new boss. The boys grinned. They had expected to rebel if he had wanted them to call him Mister, but they needn't have worried. Hardly anyone ever thought of him as Mr. Roosevelt. He was called by a good many nicknames during his life. When he was a little sick child, his family called him Teedy. This was something he liked to forget. Then he was Teddy. All his family and friends and the boys at Harvard called him that. And when he was President of the United States, he was still Teddy, but he was also T.R. and the Rough Rider.

Later, when Blackie was showing Teddy around the place, Whitey called angrily to Joe, "What's this stuff you've been fooling us with? This fellow can ride any horse."

"I was just having some fun with you, boys. He's all right. He can shoot too. He can't rope a steer yet, though. But when we were on that buffalo hunt he learned how to cook on a camp fire. First time he tried that, he burned the meat and upset the coffee and dropped the beans into the fire. But he sure was game on the hunt. Cold and hot and mud and rocks, he slugged right along. He wouldn't turn back till he'd shot a buffalo. He came through fine."

"He's got a guffle, though, when he breathes," said Whitey. "I guess he's figuring to get rid of that out in this good air."

Only once more did the cowboys wonder if Teddy was all right. That was when they saw him unpack his duffle bag and take out seven or eight big books. Those boys didn't do much reading. As long as it was light they worked or ate or lay in the sun, and when it got dark they played cards and went to bed. They couldn't understand why a rancher would want to read, especially when he was already full of book-learning from college. One day when they were out on the range teaching Teddy how to rope a steer, they asked him why he had all those books.

"Well, you know, boys," he told them, "when I was a kid and they made me stay indoors so much on account of that asthma, I got in the way of reading books. I'd pick up ants and spiders and mice when I was able to get out, and I'd study about them and take them apart, and the books showed me how to stuff them. Now, you fellows know a lot about buffaloes, and how to get them with one shot. Books don't tell you much about that. But one of those books I've got tells just what a buffalo eats and how he lives. And that taught me a lot when I went on that buffalo hunt with Joe."

But most of Teddy's books were about history. The boys became interested when he got them to read for themselves how their grandfathers left Europe to make a better living in America and how some of them hated cities and moved out West. "And," said Teddy, "that's why you and I are here."

"Jumping Jupiter, why we're part of history too," said the cowboys, and they asked Teddy to give them more history books.

"All right," said Teddy, "but wait till you read the one *I'm* going to write. I'm going to call it *The Winning of the West.*"

Years later he *did* write it and it is still a wonderful and exciting story.

For two years Teddy and his cowboys lived and worked together. He built a bigger ranch-house, bought bigger herds of steers, hired a larger crew of cowboys. And in those two years Teddy and the men who worked with him became great friends. Even when he was President of the United States, he would slip away whenever he could for a couple of weeks on a ranch with his old buddies.

He always liked to get up early and ever since he had been a thin sickly little boy, he liked to take icy showers and ride hard horses and play lively games like tennis and medicine ball and practice his boxing. He called it "the strenuous life." He seemed forever to be looking for harder and harder things to do. And after two years at the ranch Teddy found something hard enough,

and he went back East to do it. That was to fight dishonest men in government. But busy as he was in his new career, he always found time to write letters to his friends the cowboys. They were pleased with his letter telling them he was head of the Police Department in New York City and amused at the funny pictures of himself that he drew in the margins.

Years later they heard with pride that their friend had become Assistant Secretary of the Navy, and the very next year the United States went to war with the Spanish in Cuba. At once Theodore Roosevelt volunteered his services in that war. And to the delight of his old western friends, he called on them to join him. He got up a special regiment mostly of cowboys. Some of those old side-partners of his were now businessmen and ranch owners and some were public officers. But with joy they answered his call. They wore regular cavalry uniforms but they were allowed to keep their big cowboy hats. Teddy was their Lieutenant-Colonel and they were the famous Rough Riders. Whitey and Tex and Blackie were there and hundreds of others. They went into battle in Cuba. But when the war was won by the United States, Teddy had to leave them.

They eagerly read the newspapers that told when he became Governor of New York State and then Vice-President of the United States. And they were delighted when he became President. That was in the year 1901. He was only forty-three years old, the youngest of all Presidents of the United States.

He came back to see them when he could and he invited them to Washington when he could. They heard how he helped to

build the Panama Canal and how he made peace in a war between Japan and Russia. They chuckled when he told them he believed in carrying a Big Stick to scare off enemies. And the idea seemed to work. Once the head of a wild tribe in Morocco, a man named Raisuli, kidnaped an American businessman. The American was named Perdicaris, and Raisuli held him for ransom. Roosevelt would not pay any ransom. He sent one sharp message, "Perdicaris alive or Raisuli dead." Perdicaris was set free, and fast. Teddy was a natural fighter, but he never got his country into a war.

As cowboy, big game hunter, explorer, Rough Rider, and President of the United States, Teddy Roosevelt tackled one hard job after another. But all through his life he did the things boys like to do because at heart he always remained a boy himself.

His Children Thought He Was Fun

WOODROW WILSON

By Helen Woodward

THE whole world looked up to Woodrow Wilson when he was President of the United States. Europe was grateful to him. But people everywhere were in awe of him too, because he looked so stern in his photographs and because he was a man of learning.

But there were three girls who were not afraid of him at all. His daughters—Margaret, Jessie, and Eleanor—thought he was fun. They were proud of him because he was a great man, but whenever he came toward them, they would begin to smile before he said a word because they knew he would bring them news and laughter and knowledge sprinkled with nonsense.

Margaret had a lovely singing voice. Jessie was blond and beautiful. Eleanor was the one whose great blue eyes were always ready to laugh. The Wilsons were a family who always had company. In and out of their house there were always aunts and uncles and cousins. And quietly through it all moved their mother, Ellen Axson Wilson. Their mother was prettier than any of them, but, more than that, she had courage and common sense.

One summer—it was the year 1909—the Wilson family were having a vacation at Old Lyme in Connecticut. This is a lovely old town where there is good swimming in

the still salty waters of Long Island Sound.

The girls were used to the life of a college town for their father had been President of Princeton University. They were used to simple living, to informal dances, and plenty of what they called beaus among the students. This summer, though, there were men who wanted Dr. Wilson to give up his learned career and become Governor of the State of New Jersey. This would mean a big change for the whole family. If he said yes, he would enter the world of politics and government, and their days of simple living would be over. On this particular day in June, Dr. Wilson was in New York listening to these men who wanted him to go into politics.

The three girls and their cousin Helen Bones, who was staying with them, all cut their swimming short that day. They tried to play tennis but couldn't keep their minds on it. They kept walking restlessly up and down the porch, into the garden and back again. Sometimes Jessie would vanish into her room for a little while, and when she did, the others knew she was praying. Through all this their mother stayed outside, calm as always, though she was inwardly as excited as any of them. She went about her business of running the household quietly. But the girls kept looking up the

THOMAS WOODROW WILSON. 28th President of the United States. Born in Staunton, Va., 1856. Professor of political economy, Princeton, 1890–1902. President of Princeton, 1902–10. Governor of New Jersey, 1911–13. President of the U.S., 1913–21. Tried to keep U.S. out of war, but finally threw U.S. strength into World War I and helped Allies to win. Outlined Fourteen Points for peace. At post-war Peace Conference tried to make League of Nations part of Peace Treaty. Signed Peace Treaty on behalf of U.S. in Paris, 1918. Awarded Nobel Peace Prize, 1919. Wrote important books on American history and politics. Died in Washington, D.C., 1924.

road for the car that would bring Woodrow Wilson home from New York.

At last it came and Dr. Wilson stepped out. They crowded around him and looked eagerly at his face to see if they could read anything there. But he just smiled and went into the house as well as he could with the girls hanging on his arms. "Father, what is it? Did you say you would run for Governor? Did you?" they clamored.

Mrs. Wilson, wiser than they, asked nothing. She just said, "Girls, give your father room to breathe."

Dr. Wilson looked at the eager girls, but he did not answer them. Instead he began to feel around in his pockets. "By the great horn spoon," he said at last, "I almost forgot. I found something in New York I want to show you." And from his pocket he pulled a little Chinese puzzle. "This is a hard one. I worked it out on the way home. Want to try it?"

Eager as they were to hear the news, the girls couldn't help laughing. "Please, Father!" begged Margaret. But Dr. Wilson pretended not to hear any of this.

"Well," he went on calmly, "I suppose I'll have to show you how to do the puzzle." And he started to work it out. By this time the girls were exasperated.

"We don't care about that old puzzle," said Eleanor. "We want to know if you are going to be Governor of New Jersey."

Dr. Wilson gave in. "I can't tell you that," he replied. And that was all he said.

"Oh, Father!" They looked ready to cry.

"Well," he went on, smiling, "I can't tell you whether I shall be elected or not. But I have agreed to accept the nomination."

He *was* elected, as we know now, and the lives of the Wilsons changed completely. Now there had to be formal dinners and big receptions and meetings. But when they were by themselves, things were as always, except that their father had less time for family fun. He was having a stiff fight with the politicians of the State of New Jersey. These politicians looked down on college teachers and even college presidents. They thought, "Wilson is a professor. He'll be a babe in the woods when it comes to politics. We'll elect him and then we'll pull the wool over his eyes and go ahead with our own kind of politics." They were furious when they saw that he understood exactly what they were trying to do and that he would fight them and explain to the people of the state what was going on. He won that fight, but it was not easy.

To the world Wilson looked like a cool man, sure of himself. But he was really shy and a little afraid of strangers. He was tall and a fine-looking man. But he didn't think so. Once, while he was making a speech, a man in the crowd yelled out, "Go to it, Woody. You're all right. But you ain't no beaut!"

Wilson laughed and answered,

For beauty I am not a star;
There are others more handsome
   by far;
My face I don't mind it,
For I am behind it.
'T is the people in front that I jar.

When he had to meet strangers he would say to Ellen, his wife, "I really don't want to meet these people. I'd rather stay here and write them a letter."

And Ellen Wilson would say, "You have charm and wit. In a letter they may not see that."

He would not quite believe all this, but it helped him get over his shyness. He would go off and meet the important people and it was always a success.

He had no patience with people who acted big, who talked in big words but said nothing, or for people who told him things that were not so. But he was polite and would try to listen to them. At the same time he would watch their way of moving and their way of speaking. Then he would go home and imitate them for the amusement of his family. The girls thought he was the world's best mimic.

He would also imitate people he admired and even the members of his own family, but only when they were there to see. William G. McAdoo, who married Eleanor Wilson later when he was Secretary of the Treasury, said of Wilson, "He imitated me so well that he was more McAdoo than I was."

The Wilsons lived in the Governor's mansion in New Jersey for only two years. Wilson made such a fine Governor that people began saying, "We must have him as President of the United States."

Wilson himself was not sure of this. What he wanted most was to teach in college, for that was where he thought he did his best work. But his wife had more faith in him than he had in himself. When he lost courage and thought he couldn't do a thing, she assured him he could. And the wonderful thing was that he would then do it.

In the summer of 1912 the Democrats were holding a convention in Baltimore. There politicians from all parts of the United States gathered to choose the man they would nominate for President. There was great excitement in Baltimore, for any one of four men might be nominated, and it was hard to tell which would win.

The Wilsons were at Sea Girt on the Atlantic Ocean. Mrs. Wilson kept the household as calm as she could, but it was pretty hard for the young people to be calm when they thought their father might be President of the United States.

One night when the girls had all gone to bed, Governor Wilson could not sleep. He got up and looked out of the window. It was one o'clock in the morning. The beach and the boardwalk were empty and silent under a white fog. The only sound was the roar of the surf. Suddenly Wilson noticed a man on the lawn, and in a moment he reognized him as Joe Tumulty, his secretary. Wilson called out, "What is it, Joe?"

Mr. Tumulty came up closer and said sadly, "I wanted to wait till morning before telling you, but, Governor, I'm afraid we've lost." Wilson turned to his wife and told her.

She looked at him with a smile in her pretty brown eyes. "Well, then," she said, "we will go to Rydal again." Rydal was a lovely little town in England where the whole family had had a good time one summer riding bicycles, playing tennis, and singing songs around the piano. That is why Mrs. Wilson suggested going back to Rydal. "We will be happy there," she said, "and not full of worries."

But the next day two important Democrats, William McAdoo and Josephus Daniels, both called up and said, "Don't give up. We still have a chance to win."

Two days later Mrs. Wilson went to her room for a rest. There were telegraph instruments in the house and they kept ticking off the news from Baltimore. The girls waited eagerly. Even Governor Wilson sat and watched. At last came the big message. Wilson had been nominated.

Woodrow Wilson walked upstairs to his wife's room. All he said to her was, "Well, dear, we won't go to Rydal after all."

On the second day of March, 1913, Wilson, his wife, and their three daughters left home and journeyed to Washington. He was pleased with the election, but there was also sadness in his heart. He remarked to his daughters that he was no longer to have any peace.

The girls too were a little frightened. They didn't know exactly how a President's daughters ought to behave. They did not have the fine clothes they would need in Washington. Eleanor, for one, was so nervous that when they reached the White House, she found an empty room, crawled under the bed, and cried. But she learned the new ways soon enough, and a year later she had a lovely wedding in the White House, when she married William G. McAdoo, the Secretary of the Treasury.

But a great trouble came to them all.

Their mother, Ellen Wilson, had been in the White House just one year when she died. She was the one to whom all of them turned for guidance and for courage.

President Wilson was lonely. His daughter Jessie had married and was living in Massachusetts. Eleanor had her own household to manage. Only Margaret was left of the large family. In his loneliness he was married again, this time to Edith Bolling Galt.

In 1914 the whole world was thrown into a terrible tragedy when Germany started what we call World War I. Wilson tried hard to keep the United States out of war.

Some people in the United States wanted to go to war against Germany, but many did not. In the year 1916, Wilson's first term as President was over and there was a new election. This time the Democrats had a slogan: "We must have Wilson again because he kept us out of war."

Again the Democrats nominated Woodrow Wilson. The Republicans nominated Charles E. Hughes, who was later to become Chief Justice of the Supreme Court. On election day the Wilsons were torn between hope and fear because Mr. Hughes was making what looked like a good fight. But this time President Wilson really wanted to win because if he won, it would show that the American people thought he had done well as their President.

At last, on the night of election day, the newspapers said Mr. Hughes had been elected. Wilson's daughter Margaret said it couldn't be; but the President said, "I shall send Mr. Hughes a telegram of congratulation." And he added calmly, "Since we all got up so early, how would it be if we all just have a glass of milk and go to bed?"

But the next morning Margaret flew into the President's room, wildly excited. "Joe Tumulty says the California vote wasn't in when they counted the ballots last night!" she exclaimed. "But it's in now, and we're going to win after all."

The President just laughed at that. Two days passed while the votes from the West were counted. On Friday the President's valet knocked at his door and told him there was a wireless message. He had won!

Wilson tried to keep his country out of war, but the nations in Europe were calling for help and Germany did many foolish things which enraged the Americans. One day an important German official was riding on an elevated train in New York City. An American Treasury agent was keeping an eye on him. The train drew into a station. The German noticed that it was his stop. He jumped off the train and in his hurry forgot his briefcase. On the platform he missed the case, and he stood there making frantic signals to the conductor. But it was too late. The agent grabbed the briefcase, rushed off at the next stop, and delivered it to the Secretary of the Treasury. The papers in that briefcase held a terrible secret. The German government was trying to get Mexico to attack the United States on its very border. When they read about this in their newspapers, the American people were very angry, but still President Wilson hoped he would be able to keep his country out of war.

A German submarine torpedoed a great British passenger ship, the *Lusitania*, with thousands of peaceful American travelers aboard. The Germans said the ship was carrying munitions to Germany's enemies. Whether this was so or not, it was a fatal

asked nothing except that the world try to be at peace.

Woodrow Wilson had a great dream. He would get the world into one League of Nations which he felt would "make the world safe for democracy." And when trouble came, the nations would talk things over and not have to fight.

thing for Germany to do, because most of the American people, now thoroughly outraged, wanted to punish Germany. Still Wilson tried to avoid a war. But the submarines kept on and Germany showed she thought the United States would stand for anything. So at last, with deep sorrow, Wilson asked Congress to declare war.

The people of Europe had fought long and hard, and they were very tired. Now the United States sent troops, munitions, ships, and food to help the Allied Nations who were fighting Germany. And with the help of the United States, the Allies won the war. From that war the United States

But the American people, indeed the people of the whole world, were apparently not yet ready for a League of Nations. And, to his sorrow, Wilson found that out before he died. But he had given the thought to the world and ever since there has been some hope that such a thing would come about, and that the nations could find peaceful solutions to their problems.

Wilson was a great President in many ways, and this idea, that one day the nations might live without war, was the greatest of his gifts to the world.

He Sent Food to the Hungry

HERBERT HOOVER

By Will Lane

FOUR boys were ambling along a country road across the Iowa prairie. The world lay flat around them as far as they could see, as prairie country does. They were having a good time in the spring sunshine because they had been through a long, cold, and snowy Iowa winter. The boys were all barefoot and each one was carrying a bow and arrow. They were setting out to shoot prairie chickens for Sunday dinner. One of them, a chubby fellow with a round face, was lagging behind. The others turned to find out what was keeping him, and saw him bend down to pick up something off the ground.

"Hey there, Bertie Hoover," they yelled, "come on. We got to hurry."

Bertie did not answer, but began rubbing something against his pants and then licking it and rubbing it again.

"Aw," said one of the others, "he's at it again, picking up those pebbles. Let him go. No use waiting for him. When he's sot on anything, he's sot."

And sure enough, Bertie had given up all idea of hunting for that day. He was turning back to the little house where he lived. His mother looked up a moment from the pile of snowy cotton cloth in her lap. Bertie's father was dead and Mrs. Hoover supported herself and her boy by hand sewing. There were few sewing machines then in Iowa.

"I thought thee was going out hunting today." She spoke softly and used *thee* instead of *you* as the Quakers did, for the Hoovers were Quakers.

Bertie pulled some bright colored stones from his pocket and showed them to her. "Oh, thee has found more of the pebbles. Thee has many in the house already."

"I am going to show them to Dr. Walker," said Bertie.

Dr. Walker was a dentist. "How does he know so much about stones?" she asked.

"He has books about them, Mother, with lots of pictures. He shows them to me." Bertie had no trouble speaking when he had something to say, but otherwise he said little. Many years later, when he was President of the United States, he still astonished people because he said only what he meant and stuck to it. They were used to hearing politicians talk a lot and not always meaning everything they said.

Now Bertie slicked down his hair and went off to see Dr. Walker, the only person in the little town who thought Bertie's interest in stones was worth while. The dentist examined the stones carefully. "These are agates," he said. "They are not worth much money, but people make the marbles you play with from them. They are a nice

HERBERT CLARK HOOVER. 31st President of the United States. Born in West Branch, Iowa, 1874. Food Relief Administrator in China. 1900—15. Headed Commission for Relief in Belgium, 1915—19. U.S. Food Administrator, 1917—19. Secretary of Commerce, 1920. President of the U.S. 1929—33. Established Farm Loan Bank, Home Loan Bank, Boulder Dam (Hoover Dam), Reconstruction Finance Corp. Administered European Relief Program, 1946, German Food Program, 1947. Chairman, Committee on Organization of U.S. Executive Departments, 1947—49, and of Committee on Government Operations, 1953. Died in New York, 1964.

color. See, this one has the colors in stripes and that one looks like clouds in a blue sky. Once upon a time, people used to think an agate brought you good luck. We know better than that now. But these may mean good luck for you in another way. I have never seen a boy with his mind so set on stones. They're minerals really. Bertie, I don't know how you're going to manage it, but you must find a way to go to college and study geology."

As always, Bertie listened more than he spoke, but now he asked, "What's geology, sir?"

"It is the study of minerals and rocks. Geology helps us to discover mines and precious minerals and teaches us the story of how the earth is formed."

Dr. Walker was right. Bertie's interest in pebbles led him to study engineering. Mining engineers looking for new mines are often explorers too. In time Bertie's interest took him to far-off places in Africa and Asia and Australia, as well as Europe.

He became famous as a mining engineer and was a millionaire while he was still young. Later on he became President of the United States. While he was President he started projects that helped farmers and home owners. These were great accomplishments for the boy from the Iowa farm. But it is not these that people remember first when they think of Herbert Hoover. People all over the world think of him first as the man who saw that starving people were fed.

When he was twenty-six years old he was in China as a mining engineer. A rebellion

179

broke out. Many business men and missionaries were caught in the confusion and asked Hoover and his wife to take charge of getting food and water to the many wounded and starving. The refugees were forced into small space in and around the Hoover house. Both Mr. and Mrs. Hoover showed cool courage. One day Mrs. Hoover was playing solitaire when a shell came through the roof of the house. She kept right on so that the children there would not be scared.

Years later there was another war in China and once more it was Herbert Hoover who took food to the refugees.

In the year 1914 the First World War crashed on the world. For awhile it looked as though Germany would win. The United States was not yet in that war, but many Americans were caught by it in London. Herbert Hoover was one of them. The Americans wanted to get home to the United States, but the passenger ships had stopped running. And the Americans ran out of money because no one would cash their checks.

These Americans knew what Herbert Hoover had done for refugees in China, so they turned to him for help. He worked day and night to get ships to take them as passengers. He got their checks cashed. And far sooner than they expected, all who wanted to go home got there safely.

Then came a much bigger and much harder job for Hoover. The Germans had conquered Belgium and they were taking away the Belgians' food to feed the German armies.

Will Irwin, a great American newspaper man, was visiting Herbert Hoover at his house in London.

"Mr. Hoover," said Mr. Irwin, "you could not bear it if you could see the Belgian people now. They are pale and tired. The children are sick because they are hungry. I did not see a single child playing."

Mr. Hoover thought of the abundant food on the farms of his own childhood and of the fertile lands he had seen in Belgium. "But, Mr. Irwin," he said, "Belgian farmers are famous for the fine food they grow. Where is all that?"

"Some of it," Mr. Irwin told him, "the farmers are hiding for their own families. And they are selling some to very rich people who can afford to pay a dollar for a loaf of bread. The other people get nothing but thin soup. The children are too tired and hungry even to cry."

Mr. Hoover got his friends together and they bought plenty of food for the Belgians to eat. But then there was the food piled up, and they didn't know how to send it to those who were waiting for it. The British government was afraid that if the food was sent to Belgium, the Germans would take it and use it for their own armies.

Hoover went to the American State Department. But the officials he spoke to there said that since the United States was not in the war it had no right to interfere.

It looked bad. The Belgians were near by, only a few hours by a slow boat, and here in London was food and there seemed to be no way to bring the food and the hungry Belgians together. But Hoover, who had been a stubborn boy, was a stubborn man too. Now he went to the Associated Press, the biggest news-gathering outfit in the world, and spoke to the man who was at the head of it. He told this man, "If you will publish this whole story in newspapers all over the world, people will be angry. And the governments will be ashamed." And so it was.

The British asked Hoover to take charge of the operation. He got the Germans to agree to leave the food for the Belgians.

At first Mr. Hoover was not sure he could manage so tremendous a job. "We must find food for a whole nation," he said. "Nothing like this has ever happened in the history of the world. We have to get past fighting ships at sea and armies on land."

But Will Irwin said to him, "You would do it if you could see how heart-breaking things are in Belgium and in France where the Germans are winning."

Hoover gave in. "But it will not be any knitting bee or tea party," he said, "This is hard work, long hours every day and Sunday too."

First he got an army of volunteers, all working without pay. American students, Belgians, Dutch, Spaniards, French all helped. So did the Japanese and the Latin Americans. Even then it wasn't easy. Every shipload of food had to have a permit from the British, and the Germans searched every ship they saw to make sure it carried only food.

Hoover was afraid a submarine might attack a relief ship. His aides said, "They have promised not to." But Hoover was aware that a submarine could attack without knowing what the ship carried. He told a story to show what worried him. "A man who owned a bulldog said to a visitor, 'The dog won't bite. I know he won't.' And the visitor said, '*You* know he won't bite. *I* know he won't bite. But does the dog know it?'"

Still Hoover went ahead and the operation was a huge success. The Belgians got their food and clothes and blankets. The French did too. And this vast generosity brought the United States gratitude from many countries of the world.

No nation ever did a more unselfish and generous act. And the United States has given of its great wealth, ever since, to hungry and helpless people. Later, Herbert Hoover took charge of American aid to Greece, to Germany, to all of Europe.

Because of his pitying heart, and especially his love of children, Hoover was the perfect choice for Food Minister of the United States. Because of his financial brilliance, he was twice appointed Secretary of Commerce. His highest honor came when, in 1928, he was elected President of the United States by an overwhelming majority.

He was too quiet and too modest to be a good politician; so he was misunderstood by many Americans and unjustly blamed for the 1929 Depression. But twenty years later the public came to understand and he was accorded the appreciation due him.

Even after he left the Presidency, the government called on him over and over again for help. The Hoover Dam and Reorganization of U.S. Executive Departments are but two of his many accomplishments. Anyone else would have sought fame and fortune for them. But Hoover did them all quietly and without show. And often he gave his own salary to other workers who needed it more.

On October 20th, 1964, he died. It is not only for his brilliant mind that we esteem him today, but more as a humanitarian provider of food for the hungry, clothing for the cold.

He Conquered Polio and Became
President of the United States

FRANKLIN DELANO ROOSEVELT

By Corinna Marsh

A LITTLE boy five years old, Franklin Delano Roosevelt by name, was sitting on his mother's lap just before bedtime one evening. The sun, setting across the Hudson River, shone on the west windows of the big house at Hyde Park, which was then called Springwood.

"Tell me a story, Mama," said Franklin.

"Which story shall it be, dear?" asked his mother. She smiled as she asked the question, for she knew very well what the boy's answer would be. Although he had heard her tell it many times before, his favorite story was the one about his Grandfather Delano. It was the true story of how Mr. Delano, a tea merchant, went to China on business and sent word back to his wife in America suggesting that she join him in Hong Kong and bring their eight children.

Franklin's mother was one of the eight, and although she had been only a very small girl at the time, she remembered vividly the four-months-long sea voyage, in a square-rigged clipper ship, to China's famous port of Hong Kong.

Little Franklin's eyes grew bright with excitement as his mother told of the adventurous journey with the spray of the mighty waves washing over the ship that had a cow and a roost of chickens on board, as well as the crew and a whole family of Delanos.

"Oh, Mother," sighed Franklin, "do you think I could go to sea some day and maybe be a sea captain?"

"Maybe," said his mother, smiling. "But it's time now for little boys to be in bed."

That night, and on many nights for years to come, his dreams were of the sea, of ships and the far-off places he hoped some day to visit, preferably in a sailing ship.

Whenever any of his relatives planned a trip abroad, Franklin always asked them to send him foreign stamps from the places they visited. It wasn't long before the boy became absorbed in stamp-collecting. As he pasted the stamps in his album, he became more and more interested in studying the geography and history of strange places in all parts of the world. The knowledge he gained in this way served him well all his life long, and he kept up his stamp-collecting as a hobby even when he was President of the United States. After he died, his album was said to be one of the most valuable in America.

His early love of the sea stood him in good stead later in his political career too. When Woodrow Wilson was President of the United States, Josephus Daniels, then Secretary of the Navy, knowing of young

FRANKLIN DELANO ROOSEVELT. 32nd President of the United States. Born near Hyde Park, New York, 1882. Married Eleanor Roosevelt, a cousin, March 17, 1905. New York State Senate, 1910. Asst. Secretary of Navy, 1913. Stricken with infantile paralysis, August 1921. Governor of New York, 1928–32. President of the U.S., 1933–45. Launched New Deal program with benefits for labor, farmers, unemployed. During World War II drew up Atlantic Charter with Churchill. Established Warm Springs Foundation to aid polio sufferers. Died in Warm Springs, Georgia, 1945.

Roosevelt's love of the sea and knowledge of naval history, asked him how he would like to work in the Navy Department.

"The Navy!" exclaimed Franklin thrilled. "I'd rather have a post in the Navy Department than any other in public life!"

"I am somewhat at sea here," he wrote his mother in his humorous way after he had begun his work as Assistant Secretary of the Navy. But he was not really "at sea" at all, for his boyhood dream of having something to do with ships and the ocean had come excitingly true.

While he was still a child at Hyde Park, Franklin Roosevelt showed the beginning of another interest that was to play an important part in his later life. His days on the family's fine Hudson Valley estate were very full. He had governesses during the years when most children go to nursery

school and kindergarten, and he never went to an American school at all until he was fourteen. Instead he was taught by private tutors. They instructed him not only in school lessons but in all kinds of extra accomplishments from piano playing to horseback riding.

He had every advantage that the devotion and wealth and social position of his parents could provide. Yet this boy, who supposedly had everything, was unhappy because he felt he had no freedom. He thought a great deal about freedom, and about the lack of it, even then. One summer morning, as he sat at the family breakfast table, his face looked glum instead of bright and cheery as it usually did.

"Is anything wrong, son?" asked his father.

Franklin looked dreamily out of the window. "If only I could have some freedom!" he sighed.

"He-*does* have a pretty hard schedule," said his mother. "Maybe he ought to have more opportunity to play on his own."

"Well, Franklin," his father said then, "I'll tell you what we'll do. We'll give you one whole day of freedom, beginning right now. You can go off and do exactly as you please all day."

His mother was anxious for fear he might get lost or hurt. But his father said, "Don't worry, Sara. He knows every nook and cranny of these five hundred acres. He'll be careful."

When Franklin came home, twelve hours later, he was a very tired little boy. But he had had the happiest day of his life. He thought often about the joys of that day for he was not to have many like it. In his last years as President of the United States, when he left the world a creed he called The Four Freedoms, he may have thought of that precious day in his childhood as Franklin's First Freedom.

There was another occasion in his childhood that may have had some bearing on his later life. Mr. Grover Cleveland, who was then President of the United States, was an old friend of Franklin's father. One day Mr. Roosevelt took his son to see Mr. Cleveland. It was the first time Franklin Roosevelt ever saw the White House. Cleveland, beset by the cares and responsibilities of his high office, put his hand on the boy's head and said, "Son, the best thing I can wish you is that you will never be President."

Perhaps that chance remark stayed in the boy's mind as a challenge. At any rate, from then on Franklin began organizing things. His parents noticed that when he played, he was the one who planned the games and told the other children what to do. His mother told him he must wait and take his turn.

"But, Mother," he explained, "nothing gets done unless I give the orders."

But probably Franklin's ability to endure pain as a boy helped him more than anything else when he became a man. One day when he was eleven, his mother took him to the doctor because he had a sore throat. The doctor, after telling the boy to open his mouth and say "Aaaah," saw that his tonsils ought to come out.

"I'll speak to Mr. Roosevelt and let him make the arrangements," Franklin's mother told the doctor.

"Oh, come on, Mom," said young Franklin. "Why wait to ask Father? Let's get it over and done with."

It hurt, of course, after the anesthetic wore off. But Franklin never whimpered. All he said was "Won't Father be surprised!"

One summer day, a year or two later, another boy, a friend of Franklin's, accidentally hit him on the mouth with a stick. Franklin's lip was badly cut but, worse than that, one of his teeth was broken so that the raw nerve was exposed. It was almost unbearably painful, but Franklin kept his mouth tightly shut when he got home so as not to worry his mother. Finally getting the whole story from him, she took him to the dentist who said he had never known a boy to bear such extreme pain so bravely.

His boyhood grit must have become part of his character. Surely nothing but strength of will and courage could have pulled him through his great suffering when, in 1921, a grown man with a wife and five children, polio struck him.

By that time Franklin Roosevelt was on his way up in the political world. He had been nominated for the Vice-Presidency of the United States and, though his party lost the election, Roosevelt had traveled all over the country making more than a thousand speeches. He was ready for a vacation, and he and Mrs. Roosevelt and the children went off to their Canadian summer home on Campobello Island.

One day, when they came home from swimming, Roosevelt said he had a headache. The next day he was very sick. Mrs. Roosevelt sent for their doctor, then for a specialist. "It's a bad case of infantile paralysis," said the specialist. It was what we now call polio. "I'm afraid Mr. Roosevelt will never be able to walk again," he added gravely.

It was true that, at that time, he couldn't move a muscle, not even a toe. It was the worst enemy Franklin Roosevelt ever had to face. For months he lay desperately ill. It was many weeks before he could even be moved to a hospital. But as they carried him into the ambulance, his face lighted up with its characteristic grin and he said confidently, "I'm going to beat this thing. I'll walk again. You'll see."

It wasn't until Christmas that he was allowed to leave the hospital. His mother urged him to return to the comfort of the old homestead in Hyde Park where he could enjoy his books and the beauties of nature, even if he would have to see them from a cot or a wheelchair.

But Roosevelt refused. With his wife's encouragement, he made up his mind to live, as nearly as he could, the life of a normal healthy man. "I am not going to be stopped by this handicap!" he declared. And indeed he was not, for in time the American people gave him the highest honor they can bestow on any man: They elected him President of the United States—and again and again and again. He was the only President ever elected four times.

But his fight to conquer polio was a long hard struggle. Many people thought he would never again be anything but an invalid. But they did not realize how tremendous was his will. For six long years he fought his crippling disease. And then one day he announced that he was ready to go back to political life.

He had to wear heavy steel braces and he was never again able to walk without help. But he never mentioned his illness or took advantage of it in any way. He campaigned with all his old-time vigor and was elected Governor of his home state of New York in 1928 and re-elected in 1930.

In 1932 he was elected President of the United States. The country was in a deep depression. Fifteen million people were without jobs. Roosevelt took bold steps to make work for them. He pointed out that one-third of the nation was ill-housed, ill-clad, ill-nourished—a situation he did his best to remedy.

He was elected for a second term in 1936 and for a third term in 1940.

In 1941 the United States entered the Second World War which was then raging in Europe. America's decision to enter that war made possible the defeat of the Italian Fascists under Mussolini and the German Nazis under Hitler.

But Roosevelt shared Woodrow Wilson's dream of a union of nations to preserve peace. He hoped to help establish such an organization. But he did not live to see the beginning of the United Nations for which he had such high hopes.

He died, on April 12, 1945, at Warm Springs, Georgia. He had gone there often for treatments during his illness. It was there, in the swimming pool, that he learned to move his paralyzed legs, first just a little, then more and more. After he became President, he went there so often that he built himself a cottage on the grounds. It was painted white and was known everywhere as The Little White House. Before he died he established there the Warm Springs Foundation for the benefit of other sufferers from polio. It is a shining memorial to the man whose grit and courage must be admired by his foes as well as his friends.

"Duty, Honor, Country"

DWIGHT D. EISENHOWER

By Alice Q. Holby

THERE is a house in Abilene, Kansas, which is visited by hundreds of people every year. The sign in front of it says:

```
Visiting Hours
9–12 A.M.        1–5 P.M.
————————
EISENHOWER HOME
————————
Admission Free
```

When Dwight D. Eisenhower, the third of the Eisenhower brothers, became President of the United States, Abilene wanted the sign to say "This was the home of Dwight D. Eisenhower." But anyone studying President Eisenhower's modest character would know that he would refuse. "It was not just my home," he would say. "It was the home of my parents where my five brothers and I grew up. So it will be named for all of us."

When Dwight went to school he was nicknamed "Ike" and has been called that ever since. That is, he was called that by everyone except his mother. She always called him Dwight.

Ike was not born in Abilene but in the little town of Denison, Texas, on October 14, 1890. But his parents moved to Abilene before he was two years old. Their first house there was a very small cottage, too small for Mr. and Mrs. Eisenhower, Ike and his two older brothers, Arthur and Edgar. When another boy was born, Mrs. Eisenhower said to her husband, "We must get a larger house. This one is too crowded for us to live in."

An uncle moved away from Abilene and the Eisenhowers were able to move into his larger house. It was a good thing they could, for two more boys were born and they needed room for those six children. This is the house they lived in all the rest of their lives until the boys grew up and moved away and Mr. and Mrs. Eisenhower died.

On a table in the front parlor of the house, the family Bible lies open just where it always was. It is a big book with pictures of the Bible stories and many brightly colored maps of the Holy Land. All the Eisenhower boys had to read it. One evening of each week was spent in the front parlor for the Bible lesson their father gave them. In later years when the boys had grown up, many people were surprised at how much of the Bible all the Eisenhowers could quote. Other evenings they would gather in the back parlor where Mrs. Eisenhower had her piano. While Mother played, Father and the six boys would shout out hymns and the

DWIGHT DAVID EISENHOWER. 34th President of the United States. Born in Denison, Texas, 1890. Moved to Abilene, Kansas, during first year. Graduated from West Point, 1915. Member American military mission to Philippines, 1935–39. Brig.-Gen. 1941. Chief of War Plans Division, U.S. General Staff, 1942. Commander-in-Chief U.S. Forces in invasion of N.W. Africa, 1942. General and Supreme Allied Commander in N. Africa, 1943, in Europe, 1944. Army Chief of Staff, 1945–48. President of Columbia University, 1948. Headed NATO, 1950–52. President of the United States, 1953–1961. Died 1969.

old songs they all knew.

But the room they used most was the kitchen with its big wood-burning stove where Mrs. Eisenhower cooked the meals they loved to eat at the big table there. Mr. Eisenhower began every meal by giving thanks to God for all their blessings. After that they settled down to eating, joking, laughing, and arguing. They were a noisy happy family.

Nearly three acres of land went with the house and they used all of it. They grew the vegetables they ate, and the alfalfa for their horse and two cows. They raised chickens, ducks, pigs, and Belgian hares, and they planted fruit trees.

Mr. Eisenhower was the engineer in the creamery in Abilene. He had to work all day and, if anything went wrong with the machinery, at night too. So the boys had to do all the farm chores. They began working in the garden when they were only five or six years old. As they worked and played together they learned from their parents that they must always keep their bodies clean, always tell the truth, always be absolutely honest. If they wanted anything then or in later life, they knew they would have to work for it.

On Sundays the whole family went to Sunday School. While Mother and Father stayed on for the church services, the boys returned home, cooked the Sunday dinner, and washed the dishes afterward. That is how Ike learned to cook.

He always enjoyed cooking for family and friends even after he became President of the United States.

Mr. and Mrs. Eisenhower did not know until years later all that went on in the kitchen while they were at church. When the boys made a pie for dessert, they would often toss the ball of dough from one to another. If it fell on the floor they brushed it off and used it anyhow. The crust was not as tender as the crusts mother made, but everybody ate the pie with relish just the same. When they did the dishes, the boy washing would toss a plate to the one drying, and he would toss it to the one putting the dishes away. They were expert pitchers and catchers, so very few dishes were broken.

The family was always poor while Ike was growing up; so the boys had to find part-time jobs to help out. They mowed lawns, had a newspaper route, and sold some of the vegetables they raised. Edgar and Ike put the vegetables in their little wagon and sold them at the back doors of the rich families who lived on the north side of the city. None of them ever dreamed that one of the little boys peddling vegetables at the back door was to become one of America's most famous men, known all over the world as a great soldier and a great President.

Life was not all work for the boys. They played games, especially ball games, and Ike and Edgar became star baseball and football players.

Their mother believed they should be allowed to settle their own troubles. One day a friend was in the house while Edgar and Ike were having a fight. Edgar was older and stronger than Ike and had him down pounding his head on the floor.

Ike yelled and struggled to get up.

"Aren't you going to stop them?" the friend asked Mrs. Eisenhower.

"No, they must settle it themselves," she replied.

One of the younger brothers heard Ike's

better job. This meant that now Edgar and Ike had to get full-time work at home. That summer Ike worked in the creamery loading cakes of ice. These weighed 300 pounds each, but Ike was large and strong and he managed to shove the ice off and on the wagons easily.

When the summer was over, Ike had to go back to school, but he also had to keep on earning money. So he and Edgar got a job alternating as night watchmen at the creamery. Their job was to keep the fires in the furnaces going by checking the steam every hour. Between trips around the furnaces Ike studied his lessons for the next day.

That year he entered Abilene High School, and even though he worked every other night he managed to go out for the football team and soon became a football star. All that work in the summer with those

screams and ran in from the yard.

"Stop that! Stop that!" he shouted at Edgar and jumped on him trying to help Ike.

His mother picked him up. "Go back to the yard and let them alone," she told him. "If anyone interferes they will stay mad at each other. Let them fight it out and they will be friends in five minutes." And they were.

When Ike was fifteen, his oldest brother, Arthur, went to Kansas City to hunt for a

300-pound cakes of ice had made him strong as a bear. Ike always believed in fair play. He played hard and he played to win, but always fairly. In one game against a much stronger team, he and a friend, Six Mac-Donell, had to do most of the playing for their weaker team. The boys on the opposing team were mad that just two boys were spoiling all their good plays. So four of them jumped on Six at once. When they got up Six was lying unconscious on the field. The unfairness of this made Ike so mad that he went at those four boys like a fury and the next thing anyone knew, he had all four of them stretched out on the field beside Six.

By the time Ike had graduated from High School, his brother Edgar was away at college studying to become a lawyer. But Ike did not know what he wanted to be. There was not enough money for two of the boys to go to college at the same time; so Ike worked hard at all sorts of odd jobs and sent some of the money he earned to Edgar.

When not working, he passed his time reading dispatches in the two newspaper offices in Abilene as they came in over the wires.

The next year was the most discouraging one Ike ever had. He was nineteen years old and had been out of High School a year. During the long hours in the creamery he had thought a great deal about what he was going to do with his life. There was very little to look forward to in Abilene, and he knew that he must have more education. But he couldn't see how he was going to get it.

One of the friends he had made in High School, whose name was Everett Hazlett, but whom everyone called Swede, used to stop in at the creamery during the evenings to talk to Ike about his future. He was

studying to take the entrance examinations for the Naval Academy at Annapolis. He talked for hours about what a wonderful place it was and how the Government even paid you while you studied there.

"Why don't you try to get in to Annapolis?" Swede said one night.

"You have the only appointment from this district. How could I get in?" asked Ike.

"Senator Bristow has some appointments to give out. Why don't you write him?"

Ike went to two of the editors of the newspapers where he had spent his spare time, and to the postmaster, and asked them to write recommendations.

"There will be about a hundred boys after that appointment," said the postmaster. "You will have to beat them in the examination Bristow makes everyone take."

"Do you think I have a chance?" Ike asked.

The postmaster studied him and said, "It's a small chance, but I guess you can do about anything you set your mind to."

All three men wrote fine letters of recommendation for Ike. He sent them to Senator Bristow with his own letter asking permission to compete in the examinations.

Senator Bristow gave his permission. When the time came Ike went to Topeka, Kansas. It was the largest city he had ever seen. The examinations lasted several days. As long as he was there, he decided to take the examinations for West Point, too.

A few weeks later the letter with the results came. He could not open it fast enough. It said that Dwight D. Eisenhower had come out first in the Annapolis examination and second in the West Point. He ran over to Swede. Swede took one look at the grin on Ike's face and said, "You don't need to tell me. You won."

Both boys were excited and happy, planning the good times they would have together in the Naval Academy. Only Mrs. Eisenhower was not pleased. She hated war and she had brought her boys up to hate war too. But Mother Eisenhower did not let Dwight see how unhappy she was. She had always believed in letting the boys make their own decisions and she trusted her son to judge for himself.

One day Swede was reading the book with the rules for entering Annapolis.

"Say, Ike," he said, "how old are you?"

"I was twenty last October."

Swede groaned, "Then you can't go to Annapolis."

"Of course I can," said Ike. "The rules say from 16 to 20 years old."

"No," Swede said. "It says here you cannot have passed your twentieth birthday. You passed yours last October."

"Let's see that book," Ike demanded.

Both Swede and Ike had read the rules many times but had never noticed that exact wording before. Ike just knew he was not over 20 when he took the examinations. He leaned his head in his hands. It seemed the end of all his hopes.

"You don't have to say you have passed your twentieth birthday," Swede suggested. "They don't ask for a birth certificate and would never know."

"I'd know," Ike replied. "No, I couldn't do that; it wouldn't be honest."

But he was never one to give up easily. "Are the West Point rules the same?" he wondered, looking through the book. "No," he exclaimed, "the West Point entrance age is from 17 to 21."

And that is why Dwight D. Eisenhower went to West Point instead of Annapolis.

At West Point the first year men are known as plebes. The plebes have to call the upperclassmen "Sir." The plebes were called Mister. Ike remembered that only the year before these upperclassmen who acted so important and bossed the plebes around had been plebes themselves. He acted as impudently towards them as he dared, so he was always in some sort of trouble with them.

One day "Mister" Eisenhower and another plebe were ordered to appear before the upperclassmen in full-dress coats. These are short coats that come just to the waist and are splendid with shining brass buttons and white cross belts.

That evening the two plebes went to the upperclassmen's room dressed in their beautiful coats but with nothing on but their underwear from the waist down. The upper classmen were too astonished and angry to speak at first. Then one of them shouted, "What's the meaning of this?"

Ike answered respectfully, "We were told to wear our full-dress coats, Sir. Nothing was said about trousers, Sir."

He broke many of the rules in West Point. He had gone there to get a college education, and he did not take the soldier part of it too seriously until his last year. Until then almost everyone in this country was sure there would never be another war. But in the summer of 1914 World War I started in Europe. And soon our country was drawn into it too.

All the West Point drills and parades that had seemed to Ike a little like play now became very real. He settled down to becoming a true soldier, prepared to fight and die for his country.

He graduated from West Point in 1915. The graduation ceremony was inspiring and solemn. The long lines of men in their gray uniforms stood as motionless as statues, their swords drawn and shining in the sun. The band played *The Star-Spangled Banner* and the cannon was shot once. Ike had a lump in his throat.

The West Point motto—Duty, Honor, Country—became Ike's motto. From that time on he devoted his life to the service of his country.

The year after he graduated, he married Mamie Geneva Doud, a pretty girl who was more than willing to give up the gay life she had been living to become the devoted wife of young Lieutenant Eisenhower.

They had been married only a year when our country entered World War I. Ike tried hard to be sent to France with our Army. He said he had been trained as a soldier and he wanted to fight for his country. To his great disappointment he was put in charge of training soldiers in tank warfare in the United States. Armored tanks were a new weapon invented during World War I, and officers and men had to learn how to manage them. Ike, though he had been out of West Point for only two years, did such a splendid job of training the Tank Corps that it brought him to the notice of his superior officers.

For the next twenty-six years his entire career was duty so well performed that he was selected to lead the American Army in World War II. Later he was made Supreme Commander of all the Allied Forces in Europe.

As Supreme Commander he had the terrible responsibility of winning the war. Before starting any action he studied the problem from all sides and was well prepared. That was why our troops were able to land on the French coast that was occupied by the Germans and guarded by their guns at every point. The enemy thought a landing there would be impossible. But that was because they didn't know General Eisenhower's military genius.

When the war was over Ike was hailed as a hero by the entire free world. Wherever he went great crowds came to cheer him.

He returned to America and was made Chief of Staff in Washington. After two years he asked President Truman to relieve him of military duty. As a civilian he became President of Columbia University.

Meantime the Communists in Russia were forming big armies and the peace of Europe was being threatened again. President Truman asked General Eisenhower to return to France to organize the nations of Europe to defend themselves in case Soviet Russia should attack them. The President told Eisenhower he was the only man the free people of Europe wanted and trusted to do the work.

So Ike went again to France to live. During the year he was there, more and more people in this country wanted him to come home and be President of the United States. They began that slogan: "We want Ike! We want Ike!" The slogan became a mighty roar.

General Eisenhower came home and ran for President on the Republican ticket. In 1952, and again in 1956 he was elected President of the United States by a huge vote. All his actions in office were always guided by what he had learned from his parents and by his West Point motto—

"Duty, Honor, Country."

He Had a Dream — a Wonderful Dream

DR. MARTIN LUTHER KING, JR.

By Corinna Marsh

"**I** HAVE A DREAM that one day on the red hills of Georgia the sons of former slaves and the sons of former slave-owners will be able to sit down together at the table of brotherhood."

With this inspiring hope the words of Martin Luther King rang out across the United States of America one August day in the year 1963. The occasion was a great civil rights demonstration held in Washington, D.C. More than a quarter of a million people — black and white, from all walks of life — had gathered at the Washington Monument. Shoulder to shoulder they marched to the Lincoln Memorial. There the principal speaker of the day, the Reverend Dr. Martin Luther King, Jr., stood, humbly yet proudly, beneath the huge brooding statue of Abraham Lincoln, the Great Emancipator. There, a hundred years after the Civil War, a man whose people, he felt, had been too patient for too long reaffirmed Lincoln's creed that liberty and justice should be the equal right of every American citizen, black or white.

The simple sincerity of his repeated "I have a dream," the memory of past

MARTIN LUTHER KING, JR. Civil Rights leader. Born in Atlanta, Georgia, 1929. Led year-long boycott of Montgomery buses which brought about 1956 U.S. Supreme Court decision that segregation in buses was illegal. Founder and President of the Southern Christian Leadership Conference and leader of many Civil Rights marches. Won Nobel Prize for Peace, 1964. Assassinated in Memphis, Tennessee, 1968.

injustices inflicted on his people, and the hope he aroused of a brighter future — all these inspired the crowd to believe what they so fervently sang at the end of the ceremony: "We Shall Overcome." Regrettably, there were those who belittled Martin Luther King: white segregationists on the one hand and black militants on the other. But, however slowly, the vast majority of decent citizens did come to admire the unassuming non-violent preacher and to rally behind his leadership of decency and reason.

What manner of man was he? His ancestry tells us something about that. He was born on January 15, 1929, in Atlanta, Georgia, where his mother's father was pastor of the Ebenezer Baptist Church, a post held later by his son-in-law, Martin's father. Mrs. King, Martin's mother, a schoolteacher, was also religiously inclined. So young Martin and his brother and sister grew up in an atmosphere of church and the Bible. Indeed he sang solos with the church choir from the time he was a very small boy.

He was a sensitive child and he suffered from anti-Negro remarks made by white children who, alas, had picked them up from their prejudiced parents. But he held his head high and did the best he could, helping his family financially by selling newspapers after school. But he was essentially a student — so much so that he was ready at only fifteen to enter Morehouse College where he majored in English and social studies. Interesting enough, he was greatly impressed by Thoreau's famous essay, "Civil Disobedience," which maintained that jail is the place for good men when

social evils threaten their soul and their spirit. That philosophy, which so often had to fortify him in later years, loomed large in the creed of the young Martin. Before his graduation from college the boy was elected assistant pastor of the old Ebenezer Baptist Church.

By this time, his goal in life established, he entered Crozer Theological Seminary in Chester, Pennsylvania. Steeped in the peace-loving philosophy of Jesus and Gandhi, he graduated, at twenty-two, at the head of his class, with a scholarship grant for further study. He used the scholarship at Boston University where he met a beautiful girl, Coretta Scott, who was studying to become a concert singer at the New England Conservatory of Music. They were married on June 18, 1953, had four children, and lived happily in private life — if dangerously in public. So fearless was the young idealist, and so determined to find justice for his people, that he often found himself in trouble with those who, for ignoble reasons, wanted to thwart his efforts.

But he was also determined to prepare himself, educationally as well as religiously, for what he knew his calling must be. In 1955, after earning his Ph.D. in systematic theology, he accepted a post as pastor of a Baptist Church in Montgomery, Alabama. At that time many public places in the South were segregated. Hotels, restaurants, schools, even churches were for whites only or for blacks only. In transportation—trains and buses — only white people were allowed to sit in front. The Negroes had to sit in the rear. Dr. King, as he was now entitled to be known, spoke out

often, in his sermons, against such injustices. But the first person to do something about it was Mrs. Rosa Parks, a pleasant, quiet Negro dressmaker who, one day, boarded a Montgomery bus, paid her fare, and sat down in a section up front "Reserved for Whites." Refusing to stand or to move to the rear when ordered to do so by the driver, Mrs. Parks was arrested and put in jail. Hearing of this unfairness, Dr. King knew he had to do something about it. He and a group of other Negroes decided to boycott the buses. They distributed thousands of leaflets warning their fellow-Negroes not to ride the buses the following Monday to school, to work, or anywhere else. All day long the buses, which were usually jammed, carried only eight Negro passengers. This meant a considerable loss in revenue to the city of Montgomery. At a mass meeting in a church that night the huge crowd vowed to keep up the boycott. If they had to they would walk as many miles as necessary to get to their jobs or their classes, but they would *not* ride the buses. As Dr. King rose to speak, there was a sudden hush over the hall as television cameras rolled in. The bus boycott was now *news* that could be seen and heard and thought about all over America.

The crowd began to gloat, but Dr. King would have none of that. "We must heed the words of Jesus," he told them: "Love your enemies, bless them that curse you, and pray for them that despitefully use you. Protest courageously, yet with dignity and Christian love . . . This is our challenge and our responsibility."

The Negroes responded — by continuing to avoid the buses. Finally the city officials began to get tough with the boycotters. One night, while Dr. King was at a mass meeting, a bomb was thrown on the porch of his house. Mrs. King, hearing the thud, grabbed their baby daughter and ran to the back of the house. The bomb exploded, broke the windows and much of the furniture in the front of the house. When Dr. King arrived home, a group of militant Negroes had gathered there and were threatening revenge. But in a quiet voice Dr. King said to them "We cannot solve this problem through violence. Remember that 'he who lives by the sword shall perish by the sword.' We must meet our white brothers' hate with love."

Furious with frustration the Montgomery Grand Jury pronounced the boycotters' act illegal. They arrested one hundred of them, including Dr. King. But by this time the whole world knew about the case and the outrage of decent people everywhere influenced the outcome. Finally, after much bitter fighting on the part of Montgomery's white officials, the Supreme Court of the United States declared Alabama's bus segregation laws unconstitutional. The ruling came in November of 1956 after Montgomery's fifty thousand Negroes, led by Dr. King, had walked for freedom every day for more than a year.

By now Martin Luther King, Jr. was a famous man. He had succeeded in awakening his people to their rights and he felt it was his mission to lead them on to freedom and justice. A central organization was formed, called the Southern Christian Leadership Conference, and Dr. King was elected its president.

Membership in what came to be known as SCLC increased all over the country, and soon the members were going on "freedom rides." Groups of people, black and white, from all over the United States, boarded buses in the South and sat together. They applied for service at restaurants and, when denied, they made world-wide news of it. Hundreds of them were clapped into jail where they went on hunger strikes and sang "We Shall Overcome."

Other protest groups supported them

and white clergymen of all faiths joined the movement. Dr. King addressed rallies wherever he could. His growing family saw less and less of him at home, but they saw more and more of him on television, and his wife supported him in every way she could. She knew his life was in danger but she felt that his cause was of first importance. His life was indeed in peril. He was often in jail for leading protest marches and he was occasionally stabbed—sometimes critically —and frequently shot at. Once he was held in solitary confinement in jail. Mrs. King was terrified for fear he might be the victim of some hate-monger's violence. But she had no way of finding out. That evening she received a long-distance telephone call from none other than President Kennedy. He assured her that Dr. King was safe.

Many terrible things happened while Dr. King was leading the freedom movement. Churches were burned, Negroes were shot, martyrs were killed. But indignation raged, and just before his assassination in 1963, President Kennedy presented a Civil Rights Bill to Congress, and finally, almost two years later, it was passed by the Senate and signed by President Johnson.

Dr. King, feeling all the sacrifices he and his family had made were producing results, ended a speech he made at the time by quoting an old-time Negro slave preacher who had said "We ain't what we ought to be, and we ain't what we want to be, and we ain't what we're going to be, but thank God we ain't what we was."

Up to that time people in power all over the country came to see the importance of this humble preacher whose non-violent humility was so much more effective than the strident voices of the militants. He received more awards than he could count. In 1964 he won the Nobel Prize for Peace — a world-wide tribute to his greatness as the person "who has done most for the furtherance of brotherhood among men."

But this high honor affected the modest man's behavior no more than had all the slings and arrows he had suffered from the opposition. He just continued his life's work.

On April 4, 1968, Dr. King was in Memphis, Tennessee, where he had gone to organize support for a group of miserably underpaid striking garbage workers. As he was preparing his speech he was shot and killed, in his motel room, by a sniper's bullet. In understandable fury Dr. King's supporters, ignoring his many pleas for non-violence, broke out in rioting and looting all over America. President Johnson ordered

Federal troops to protect the nation's capital. National Guardsmen were called out in other cities. President Johnson, visibly moved, went on television to express his esteem for the fallen leader, urging us to "reject the blind violence that had struck Dr. King who lived by non-violence."

After funeral services at Atlanta's Ebenezer Baptist Church and memorial services at Morehouse College, scores of national leaders joined the thousands and thousands of marchers who followed the coffin which had been placed, symbolically, on a farm wagon pulled by two Georgia mules. The services were shown on television to the entire nation and abroad. The day was observed everywhere, at President Johnson's direction, as a national day of mourning.

Mrs. King, bowed by grief, nevertheless took her husband's place at the head of the silent marchers, black and white. With infinite courage and dignity she has carried on the work of her slain husband. Her book, "My Life with Martin Luther King, Jr." has touched the hearts of thousands of readers with whom it has become a best seller. More than anything else, perhaps, it reveals the humble yet great humanity of the man. The award that would perhaps have pleased him more than any other was the Eleanor Roosevelt Peace Award presented posthumously to Mrs. Coretta King by the National Board of SANE at the Americana Hotel in New York on December 14, 1969. Listening to the accolades he received on that glittering occasion, one grieves once again that so lofty a spirit was wantonly slain, but we can all rejoice that his beautiful widow lives "to be dedicated here to the unfinished work that they who fought here have thus far so nobly advanced."

"Ask Not What Your Country Can Do for You— Ask What You Can Do for Your Country"

JOHN F. KENNEDY

By George W. Cooke

JOHN F. KENNEDY was born second in a family of nine children, four boys and five girls. The Kennedy children's father, Joseph P. Kennedy, was a banker, businessman, and government official. He was a very busy man indeed, and yet his greatest joy in life was derived from his children and their accomplishments. The Kennedys' father always found time to be vitally interested in everything they were involved in, and he inspired them to stick together in work and in play, a lesson they never forgot.

Although the Kennedys were descended from a poor Irish immigrant to America, Joseph P. Kennedy became one of the richest men in the world, and because of this he was able to afford his children great privileges.

Despite their father's immense wealth, the Kennedy children were never allowed to lead lives of idle pleasure. Each child was urged to work as hard as possible and to play as hard as possible. Discipline in the Kennedy family was very strict. John F. Kennedy, or Jack as his friends called him, the future President of the United States, was spanked along with his brothers and sisters when they misbehaved. In spite of the rigid rules their father and mother laid down, the Kennedy children flourished because of the constant love

and encouragement they received from their parents.

And although Mr. Kennedy set up a trust fund of one million dollars for each of his nine children, and later increased this to ten million dollars each, the children were not permitted to be extravagant. In fact, when Jack was a boy he once wrote a letter to his father from school, listing all the reasons why his allowance of forty cents a week should be increased slightly.

Young Jack Kennedy was not a very good student in school. He did not always pay attention to the teachers as well as he should have and he was not always interested in his subjects. Jack's father, like most other fathers, was upset when Jack

JOHN FITZGERALD KENNEDY. 35th President of the United States. Born in Brookline, Massachusetts, 1917. U.S. Navy, 1941-1945. United States House of Representatives 1947-1953. United States Senate 1952, 1958. Married Jacqueline Bouvier, 1953. President of the United States, 1961-1963. Instituted such New Frontiers programs as the Peace Corps, Alliance for Progress, aid to Appalachian poor, nuclear test-ban treaty with Russia and Great Britain, space program to land men on the moon by 1970. Assassinated in Dallas, Texas, 1963.

came home with poor grades, but he would say, "I will not be disappointed if you don't turn out to be a genius, but I will be sad if you don't show yourself to be a boy who always does his very best." Talk like this made Jack try a little harder, and most importantly, it kept him from becoming altogether discouraged.

Jack was sent to exclusive private schools and graduated from Choate, a famous boarding school in Connecticut. His summers were spent at the Kennedy home at Hyannis Port, Massachusetts, which is located by the ocean on Cape Cod. The summers on Cape Cod were happy times for Jack and his brothers and sisters. Their days were filled with swimming, sailing, tennis, and other sports, and in the evening there were movies in the private theatre in the basement of the Kennedy home. But often Jack was not able to participate in the fun because he was frequently ill. He tried to hide his ills so that he would not spoil the others' fun.

The Kennedys owned a fleet of small boats and the children enjoyed competing in sailing races. Jack's favorite sailboat was named the *Victura* and with it he won many public races. Jack's knowledge of boating and swimming was to stand him in good stead in later years when he was a Navy Commander.

After graduating from the Choate school in 1935, Jack took a trip to England to study at the London School of Economics. In the fall he enrolled at Princeton University in New Jersey, but he was unable to complete his freshman year because of illness. The next fall he started over again in Massachusetts at Harvard College where he remained until he graduated in 1940. At Harvard as at Choate Jack was only an average student, although he wanted to be outstanding. He simply could not shine in school like his older brother Joe, who seemed to excel in everything he tried. While playing football, Jack suffered a severe back injury which brought to a sudden end any hopes he had of becoming a football star. His injured back was to trouble him for the rest of his life.

In order to graduate with distinction of one kind or another, Jack decided to do a great deal of extra work and write a scholarly thesis that would bring him honors. His subject was the political situation in England before the outbreak of World War II. This essay brought Jack Kennedy some of the fame he so strongly desired. Not only was he graduated from Harvard with honors, but his thesis was published and became a best selling book entitled *Why England Slept*.

The lesson in Jack Kennedy's example is that you do not need to be a brilliant student in order to accomplish really worthwhile things in life. But you do need to have plenty of ambition, patience and persistent effort.

Just as Jack was graduating from college, the world was entering upon troubled times. The most terrible war in history was underway and soon the United States joined Canada and the other Allies against Germany and Japan.

Even before the United States entered the war, Jack had volunteered to serve in the Army. But he was promptly rejected because of his bad back. Rather than give up and stay safely at home during the war, Jack took special exercises and followed a training program to build up his muscles and improve his health. Then he volunteered again, this time for the Navy, and he was accepted.

Jack was placed in command of a motor torpedo boat in the South Pacific. This was a dangerous assignment, and in August 1943 his PT boat was rammed and sliced in two by a Japanese destroyer. A report came back to Navy headquarters saying that PT boat 109 had burned and sunk with no survivors. Actually, Jack and ten of his men had survived the collision, although some of them were burned and injured. They managed to swim to an uninhabited island inside enemy territory where they hid in constant danger of being captured by the enemy. They had nothing to eat but coconuts. Jack did his best to keep his men safely hidden while he worked out plans for getting help. Finally he managed to persuade a native to slip through the enemy lines and get to an American naval base, carrying with him a message asking for help. Jack had carved the message on a coconut because he had no paper. Help soon arrived and only after his men had been rescued did Jack reveal that he himself had been badly injured in the back. He was later decorated for heroism, and after an operation on his back he was discharged from the Navy. It was now 1945 and World War II was over.

Jack's older brother Joe had joined the Air Force and was killed in an explosion while flying a plane on a dangerous mission against the enemy in Europe. Next one of Jack's sisters lost her husband, who was also killed fighting in the war. Later Kathleen herself was killed in a plane crash. These deaths were very heavy blows to all the Kennedys, but to none more than to Jack. After his talented older brother Joe was killed, it seemed as if all the responsibility for achieving great things fell on Jack. His family expected it of him.

After his discharge from the Navy, he was not sure what he wanted to do. He got a job as a newspaper reporter and covered the founding of the United Nations and the election campaign in England. But now Jack's father began urging him to enter politics where, his father felt, he could do more good for more people. So Jack went to Boston and, as a Democrat, campaigned successfully for Congress. John F. Kennedy was only 28 years old when he went to Washington for his first term as a Congressman. He was re-elected in 1948 and 1950. In 1952, Congressman Kennedy, who was still Jack to his friends, challenged the popular Henry Cabot Lodge in Massachusetts for the office of Senator. Kennedy won the Senate seat in a brilliant upset victory.

In 1953, when he was 36 years old, Jack married the beautiful and talented socialite, Jacqueline Bouvier. This was the beginning of a marriage that was blessed with the birth of Caroline and John Jr., children whose high spirits and joyful antics later, in the White House, were to make them known in every American household.

The Kennedys' marriage was saddened, however, by a recurrence of Jack's back trouble. By 1954 the Senator had to walk on crutches most of the time. Finally, he decided to undergo surgery on his

spine, even though doctors warned him that his poor health might mean that he would die from the dangerous operation. Senator Kennedy did barely manage to survive and his recovery was very slow. Soon it became apparent that a second serious operation would be necessary. While recovering in Florida from these operations, which left him in severe pain most of the time, the Senator decided to try to distract his mind from his suffering by writing another book. This one he called *Profiles in Courage*, and it too, became a national best seller and won a Pulitzer Prize for its author.

In 1956, however, Senator Kennedy received another disappointment when Senator Estes Kefauver defeated him in a bid for nomination as the Vice-Presidential candidate to run with Adlai Stevenson. But Senator Kennedy's popularity as a public speaker continued to grow as his own speaking ability improved with long hours of practice. He found himself spending more and more time filling speaking engagements. In 1958 he ran for reelection as Senator and received the greatest landslide vote ever received by any candidate in Massachusetts.

On January 2, 1960, Senator Kennedy announced that he would be a candidate for President of the United States. Many people thought he was too young at 42. Others argued that he could never win because he and his family were too rich. People said that so rich a man could never have any sympathy for the problems of ordinary citizens and the poor. Still others said that it would be impossible for him to win the election because he was a Roman Catholic and no Roman Catholic ever had been or ever could ever be voted into such high office. Despite these gloomy warnings, Senator Kennedy fearlessly entered seven state primary elections and won every one of them! At the National Democratic Convention in Los Angeles, Kennedy defeated Lyndon Johnson and Adlai Stevenson for the nomination for President. He chose Lyndon Johnson, a Protestant with popular Southern support, as his running mate for Vice President.

In the great election campaign that followed, Jack's brother Robert, later Attorney General of the United States, served as campaign manager, and the whole Kennedy family excepting only the founding father who contributed power and money from behind the scenes, toured the country seeking votes for Jack. After a spirited campaign, which included a series of famous television debates with Richard Nixon, the Republican candidate, Jack, or John F. Kennedy as the world now knows him, won the election. He took office on January 20, 1961, as the thirty-fifth President. John F. Kennedy was the youngest American ever elected to such a high office.

Life in the White House was happy for President Kennedy and his family. Despite his great responsibilities and the many world problems that he had to deal with daily, the President retained his good nature and unfailing sense of humor. Little Caroline and John, Jr. made the President's elegant mansion seem like a real home.

A time of great sadness came to the President and Mrs. Kennedy when their infant son Patrick died soon after birth in 1963. But the President could not let his personal grief interfere with his duties as

Chief Executive. He continued to work long hours planning a crusade for new civil rights legislation, programs for the poor and underpriviledged, and new proposals for peaceful solutions to world problems. The President's tanned, healthy, handsome face was an inspiration to his country as he called upon Americans to explore New Frontiers. He confidently proposed that we send men to the moon before 1970, a goal that very few people then believed we could achieve.

What most Americans did not suspect was that behind the calm, confident voice and handsome face they saw on television, their inspiring President lived in almost constant pain from his back injuries. Everyone knew about his long hours of study and work as President, but they did not know about the back braces, the hot baths, heating pads, medical treatments, and calisthenics that were also a part of his daily routine to ease the pain and help him perform his duties as President.

President Kennedy's administration was largely a time of peace and prosperity. His programs were designed to provide more benefits to the unemployed, to increase Social Security payments to retired people, to raise the minimum wage, and to give aid to farmers, and help clear city slums.

One of the programs President Kennedy was proudest of was his founding of the Peace Corps. This organization trained young men and women volunteers to live among the poor of foreign countries for a year or two with only little pay, in order to teach the underpriviledged how to make better lives for themselves. In addition to his program for the poor of other nations, the President provided special aid for the poverty-stricken coal miners of the Appalachian states and eastern Kentucky in his own country. And to help keep prices down, he forced the big steel companies to turn back price increases that he considered excessive.

But of all his efforts to make America a better place to live, none was more important that his struggle to outlaw racial discrimination. President Kennedy saw to it that Negroes received important government jobs as judges, ambassadors, and supervisors. He sent 600 deputy U.S. marshals to Alabama to protect the Freedom Riders who helped bring about integrated buses in the south. At one time the President was forced to call out the army to restore order at the University of Mississippi after the first black student, James Meredith, attempted to enroll as a student in 1962. Again President Kennedy had to call out the army in Alabama after terrorists bombed the homes of blacks in Birmingham. Kennedy sent to Congress the most comprehensive civil rights bill ever devised. It was designed to end all types of racial discrimination in hotels, restaurants, theaters and schools. But the President recognized that racial discrimination existed all over the country, in the north as well as the south, and he called upon people everywhere to help him bring about a change that was long overdue. All over the country citizens' groups and churches responded to Kennedy's proposals with voluntary efforts to end racial discrimination once and for all.

President Kennedy made strides toward achieving world peace by establishing the United States Arms Control and Disarmament Agency. His goal was to eliminate the international arms race and use the vast sums being spent on bombs and weapons for health and education.

Concerned with the dangers of poisoning the air with nuclear fallout from the continued testing of atomic bombs, President Kennedy strove to persuade the Soviet Union to agree to a test-ban treaty. And in 1963, an important step toward world peace was taken when the United States and Russia and Great Britain signed the Test Ban Treaty. This treaty was designed to halt atmospheric testing of nuclear weapons and slow down the arms race. It paved the way for further disarmament proposals which are so necessary if the world is to survive.

A low point in President Kennedy's career came in April of 1961 with a disastrous attempt to invade Cuba at the Bay of Pigs by 1400 Cuban exiles trained and transported by the United States. The U.S.-sponsored forces were totally defeated and U.S. ships and planes were destroyed. The President was deeply distressed by this catastrophe, but he courageously took all the blame upon himself. From this experience he learned to be more cautious in foreign affairs, just as he learned from everything he did.

The high point of the President's career came in October of 1962 when he forced Soviet Premier Krushchev to remove from Cuba the Russian nuclear missile bases capable of striking the United States. This confrontation could easily have resulted in another world war, but it was ended peacefully due to the President's diplomacy. As part of the agreement, the United States promised not to invade Cuba.

The President faced many other crises in foreign policy during his term in office, such as the turmoil in the newly liberated Congo, the invasion of the border of India by China, wars in Laos and Vietnam, and a crisis in Berlin. In all these situations, President Kennedy strove to restore peace and prevent the spread of war.

On November 21, 1963, his active mind full of plans for the future benefit of his country and all mankind, the President flew to Dallas, Texas, to make a speech on his new ideas. The next day he was assassinated as he rode in an open car through the streets of Dallas. This terrible tragedy ended the career of one of America's most beloved Presidents. He was killed before most of his dreams could be realized. John F. Kennedy left the task of continuing his work for peace and prosperity to all of us. The eternal flame that burns over his grave in Arlington National Cemetery in Virginia is a reminder to each of us that President Kennedy's spirit should live forever in our hearts and minds.

Lives of Kindness and Courage

Brother to All the World

ST. FRANCIS OF ASSISI

By Rhoda Power

A RICH Italian merchant who lived in the town of Assisi had a son called Francis. He was so rich that he could give the boy whatever he wanted. In the summer Francis wore clothes made of soft fine silk embroidered in gold and silver, and in winter he had velvet coats lined with fur. If he asked for jewels, his father bought them for him, and if he wanted anything to eat, a servant brought him a tray piled high with every sort of delicacy. He had horses and money, and he led a gay happy life.

One night, when Francis was lying in bed under a silken canopy, his head began to ache and his body to burn with fever. The next day he was very ill, and for a long while he lay on his couch suffering great pain. The best doctors came to see him and he was tenderly nursed.

While he was still too weak to leave his bed, Francis began to compare his own gay life with the lives of all the poor and the sick who lived in Assisi; and he thought, "It is wrong of me to waste my youth and my strength seeking pleasure. I must try to help people who are as ill as I have been, yet have no one to care for them."

When he was well, Francis sold his jewels and his fine clothes, and gave the money to the beggars he met at the roadside.

When his father saw that his son was living like a beggar, he was very angry. He seized Francis and shut him up in prison, thinking, "When I set him free he will come back and live in this fine house. He will be tired of suffering, and he will be afraid to disobey me."

But Francis was not afraid. When he came out of prison he went back to the poor. He even went and lived with the lepers, who had such a terrible illness that people feared to touch them.

One day Francis sold a piece of cloth from his father's warehouse and gave the money to a poor priest who was repairing a shrine. His father was angry and took Francis before the judge.

"Francis," said the judge, "you wish to help God by repairing this shrine, but God cannot accept from you something which is not yours. You have no right to your father's money."

Francis bowed. "I understand, sir," he answered. "All that I have belongs to my father. I will give it back to him." Then he took off his clothes and gave them back to his father and left the court, wearing only a hair shirt.

ST. FRANCIS OF ASSISI. Preaching friar who considered flowers and animals his sisters and brothers. Born Giovanni Francesco Bernardone in Assisi, Italy, 1181 or 1182. Led a frivolous life as a youth. After a serious illness in 1202 sought solitude and prayer, and lived among the poor. Obtained permission from the Pope to preach. Wrote fine books on the Christian way of life. Made a Saint by the Pope two years after his death in 1226.

So Francis went away from his father's grand house, and put on a coarse, brownish-gray coat, like those which only the poor country people wore, and he made friends with the sick and the needy, sitting up with them all night and washing their wounds. He remembered how Jesus had washed the feet of the poor and he wanted to be like Him.

Very soon all the friends who used to dance and hunt with him began to desert him. They thought he was a madman, and they pelted him with mud and stones. But Francis took no notice. He wandered about the country, caring for the sick, making friends with the poor, and teaching everyone about the goodness of God. He had neither money nor food; but because he was always so kind and so cheerful people began to love him. When they saw him coming along the road barefooted and bareheaded, they came to meet him and gave him bread. Then Francis would sing to them the old happy songs that he had learned as a boy, and talk to them about the love of God. And the people would look at him gently and say, "He is our brother, and a friend of all the world."

Francis *was* a friend of all the world. Indeed, his heart was so full of love that he called everyone and everything his brother or his sister. The flowers in the fields were his "little sisters," the animals in the woods his "little brothers." In summer, when the weather was hot and Francis was parched with thirst, Brother Wind and Sister Water refreshed him. In winter, when snow lay on the ground, Brother Fire warmed his shivering body. At night Sister Moon gave him light, and in the morning when he awoke he used to sing, "Praised be Thou, Lord, with all Thy creatures, especially for my Brother Sun which gives us the day."

He was so well loved that people wanted to be like him. One day a rich nobleman called Bernard and a famous lawyer called Peter gave up all they had and followed Francis. "Let us be your brothers too," said they. Then Brother Bernard, Brother Peter, and Brother Francis built a hut out of branches and mud, and lived together, praying, preaching, and doing good.

Not long afterwards, Francis was walking through the forest when he came to a little patch of bare ground, and there he saw a ploughboy kneeling at prayer. When he heard Francis coming, the ploughboy rose and said, "My name is Giles. Will you have me too?" And Francis took him by the hand.

They all sat under a tree, the wealthy merchant's son, the young nobleman, the famous lawyer, and the poor ploughboy, and each called the other "Brother."

Little by little many people gave up everything and followed Francis and his three friends. Men called them the Franciscan friars, which means the Brothers of Francis. Barefooted and dressed in the coarse, gray-brown robes, with ropes knotted round their waists, they wandered into the dirtiest parts of the town, where people were suffering from fevers, and they nursed the sick. They never asked for payment. They were content to live on what people gave them. They were never weary of helping and serving, for they believed that "God is love," and this made them happy.

One day, when Francis was walking through the woods, he saw all sorts of birds gathered together, so he ran to the spot and greeted them. The birds were not afraid.

They waited till he drew near, and those which were on the ground gazed upwards, and those which had perched on branches bowed their little heads and looked down at him. Then Francis preached them a sermon. He said, "My Bird Brothers, you ought to praise God who has clothed you with feathers, granted you wings to fly, and given over to you the pure air." While he was speaking, the little birds all began to stretch their necks and open their beaks and look intently at him. He walked among them and touched them, and not one of them moved away until he had blessed them all. Then they flew singing and twittering above the tops of the trees.

Once, one of the brothers brought Francis a little lame hare which they had rescued from a trap. "Come to me, Brother Hare," said Francis, and when the little creature loped towards him, he picked it up and caressed it. But when he put it on the ground so that it might run away, it returned again and again.

As time passed, Francis gathered more and more friars round him, and he made rules for when he was with them and when he was away. Because of these rules his brotherhood was called the Franciscan Order.

One day, when the sun was shining brightly, Francis went on a journey.

"Where are you going?" asked the people along the way.

"To Rome," said Francis, "to ask the Pope to read our rules and bless our Order."

People say that when the Pope saw the shabby, gray-brown robe which Francis was wearing, his dirty hands and dusty naked feet, his shaggy hair and beard, he was very much astonished. He read the rules

and he thought that they were almost too difficult for any man to obey. "Brother," said he, smiling at the barefooted, untidy man who stood so humbly before him, "go to the pigs, for you are more like them than a man. Read them your rules."

And Francis went out into the fields. He saw the pigs wallowing in the mud, and he sat among them and read them his rules. Then he went back to the Pope and said, "Father, I have done as you have commanded. I pray you, grant me now your blessing."

The Pope was amazed at the humble way his words had been obeyed. He gave the Franciscan Order his blessing.

Francis now began to think that he ought to help other countries besides Italy, for he knew that everywhere he would find the sick and poor. So he divided his brothers into little companies and sent them far and wide to carry their message of healing and love into different parts of the world.

The brothers set out bravely. Sometimes people treated them unkindly and mocked them because they were barefooted and poor, but gradually they made friends and, little by little, men came to them and said, "Let us be brothers too."

And so it happened that in many different lands there were groups of Franciscan friars tending the sick and caring for the poor. At first they lived in little huts, but after a while people who loved them began to give them land, and they built themselves monasteries where they could live and churches where they could worship.

But Francis stayed in Italy. Year after year he and the brothers who were with him wandered about, doing good and preaching the word of God, until Francis began to

"Amen," whispered one, and as he did so the air was filled with sweet music. It was as though soft bells were ringing and heavenly voices were singing. The brothers stole to the door and looked out. On the roof of the hut, in the trees and bushes, on the rocks and among the reeds were birds of all kinds, piping, singing, and twittering. These "little brothers" whom St. Francis had loved were still praising God, although their old friend could no longer tell them to do so.

grow old and blind. Day by day the brothers watched him growing weaker, until at last his strength failed. He gave them his last sweet smile, and murmuring, "Welcome, Sister Death," he died.

With the tears falling from their eyes, the brothers knelt by his bed and prayed.

Many years later, people remembered how good and loving Francis had been, and they made him a saint.

Because of Him the Blind Can Read

LOUIS BRAILLE

By Bella Koral

ONE spring day, about one hundred and fifty years ago, a small boy, Louis Braille, was playing happily in his father's workshop in the village of Coupvray near Paris, France. Monsieur Braille, Louis' father, was a harness and saddle-maker and three-year-old Louis' brown eyes sparkled as he watched his father swing the shining knife through the tough leather hides.

Thick scraps of leather dropped on the floor around the harness-maker. Sometimes they were round. Sometimes the thick slices were like half moons. Other times they were triangles. But mostly they were leather slabs with no shape at all. Little Louis loved to play with the pieces, fitting them together to make new shapes and patterns.

Monsieur Braille picked up his awl to bore a hole in a heavy piece of leather he was working on. He exclaimed impatiently as the awl slipped off the hide without going through it. He laid the tool on his bench and crossed the room to get a stronger awl from the rack on the wall.

Little Louis picked up the awl and made a stab at the leather. As he bent down, the awl suddenly flipped up and pierced his eye. The little boy's scream brought his father rushing to his side. But it was too late. The injury was serious. Unfortunately, as often happens in such cases, the other eye soon became infected too. His parents took Louis to several doctors hoping to save his sight,

but it was no use. Before long, three-year-old Louis was in total darkness, never to see again.

In Louis Braille's day, and for hundreds of years before that, blind people in backward parts of Europe and Asia were often treated cruelly. They were hired out as beasts of burden, costing less than horses or oxen. Others were put to shoveling coal in factories or manure on farms all day long. But mostly they were trained to be beggars, to whine on street corners or on the steps of temples or churches for a piece of bread or a copper coin.

It was not that people wanted to be cruel. They just didn't know what else to do with the blind.

It was not like that in the little village of Coupvray, where everyone loved the little blind Louis. Poor Monsieur Braille could never forgive himself for the accident to his son and everybody tried to make life easier for him.

The boy had a cane and soon learned to tap his way around the village. At first he could recall the shape of a tree, or the look of clouds floating across the sky. But after a while these mind pictures faded away and Louis could not remember them any more.

"There comes little Louis," the villagers said when they heard the tap, tap, tapping of his cane. They scratched out grooves on the road so he could follow a straight path

LOUIS BRAILLE. Teacher of the blind. Born in France, 1809. Lost his sight at age of three. Studied music. Became organist in Paris church. Taught the blind. Devised system of printing with raised dots, called Braille, used all over the world. Died 1852.

to the school. Louis would count out the exact number of cane taps it took him to reach the road. Tap, tap, tap—so many taps to the big tree. So many more to the pond. That many more to the hills. This tapping stayed with him through his life and was to mean much to the world later on.

At home as he grew older, Louis tried to help his father in the harness shop, handling the tools and bits of leather. Louis' fingers grew nimble and strong, his hearing became very keen. At the village school his teacher was amazed at how well Louis learned his lessons by ear and memory.

Yet he was unhappy, for Louis wanted to learn to read and write like other children and he knew he couldn't. Then it happened that the schoolmaster heard of a school in Paris called the Institute for the Young Blind. There the blind children of well-to-do people did have books of a kind. When Louis found out about this school he begged to go there to learn what he could. His parents did not expect him to learn much at the Institute for in those days schools for the blind were not well equipped at all. But they wanted to do the best they could for their boy.

When Louis was ten years old he was sent to this Institute in Paris. The head of the school soon found that Louis learned quickly whatever was taught him and that he was especially talented in music. It became his favorite study. With his keen sense of hearing, his nimble fingers, and his fine memory, Louis Braille learned to play the piano and the cello expertly. His very happiest hours were those he spent at the organ of a nearby church. And when he was still a young boy he was asked to play at church services.

After eight years at the Institute Louis was graduated. Then the Institute appointed him as a teacher of the blind children. For the rest of his life he devoted himself to teaching and helping those who were afflicted as he was.

When as a ten-year-old boy Louis had first come to the Institute, the first question he had asked his teachers was, "Can you teach me to read?"

The teachers would make no promises. Few blind people could ever learn to read well, they told him. In those days blind children learned the alphabet in this way: The teacher arranged little twigs in the shape of letters. Then the teacher would guide the child's fingers over these letters and explain them. Soon the child could take a pile of twigs and spell out words. But that was as far as he could go.

At about the time Louis Braille came to the Institute, a new way of reading for the blind was being tried. This was to print or press the letters very hard on to a page. In this way the letters were "embossed"— that is, "raised" on the other side of the heavy paper so that the blind person could trace their shape with his fingers.

Louis would trace each letter over and over again. "I *will* learn to read," he said determinedly. And he did. But for a quick mind like Louis Braille's, this was much too slow a way to read, for the letters had to be very large—at least an inch high. So even a very short story would fill many heavy volumes. And a blind child would have to spend a long time doing just a little reading.

Besides, it was hard and expensive to print books with embossed letters; so there was very little for the blind to read. For long or important books, a blind person had to depend on friends to read out loud to him.

Above all, a blind person couldn't write unless he had learned how before he became blind. He could only dictate his ideas for someone else to write down. And there was no way of reading or writing musical notes and music was what Louis Braille especially loved.

As he helped the blind children to learn to read the embossed books, Louis worried more and more about their painful struggles. Many gave up in despair when they found the going too hard and their progress so slow.

"There must be an easier way for the blind to read and write," young Braille said over and over. "Only books can free the blind. A person can never be truly educated unless he can read quickly and easily."

Louis was only seventeen years old then. He thought there *must* be an easier, quicker way for the blind to read than by trying to feel all the way around each letter. He was looking for a code—that was what he wanted!

Should his code be a symbol for every word in the dictionary? Or a shape like a square, circle or a triangle for each letter of the alphabet? He thought about it for months and months.

One evening he found the answer. He was sitting in a restaurant listening to a friend read aloud from a newspaper. Suddenly he heard something that made him jump up. In his excitement Louis pounded on the table, shouting, laughing, and crying all at once.

The people in the restaurant stopped eating and the room became quiet as the blind young man waved the paper.

The restaurant owner ran over and said kindly, "Monsieur Braille, calm yourself, I beg of you. You are disturbing my guests." Louis calmed down and said, "You must forgive me, but I am very happy."

Then Louis explained to his friend that the item he had been reading to him from the paper had solved his problem.

The news article was about night-writing —a new signal code in the French army. An artillery captain named Barbier had invented a method of sending messages by means of dots and dashes "in relief," that is, standing above the surface of the paper like embossed type.

This code could be used in the dark because it could be felt with the finger-tips. If a man could read and write a message in the dark without using his eyes, then a blind person could do it too!

Braille could not rest. The very next morning he found out where Captain Barbier lived and went to see him. The Captain explained his code to Louis. He punched some holes in a sheet of paper with a simple awl not so different from the one that had cost Louis his eyes. The Captain made Louis feel the bumps or dots that he made on the other side of the paper. A certain combination of dots meant a certain army command like, "Retreat to the main line," or "Cease fire," and so on.

Louis Braille was overjoyed. Punching dots on paper was easy, fast, and inexpensive. Now he could figure out a way by which the blind might punch out all words in a code made of dots.

Louis thanked the Captain and went home to work on the idea.

Many long and weary months went by. Except for his beloved music, all of the

young man's time and energy went into his endless experiments.

To make this "night-writing" really useful for the blind, Louis worked out an easy-to-read alphabet by means of raised dots. By the time he was twenty, in 1829, Braille had worked out his system. He designed a little hand punch that could be used with an oblong "cell" containing six holes. There was a special combination of dots for every letter of the alphabet, for every number and for every punctuation mark. Another blind person who knew the code could now feel the dots made by the punch and read what Braille had written. Louis practiced and practiced even when he should have been sleeping, and often his friends would find him in the morning asleep over his piece of cardboard and his punching tool.

After a while Louis learned to punch-write almost as fast as a person could talk and he could identify dot writing with his fingers almost as quickly as sighted people could read printed type.

Louis punched out a number of stories as they were read to him from books. He was ready at last to announce his new method. But now the authorities of the Institute would not accept Braille's idea. People who could see were satisfied with the old methods and felt there was no reason to change to something new. Printers of the old-style "embossed" books were afraid they'd lose business if Braille's system were adopted.

Braille went on with his work. He taught his blind pupils in private after school hours. They soon realized how much better his method was, and they told other blind people about it. Braille began to get letters begging for instruction, from the blind in every country in the world.

For the next few years Braille worked to improve his system. He worked at his teaching and his music, too. He designed a special code for musical notes so that a blind musician like himself could learn to play a score by reading the music with his fingertips.

Little by little Braille and his friends punched out textbooks, story-books, and song-books. Then some printers invented machinery for making copies of these books. But still his system was hardly known to the public. To Braille's great disappointment, it had not caught on.

Louis' health began to fail and it seemed to him that the work of his lifetime might die with him.

But he was still to have his moment of triumph. Among his music pupils was a blind young girl who was a very fine pianist. Braille had taught her his dot method of reading and writing music.

One evening she gave a concert before a most enthusiastic audience. The applause was tremendous. The young girl held up her hand for silence. Then she made a speech about Braille and what his method had meant to her. "I beg you to applaud *him*, not me," she said. "I play through his eyes."

The next day the Paris newspapers were filled with stories about Braille and his work

with his blind pupils. So much interest was aroused that many schools finally agreed to use his system.

When Braille heard about this, he wept for joy because, as he said, his life had not been a failure after all. This was in 1852 when Braille was forty-three years old.

Two years later the Institute officially adopted the Braille system. Books were translated into "Braille" and through books, the blind found happiness they had never before dared to hope for.

But it took many more years before Braille became the method of teaching the blind all over the world. Blind students taught it to one another. Then, finally, blind people persuaded every government to teach Braille in every school for the blind.

Today most blind students learn it. They go to regular colleges and punch out their own lecture notes. They can study and teach almost any subject. And they can read and write in Braille almost as fast as you and I can write.

Of course it takes many more pages to write a book in Braille than in ordinary print. The pages are large and the volumes are bulky. The Bible in Braille occupies several shelves. And, too, the cost of the books is too expensive for individuals to buy. In most countries government libraries provide these books free.

In April, 1929, the whole world celebrated the one hundredth anniversary of the publication of Louis Braille's code. A granite statue of him was set up in his little French village of Coupvray. From all over the world people came to honor him—both those with eyes to see, and those who could "see" the granite outlines of the statue's face only with their grateful hands.

The Lady with the Lamp

FLORENCE NIGHTINGALE

By Rosemary Nicolais

WHEN Florence Nightingale was a very little girl she loved dolls. There is nothing strange about that, but there was something strange about Florence's dolls. They were always sick or breaking bones or hurting themselves in some way or other. And that gave Florence a chance to put them to bed and bandage them and give them medicine.

One day the little girl had an opportunity to nurse a live animal instead of a doll. She loved to ride on horseback, and this day she and the vicar of the village were having a little gallop on the smooth low hills near her home. They had to stop to let some sheep pass and the vicar spoke to the shepherd.

"Good morning, Roger," he said. "Where's your dog, Cap, today?"

"I think his leg's broken, sir. Those boys were throwing stones at him."

"Oh!" cried Florence. "Poor Cap! Are you sure his leg's broken?"

"No, miss, but if it is it'll be best to put him out of his pain."

But Florence wouldn't hear of it. She and the vicar must go and see what could be done for poor Cap. They rode back to the shepherd's cottage and found the dog lick-

FLORENCE NIGHTINGALE. British hospital reformer and nurse. Born in Florence, Italy, 1820. First woman to organize nursing of the wounded on the battlefield. Took a group of nurses to the battlefront of the Crimean War 1854–56. Laid foundations of modern scientific nursing. Died in London, 1910.

ing a badly swollen leg. He made no objection when the vicar examined it.

"Is it broken?" asked Florence anxiously.

"No," said the vicar. "All it needs is a hot compress."

As soon as Florence found out what a hot compress was, she set about making one. She found a freshly washed smock of Roger's hanging on a door, and she tore it into strips. "My mother will send you a new one," she said as she worked.

She boiled some water, then wrung out strips of the smock and lay them, hot and wet, over the dog's wound. It was a real first-aid experience. She danced with joy when Cap got better and was able to go back to take care of the sheep.

From then on, Florence, mostly alone but sometimes with her sister Parthenope, visited all the people in the village who had anything the matter with them and tried to help them. Their parents were happy to see their daughters so well occupied. But as Florence grew older and wanted to learn seriously about nursing and caring for the sick, her father and mother became anxious.

Florence was born in the town of Florence in Italy, in 1820, about the same time that England's Queen Victoria was born. Her parents were traveling in Italy at the time, but they were English. Their real home was a fine mansion called Lea Hall in the middle of England. In those days girls belonging to wealthy families were supposed to spend their time at home doing needlework, playing the piano, or reading. Occasionally they were allowed to go to parties and dances. They could help the poor with a bowl of soup or a basket of fruit now and then. But it was thought unladylike to go out into the world and

work. So only a girl who knew exactly what she wanted to do and was quite determined to do it had a chance to make a working life of her own.

Florence Nightingale was just such a girl. She loved her parents, but she would not let them stop her from doing the work she was fitted for. And she met two or three people able to help her just when she needed help. One of these was an English Quaker lady, Mrs. Elizabeth Fry, and another was Dr. Samuel G. Howe, an American. Elizabeth Fry worked all her life long to improve prison conditions in England. Dr. Howe built and equipped a home for the blind in Boston. Florence loved and admired them both. They gave her strength and encouragement to carry out a plan she had been dreaming of for some time—to go to Germany where she could learn to be a professional nurse.

In France the Catholic Sisters of Mercy were trained to care for the sick, but there was no place in England where nurses could be trained. But a German Lutheran minister, Pastor Fliedner, saw what Elizabeth Fry had done for prisoners, almost alone, and he made up his mind to do the same for the sick in his own country. He scraped and saved and begged until he had enough money for a small hospital in Kaiserswerth, Germany. It was to this Protestant hospital that Florence at last made her way to learn to become a good nurse. Later she visited hospitals in France to learn what she could from the Sisters of Mercy there.

One day, soon after her return to England, Florence Nightingale picked up a copy of the *London Times* and read these words:

"Are there no devoted women among us able and willing to go and minister to the sick and suffering soldiers of the East in the hospitals of Scutari?"

"There is one," she said to herself, and immediately sat down and wrote a letter to the War Department. She offered her services and said she would train a band of other women to nurse the soldiers too.

Scutari was a small Turkish town opposite Constantinople on the Straits of the Bosporus. Ships had to pass through these straits on their way from the Mediterranean into the Black Sea, south of Russia. On the north coast of the Black Sea there is a peninsula called the Crimea. Here, during the years from 1854 to 1856, a terrible war was being fought by Russia against France, England, and Turkey.

There had been no wars in Europe for a long time. Most people seemed to have forgotten that soldiers must have good food and clothing, and that if they are sick or wounded they must be taken care of. There was no Red Cross then, no field service, no one to give first aid to injured men. The Crimean battles were fierce and cruel. Lord Tennyson, England's Poet Laureate, has left us a picture of an incident in one of these battles. He calls it *The Charge of the Light Brigade,* and here is one verse:

"Forward the Light Brigade!"
Was there a man dismayed?
Not though the soldier knew
    Someone had blundered.
Theirs not to make reply,
Theirs not to reason why,
Theirs but to do and die.
Into the valley of Death
    Rode the six hundred.

Florence Nightingale's letter to the War Department need never have been written, because at the same moment that she was writing it the head of that Office, Mr. Sidney Herbert, was writing to urge her to do just what she most longed to do. Their letters crossed in the mail. Sidney Herbert wrote "You are the one woman in England capable of performing this great task."

Today it seems natural that trained nurses should be sent to a scene of war. But in the year 1854 there was a great outcry when the newspapers announced that Florence Nightingale was planning to take English women to the Crimea to care for wounded soldiers. It was a new idea and people were afraid of new ideas. "Miss Nightingale! Oh, dear! Miss Nightingale! Shocking!" they said. Meanwhile Florence Nightingale and her band of nurses slipped quietly across the English Channel to France on their way to the East.

When they reached Scutari, they were taken to a large Turkish barracks. This was the hospital. Their first shock was the sight of wounded men lying in the snow outside. When they entered the building they saw hundreds of men, most of them badly injured, many dying, lying in rows on the bare floor. Hundreds more, they were told, were at that very moment being landed from the battlefields, and more were on their way across the Black Sea. All still wore their ragged, blood-stained uniforms.

Where were the soap and towels to wash their patients? There were none to be found. There were no bowls, no dishes, not even any medicines. And the food, what there was of it, was uneatable. A few fortunate soldiers lay in beds, but the sheets on these beds were of such rough canvas that the men begged to have them taken away.

Miss Nightingale set about discovering the reason for such a dreadful state of affairs, and she found the main reason to be—red tape!

This is the way Miss Nightingale dealt with the red tape monster:

She knew that large stocks of supplies of all kinds had been sent from England. Where were they? Probably, she thought, locked up in warehouses along the docks. So, as she must have towels, soap, medicine, and food at once, she made her way to one of these warehouses. She asked in gentle tones for the man in charge. She was shown into his office.

"What do you want?" the man asked gruffly.

"Will you please open the warehouse for me? I need supplies."

"Can't do it, ma'am," he replied. "Have to have an order from the Board."

Miss Nightingale thanked him and went to seek the chief officer of the Board.

"I'm sorry, ma'am," the officer said, more politely, "but before I can open the warehouse, I must have authority to do so."

"Who can give you the authority?" Miss Nightingale asked with a friendly smile.

"The entire Board has got to meet."

"Can you give me the names of the members of the Board?" the lady asked reasonably.

"Well, there's Colonel Dash, and Mr. Doe and Mr. Roe," the officer said unwillingly, and added a few more names, all of which Miss Nightingale was careful to remember.

"Where can I find these gentlemen?" she asked.

"Well, the Colonel's gone riding. I know that. And Mr. Doe's not feeling well. I can't say where I'd find the others at this time of day, ma'am. I really can't."

"Will you please call them all together to a meeting—now?" she went on, gently but firmly.

"I'm very busy just now, ma'am, but to-morrow, say, or the day after, I'll see what can be done."

"Will you come to a meeting if I get the other members together right away?" she asked.

"We-ll, I—er, I—er, I daresay."

An hour later Miss Nightingale had rounded up every member of the Board. She got them to open the warehouse a few minutes after they met, and soon all the supplies she needed were delivered at the hospital.

A few months later Scutari Hospital was a well-equipped institution. It even had a wonderful kitchen, presided over by Monsieur Soyer, a Frenchman who greatly admired Miss Nightingale's intelligence and tireless devotion. Before the nurses arrived, sixty patients out of every hundred had died. Now it was only one out of a hundred.

At the end of the war the name of Florence Nightingale was on the lips of all her countrymen. Returning soldiers told how she toiled twenty hours out of the twenty-four to save their lives and cheer their spirits.

"We kissed her shadow as she went by our beds," some said.

"The Lady with the Lamp was her name out there," a young man told his mother. "She carried a lamp with her through the wards at night. If anyone was awake and in pain, sure enough there was always something she could do."

Everyone spoke of her courtesy, her sweet and unfailing kindness and patience, of the letters she wrote for men too sick to write themselves, the hours she spent comforting

the dying.

"What can we do for her?" was what everyone wanted to know.

Sidney Herbert gave the answer. "One testimonial I know would touch her deeply," he said, "and that is—enough money to found a hospital in London. It must be a hospital such as she dreams of, where she will be able to reform the nursing system of England."

Immediately money began pouring in for The Nightingale Hospital Fund. At the end of a year Miss Nightingale herself said "No more!"

She returned to England as quietly as she had left. The British government held a man-of-war vessel in readiness to carry her home, but she insisted that that was much too grand for her. Instead she stepped aboard a French steamer that took her from the Crimea to France. From there she crossed to England and made her way home. Florence Nightingale thought so little of her own importance that she did not even let her family know when she was arriving. She was content to have saved the lives of thousands of British soldiers and to have made people respect the profession of nursing.

They Helped to Free the Slaves

HARRIET TUBMAN AND THE UNDERGROUND RAILROAD

By Bella Koral

"THERE's two things I've got a right to," Harriet said to herself. "These are death and liberty. No one will take me alive."

Harriet was a Negro slave on a plantation in Maryland. From the time she was very small, one of eleven children of a slave father and mother, she had rebelled against her slavery. On the very first day she was sent to work in the Big House, her mistress whipped her four times. Once she ran away and hid for a few days in a pigsty, sharing with the pigs the scraps thrown to them. When her father finally found her late one night and tenderly carried her home, she pointed to the sky.

There was one special star she had watched each night. When the other stars moved across the sky, this one stood still.

"What do they call that star—the one that never moves, Pappy?" she asked.

"That's the North Star," he said, "the best star there is." It was the star that pointed North, to freedom.

Since her owner saw that Harriet would never make a good house servant, she was sent to work in the woods and fields. One day, when she was in her teens, a slave had gone without permission to a country store. The plantation overseer followed to whip him and bring him back. He ordered Harriet to help tie him up. As Harriet refused, the young slave ran off. The overseer picked up a heavy iron weight and threw it after him. But he did not hit the fellow. The weight struck Harriet's head.

She was unconscious for many, many days. Even after she was able to work again, and for the rest of her life, she suffered spells of unconsciousness. More and more after this she longed and prayed for her freedom.

A few years later when her master died, Harriet heard she was to be sold. She was afraid her new owner might be even worse than the one she had had. And she might be taken to the deep South and never see her loved ones again.

She made secret plans to run away. She could not let even her mother know. It would be too dangerous.

On the evening she was to leave she went about the fields and slave quarters singing:

> I'll meet you in the morning,
> Safe in the Promised Land,
> On the other side of Jordan
> Bound for the Promised Land.

Harriet knew some slave would hear her song and let her family know that to her the Promised Land meant the North.

Late at night Harriet slipped into the woods. She had only her instinct and the North Star to guide her, and she had faith that God would help her.

By a roundabout way, she reached the home of a Quaker woman she knew who

HARRIET TUBMAN. American Negro rescuer of slaves. Born in Maryland about 1820. Most of her life was devoted to fighting slavery and to assuring freedom for Negroes after slavery was abolished. In her Underground Railroad activities she rescued more than three hundred slaves. Died in Auburn, N.Y., 1913.

might help her. The woman wrote a note and gave it to Harriet. But Harriet did not know what it said. Her owner had never allowed her to learn to read and write. The woman told her how to get to a certain house far to the north. This was a "station" on the Underground Railroad. Harriet understood very well what she meant.

The Underground wasn't a real railroad, of course. It was the secret route by which Negro slaves escaped to freedom.

At this time there were many other white people, too, in the North as well as in the South, who hated slavery and believed it should be done away with.

There was William Lloyd Garrison, a young printer and editor, who started a newspaper in Boston called the *Liberator*. In it he took up the cause of the slaves. He went to jail for expressing his anti-slavery views.

Wendell Phillips, one of New England's ablest preachers, lent his voice to the cause too. Among others who sided with the foes of slavery were the famous poets John Greenleaf Whittier, James Russell Lowell, and Ralph Waldo Emerson.

Frederick Douglass, himself an escaped slave with a wonderful gift for speaking and writing, also lectured against slavery throughout New England.

Many foes of slavery banded together, often at the risk of their lives, to help slaves escape to the North. Their homes and barns were the "stations" of the Underground Railroad where the "passengers," the escaped slaves, could hide, eat, and rest before going on to the next "station." The "conductors" of the Underground Railroad were free Negroes, kind Quakers, ministers or workingmen who guided the escaping slaves and helped them on their way. The "conductors" knew the roads and trails that led to the North, and they knew how to keep out of the slave catchers' way.

For several days Harriet Tubman made her way from one "station" to the next. Sympathetic "conductors" helped her hide from the slave catchers who had been searching for her ever since her escape had been discovered.

Handbills and posters describing her had been posted on every bridge, railroad station, and courthouse all the way north to the Pennsylvania border. Armed men watched the woods hoping to get the reward offered for her capture.

Harriet managed to elude them all. Near the end of her journey, Harriet's "conductor" was a farmer who hid her under a pile of vegetables he was taking to market in his wagon. It would have taken very sharp eyes to notice that a dark-faced woman in dark clothing had climbed out of that vegetable wagon in the night.

As soon as Harriet reached New Jersey, she knew she had crossed the line. She would never be a slave again. Later she told a friend, "When I found I had crossed that line, I looked at my hands to see if I was the same person, now I was free. There was such a glory over everything. The sun came like gold through the trees and I felt like I was in heaven."

Harriet got work and began to earn money. But she could not enjoy her freedom while all her family were slaves. So, some months later, Harriet herself became a "conductor" on the Underground Railroad. Walking over long stretches of the way, she secretly returned to Maryland several times within two years after her own escape, and brought out two of her brothers, a sister, and a dozen more slaves.

Then a new law was passed, the Fugitive Slave Law of 1850. It became a crime for anyone even in the North to help runaway slaves. Now they were being hunted down in places where they had been more or less safe before. Only in Canada could they really be safe, for Queen Victoria of England had forbidden slavery there. The Underground Railroad went up to Canada now. More and more secret "stations" were being set up. And the Fugitive Slave Law did not stop Harriet.

Negro slaves were beginning to call her Moses. Like that great leader of the Hebrew people, she was taking her people out of slavery into the land of freedom.

At about this time there appeared a sensational book called *Uncle Tom's Cabin*. It was written by Harriet Beecher Stowe and had a tremendous influence on America's history. Through its vivid tales of the slaves' suffering, it inspired sympathizers to work with Harriet and others in the Underground Railroad.

Harriet knew the hidden paths through woods and swamps. She knew when it was safe to go ahead, and when to hide. She knew where people lived who would feed and help runaways, and just the spot where a boat waited to take her group many miles northward during the night.

When slave owners hired men to put up posters advertising her runaways, she paid others to tear them down. If the roads were blocked by posses of slave catchers, she turned her party around, putting them on a train going south for a few stops. No one would suspect that Negroes heading for the cotton fields were running away!

Sometimes Harriet waded for hours upstream to throw the hounds off scent. When the nights were dark and there was no North Star, she would feel the trees for the moss that grows on the northern side. That would be the guide toward freedom.

Harriet sometimes disguised herself as a man. Many of the Southern plantation owners believed she *was* a man—for they could not imagine a woman with such courage and daring! The rewards for her capture rose. At one time there was a price of $40,-000 on her head, dead or alive. Her pictures were posted everywhere. Armed men were sent out to watch for her. Every moment she was in the South her life was in terrible danger. But when her followers lost courage, it was Harriet's bravery that strengthened them. In twelve years she made nineteen trips into the South, rescuing three hundred slaves by means of her Underground Railroad. She herself said, "I never ran my train off the track, and I never lost a passenger." Everyone who started out with Harriet Tubman lived to thank her for freedom.

Later Harriet enjoyed telling of some of her narrow escapes. Once, not being able to read, she sat down and fell asleep on a park bench right under a sign offering a big reward for her capture! But, miraculously, she was not recognized.

Another time when she was in Maryland to rescue some relatives, she had to pass through a town where there was danger of meeting a slave catcher who knew her well. She covered her head with a shawl and hobbled along all bent over like an old woman going to market. Harriet was a good actress and her disguise was perfect. But she wanted to be absolutely sure. So she bought some live chickens, tied their legs

together, and hung them head down around her neck. As she shuffled down the street she saw the slave catcher heading toward her. He might recognize her in spite of her disguise. Quick as a flash she slipped the knot that tied the chickens and they all scattered, squawking, in different directions. Harriet, purposely not catching them, limped after them, away from the man who could have captured her. He just stood there laughing!

One of Harriet's most daring exploits was the rescue of her father and mother. They were both well over seventy years old when she brought them from Maryland to Canada. But it was too cold there for the old people, so she brought them to a home she had begun to buy in Auburn, New York. By this time she had become so well known in the North that Anti-Slavery groups often asked her to speak at their meetings where money was raised to help her in her work. She came to know well such Abolitionists as Ralph Waldo Emerson and Bronson Alcott, Louisa Alcott's father. Between trips Harriet worked as a cook and cleaning woman, and most of her earnings went to the cause of freedom.

When the Civil War broke out, Harriet's work of helping slaves journey to freedom kept right on. It was not long before she became a nurse for the Union Armies of the North and was sent to Florida to care for soldiers there. Then she became a Union Army scout and carried out dangerous missions within the Confederate territory of the South, though she knew that whenever the Confederate soldiers found a scout behind their lines, they shot him as a spy.

She secretly organized a group of scouts and river pilots, and with a Union Colonel named Montgomery, she led a raiding party of three gunboats and about one hundred and fifty Negro troops up the Combahee River in the middle of the night.

The unexpected daring of this raid caused panic and confusion on the Confederate side. At first the slaves were frightened too, but they remembered the plain little woman who had promised to come back with "Lincoln's gunboats to set them free." Mothers ran down to the river with their babies in their arms and older children clinging to their skirts. Barefoot men dashed out of the fields.

In all, about eight hundred slaves crowded aboard those little gunboats and shoved off to freedom and safety. And Harriet Tubman had not lost a single soldier on her greatest rescue mission!

She was over forty years old when President Lincoln signed the Emancipation Proclamation, on January 1, 1863, outlawing slavery. Now the freedom Harriet Tubman had fought so hard to secure was legal for all.

After the Civil War ended, Harriet was soon supporting two freedmen's schools in the South, buying clothes and books for the students with money she earned at housework.

Harriet's trips on the Underground Railroad were over, but she kept on traveling for more than fifty years. The ending of slavery did not mean the end of injustice for the Negroes. So Harriet made more journeys speaking for justice as well as freedom.

Much as she had done for her country, Harriet was never allowed to vote. Neither white nor Negro women had as yet been granted this right. Harriet made speeches all over the country for women's rights and shared the platform with such famous suffragette leaders as Susan B. Anthony and Elizabeth Cady Stanton.

In 1913, just fifty years after Lincoln had set the slaves free, Harriet Tubman died in her Auburn home at the age of ninety-three. The people of Auburn held a great mass-meeting and a bronze tablet was erected to her memory on the city's courthouse. It is still there, honoring one of the bravest, most devoted fighters for freedom America has ever had.

Pioneer American Battlefield Nurse

CLARA BARTON

By Toby Bell

THE bullet zinged straight through Clara's sleeve and killed the soldier she was nursing. She was a tiny thing, strange to see in the wild battle that raged all around her. She was not dressed as a nurse. She had on one of the long full skirts women wore in her time. A young Lieutenant, whose own head was bound by a bloody bandage, touched her on the arm.

"Ma'am," he said, "you shouldn't be here. This is no place for a lady."

Clara looked up at him for a second. Her eyes were full of tears for the poor young soldier she had tried to save. But she said, "Don't bother me, young man. I'm busy." And she went on to take care of another wounded soldier.

This happened during the American Civil War when the Southern States fought the Northern States. This battle, at Antietam, was one of the bloodiest in American history. Clara Barton, tending the wounded,

CLARA BARTON. Founder of American Red Cross. Born in Oxford, Mass., 1821. Taught school, 1836–54. Collected and distributed supplies for wounded during Civil War. Aided wounded and destitute in Europe during Franco-Prussian War, 1869–73, in association with International Red Cross. First President of the American Red Cross, 1882–1904. Wrote *History of the Red Cross*, *Story of My Childhood*, and other books. Died 1912.

225

looked out of place to the Americans of both sides. They were not used to seeing women on battlefields. In Europe Florence Nightingale had fought for the right of women to nurse in battle. But in the United States they were allowed only in hospitals, not on battlefields. It wasn't lady-like, said the Americans. But the soldiers Clara Barton nursed didn't care about that. They thought she was wonderful.

The Lieutenant who tried to get Clara to leave the battle was wasting his breath. She was determined to give the wounded men all the nursing care she could. Clara Barton was the youngest child and the favorite in a farm family in Massachusetts. While she was still a little girl, she began to nurse her kittens and her dog, Button.

We do not know whether she nursed her dolls, but maybe not, because she was a tomboy, and when there was no school, she was outdoors with her brothers and the many animals on the farm. She loved them all. She even made a pet of a turkey, and a turkey is a most unfriendly bird. She was about thirteen when one of her brothers caught smallpox. That is a disease to scare anyone. She knew how catching it was, but she begged to be allowed to nurse her brother. At last he was cured, but then Clara caught smallpox herself, and she had a bad time of it.

When she was well again, she wanted to go ice-skating with her brothers. She pleaded with her father, "Please, Father, may I go too? I'll be very good."

Her father shook his head and said, "I'm sorry, dear child. I wish I could say yes. But you know it isn't lady-like for girls to skate. The neighbors would be shocked."

But Clara made up her mind. Without a word to anyone, she borrowed a pair of her brother's skates, and off she went. The skates were too big for her and she fell and hurt her knee badly. She was ashamed to tell her father what she had done. So she bound up the wound on her knee with a woolen scarf and tried not to limp. Of course the knee got infected and she had to stay in bed a long time. In those weeks she learned how a wounded person feels.

In her teens she wanted more and more to be a nurse. But in her day girls didn't make a career of nursing. The women who did nursing were untrained and often ignorant. A sick patient was lucky if a kind neighbor knew something about sickness. For several years Clara taught school. Later she went to the city of Washington and worked in the United States Patent Office as a clerk. Then came the Civil War.

One day, in her office a man said to her, "Miss Barton, do you know that there's a regiment here from your home?"

Clara was excited and asked where they were camped.

"They're in a queer place for soldiers," said the man. "They're camped in the meeting room of the Senate. You know how crowded everything is with soldiers coming in from all directions. There isn't any other place for them to go."

"Oh," said Clara, "may I be excused from work? I must go to see them. I'm sure they're uncomfortable. The Senate is a grand place but it has no beds and no kitchen."

When she got to the Senate Building, Clara found that some of the men were wounded. On the way through Maryland, they had been mobbed by Southerners. They were all tired and hungry. There was plenty for Clara to do. She tended the wounded and soothed the sleepless. She gathered so much food and clothing that it took five porters to carry it all.

Now she felt bold enough to go to the office of the Secretary of War, and in her soft voice she asked his permission to go to the front lines as a nurse. The Secretary looked at the little lady whose feet didn't reach the floor when she sat in the big chair in his office. She wasn't a pretty girl, but her face was warm and kind and she had a dimple in her cheek. The Secretary said "No." He was sorry but it wasn't a place for a lady.

Of course she didn't give up. At first she was allowed only to drive wagons with medicines and bandages to the soldiers. She was used to horses and bad roads and she did that job well. She had great courage and common sense too. One day she was unpacking some bottles of medicine at a camp when a doctor remarked, "We are glad to get these medicines. We need them. But right now the men are hungry. We are running low on food."

Clara glanced down at the case she was unpacking. "Look!" she said. "They packed these bottles in cornmeal to keep them from breaking." And in a jiffy she had the cornmeal cooking in a big pot. That night the men had hot cornmeal mush for supper.

Bit by bit, doing each job as it came along, Clara Barton became a nurse for the Army. And other women got courage from her and became nurses too.

About three months after that bullet went through her sleeve at Antietam, Clara was busy in the roar and smoke of another battle. This was at Fredericksburg. It was December and bitterly cold. There were so many thousands of wounded that most of them could not be moved soon enough and actually froze to death on the ground. Again Clara had a narrow escape. A shell screamed overhead and a piece came right at her, tearing a hole in her coat and her dress. But once more she was not touched. And again she went on about her work as though nothing had happened.

Then one day she got a letter from her home town. "Please, Miss Barton," wrote a neighbor, "will you please try to find out what has happened to my son? We haven't had any word from him in three months. Is he a prisoner? Is he wounded? The Government just says he is missing."

And from that one letter grew another great part of Clara Barton's work, that of finding soldiers who were missing. After the war was over and others went home, she went on with that search. Clara Barton's nursing and her search for missing soldiers came to be the beginning of the Red Cross in America.

This is how it happened. Clara Barton broke down after her years of hard work. The doctors sent her to the mountains of Switzerland to get well. All the public buildings there flew the Swiss flag with its white cross on a blue field. But one day she saw flying over the Town Hall a flag with a red cross on a white field. She asked what it was.

Her Swiss doctor looked surprised. "Don't you know?" he asked. "That is the flag of our International Committee of the Red Cross. That committee does, on a large scale just what you did when there was a war in the United States. It nurses the wounded, takes food to the hungry in war."

"But Switzerland does not have any

wars," said Clara. "Oh," she added quickly, "I see. It is because the Swiss are never at war that the Red Cross Committee can go in and help both sides. For them there is no enemy. Only friends. How wonderful!"

Clara got well quickly after that. She was in a hurry to get home and start a Red Cross in the United States. She went at it tooth and nail, yet it took her thirteen years to get the United States Government to let her start the American Red Cross. But she did get it started at last, in the year 1882. Clara Barton was its first President, and she was its President for twenty-two years. Before she was through, the Red Cross flag flew in disasters of peace as well as in war. Where there is a flood or a drought or a tornado, there you will find the Red Cross.

The Red Cross brings nurses and doctors, food and clothes as well as medicine wherever there is need.

Clara Barton began with nothing, but today the American Red Cross does so much good that the American people contribute many millions of dollars to help the good work.

Boys and girls play a big part in the Red Cross. Through their schools and their teachers, millions of children do their share in taking care of others and making friends at the same time. They are members of the Junior Red Cross.

The Junior Red Cross does not wait for war or disasters. It works all the time. The Junior Red Cross does many, many things for its own members and through them for children all over the world. No boy or girl has to give money to join the Junior Red Cross. But all children who belong do what they can to help. In New York and some other states, every member gets a pin or a tab to wear.

This Junior Red Cross is now an important part of the American Red Cross, and it all grew out of Clara Barton's work. She never dreamed she was starting such a huge organization. But those bullets whistling around her, during the American Civil War, left us something very wonderful. Because of them Clara Barton made the American Red Cross a sign of hope and help for people in distress everywhere.

Newspaper Wonder

JOSEPH PULITZER

By Will Lane

A YOUNG man, Joseph Pulitzer by name, was looking out across the rail of a small westbound ship as it fought the waves of the Atlantic Ocean about a century ago. He had no right to be on deck, for his berth was in the cheapest part of the boat and he was supposed to stay in the dark and dismal place they called the steerage. The ship pitched and rolled, but Joseph did not mind that. He didn't even mind the uncomfortable, crowded steerage. He was excited about the new life he was planning to live in the United States. He was seventeen years old, strong and healthy. But he was very thin, because he had shot up to his height of over six feet much too fast. He was peering ahead, trying to catch sight of land, but his eyesight was bad and he could make out nothing.

As he stood there, he did not dream that in the future he would cross this ocean many times in his own yacht with its crew of forty-five men.

Now from a hatchway he heard one of his fellow-passengers from the steerage calling to him, "Joey, Joey, come down and eat." And then came the voice of another, "Where is that Joe? He's so full of jokes and tricks I bet he's hiding from us."

Joseph was indeed hiding. But now he was hungry. And he was homesick too. He thought of his father, buried in the Jewish cemetery of a little town back home in Hungary. And of his mother who would be praying for his journey in her little Catholic church.

Down below, in his berth, there was still some of the sausage and herring she had given him when he left, and even a little of the black bread she had baked. He thought to himself, "Should I go down and eat?" And then he heard another call from above him. "Land! I see land!"

No, he would not go down. He was not going to spoil his plan just to get a little something to eat. If the ship was approaching Boston, he must stay where he was, for he knew he must not be on the ship when she docked in Boston Harbor.

What he wanted was to join the United States Army. It was for this that he had passage on the ship. He had learned in Hungary that the United States was fighting a terrible Civil War.

Joseph wanted to fight for the North, but he was afraid the Army might not take him because of his poor eyesight. Besides, he was too young. In Europe he met a man who said, "I'll get you in. Don't worry. Just stick to me."

But on the ship he began not to trust this man. He heard that make-believe friends sometimes got young men into the United States and then sent them off to work in mining camps and swamps. Joseph could speak only a few words of English and he

JOSEPH PULITZER. American newspaper publisher. Born in Budapest, Hungary, 1847. Came to America, 1864. Enlisted in 1st N.Y. Cavalry during Civil War. Publisher of *St. Louis Post-Dispatch, New York World.* Founded Pulitzer School of Journalism and established Pulitzer Prizes. Died in Charleston, S.C., 1911.

would not be able to defend himself against such a plot.

No, he must not land in Boston with this man. So now, without making a sound, he slipped over the ship's side and began to swim to shore. If he had done this in later times he would have been breaking the law. But in 1864, when Joseph dived into Boston Harbor, there was no such law. He swam a few strokes under water and when he came up above, he could make out the lights of the city and he knew what direction to take. When he reached shore, he was sorry he had not had time to make a bundle of a few extra socks and some sausage. In his wet clothes he spent the rest of the night on a park bench. Next day, he had no trouble at all in enlisting in the Union Army. The war had been going on for three years and there was a great need of men. The recruiting officers didn't find out about his poor eyesight. And he cheerfully added a year to his age. His joy was great when he heard that he was to be sent to a cavalry regiment, because he loved horses and was a fine rider.

But when he reached the regiment, he was not so pleased. The men in his company were almost all Germans and he wanted to be with Americans. And for some time they did not get into any fighting. The Germans treated him roughly. They made fun of his long thin body, his long nose, and his Hungarian accent.

One day he saw a corporal bullying a small, helpless private. Joe always had a hot temper and now his temper flew out and he punched the corporal. That was a thing a man can't do in any army, so he was put under arrest. But before anything further could be done, he was saved because he was a good chess player. It happened that the colonel in command like to play chess and there was no one else in the regiment who could play as well as Joe. Besides, the colonel liked Joe's good humor, and admired his mind. So he made Joe his orderly. Soon after that they left camp and there was plenty of fighting.

In another year the Union Army won the war and the soldiers who were left went home. This time Joseph thought he'd better go to New York where he supposed there would be more chances to get a job. The United States Government did nothing for the veterans of the Civil War until years later when Joseph no longer needed it. In 1865, when the war ended, there were thousands of ex-soldiers looking for jobs. Those who had trades or some experience got work. But Joseph didn't have a chance. He had no trade and his English was still pretty poor. He lived for a while on the few dollars he had saved from his pay as a soldier, thirteen dollars a month.

One day, he sat on a bench in a park in New York not knowing what to do next. He sat there in his old uniform. It was worn almost to rags and he needed a shave. He counted the few pennies he had left. Like many Europeans he was fussy about having his shoes shined. He had enough money for that, so he got up and walked to a shoe-shining place, but the man would not let him in. "The way you look, you'll drive away my customers," he said. Joseph went back to the bench. He was cold; someone had stolen his Army overcoat.

He couldn't know, as he sat there, that the time would come when across this very square there would be a tall building with a golden dome that was to be known as the Pulitzer Building. He could not know that

he, Joseph Pulitzer, would own that building and that his mighty newspaper, the *New York World*, would be published there.

Not dreaming any of this, sitting on that park bench, he made up his mind to get away from New York. He thought the city of St. Louis would be a better place for a young man starting out. Besides, some joker told him that there weren't any Germans in St. Louis and that he would learn English better there. But St. Louis was full of Germans, some of them great men. This turned out to be just as well for Joseph.

He hadn't enough money for train fare. So he did what many a poor workman did; he "rode the rails." On a dark moonless night, he slipped into the railroad yards across the Hudson River and lay down on the underbody of a railroad car. There he hung on until he saw that the train was getting into a station. Then he jumped off and waited on the side away from the depot. Sometimes he crouched between two cars and once he was almost crushed when they

231

banged together. When he was in luck he could climb into an empty express car. It was all very dangerous, but not as dangerous as it would be now because there were no electric wires or connections in that day.

When at last he jumped off in St. Louis' dingy railroad yard, he was covered with soot and his face was black with coal dust. And then he found that between the station and the city, three great rivers meet, the Missouri, the Mississippi, and the Ohio. They were much too wide to swim. Every cent of his money was gone. He did not have even a penny which was the fare for crossing the rivers on a ferry.

He was hungry and he was shivering with cold. The lights of St. Louis looked like the promised land to him, but how could he reach them? A ferry-boat came into the slip. Joseph called out and asked if there was any way he could earn his way across the ferry. The ferry man asked if he could fire a boiler. He said yes, though he had never done it. All night he poured coal into the fiery furnace. And that is how Joseph Pulitzer, who was later to become one of the world's greatest publishers, reached the city of St. Louis.

He had many odd jobs after that, each for a short time. He was a gate-keeper for the ferry; he unloaded freight from the river boats; he was a "mule skinner" for one day. For another day he was a waiter, but he was nervous and he lost that job when he dropped a steak on a customer's head.

Through it all he found hours to spend at the library. And no matter how little he earned, he put some aside each week. And he would always pay for his room and board ahead of time. That made him feel safe enough to look for a better job.

He took one where he was in greater danger than he had been during the war. The Atlantic and Pacific Railroad sent him on a legal errand to every county in the state of Missouri. It sounded safe enough. But far from it. Joseph had to go through long stretches of wilderness and the country was overrun with bandits, like Jesse James and his brothers. But he made good at this job and after that things went better. He made friends through his chess playing and through these friends he got a job on a German magazine.

Then came a big year for him. He had been in the United States for four years and now the great future that lay before him opened its door. It began when, without his even asking for it, a friend got him a job as a reporter on a German newspaper. "But why do they choose me? I am unknown, I have no luck. Why do they give me this important job? It seems almost like a dream," he said.

But it was no dream. He loved the work, though it was hard. His working day was from ten in the morning until two the next morning.

He was still thin, tall, and gaunt. His English was still not perfect and the reporters on the other papers played tricks on him. They sent him out on wild false tips to out-of-the-way places. But he always laughed at their tricks. He was good-humored and full of fun and jokes. He was bold and he always managed to be on the spot when things happened. He would come running, with no coat or collar, with a pencil in one hand and a note-book in the other.

He had so many news "scoops" that the editors of American newspapers began to say to their young reporters, "You'd better

stop kidding Joey and try to imitate him instead. We're tired of getting our news by translating Joey's stories from the German paper."

One of these papers was the *St. Louis Post and Dispatch*, later called the *Post-Dispatch*. Joe heard it was for sale. Its machinery was broken, and it had few readers. Joe took it over and built it into one of the great papers of the United States. He worked so hard that he had a breakdown and, for a rest, he went back to Europe to see his mother.

Joseph now began to play a big part in politics. Under his leadership the *Post-Dis-*

patch fought the cause of the weak. People in and out of St. Louis read his paper. In Arkansas, in Tennessee, and in other states they waited for Joe's newspaper.

Joseph Pulitzer moved on swiftly to bigger success. He had grown a reddish Vandyke beard and a mustache, so his face seemed to have a better shape. He was no longer a figure to laugh at. He was a powerful and able newspaper publisher. But he was not yet a rich man. Yet when he heard that the *New York World* was for sale, he wanted it. Like the *Post-Dispatch*, the *World* had been a failure. Pulitzer bought it and built it up into one of the most powerful newspapers in the world. It was a fighting paper. Pulitzer hated tyranny. He fought against too much power for the President of the United States and fought for more power for Congress and the states because he said that was true democracy. He opened the pages of the *World* to many a great fight for liberty.

The *New York World* became a smashing success, and Pulitzer was now a millionaire. But his eyesight grew worse. He liked to play cards but he had to have special cards made with very large figures so he could see them. His chessmen and board also had to be made larger than the usual sets. He grew slowly blind and he had to have his secretaries read even his own paper to him. He looked handsome and dignified in his great sweeping overcoat and a big soft hat. But he was ill as well as blind. He had a yacht built for himself in Scotland just the way he wanted it. The yacht was magnificent, 300 feet over all. On the main deck there was a dining-room, a music-room, and a sitting-room for Mr. Pulitzer. For his crew of forty-five there was a gymnasium.

He said, "I love this boat. In a house I am lost in my blindness, always fearful of falling downstairs. Here the narrow companionways give me safe guidance and I can find my way about alone."

He no longer went to his office. Far off from the hurry and excitement of his newspapers, Joseph Pulitzer wanted to leave behind him something that would last a long time. He thought out a plan to make newspapers better, not just his own but newspapers everywhere. So he planned a college that would teach journalism. Up to that time, most newspapermen had learned their business while they were working at it. Now he wanted to prepare them for their life work in the way a doctor or a lawyer is prepared in a college. He offered one million eight hundred thousand dollars to Columbia University in New York for such a school. But the trustees of the University said no, it wouldn't work. Later on, wiser heads at Columbia accepted the gift. And the Columbia School of Journalism was built. It has become a large and powerful college, and there are now schools of journalism in many places.

But Joseph Pulitzer did more than that. He left money to send poor boys to college both in America and in Europe. He set aside half a million dollars to be used for prizes. Each year there would be prizes for the best book of the year, the best play, the best poem, the best cartoon, the best news story, the best editorial and many more. They are known as the Pulitzer Prizes and greatly coveted.

And so the tall, gangling Jewish immigrant, though he is dead, is still doing great work for the newspapers and the talented people of the United States.

Parks and Homes in Place of Slums

JACOB RIIS

By Catherine Cate Coblentz

JACOB RIIS was born in Denmark, but when he was little more than a boy, he decided to go to America.

Before he was allowed to land in this country, he was asked many questions, as all immigrants are. One of the questions was, "How much money do you have?"

Jacob had forty dollars, which the people of the small town in Denmark had given him. That was all he had besides his fare in the steerage, for Jacob's family did not have much money. His father was a teacher.

After he came to America, Jacob thought a good deal about the questions he had been asked when he came knocking at America's gate. "It would have been much wiser if I had been asked what I brought in my head, rather than how much I had in my pockets," he decided. "They should have asked me whether I was bringing with me to America a love of the heroes of the part of Europe from which I came. The heroes a man has in his heart are a good measure of the kind of citizen he will be."

He thought about the men he admired. Finally he wrote a book about his heroes. The last two in the book seem especially important, because we can see how Riis learned from them, how they became part of his own measure of citizenship.

The next to the last hero in the book was a Swede, Carl von Linné, more generally spoken of now as Linnaeus. Linnaeus loved and studied flowers and made it possible for people all over the world to learn about them. Riis calls him the King of the Flowers.

The last hero in the book was Niels Finsen. He was born in Iceland. He became interested in light. He saw how a cat always moved out of the northern shadow and slept in the sun. He discovered that he felt better and could do more in a well-lighted room than in a dark and gloomy one. Niels Finsen was not a strong man, and many who are as ill as he was for most of his life would not have tried to help other people. But Niels Finsen did. He carried on researches and before he died he was able to find a cure for a terrible skin disease which was widespread in Denmark, a disease so awful it was called the Latin name for wolf—or lupus. Even invalids can be heroes.

But Finsen's great work was not done until after Riis had come to America. Riis heard of him through letters he had from home.

There was one hero, however, whom Riis did not include in his book and that was a storybook hero. His name was Lumpy Dumpy, and he is found in a story written by Hans Christian Andersen, the Danish writer. In the story, a little pine tree overheard people talking about Lumpy Dumpy. The tree didn't hear much about him, only that Lumpy Dumpy was a clumsy lout, and

JACOB AUGUST RIIS. Writer and journalist. Born in Denmark, 1849. Came to New York, 1870. Did much to improve conditions in slums and tenements. Introduced parks and playgrounds. Author of *The Making of an American* and other books. Died in 1914.

fell downstairs, but that it didn't matter really, for in the end he got the Princess after all.

Now Jacob Riis was rather short, and he was nearsighted. So, it is altogether possible that as a boy, he sometimes felt rather like a clumsy lout himself. And probably he even stumbled and fell downstairs. But we do know that Jacob Riis always said the pine tree story was a favorite of his, and that he loved a Princess—that is, a girl whom he thought as fair and as far beyond him as a Princess could have been.

He was told, however, that he had no chance of winning her. And so when he went to America he thought he might never see her again. But he carried her picture with him in a locket, which he wore hidden beneath his shirt. Her name was Elizabeth.

After he came to America, Jacob Riis had a hard life. His forty dollars were soon gone. And he had terrible experiences at different jobs. He worked in a coal mine in Pennsylvania a whole day and was paid only sixty cents. He picked cucumbers until he could not stand the hot sun any longer. He worked on a clay bank, and his employer did not pay him at all. He toiled as a hired man. He was often hungry. Sometimes he didn't have a penny.

Then just when things were at their very worst, Jacob Riis found a friend. It was only a little dog, but in a strange country it meant a lot to Jacob to have a dog wag his tail in a friendly fashion. To be chosen as a friend by a dog shows that one is a pretty fine fellow after all, he thought.

One night, followed by his dog, Jacob went to a police station. In those days in New York there was almost no place for a man without money to find a night's shel-

ter except in these police lodging basements. And men did not go to these unless the weather was too bad for them to stay outside. The shelters were dark, filthy basements with wooden planks for beds. You made the bed simply by turning the plank over. The shelters were filled with thieves and pickpockets, as Jacob had good reason to find out. For in the morning he discovered that the locket with Elizabeth's picture had been stolen from him during the night.

When he complained of what had happened, the policeman put him outside the building. His little dog was there waiting. He had waited all night. When he saw his master being thrust forth, the dog growled, and one of the attendants seized the dog and flung it aside so roughly that it was killed.

Jacob Riis never forgot that night and that morning. He determined that his little American dog should not have died in vain.

Brighter days were ahead for Riis, for he finally found a job for which he was suited, a job on a newspaper where he could write about human beings. At last he sent a letter to Elizabeth in Denmark, asking her a very important question. And Elizabeth wrote back, "Yes." So Jacob Riis married his Princess. And they lived happily in America.

But now that he was happy, Jacob Riis did not forget the days of suffering he had known. For one thing, his work for the newspaper kept him from forgetting. He was a reporter for one of the most crowded districts in New York City—a place called Mulberry Bend. And every day he saw much and terrible suffering.

He wrote many newspaper articles about what he saw. By this time Jacob Riis himself had a home in the country, and his children used to gather flowers for their

father to take into the city with him. The children on Mulberry Street clustered about the newspaper reporter on his way to work, begging for just one flower.

So Riis wrote in his paper about their eagerness for flowers. Somehow that story reached people's hearts, and they began sending flowers in bouquets, boxes, barrels, even whole wagonloads of them. Riis and the rest of the newspapermen gave them away. So for a time Riis was himself a sort of King of the Flowers in New York's slums.

But flowers were not enough. Jacob Riis wanted green grass and sunlight and air for the people of the slums. He wanted the crowded buildings, where whole families slept on the floors of a single room, torn down. Many of these buildings were dangerous, with rickety stairs and no fire escapes. He wanted—oh, how he wanted!—the terrible police lodging basements done away with.

Finally he wrote a book called *How the Other Half Lives*. Day after day, in the newspaper, Riis had been telling these things about life in the slums. But it was not until people read the book, read all the stories, that they began to understand.

One of the people who read the book had, like Riis, known a personal struggle. Only his struggle had been to gain health. After this man read the book, he put on his hat and went at once to Jacob Riis's office. But the newspaper reporter was out, hunting other stories to write. So the visitor left his card. On the back he had written:

"I have read your book, and I have come to help."

The note was signed *Theodore Roosevelt*.

Theodore Roosevelt was not an important man at that time. But he promised Jake Riis, as he always called him, that if he ever did have sufficient power, he would see that reforms were made.

Not long after that Theodore Roosevelt became President of the Police Commission. He lived up to his promise, and things began to happen at Mulberry Bend, and in other slum sections of New York.

Night after night Theodore Roosevelt and Jake Riis went through the slums, the newspaper reporter showing the new President of the Police Commission all the horrible places he knew so well.

And when Roosevelt was shown a police lodging room such as his friend had told him of, he asked, "Did they do that to you?" Then he shut his fists together and fairly hissed through his teeth, "I will smash them tomorrow."

Nobody knows what Riis said. Perhaps it was "Hallelujah." We know he thought of his little dead dog and of other slum victims.

Anyway, Riis and Roosevelt went on, inspecting the crowded tenements, and every crime-ridden hole Riis had written about, every new one he found.

And things began to improve. Policemen caught sleeping on their beat became very wide awake. And the terrible police lodging basements were banished. Buildings which were dangerous to live in were condemned and torn down. Flashlight photography came in, and Riis took pictures night after night which helped spread the truth.

Slowly but surely the Mulberry slum was disappearing. But it was still a long while before Jake's dreams of parks and playgrounds came true. Yet come true they did. Mulberry Bend Park appeared, with sunshine and air and green grass for children and their parents to enjoy, and green trees to shade them from the hottest sun.

Next, Theodore Roosevelt became Governor of New York. He went into the homes where people toiled at sweatshop wages, and saw little children sitting hour after hour making paper flowers for sale. He learned how long grown-ups must work to make barely enough money to live on.

More reforms came to New York State. Old buildings were torn down. Playgrounds and parks seemed to spring up over night. And with the coming of light and air and hope, there was new interest in hospitals and in the well-being of people, who before this had not been considered very much.

Jake Riis' American hero, Theodore Roosevelt, became Vice-President of the United States. Reforms, started in one city, one state, were spreading through the nation.

Many people expect their country to give them a great deal. Some people are glad to give free and voluntary service to that country. Jacob Riis was one who gave. He gave

beauty and air and light to what had been the dreariest, ugliest section of the city he lived in. He opened the eyes of other people, so that they too gave these things.

Jacob Riis himself never held any important office. He was not interested in position or in honors. He was doing for others what the little mongrel dog had done for him, being a good friend. He was helping those who could not help themselves.

Riis was one of those who helped organize the Boy Scouts of America. Theodore Roosevelt said that when he preached citizenship, he could turn to Jacob Riis as an example of what he had been preaching. Jacob Riis was one the best citizens this country ever had. It was a good thing for us that he chose to come to America.

And Denmark was so proud that Jacob Riis had been born there that the Danish King sent him a golden cross. It was the old crusaders' cross, which crusaders from Denmark wore when they left their country to go to Jerusalem. Jacob Riis was certainly a good crusader.

His Life Was a Field of Honor

WILFRID GRENFELL

By Rosemary Nicolais

WILFRID GRENFELL was born on a winter's day in 1865 in a big old house on the banks of the River Dee in the West of England. This was just the place for an adventure-loving boy to grow up in. He was only eight years old when he started going off all day exploring the fields and streams in the neighborhood.

One summer afternoon he and his older brother Algernon were walking home after a long day on the water with some fishermen, and they were talking about boats.

"If we could only have a boat of our own," said Wilfrid, "we could go out whenever we liked and wherever we liked."

That night at supper Algernon told his father he and Wilfrid wanted a boat.

"You do?" Mr. Grenfell replied. "Well, you can have one. You can have any boat you can build yourselves."

The boys looked at each other. Did he mean it? Could they really build a boat? How did you go about it? They were too excited to sleep much that night, and early next morning they were down at the shore examining boats to see how they were made.

The village carpenter gave them a few tips about what wood and nails to use. A big empty room at the back of the house became a shipyard. Soon the boat was finished. It was a funny-looking tub. But Mr. Grenfell suggested, "Give it a coat of red paint and it'll do."

They called their boat the *Reptile*. It carried them on wonderful voyages of discovery. They tied up at any spot on the river that looked promising, and went duck-hunting and oyster-fishing. They collected sea-shells and birds' eggs and butterflies.

Their father gave them one important rule to follow: "Never take the life of any living creature," he said, "except for food, or for study when that is the only way to learn what it is important to know, or in self-defense." The boys agreed.

The time came when Wilfrid had to leave home and the River Dee and the *Reptile* and go to boarding-school. But, to his delight, after a year or so at school his father told him, "You seem to learn more at home than you do at school. I'm going to engage a tutor to teach you here."

A few years later, when the boy was ready for college, his father asked him, "What do you want to do, Wilfrid, after you graduate?"

His son replied, promptly, "I'd like to go tiger-hunting in India, Father."

"A man can't earn a living hunting tigers," his father laughed.

One day Wilfrid ran into a friend of the family, a doctor. He was a man of good plain sense who thought being a good doctor was a very satisfying kind of life. They walked towards his home.

"I hear you haven't the ghost of an idea

WILFRED THOMASON GRENFELL. Doctor, missionary, explorer. Born in England, 1865. Devoted most of his life to providing for the needs of Labrador fishermen. Built and equipped the first hospitals there. Wrote many books, including *A Labrador Doctor* and *Religion in Everyday Life*. Died 1940.

what you want to do next?" the doctor said.

"No, sir."

The doctor looked at the boy sideways. He had watched him grow up. He had seen him run with a football as if nothing else in life mattered. He had seen him sit patiently for hours in the rain to observe a rare bird, or tread swiftly and silently through the fields with a butterfly net.

"If you could direct all that intelligence and energy of yours properly," he said at last, "you might do something big. You have a fine muscular body. Your eyes are clear and honest."

Then the doctor began to talk about his own work. The boy listened, and his interest and wonder grew. Here was a man who spent his life driving from house to house in all weathers, putting splintered bones together, poulticing, bandaging wounds, and sometimes bringing back to life a heart that had almost stopped beating! There was a kind of magic in that, Wilfrid thought, much more wonderful than hunting tigers.

He followed the doctor back to his office and saw on a shelf a jar containing a greyish shapeless object in alcohol.

"That's a human brain," the doctor said, and he went on to explain the marvellous way the brain telegraphs messages to all parts of the body.

"I'm going to be a doctor," Wilfrid announced to his family as soon as he reached home that night. His father breathed a sigh of relief.

Wilfrid Grenfell became a doctor and surgeon. But his eager and enthusiastic nature would not let him rest content with being a fine surgeon. He felt he must do what he could to help his patients in other ways. When he was still training in a hospital in the slums of London, he started clubs for boys and girls. He even found time to take hundreds of them to the country and on sailing trips in a boat he bought especially for them.

His first job took him out to the cold North Sea off the East Coast of Britain, as doctor to the fishing fleet that stayed at sea for months at a time. There he not only mended broken bones and tended the sick fishermen but was ready to lend a hand at the ropes and man a boat when necessary.

A few years later he became doctor and life-long friend to the fishermen and their families off the ice-bound coasts of Labrador. That was a job that suited him perfectly. He stayed with it all his life.

The young doctor thought he knew, before he arrived, how difficult the work was going to be. Everyone he met told him discouraging stories.

"If ever a land warned men to keep off," said one friend, "Labrador does."

Another told him of the ships that were battered and torn to pieces by mountainous seas. "Fishermen drown, freeze, and starve to death up there with no one to hold out a helping hand."

Dr. Grenfell found these tales to be true, and the suffering of the fishermen in those frozen seas were far worse than anyone who had not seen them could believe. Yet the young doctor was not discouraged. Indeed Labrador was always beautiful to him, both because he loved the wild and terrible land itself, and because of its great need for his services.

His fee was sometimes nothing more than a tiny pat of butter, sometimes a sack of potatoes. But a look of thankfulness on a mother's face when her child grew well again was all the fee the good doctor wished.

During his sixteen years of hard but happy service, the fishermen's beloved doctor built them four hospitals and equipped a floating hospital, a ship named the *Strath-*

cona. The thought of these hospitals gave him comfort one day when he himself lay close to death on a raft of ice drifting helplessly out to sea.

This nearly fatal accident happened because the doctor was determined to save a little boy's life. Some men had come across the ice to tell him that this boy, who lived on the far side of a certain harbor, had hurt his leg badly, and his mother believed only Dr. Grenfell could save it. The doctor immediately loaded his dog sled with blankets, medicines, food, and firewood and set out on his long trip, in high spirits.

"Come on, Jack! Haul up, Brin, Moody, Jerry, Sue, Watch, Spy! Haul up!" he cried to the dogs.

It was a crisp sunny morning and the dogs needed very little urging. Jack, the little spaniel, ran on ahead setting the pace. By nightfall they had reached a small cottage and they rested there. Next morning, as they were setting out again, Grenfell heard what seemed to be a cracking of the ice. It began to snow too. He was disturbed, but not seriously. The ice was still thick even if there were a few cracks, and he would travel more slowly and carefully. A wind was blowing from the sea, and that, he thought, would keep the masses of loose ice from drifting apart.

Then Dr. Grenfell began to figure that the boy with the broken leg would stand a better chance if he arrived a few hours earlier than he was expected. He thought he could do that if he crossed the harbor to a small island near the middle instead of going all the way around it. It would take only four hours to get from the island to the boy's house. The doctor decided to risk it.

He reached the island safely and started

on the last four-hour stage of the journey.
Two, three, three-and-a-half hours! In only
half-an-hour now he would be there! But
suddenly the wind changed. Instead of
blowing the blocks of ice together, it blew
them apart, and out to sea. Dogs and sled
were marooned on an icepan, as these
masses of loose ice are called, and surrounded by gaps of icy black water.

The icepan began to sink. The doctor cut
the traces of the harness so that the dogs
would be able to swim. But not understanding what he wanted, they climbed back
onto the sinking icepan. Once more their
master pushed them off, but back they
climbed again. There was a larger icepan
not far off where they would be safer. But
no, they wouldn't go near it. At last little

Jack, the spaniel, turned his brown eyes up
to his master's face, seeming to ask "What is
it you want from us?" The doctor threw a
piece of ice onto the big icepan, pointed to
it and shouted, "Over there, Jack!" And
after he had done this several times Jack
understood and dashed after the piece of ice
to safety. The other dogs swam after him
and their master followed.

The immediate danger was over. But as
the doctor looked about him he realized
that he and his dogs now faced other and
greater dangers.

The icepan was drifting out into the bay.
The bay was an isolated one that fishermen
never used, so there was scarcely any hope
of being seen. And even if someone did see
them no boat could be put out. It would be

243

ground to bits, because the wind kept pounding great masses of ice to and fro, smashing them against the rocks. Apart from all this, Dr. Grenfell thought, he himself would be frozen to death before long.

All the warm clothes he had brought with him had sunk with the sled, so he cut up a pair of seal boots he was wearing and tied them together to make a rough wind-breaker of them. But it wasn't enough.

His dogs nestled close to him. They would keep warm, anyway, in their heavy coats, he thought. He wondered whether it was more painful to freeze to death than to die of slow starvation. They would all die anyway.

A thought formed itself in his mind. If he had the skins of some of his dogs he could be warm in a moment. As for the dogs—surely they would prefer to die quickly rather than wait who knows how long to die of hunger on a raft of ice in the end.

He seemed to hear his father's voice saying, "A man may kill an animal, if he must, to save his own life." Quickly, before his courage failed, he killed three of his sled dogs, as painlessly as possible, and skinned them.

He was warm at last in the deep furred wraps, and was suddenly overcome by drowsiness. As he dozed, surrounded by his four remaining dogs, he thought of the hospitals and the hospital ship, the *Strathcona*, that he had built, and was glad he had been able to complete them for his Labrador friends before he left them.

Waking with a start he saw that the ice-pan was still being driven out to sea. He had made no effort to signal for help because there had been nothing to signal with. His matches were wet, so he couldn't light a fire. But now that he was warm, he could take off his woollen shirt, and use it as a flag. He could make some sort of flagpole out of the bones of the slain dogs.

That was the strange signal a group of fishermen saw at dawn after a night-long search for their beloved doctor.

"I'm terribly sorry to have given you so much trouble," said Grenfell to his rescuers. His voice was low, and the men hardly recognized him, his face was so old.

Little Jack, the spaniel, jumped all over the men trying to make them understand his part in the grim adventure. But Grenfell couldn't rejoice as the others did. He kept thinking of the dogs he had had to sacrifice. When he recovered from the illness caused by his long exposure, he had a bronze plate made to hang on the living-room wall of his house. On it he had inscribed:

"To the Memory of Three Noble Dogs,
Moody, Watch, and Spy,
Whose Lives Were Given for Me on the Ice,
April 21, 1908."

The boy for whom Dr. Grenfell had risked his life was brought to the hospital by boat as soon as the ice melted. The doctor was very happy when he was told the boy would not lose his leg.

The name of Wilfrid Grenfell became famous all over the world. King George V of England made him "Sir Wilfrid Grenfell" in 1928. But to all the fishermen in Labrador he was still "The Doctor," and so, with respect and affection, they thought of him to the day of his death. A rock above his grave in Newfoundland is inscribed with his name, age, and the words "Life is a Field of Honor."

Honor was like a star towards which Wilfrid Grenfell aimed all his life long.

Champion of Homeless Boys

FATHER EDWARD JOSEPH FLANAGAN

By Elma Martens

A GRIMY little boy came into the kitchen from his play and sniffed. "Mmmmm—! Fresh bread! May I have a piece, Mother?"

"One piece, Edward," answered his mother. "It's almost too fresh to cut. But wash up first."

Edward went to wash. "There's no water," he said, returning with a pail. "I'll pull some up—"

"You're not to carry it in alone," his mother called after him.

"I'll help him," offered his sister Nellie, and followed him out to the well.

Their father, just in from the fields, appeared in the doorway. "You'll spoil the boy, Mother," he objected.

Mrs. Flanagan shook her head. "I worry about him," she said.

Mrs. Flanagan never could forget how near they had come to losing the boy when he was not yet two. Very ill with pneumonia, for days he had just lain quietly on his bed, not moving and apparently not breathing. They thought he was dead, but presently he sighed, ever so little. Loving care had nursed him back to health.

Now, when Edward came in again, clean and freshly combed, there was a huge glass of milk on the table and a thick crust of bread, generously spread with rich butter from Nellie's churn.

EDWARD JOSEPH FLANAGAN. Roman Catholic priest. Born in Ireland, 1886. Came to America 1904. Pastor in Omaha, Nebraska, 1913–17. Founded Home for Boys, Omaha, 1917. Boys' Home—farm and village—incorporated as Boys Town. Died 1948.

"Come along to look after the sheep," his father said, when Edward had finished eating.

"And the cows, too," answered Edward, as he hurried to join his father.

Edward loved these walks. His father would tell stories of Irish heroes and saints.

"Do you think anyone could be really great now, like Saint Patrick was in the old days, Father?" Edward asked earnestly.

"I'm sure of it," answered his father, "but the good Lord picks those He would make great. If you work hard and honestly and pray for guidance, the greatness will take care of itself."

Edward Joseph Flanagan was born on his father's farm in Ireland, on July 13, 1886. His early illness had left him frail and small. When he was old enough, he went to school with his older brothers and sisters, eleven of them in all. Edward looked scarcely able to carry his load of books as he trudged the two miles to the country school.

After Edward had finished school, he went north to Summer Hill College in Sligo, and after four years graduated with high honors. He had taken a lively interest in athletics and sports while at Summer Hill and had grown tall and wiry.

Meanwhile, his brother Patrick had been graduated from a seminary in Dublin and had been ordained as a priest. Patrick went to America to establish a parish in Omaha, Nebraska.

Edward was determined to become a priest too. His sister Nellie was then living in New York, and when she came home for a visit she suggested that Edward come to the United States and study there. He came to America in 1904 at the age of eighteen, and enrolled at Mount Saint Mary's College at Emmitsburg, Maryland. He received his Bachelor of Arts degree in the spring of 1906.

That fall he enrolled at St. Joseph's Seminary in Dunwoodie, New York, for his Master's degree. Here he again developed pneumonia and was in bed for months. Still, he continued with his studies and completed his term in spring. A stubborn cough persisted, and the doctor ordered a change of climate.

Edward thought of his brother Patrick, who had a parish in Omaha. He persuaded his parents, who had come to America, to move there too.

The prairie climate proved beneficial to Edward, and in August the Bishop sent him to Rome for further preparation.

In Rome the halls, classrooms, and dormitories were unheated. Before winter was completely over, Edward's cough had returned, worse than ever. Soon he was on his way back to Omaha.

There was nothing to do but give up his studies, at least for the present. In line with the doctor's orders, his family urged him to put his books away.

The warm dry Nebraska summer worked its miracle a second time. Edward slowly regained his strength. He took walks around the neighborhood, and long streetcar rides through the city, to get acquainted with his surroundings.

Coming home from one of these jaunts, he announced, "I'm going to work in South Omaha."

His father and mother were surprised and exclaimed in unison, "At the stockyards?"

"Yes," said Edward, "in the office of one of the packing plants."

For a year Edward worked at the packing

plant, and by the end of the following summer he was ready to take up his studies again.

This time the Bishop sent him to the Jesuit University at Innsbruck, in the lovely Austrian Alps. His health improved rapidly in the dry inland climate. Edward completed his studies without further difficulties and was ordained as a priest at Innsbruck on July 26, 1912.

He returned to Omaha in August and celebrated his first Solemn High Mass at Father Patrick's Holy Angels Church. For three years he was assistant pastor at St. Patrick's Church and for one at St. Philomena's Church, in Omaha.

Father Flanagan spent all his spare time getting acquainted with people, especially poor people or people in trouble. In 1913 he turned his attention to the vagrants. Because of poor harvests that year, the men who migrated from farm to farm helping to harvest crops were unable to make even a bare living. They had no homes, no jobs, no money.

Father Flanagan started by giving them food. Soon he opened what he called a "Workingmen's Hotel," in an abandoned building. Here he offered food and a place to sleep free of charge to any man who needed help. He asked a dime from those who could pay.

Father Flanagan hunted out jobs for them, tried to put them back on their feet, to bring back their self-respect. With a few he succeeded, but the majority drifted back to their vagrant habits.

"Aw, Father, I'm too old to change my ways," was the common excuse when he tried to appeal to them.

Father Flanagan began to question all of them about their past, their childhood, their homes. It was always the same story. "Home? When I was a boy there was no one to care whether I did an honest day's work or not."

This was the keynote. "No one to care." Father Flanagan realized it was the children with no one to care for them that he must reach and prevent from becoming bitter, hardened men.

Almost four years passed before Father Flanagan made up his mind what to do. It was 1917, the year of World War I. With the war work there were jobs for all now. Father Flanagan closed his Workingmen's Hotel.

The following day, as a result of his eloquent appeal, he secured permission from the Bishop to establish a home for boys. He was released from his duties at St. Philomena's Church, but the Bishop told him he could give him no financial help whatsoever.

His next problem was to find a house which he could use. He located one on a hill at the edge of Omaha's business district. The owner wanted ninety dollars for one month's rent. He did not have it, but by persistence Father Flanagan was able to make the payment. No one knew who loaned him the money for this first payment, and Father Flanagan never would tell.

It was December 12, 1917, when Father Flanagan moved into the house with five boys. The Archbishop sent two nuns and a novice to help him out.

By Christmas their family had grown to twenty-five, and more came each day. There were boys of all faiths and creeds. As winter melted into spring it became obvious that they would have to move. They had outgrown their house on the hill.

In June they moved into the home of the German-American Club. It was inactive then on account of the war. Here there was room for 150 boys and sufficient grounds for a good-sized garden.

Instead of sending the boys out to schools, Father Flanagan brought teachers into the Home. He also organized handicraft classes and hobby groups. The boys had always sung together, even from the beginning, and Father Flanagan had often sung with them. Now he organized a choir and encouraged the boys to start a little band.

"As soon as we can really play something," he promised, "we'll have a parade."

One fine day they took their instruments and had a parade up and down the streets of downtown Omaha. The boys played lustily, if not always tunefully. The little band marching along behind the tall priest soon became a familiar sight to the citizens of Omaha. There was something appealing about them that made people ask to do something for them, even when it could be only a little.

As a consequence, small glass-front banks appeared beside cash registers in drug stores, grocery stores, and elsewhere. They were captioned "For Father Flanagan's Boys," and into them went the nickels, dimes, and pennies of the many who wanted to help out but had little to give.

In 1918 Father Flanagan received his final American citizenship papers.

"You see," he told his boys, "I first had to prove myself worthy of being a citizen of this great country of ours. You were born here, so you are citizens automatically. But you should never forget that it is a privilege that many people have to earn first. You must always live up to that privilege."

For about three years they lived in the German-American Club, striving and growing, until in 1921 they had again outgrown their quarters.

"This time," said Father Flanagan, "we are going to where we can stay put. What we need is a farm."

In October, 1921, Father Flanagan, a small teaching staff, and his 150 boys moved to Overlook Farm, a rolling tract of land ten miles west of Omaha. As there was no money for building, wooden barracks were erected for the boys. Father Flanagan used a garage for his quarters.

Now Father Flanagan's friends went into action. Headed by two prominent businessmen, they organized a drive among the business and professional men of Omaha for a building program. Within a year enough money was raised to build the first permanent building, a five-story brick structure. The next year Father Flanagan moved his boys from the wooden barracks to the new house.

Once they were established in their permanent quarters, new trades were taught, and the farm program was developed. Music, athletics, and sports were important parts of the training. Both lay teachers and nuns comprised the teaching staff.

In addition to the regular curriculum, religious instruction was an important part of the educational program. Protestant ministers instructed the Protestant boys. The Jewish boys were taken to synagogues in town by special arrangement. Into the hearts of all the boys there crept a deep and lasting affection for Father Flanagan.

Father Flanagan's heart went out to every boy in need. When he read in the papers about a boy in trouble for theft or even

murder, he would reach for the telephone, or for pen and paper.

"Send the boy to me," he would say. "Please don't send him to prison or the reformatory. Send him here and I'll straighten him out."

His vigorous defense of boys in trouble gave most people the mistaken impression that his boys were mostly delinquents. As a matter of fact, most of his charges were merely boys suddenly orphaned, whose relatives could not or would not take them; or boys whose widowed mothers could not afford to support their families; or simply boys who had never known the security of a real home. They came from every state in the Union and from many other countries.

In an effort to tell people the real aims and purposes of his Home, Father Flanagan wrote articles for magazines and newspapers, lectured to civic and educational groups, and spoke over the radio.

As his ideas became better known and understood, Father Flanagan came to be much in demand as a speaker. His statement, "There is no such thing as a bad boy," became famous. "Expect only the best from a boy," he would say, "and he will live up to your expectations."

The Home gradually became known as "Boys Town." In 1936 it was incorporated as a village. It was, indeed, a small town. It had its own post office, power plant, shops, and a population of two hundred and seventy-five people.

Under Father Flanagan's watchful eye the boys now learned self-government. They learned to hold elections, to make just laws as needed, and to enforce these laws.

"The boys must learn," declared Father Flanagan, "that laws must be obeyed. They also should know that they have a right to help in the making of such laws."

The government of Boys Town is patterned after that of the city of Omaha. From among their own number the boys elect a mayor, four councilmen, and seventeen commissioners. These officers have charge of Boys Town.

In 1946 so many applications were received in behalf of boys left fatherless by World War II that another building program was started. When these buildings were completed, one thousand boys could be accommodated.

Under the new program there was to be an entirely new high school section with its own administration and welfare building, dining hall, music hall, cottages for dwellings, field house, and a trade building where nine major trades would be taught.

There was an orchestra too, and no civic parade in Omaha was complete without the Boys Town Band which had such humble beginnings. The Boys Town Choir has appeared in performances throughout the United States, including one in Carnegie Hall.

One would think Father Flanagan might have relaxed a bit by this time, but not so. In April of 1947 he was asked by the Government to go to Japan and Korea for consultations regarding their homeless youth problems. He found the need appalling. Many youth centers were started as a result of Father Flanagan's recommendations.

Father Flanagan returned to Boys Town in July. Less than a year later came another request for a similar mission to Austria and Germany.

"This country has been good to me," he said. "If there is a service I can render it, I cannot refuse."

He left on February 26, 1948. Though the situation in Europe looked hopeless, he held endless conferences, worked out plans, and made recommendations.

In the midst of all this activity, Father Flanagan was stricken with a heart attack. Within two hours he died.

Father Flanagan rests now in the lovely chapel, in Omaha, as was his wish. Here his boys can visit him. The marble slab bears the simple inscription:

Father Flanagan—Founder of Boys Town
Lover of Christ and Man
July 13, 1886–May 15, 1948

Deaf, Dumb and Blind, She Spoke to the World

HELEN KELLER

By Rosemary Nicolais

HELEN was the first baby in the family of Captain and Mrs. Keller of Tuscumbia, Alabama. She was a very clever little baby. At the age of six months she began to talk. She said, "How d'ye?" to visitors, and cried out for "tea, tea, tea!" or "wah-wah!" when she was thirsty.

Then, after nineteen months of life as a healthy happy baby, Helen became very ill. She recovered, but never again saw anything or heard any sound.

It was very hard for the little girl. For a very short time she remembered the sound of her mother's voice and what trees and flowers looked like. But these memories faded, and she was shut up in a pitch-dark, absolutely silent world. She couldn't see her father and mother. She didn't know what she looked like herself. She couldn't run about and play. She could only hold on to her mother's skirts and try to make signs for what she wanted to say. She had to feel the chairs and tables and her toys with her hands to find out what they were.

Sometimes Helen got into violent tempers during those early years. It is easy to see why. She was a very intelligent, quick-witted little girl and wanted to do and say a great many things. She said later that she felt as if invisible hands were holding her. She tried hard but she could never escape from these invisible hands. She didn't even know it was wrong to get into rages. No one was able to explain right and wrong to a little girl who couldn't see or hear, any more than they could explain sunshine.

The Kellers tried to make their little girl happy, but sometimes they lost hope. "What can we do?" Mrs. Keller exclaimed to Mr. Keller one day after Helen had had one of her tantrums. "She can't see us! She can't hear us! She can't speak to us!"

Yet Helen kept on trying to do things a seeing and hearing child could do. She dressed and undressed her dolls, folded their clothes and arranged them in neat piles, and in this way came to understand how to take care of her own clothes. She discovered that her mother always dressed with more care than usual when she expected guests; so one day, feeling the commotion of people arriving at the house, she hurried upstairs to change her clothes. After a while she appeared in the living-room with her face thickly powdered, a long veil covering her face and neck, and a bustle tied on behind. It was her idea of the way to make guests feel welcome. She looked very comical, but the visitors were deeply touched to think of her dressing up for them.

When Helen was about six years old, her parents took her to a famous eye-doctor in Baltimore. Of course the doctor couldn't give her back her sight, but he did some-

HELEN KELLER. Blind deaf-mute. Born in Tuscumbia, Alabama, 1880. Under the guidance of her beloved teacher, Anne Sullivan Macy, learned to read and write in several languages, developed fine literary style. Mastered the difficult art of speaking by mouth, and lectured on aid to the blind. Author of *Story of My Life* and other books. At 75 traveled on a good-will tour around the world with her secretary and friend, Polly Thompson. Died 1968.

thing she was grateful for to the end of her life. He introduced her mother and father to Dr. Alexander Graham Bell. Dr. Bell was the scientist who had invented the telephone, but he was almost as well known for his good work in educating the deaf. He took Helen on his knee and let her feel his watch. He understood exactly what she meant by her sign-talk and that made him her friend at once. And it was Dr. Bell who found Helen her wonderful teacher, Miss Anne Mansfield Sullivan who taught her to "speak" by hand-spelling and to understand that way too.

Miss Sullivan had been blind herself when she was a child, but she was lucky: doctors were able to give her back her sight. When she was older she went to the Perkins Institution for the Blind in Boston to learn how to teach blind children to read and take an active part in life.

It was the third of March, 1887, when Miss Sullivan arrived at the Kellers' little house in Tuscumbia. Helen Keller said some time afterwards that the third of March was her real birthday. Describing what happened that day, she said:

"I felt approaching footsteps. I stretched out my hand, trying to touch my mother. Some one took it, and I was caught up and held close in the arms of her who had come to reveal all things to me, and, more than all else, to love me."

Anne Sullivan understood from the start that little Helen didn't know what love was. Other little children can see love in their mothers' eyes, and hear all the loving words and tones parents and brothers and sisters use. But this little girl who could not see or hear had to learn about love in some other way. Her teacher began this lesson by giving her pupil a doll.

"D-o-l-l," Anne Sullivan spelled into Helen's hand. Helen learned the word at once. She ran to show her mother the doll and spell out the letters. She was proud and happy. But she still didn't know how to love the doll.

One day she grew angry at her teacher who kept trying to make her learn the word "water," so she threw her doll on the floor and broke it. Her teacher said nothing. She just swept the broken pieces into the fireplace and took Helen out into the sunshine.

On they went down a garden path to a well. It was covered with honeysuckle that the little blind child loved to smell. Anne Sullivan took Helen's hand and held it under the water-spout. At the same time she spelled into her other hand the word "w-a-t-e-r."

Anne Sullivan described what happened when her little pupil felt the wonderful cool water flow over her hand and learned the word "water" by the finger alphabet at the same time:

"A light came into her face. She spelled 'water' several times. Then she dropped to the ground and asked its name. I told her. She asked my name. I spelled that out. Just then the nurse brought Helen's little sister into the pump-house and Helen spelled 'baby' and pointed. All the way back to the house she was highly excited and learned the name of every object she touched. In a few hours she had learned thirty new words. Here are some of them: door, open, shut, give, go, come."

As soon as Helen reached the house, she remembered her doll and ran to pick up the pieces her teacher had swept into the fireplace. Her eyes filled with tears. She understood what she had done and was sorry.

Still she could not understand exactly what love was. But one day in the garden the meaning burst upon her.

"Is love the sweetness of flowers?" she asked her teacher.

"No."

"Is this love?" she asked, pointing to where the heat of the sun seemed to come from.

Anne Sullivan said no, that was not love.

Helen sat down under a tree, opened a box of beads she had brought with her, and began stringing them. She threaded two large beads, three small ones, and so on; but she kept making mistakes.

"Think!" Anne Sullivan spelled into her hand.

Helen turned her face up to her teacher's.

"In a flash," Anne Sullivan wrote in one of her letters home, "Helen understood something new and exciting. She realized that thinking was what she was doing when I said the word 'think'. Thinking, then, wasn't a *thing*, like water. It was something that went on inside your head."

The time had come, Anne Sullivan realized, for her to make little Helen understand something else—that love too was something that came from inside.

"You know about the clouds," she told Helen. "You cannot touch clouds. But they come down as rain, and the rain refreshes the flowers on a hot day. Well, it's the same with love. Love pours its sweetness into everything, and you feel that sweetness inside yourself.

"Next morning Helen woke up like a radiant fairy," Miss Sullivan wrote in her letter. "She flitted from object to object, asking the name of everything, and kissing me for gladness. My heart was full of joy."

So that was what love was! At last Helen knew. Suddenly she felt that there were threads she couldn't see—but no one else could see them either—binding her to all the people around her. She would never be alone any more.

Helen's love seemed to have no bounds. She was eager to reach out to people, animals, trees and flowers now that she knew they not only had names but could be loved. Anne Sullivan began to spell into her hand whole sentences, not merely words, and Helen learned them just as a baby learns to speak, only much faster. Her father and mother learned to spell into her hand and so did many of their friends, and soon Helen was hand-chattering all day long, asking so many questions that Anne Sullivan had to say, "No, I can't tell you anything more today." Then her teacher found her spelling words into her dog's paw, hoping she could teach *him* to talk to her.

At the same time Helen was learning to read. Her books were printed in Braille, letters made up of raised dots that blind people can read by touch. But her teacher's greatest surprise came when she found Helen busily writing letters. Her first letters read like baby-talk. But by the time she was ten years old she could write very pleasing letters. She wrote one to the famous Dr. Oliver Wendell Holmes who had visited her home some months before. Dr. Holmes thought it was a beautiful letter and had it printed in a magazine. It starts:

"Dear, Kind Poet:

I have thought of you many times since that bright Sunday when I bade you good-bye; and I am going to write you a letter because I love you. I am sorry you have no little children to play with you sometimes; but I think you are very happy with your books and your many friends."

Then Helen went on to tell her poet friend a story about a little blind boy, Jakey, "the sweetest little fellow you can imagine." And she told him she was studying about insects. "Butterflies," she wrote, "do not make honey for us, like the bees, but many of them are as beautiful as the flowers they light upon."

That same year, 1890, Helen made up her mind she was going to learn to speak with her mouth. She had heard of a deaf and dumb girl in Norway, Ragnhild Kaata, who had been taught to speak, and she was willing to work just as hard as Ragnhild had.

Anne Sullivan was not sure even her clever little Helen could be taught to use the spoken language the way seeing and hearing people do, but she was glad to let her try. She took her to Miss Sarah Fuller at Horace Mann School in Boston for lessons.

Miss Fuller's method of teaching was to pass her pupil's hand over her (Miss Fuller's) face, then put the child's fingers into her mouth so that she might feel the movement of the tongue and teeth and at the same time feel with the other hand how the jaw and the windpipe moved. She was delighted when Helen uttered her first sound almost like an echo.

A month after that first lesson Helen and Anne Sullivan were going home on a streetcar. Tears came to the eyes of the teacher who loved her little pupil so much when she spoke to her for the first time. Helen's voice was hollow and breathy, but the words were perfectly understandable. With what happiness she said, "I am not dumb now!"

Only the deaf and dumb person can understand the eagerness with which Helen talked from then on to her toys, to stones, trees, birds and animals. It was a special delight when her little sister, Mildred, came running at her call, and when dogs obeyed her voice.

Helen entered Radcliffe College when she was nineteen, and graduated with honors. Anne Sullivan went with her into the classroom and spelled the lectures into her hand. At home Helen tapped out on a typewriter all she remembered. She became a thoroughly well-educated young woman, able to speak several languages. She wrote *The Story of My Life* and other books, gave lectures that crowds of people came to hear, and had some of the most famous men and women of her time for friends.

Blind people have their own way of knowing color. To Helen Keller pink was a baby's cheek, or a soft breeze; gray was a shawl around the shoulders; brown was withered hands, warm and friendly, or leaf mold or the trunks of trees; lilac was kissing a face she loved; yellow was the sun.

It is a good thing to remember that after her teacher came to her, even as a child Helen enjoyed life. She rode a tandem bicycle, played chess and cards, and she saw the World's Fair in Chicago with Dr. Bell, and Dr. Bell arranged for her to be allowed to touch all the exhibits.

In 1914, when Helen was thirty-four, she realized that her dear Anne Sullivan was losing her sight again, and was no longer able to keep up with a young woman as strong and healthy as herself. She was heartbroken. But Anne Sullivan took things into her own hands. She looked about and found a young and capable secretary for Helen. Her name was Polly Thompson, and she came from Scotland. The two young women, Helen and Polly, took long, exciting trips together. They voyaged to Europe and the Far East, and everywhere they went Helen Keller made time to meet the blind and the deaf and help them. They were all her friends, and she was theirs. She loved especially to talk to children who couldn't see or hear. Their small fingers, spelling into her hand, were, she said, "like the wild flowers of conversation."

Helen liked to read people's lips by their vibration. She placed her middle finger on the nose of the person she was "talking" to, her forefinger on the lips, and her thumb on the throat. She found Franklin D. Roosevelt and Dwight D. Eisenhower very easy to understand by that method, and she enjoyed Mark Twain's jokes in that way too. The great operatic tenor, Enrico Caruso, sang for her with her hands on his face. The violinist, Jascha Heifetz, the poet Carl Sandburg, and many other famous people were happy to entertain this heroic woman who had done so much to overcome her own cruel handicaps, and to help others.

It was a great sorrow to Helen Keller when, in 1936, her old friend and teacher, Anne Sullivan, died. But Anne had lived long enough to receive the Roosevelt Medal for Cooperative Achievement, which had been awarded to Helen Keller and herself jointly that year.

Ten years later, Helen had another loss to bear. She and Polly Thompson were in Greece. They had gone there to help the men blinded in World War II. And the news came to them that Helen's house in Connecticut had burned to the ground. It was a great grief to Helen to lose her beau-

She
Proves
the
Wondrous
Talent
of
the
Mind
to
See
in the
Darkest
of
Ages

tiful home, but it grieved her even more to hear of another loss. She had spent years getting together notes and letters so that she could write a book about her beloved teacher. And every one of these papers had gone up in flames. She had to start all over again when she came back from Europe. But in 1955 the book *did* get published.

The approach of old age made very little difference to Helen Keller's interest in life and people. When she was seventy she and Polly Thompson went together on a tour of France and Italy. Five years later the two friends set out on a 40,000-mile journey through India, Pakistan, Burma, the Philippines, and Japan. But there was one thing she had to be more careful about as she grew older. She had to try to rest her hands.

Nobody's hands had ever had more work to do than Helen Keller's. They listened for her, they read for her, they told her where she was, and felt all the objects about her. And they did a great deal of typing for her. So naturally these busy hands tired.

All over the world men and women who took care of the blind and deaf loved Helen Keller for the help she was to them. Mrs. Eleanor Roosevelt said to her, "All people are part of your family." A famous sculptor who was an old friend of Helen's, Jo Davidson, said, "We are all good when we are with Helen."

Deaf, dumb, and blind, Helen Keller spoke to the world. And in gratitude and admiration the world listened and wondered and learned.

They Gave Their Lives That Others Might Live

THE FOUR CHAPLAINS OF WORLD WAR II

By Joanna Strong and Tom B. Leonard

THE soldiers in the ship sat up sharply in their bunks. The cry had just been heard, "German submarine ahead!" In tense silence the soldiers looked up, each one concealing as best he could the fear that gripped his heart.

Then, suddenly, the giant ship heaved and trembled as a torpedo cut a jagged, gaping hole in its side. With a roar, the water rushed into the hold. Then another torpedo struck—and another!

In desperate haste, the men of the U.S.S. *Dorchester* put on their life-jackets. When the order "Abandon ship!" boomed over the loudspeaker a few moments later, the decks were covered with a streaming swarm of men, struggling desperately into life-jackets, stumbling, shouting, running toward the life-boats. As an icy wind whistled through the masts and funnels, frightened men jumped overboard into the freezing North Atlantic.

But throughout the terrible confusion, four men calmly went among the soldiers, quieting their fears, encouraging them when they were afraid to jump, steering them to life-boats, and helping into life-jackets boys whose hands were too nervous to fasten the strings themselves.

Who were these men of mercy? They were four chaplains of the U.S. Army— one John Washington, a Catholic priest; another, Alexander P. Goode, a Jewish rabbi; and the two others, George Fox and Clark Poling, Protestant ministers. These men had joined the U.S. Army of World War II, not to fight but to help soldiers when they were frightened, and to advise them when they were troubled. And now, in this hour of greatest need, these four men seemed to be everywhere at once, helping everybody, thinking of nothing but how they could be of service to their fellowmen.

Many men were rescued from the sea that day. But the four chaplains were not among them. In all the terror and excitement, few had noticed that the four chaplains had taken off their own life-jackets and given their life-preservers to men who had none.

As the ship went down, the soldiers in the life-boats, turning to take a last look at the sinking ship, saw the four chaplains standing arm in arm praying.

Who knows what they said? The young Catholic priest may have prayed in Latin, the Protestant ministers in English, and the young Jewish rabbi in Hebrew. But whatever their words were, the spirit of what they said must have been the same.

What they had done was what all their religions had taught them—to give to others without any thought of self. They had all given help to every man who needed help, without knowing what his religion might be, without questioning whether he was Protestant, Catholic, or Jew. For these great heroes knew that an American is an American, regardless of his religion; and that all men are brothers and children of one God.

Man of Peace, Medicine, and Music

ALBERT SCHWEITZER

By Charlie May Simon

A FEW years ago, a message was sent by radio and telegram throughout the whole world. The 1952 Nobel Peace Prize was to be given to Dr. Albert Schweitzer.

"The greatest man in the world" he has often been called, and many must have repeated the words as they heard his name over the radio or read it in their morning paper.

Many sent messages of congratulation. Presidents and Prime Ministers put aside their affairs of state to say how pleased

ALBERT SCHWEITZER. Protestant clergyman, philosopher, physician, and musician. Born in Alsace, 1875. Studied medicine to devote his life to healing the sick in French Equatorial Africa, 1913. Also directed them in spiritual and practical matters. Built and equipped hospitals. Cleared the jungle to grow food for the people. Author of many books on religion, on his work in Africa, and on the music of Bach. Died 1965.

they were. Doctors, ministers, philosophers, writers, and musicians could all claim him and be proud that one of their own had been so honored, for Dr. Schweitzer has won fame in all these fields.

Even in his youth, Albert Schweitzer thought of the many unfortunate people of the earth, living in faraway places, suffering and dying needlessly for want of doctors and medicines to heal them. He remembered the words of the Bible, "All ye are brethren." And so, in 1914, he left his home in France and went to a place where he felt he was most needed, in the jungles of French Equatorial Africa.

Seven years went by, though, before he was fully prepared to start on his new life. He was a learned man and a fine musician, but he had no medical training. So he had to study medicine. At the same time he taught himself many other things he knew he would need to know in Africa. He read books to find out all he could about the Africans and thought about what he would teach them. He learned, too, how to grow food in a tropical land, and how to build houses, hospitals, and boats.

The doctor's life was spent teaching the natives and preaching to them; planting trees and gardens; and building hospitals. He lived his religion and philosophy in his everyday life. He put aside his music until his daily work was done. Then, in the tropical night, there came from the open windows of his hut some of the sweetest melodies of his beloved Bach. The wind in the palms and the gently flowing river murmured their accompaniment.

Dr. Schweitzer was one of the world's greatest authorities on the music of Bach—not only in playing it on the organ but in understanding what the master-musician meant by his magnificent music.

While the news that the Nobel Peace Prize was to be given to Dr. Schweitzer was being read and talked about over the rest of the world, a small canoe could be seen pulling away from the landing of the little village of Lambarene, in the heart of Africa, close to the equator. For an hour it glided in and out among the many papyrus-covered islands of the Ogume River. Kingfishers and white herons flew up with a startled whirr at its approach. On each side of the river, where the dark mysterious jungle stands like a high green wall, trees grew close to the water's edge and formed a shady arbor.

At last the boat pulled toward a clearing in the forest, where Dr. Schweitzer's hospital stands. A group of women washing clothes on the bank looked up with ready smiles, and on a level terrace above them the men at work in the vegetable garden called out a cheerful greeting.

Two boys who had helped with the rowing at the stern of the boat, jumped out and waded barefooted to push it ashore. The other passengers followed, carrying supplies bought at the village, and a pouch filled with letters and telegrams.

The long, low-lying hospital buildings could be seen through the trees, and beyond them the simple wooden house where Dr. Schweitzer and his staff lived.

The courtyard was a scene of great activity on weekdays. Everyone who was able to did his share of the work for the hospital that had been built for them all. Many of the people were friends or relatives of some sick person, there to keep him company. Some were patients who were almost well enough to return to their homes.

And there were some who had been entirely cured, but who stayed on because they were happier there, and life was better than it had been where they came from.

There was a constant chatter as they talked among themselves. Two women, pressing clothes with a charcoal iron, told about one of their kin, a husband or a child, or perhaps a parent, who had been brought to the hospital, and how the doctor had made him well again. The Grand Docteur, they called him, and he was known by that name far and wide in Africa.

"Yes, there was a fire burning inside my child, and his body was as hot as this iron almost, when I held him in my arms, even though he always wore the fetish charm around his neck. But the Grand Docteur has made the fever go away, and now my child sits up in bed and laughs and talks again, and soon I'll take him home."

A man sitting on the ground stringing palm branches together to make thatches for a roof, told about his operation:

"Ayi, I was in pain when they brought me here. Then the nurse gave me something that smelled queer, to breathe. I died for a little while, and when I came to life again, the pain was gone. The Grand Docteur cut a place here on my body to let the pain out."

A bright-eyed leper boy, sitting with others in the shade of a cinnamon tree, split lengths of cane into thin strips each morning. It was the sort of thing school children do during their recreation period. But these strips were used to weave bamboo poles together to make the walls of a house in the leper village. He was almost well now, and would soon be going home. He could still remember how the boys in his village had thrown sticks at him and had not let him come near them. But now he was going to be one of them again, and run races with the swiftest. And wouldn't they all look up to him when they learned that he could read and write his name! There was no school in his village, such as there was here for the leper children, and he would be the only one there who could read written messages.

An old man with kinky gray hair and a face that was black and wrinkled, drowsed as he smoked his pipe, with his thoughts on the days of his youth. He scarcely noticed the smaller children shouting and laughing in their play close to where he sat. The little girl twins were like frisky puppies as they jumped about playing tag with each other.

The old man saw the boat as it pulled up to the landing, and he watched the people in it step out and come walking up the slope. And he thought of the times when he could row all day, balancing himself as he stood in a canoe.

Ah yes, he sighed, when a man was young and strong he had many friends in his village. It was when he grew old and his days of usefulness were over, that he was no longer wanted. But here at the hospital of the Grand Docteur, it was different. He had come here to die, so he had thought. But to his surprise, he had been made well. And new hope had come to him; the joy of life had returned.

One of the twins rushed past him as she ran to catch up with her sister. The old man smiled to see them tumbling to the ground, laughing. There were some tribes that looked upon twins as bad luck. The mother and children were turned out and sent to the jungle alone, at the mercy of wild beasts. But these little girls were going to grow up healthy and happy. Their shouts

could be heard above the clucking of hens and the bleating of goats that roamed about the place.

The chickens and goats served to keep down the high weeds and enrich the soil. They were a common enough sight in every African village. But where else except here, could a wild boar, one of the most savage of the jungle animals, be seen behaving like an affectionate kitten that wanted to be petted? And antelopes, with no thought of fear, ate fresh green leaves from the hand of anyone who fed them. The pelican that flew in each night to roost on the porch rafters above the doctor's door, sometimes flapped his wings impatiently, but only because he wanted to be fed. Monkeys and parrots also knew that they were safe here. It was as if they too understood that to Dr. Schweitzer all life was sacred.

It was to this place, that the message came to Dr. Schweitzer, telling him of the Nobel Peace award. And the letters and telegrams of congratulation came in the same little boat from Lambarene, an hour's boat-ride away.

The people in the courtyard and in the hospital, and in the leper village farther up the hill, knew little of the world outside. Perhaps they would not understand if anyone tried to explain to them the meaning of the Nobel Prize for Peace. But if they were told that it was given to the Doctor because he was considered a very great man, the answer of everyone of them would be, "Of course he is great. The greatest man in all the world. Has he not saved my life and made me free of pain?"

The Maid Who Saved France

JOAN OF ARC

By Rhoda Power

Once upon a time, more than five hundred years ago, there lived a little French girl whose name was Joan of Arc. Her home was in the village of Domrémy, where her father had a small farm.

Joan did not learn to read or write. She spent her time sewing and spinning, or watching her father's sheep as they nibbled grass in the meadows. She was a quiet little girl but, like all the children in the village, she sometimes wanted to play, and then she sat with her friends plaiting garlands of flowers to deck the branches of an old tree near the woods. The children called this "The Ladies' Tree," and they thought that every night the fairies danced around it. They believed in witches too, and thought them so wicked they ought to be killed.

As Joan grew older, she became quieter and more thoughtful. She would steal away to the village church or say her prayers alone in the woods, and the prayers Joan said were nearly always for her native land.

These were unhappy days for France. The young King had not been crowned; a stranger was ruling in Paris. Enemies were pouring into the country and, little by little, they were winning more and more land. The enemies came across the sea from England, and every day Joan prayed that God would save France from the English.

One morning in August, when Joan was about thirteen years old, she heard the villagers talking in grave distress. The French had been defeated in a great battle, and the poor people thought that before very long the English soldiers would drive them out.

When she heard this Joan was very unhappy. She left her sheep in the field and went alone to the woods. For a long time she knelt there very quietly. Suddenly she seemed to hear a voice speaking to her. "Joan!" it said, so softly that it might have been a leaf falling upon moss, "Joan! Be a good girl, and God will show you how to help the King of France."

Joan was puzzled but not afraid. The voice was too sweet and gentle to frighten her. She listened, but she heard nothing more, so she wandered back to her sheep. When the shadows were lengthening and the sun was setting in a pink sky, she took up her crook and, calling her flock, walked home through the village. The church bells were ringing and, as the chimes died away, Joan heard the same sweet voice calling her. Still it said, "God will show you how to help the King of France."

JOAN OF ARC. Savior of France. Born in Domrémy, France, 1412. Voices spoke to her telling her to help her country. Journeyed to Orleans to crown the Dauphin King. Led him to victory over the British, 1429. Captured at Compiègne, 1430. Burned at the stake, 1431. Made a saint by Pope Benedict XV, 1920.

Joan told no one about her adventure, but from that day she spent more time in the little church of Domrémy, and, although she was always kind to the children, they noticed that she liked to be alone and that she slipped away to the woods whenever she could.

As time passed, Joan began to hear more voices than one. They spoke to her when the church bells chimed and when she was alone. They called her when she was keeping her father's sheep and when she was picking flowers in the wood. The voices made her happy, and she whispered to herself, "They come from God and the blessed saints."

Three years passed, and Joan wondered when God would show her how to help the King of France. The English soldiers were winning more battles, and at last they reached the beautiful city of Orleans and began to besiege it. The peasants of Domrémy wrung their hands. They were in despair. When they saw Joan driving her sheep along the road they said, "Soon we shall have no sheep to drive." But Joan only smiled when she heard them. She felt no fear. She knew that her voices would bring her some message of comfort.

That evening when she came home her eyes were shining and her mind was busy with many plans. Her voices had told her to go to the village ten miles from Domrémy and tell the French captain to take her to the young King of France. "God will help you to raise the siege of Orleans," said the voices. "God will help you to crown the King."

Wearing an old red woollen dress, which was patched and darned, and with wooden shoes on her feet, Joan left Domrémy and trudged to the village of Vaucouleurs.

At first the Captain of Vaucouleurs took no notice of the young village girl. But the peasants and the soldiers listened to her. When she told them of the voices which she had heard in the woods, they believed that God had sent her to help them, and they persuaded the Captain to let her go to the young King.

Full of hope, Joan set out on her journey. She had cut off her hair and was dressed like a boy, in a tunic, leather breeches, and high laced boots. On her head was a little black cap, around her shoulders a cape.

For eleven days she rode with two soldiers to guard her, until at last she came to a great rock which towered three hundred feet above an old gray city. On the rock was a castle, and in the castle Charles, the Dauphin, the uncrowned King of France, held court.

When Joan came into the big hall, Charles, the Dauphin, was walking among the courtiers and their ladies just like any ordinary gentleman of the court. Nobody helped the poor little peasant girl to find him; but she needed no help. Scarcely pausing, she walked straight up to Charles and knelt on one knee. She gave her message very clearly, but Charles could not believe that a village girl would be able to drive away his enemies.

"Send me to Orleans," Joan implored, "and with God's help I will raise the siege." Day after day she begged him to grant her wish, and at last, when the days had passed into weeks, he sent her to Orleans with his soldiers.

Then Joan, the young peasant who used to pray in the woods, rode at the head of an army. They made her a suit of white armor and mounted her on a white charger. They gave her a fine old sword and a banner fringed with silk and embroidered with lilies. When she passed through the villages the people ran out and tried to kiss her feet. "An angel has come to help us!" they cried.

Joan knew that she was not an angel, but she believed that the angels were helping her, and this gave her courage. At Orleans she was so strong and brave that the soldiers took heart and forgot their fear whenever they saw her white silk banner.

"Follow the Maid! The Maid of France will save us!" they cried, and their arrows flew swiftly through the air, until the English were driven back and Orleans was saved.

Then the soldiers and the townspeople shouted, "Long live the Maid!" As she rode through the city the women lifted their children up to see her pass. "Look," they said, "it is the Maid who was sent by God!"

But the English were angry and afraid. They looked at one another with frowning faces and said, "A witch is fighting for the French." They wanted to catch Joan and kill her, for in those days when people thought a woman was a witch, they treated her with great cruelty, sometimes burning her alive in the market-place.

Joan paid no heed to what was being said. She went on fighting for her own people. The French soldiers adored her and followed her everywhere. They fought so bravely at her side that she won many a victory, and before long she had driven the English so far away that she was able to take the young Dauphin to Rheims. He was crowned in the cathedral where his father, his grandfather, and nearly all the Kings of France had been crowned.

It was a wonderful sight. The roads were crowded with peasants and townspeople in their best clothes. Soldiers guarded the doors of the cathedral. Joan in her gleaming armor stood besides Charles, and behind knelt all the ladies and gentlemen of the court in scarlet, purple, and gold, in crimson silk and green velvet. Jewels glittered, swords and spurs shone. The sounds of music passed through the open doors and were carried by the wind to the ears of the waiting crowd.

When the crown was placed on Charles' head there was a great noise of trumpets, and the people outside knew that at last their young lord had been crowned and was indeed King of France.

Joan left the cathedral with her heart full of joy, but her happiness did not last long. She wanted to win more victories for France. But King Charles was afraid to follow her advice. When she went to battle without him, he did not send her enough help, and one day, while she was bravely fighting, she was surrounded by her enemies and taken prisoner.

Sitting alone behind locked doors, Joan thought of King Charles. She said to herself, "He will soon come to my help. He will send some money for my ransom, and then I can go home." She looked through the window across the green fields dotted with her enemies' tents, and she thought of the voices which had spoken to her in the woods of Domrémy. She was full of peace and patience.

For many days she waited, but King Charles was ungrateful. He forgot all the help Joan had given him. He never sent money for her ransom, and he allowed the English to carry her away to Rouen and

shut her up in a dungeon, with chains on her ankles, and with no women to look after her but only five rough soldiers who teased and tormented her. Charles did not even try to save her when she was taken before the judges, who said she was a witch who must be burned in the market-place.

So this poor village girl, who had never done anything but good, was led out of prison to a great pile of faggots and tied to a stake. Someone set fire to the faggots. As the flames crept higher and higher, Joan begged for a cross. An English soldier made one from two sticks and gave it to her. This was probably the only kindness which she had ever received from an Englishman. She died holding the cross and whispering "Jesus."

As the flames shot up and hid her from view, an English soldier turned away and murmured, "God help us, we have burned a saint!"

Hero of South America

SIMON BOLIVAR

By Toby Bell

LONG ago in Spain three men rode their horses out from behind a wall. They wore stiff coats with high boots and three-cornered hats, but all their clothes were shabby and dusty.

"Here he comes," said one of the riders. "Thinks he's mighty fine, doesn't he?" With grim faces they watched a young man galloping down the road toward them on a lively Arab horse.

The young man did look as though he thought he owned the world. Everything about him and his horse looked rich. The saddle, made of famous Cordovan leather, glowed with polish. The young man's clothes were embroidered in gold. His shirt was fastened with diamond studs.

As he came up to the three riders, young Simon Bolivar smiled and saluted.

The three riders did not smile back. Instead they spread their horses right in front of him, blocking the road. Simon had to pull up his horse so sharply that it reared up on its hind legs. In a flash Simon drew his sword, but the three men pointed pistols and rode at him. Against the three, armed like that, Simon could do nothing.

"What do you want," he called. "Are you bandits?"

"We are the King's police," they yelled.

"You are under arrest."

"What for? I've broken no law."

"You are breaking the law right now. Look at those diamonds on your sleeves. You are nothing but a Creole from a colony in South America—Venezuela. Creoles aren't allowed to wear diamonds in Spain. Hand them over."

"Of course, I am a Creole," he said, "and proud of it. After all, a Creole is a Spaniard born in America."

And before Simon could move, two of the men pinned back his arms while the third tore off the diamonds.

"So," said Simon, "you are just thieves dressed like police."

The men's laughter was loud and rough. "Turn your horse, my fine young bucko," said one of them, "you're going back to Madrid and there you'll see the inside of a prison."

Then they pricked his horse with their knives till the frightened creature whirled about and all four of them tore down the road to the city of Madrid.

There Simon tried to tell them that his uncle was a grandee of Spain and a close friend of the King. He tried to tell them that his mother had been born in Spain and his father's people had gone to America

SIMON BOLIVAR. South American soldier, statesman and revolutionary leader. Born in Caracas, Venezuela, 1783. Took part in revolt against Spanish, 1810, and had to flee. Led many revolts in Venezuela and Colombia. Defeated Spanish in 1819 and was made President of Colombia. Made Venezuela an independent republic in 1821. Freed Peru from Spain in 1824 and was made President of Peru. Organized new republic north of Peru, named Bolivia after him. Resigned as President of Colombia, 1830. Died 1830.

from Spain long ago. But they just pushed him into a dirty prison cell and walked off with his sword.

The cell was pitch dark. Stretching out his arms, Simon felt around the walls and found no bench or cot. He had to huddle on the muddy floor. With his arms clasped around his knees he stared into the darkness. He was afraid that the police would not tell his uncle where he was and that he might be shut in here forgotten for years.

He thought of the gay days when he had been a boy in Venezuela. In the city of Caracas he had lived in a great house with a red roof. There were patios with bright flowers where he used to play.

In the summer, all of them rode up to the family ranch in the mountains. Some rode on horses, some on burros, and his mother rode in a sedan chair that was carried by two slaves. Simon's father was dead and his mother ruled an estate that was as large as a small kingdom. Simon was rich, he was good-looking, with black curly hair and dark eyes. He rode and swam well and he was a little spoiled.

He was courageous and charming but he sometimes annoyed people by his toplofty ways. But then the next moment he would do something to make up for it, and people forgave him and loved him. He was so full of fun and so lively that rather than sit still he often did mischief.

When Simon was nine years old his mother died. For the first time in his life, Simon felt lonely. And to comfort him his uncles sent him a tutor from Spain by the name of Rodriguez. Simon grew to love him better than anyone else he knew.

Now, sitting in the prison cell, Simon thought of the days Rodriguez and he spent together, their long rides on their horses on the slopes of the Andes under the high snows. He remembered that Rodriguez was the first one who told him that the people in Spain looked down on the colonists in America, even though they were really Spanish too.

Rodriguez was a wonderful teacher, and he was always telling the boy about things and places that were new to him. One day he told him about a country in North America called the United States.

"Where is that place, *amigo?*" asked the boy. "Is it on the other side of our Andes Mountains?"

"No, no," said the tutor. "The United States is far north of here. It would take months to get there from here. We would have to take a ship to Spain and then another to England and from there a third ship to the United States.

"Simon," he went on, "I am now going to tell you something that I am not supposed to. It is about a study called geography. The King of Spain does not allow any of the boys here in the Spanish colonies to learn geography. He is afraid that if you see a map of the world and find out how much bigger these colonies are than all of Spain, the people here would rebel and stop paying taxes to him. Wait, I will show you."

From a hidden place in his box of clothes, Rodriguez drew forth some sheets of heavy paper. On them were little gay pictures, in jolly colors, of ships on the ocean and people and animals in their native places. They were picture maps.

Simon had never seen any kind of map. He looked at these in wonder and delight.

"Why look," he said, "here is one of our own llamas." And he pointed to the animal that looks like a camel without a hump.

"Yes," said Rodriguez, "and right here on this map is where you live." He showed the boy Venezuela and the grand stretch of land along the north and west coasts of South America from Cartagena to Peru. "See," he said, "you could tuck all of Spain into one corner here. And that is what the King doesn't want you to think about."

Rodriguez owned books that the Spanish were not allowed to read, books about freedom. One night a servant slipped into Simon's room and told him that the King's soldiers were coming to arrest the tutor because of those books and because he had taught Simon how colonies could be free. In the night and in disguise, Rodriguez had to flee. And in all the long years since then, Simon had not seen him again. He did not even know where he was.

All this Simon remembered as he sat on the dirty floor of the dark cell. He stayed in the cell overnight, long enough for his uncle to go to see the King and demand his release.

Soon the guards came to Simon's cell, and with black looks they set the young man free. He got back his diamonds and left the prison, dressed once more in silks and velvets. But the young man under the fine clothes was different. He had learned a hard lesson. He knew now what it meant not to be free.

After he got out of prison he made up his mind that South America must be free from Spain. He knew that meant a fight and he wanted to take a part in it. But he never dreamed that he would be its great leader and hero. He wanted to start at once, but he did not know what to do first. He thought "Rodriguez would know. I must find Rodriguez again."

He asked everywhere, and he asked everyone who might know. He wrote letters, and he hired men to search. And at last he found that Rodriguez was in Paris. He was glad of that because the French had rebelled against their King too and he wanted to see how it was done. If he could get to Paris and find Rodriguez, he would learn how to make his own nation free. So to Paris he went, and at last he found Rodriguez there.

In Paris Rodriguez warned Simon, "When we have our revolution in Venezuela, we must be careful that we do not later get a tyrant to take the place of the King. That is what has happened here in France under Napoleon Bonaparte."

Simon was twenty-two years old when he left Europe and went back to Venezuela. He made a long roundabout journey, for he went by way of Washington, D. C., and while he was there he talked for a long time with Thomas Jefferson who was then President of the United States. There, too, he went to see the home of George Washington, who had become the greatest hero in the world to him.

Back in Venezuela, he found that the Indians would not help him. They could not read and they did not care who ruled them because they thought each new master would be as bad as the old one.

Simon started to hold secret meetings with his friends. Little by little they began to drive the Spaniards out of Venezuela. But not all his fellow-countrymen sided with him. Some slave owners did not want to lose their slaves. And some were afraid even to talk to him for fear the Spanish troops would arrest them.

The fight went on and on. Six years went by. Many who were schoolboys when Simon began his fight were now old enough to be part of his troops. They were beginning to win. And then disaster hit them. In the year 1812, a frightful earthquake hit Venezuela during Holy Week. The Spanish spread the story that this was a punishment for rebelling against the King.

The Venezuelans were so afraid that they almost gave up and the Spanish took Bolivar's leading officer, the great General Miranda, prisoner. That was a blow. But then came a worse one. They took Bolivar himself prisoner. It looked as though the revolution was really lost. Miranda died in prison.

But then the Spanish made a mistake. They made Bolivar march on foot between their men who were on horseback. He was ragged and weary as he slogged along behind his captors. As he lifted his tired feet, Simon thought to himself, "They will shoot me as soon as they get to their headquarters. Miranda is gone. I will go next. Our cause is lost. This is the end."

But Simon was not a man who gave up. The next moment he was making plans for an escape. So he went from gloom to hope, though the hope seemed foolish.

The guards led him into a fort and pushed him before the commanding officer. "Here comes the order to shoot me," thought Simon. But that was when the Spanish made their mistake. That puffed-up commanding officer did not understand the colonials at all. He looked at the shabby young man before him.

"What do we want with this person?" he said. "We have General Miranda and he is the head man of all this rebellion. This youngster can't be anybody."

And then came the words that Simon never expected to hear. "Let the fool go."

Simon could hardly believe it when they pushed him out of the place and set him free.

When his people heard about this, they thought it showed that God was not angry with them after all for rebelling against the King.

But though Simon was now free, he had lost everything he owned. The Spanish took his house, his ranch, his horses, and all his money. They even took his clothes. And he knew he had to get away before the Spanish learned their mistake and took him prisoner again. He went off to a rocky island in Colombia where he walked for hours and looked across the sea thinking of Venezuela, the land he loved.

One day he got good news. A boat approached the island and brought word that other colonies in South America were ready to join Bolivar. But he must find a way to get to them. That cost money and he had none. He strode up and down wondering what to do. He was carrying his old coat and, in a burst of impatience, he threw it down on the rocks. There was a small thud. Bolivar looked to see what it was. A lumpy little package had fallen out of the torn lining of the coat. Bolivar unwrapped the package, and there, gleaming before him, were his diamonds! One of his men had sewed them into the lining of his coat before he was taken prisoner, so that they would not be stolen. In all the excitement Bolivar had forgotten all about them.

Joyfully, now, he sold the diamonds, and

then he had enough money to reach his new allies. But he did not have enough to outfit an army. His soldiers were in rags. All they had were a few pistols. But they had plenty of courage. And once more the Spanish made a foolish mistake. They thought the revolution was over. Bolivar caught them by surprise. It was a desperate fight, but little by little, town by town, mile by mile, Bolivar and his men began to make some headway.

They had to climb the Andes to outwit the enemy. The Andes are among the highest mountains in the world, freezing cold and snowy. Bolivar's men were from the low coast where it was warm. They were not prepared for the icy cold. They had no warm clothes, no shoes. There were no roads. On hands and knees Bolivar and his men crawled up the pathless peaks.

Simon gave them everything he had—money, clothes, food. He got up before daylight while his men were still asleep. Often he did not sleep at all. He went without food when stores were low. His fine friends in Spain would not have recognized this ragged, sunburned General.

Slowly the small army began to wear down the Spaniards, and at last drove them from Caracas.

The people went wild over Bolivar when he entered the city. They would not let him show himself in his shabby fighting clothes. They went to meet him and presented him with a white Arab pony and a white uniform trimmed with blue. And so he rode into the capital city. There twelve pretty girls were waiting for him with a flower-trimmed chariot. He had to get into the chariot and the girls with silken reins pulled him into the center of the city. Cannon roared, church bells rang and bands played a welcome for the hero.

The people wanted him to be their Emperor. Most of the people, though, could not read, and did not really understand what was happening. He tried to make them see that an Emperor would become just another tyrant and that they should vote for a President instead. Also many of the rich and powerful people who could read did not want a President because each of them wanted to be an Emperor or a King of the new Venezuela. So they plotted against

Bolivar. They forced him to flee from the country he had rescued from Spain. And once again he had to fight for freedom—his own and his people's.

Simon Bolivar went on fighting until he had set free not only his own Venezuela, but three other countries as well—now called Peru, Ecuador, and Bolivia. And soon, because neighboring countries took heart and imitated Simon's bravery, the Spanish were forced to flee from all of South America.

But the struggle lasted many years, and left Bolivar poor and tired. Because of enemies at home, he lived in Colombia towards the end of his life. When he was forty-seven years old, the Venezuelans asked him to come back and govern them. But it was too late. He was sick and about to die. He died, far from home, in Colombia.

His death made his people realize how much he had done for them. He was mourned in Europe and America too. The people there flew their flags at half-mast when they heard he had died. The Colombians honored him by sending his body home to Venezuela under a heavy naval escort. From all over the world people came, and still come, to see his grave.

Today hundreds of streets, ships and schools and even cities are named Bolivar. A whole country, Bolivia, is named for him. He had refused to be an Emperor but the world has given him greater titles. Many call him the *George Washington of South America*. That name would have pleased Simon Bolivar because George Washington was his ideal of what a national leader should be. And he would have been proud of the title engraved on most of the statues that have been raised in his memory. That title is simply *The Liberator*.

He Fought to Set Italy Free

GIUSEPPE GARIBALDI

By Will Lane

THE redhead was winning the race. The two other boys gave up and yelled after him, "All right, Peppino, you win!" Peppino turned and waited for them. He looked fine standing there, his back to the blue waters of the Mediterranean, his bare feet on the packed white sand of the beach.

"You always win, Peppino!" Carlo growled as he caught up. "But look, I've got something you haven't got." And from his pocket Carlo pulled a compass. "My uncle gave it to me."

"It's broken," said Cesare, as he too caught up. "What good is it?" Peppino took the compass and looked at it, and an idea popped into his head. But it was so bold that he didn't speak of it for a moment.

The boy they called Peppino was Giuseppe Garibaldi, and on this day in the year 1817, he was ten years old. The beach was at Nice in France, but the three boys were not French. They were Italian, living in France because their fathers had had to flee from Italy. Italy was torn to pieces by the tyranny of Austria, France, and some of the Italian princes.

Giuseppe ran faster, fought better, and talked more than any other boy around. He won every game. But the boys liked him because he was good-natured and always fair. He loved a fight but he never took on a smaller boy. He was always ready with a laugh. Where he went others followed.

Now the three boys stood a moment and looked out over the blue harbor of Nice. "There's your father's boat, Peppino," said Cesare. He was pointing to a fishing boat so far out that no ordinary eye would have been sure. But these boys, all the sons of sailors, were used to looking off long distances.

Giuseppe grinned. "My father's the best sailor on this coast," he boasted. The others nodded. Everyone knew that Captain Garibaldi was a great sailor.

Giuseppe looked again at the broken compass that he still held in his hand. He said, "I ought to be out there! What am I doing here? Ten years old and fooling around on land!"

"The sea's not for you, Peppino," said Carlo. "You're going to be a priest. You've got to study." And then, teasingly, "Cesare and I will go off to foreign places and see strange things. You'll have to stay here and be good and take care of us."

"A poor priest *he'd* make," said Carlo. "He'd rather fight than pray."

Giuseppe's laughing face turned a little sad. He knew his mother and father had their hearts set on his becoming a priest. He was a good Catholic, but he was beginning to think that he would not make a good priest. He knew well that when he saw someone being ill-treated, he wanted to use his fists. But he tossed that out of his mind.

GIUSEPPE GARIBALDI. Italian patriot. Born of Italian parents, in Nice, France, 1807. Fought for Italian freedom in Army of the Roman Republic. Fled to United States, 1849, and became naturalized. Returned to Italy, 1854. Organized famous Red Shirts. Elected Deputy to Parliament in Rome, 1874. Died 1882.

He was a boy who sometimes acted first and thought afterwards. And now he was bursting with that wonderful new idea.

"Look," he said, "let's get a big boat and go out on a real trip. Not just here in the harbor. We've all been out often enough with our fathers. We know how to sail and how to fish. What's holding us back?"

"Well, one thing," said Cesare, "we've never taken a boat out alone outside the harbor. Another thing," Cesare laughed. "We haven't got a boat big enough."

"Oh, haven't we!" exclaimed Peppino. "What's the matter with the *Red Dragon?*"

"But that's my cousin's," said Cesare. "He'll never let us take her out. We're supposed to paint her tomorrow while he's away."

"Then tomorrow is a good day for us to take her out," said Peppino. The others were used to Peppino's wild ideas. They just shrugged and didn't bother to answer.

"I mean it," said Peppino. "Here's that compass of yours, Carlo. We'll take things to eat from home. I'll bring sausage. Carlo can bring bread and olives. Cesare can bring cheese."

His plan was beginning to excite the other boys. "But," still objected Carlo, "what good is a broken compass?"

Giuseppe didn't like to give up the compass because it looked business-like. But he was always able to make the best of a situation. "Oh, well, we don't really need a compass. We'll be able to see the coast line nearly all the way."

"All the way to where?" asked the others.

Giuseppe was surprised that they should ask. "Why to Genoa, in Italy, of course. There we'll find the leaders of the Revolution and we'll fight for Italy."

Carlo and Cesare liked that. They had been brought up to look for the day when they would fight for Italy against its tyrants. Carlo had a last doubt. "Suppose the sun doesn't come out tomorrow. How will we find our way with no compass?"

"Suppose, suppose," said Giuseppe impatiently, "Why not suppose the other way, that the sun will be here and we'll have a fine sail?"

So in the year 1817, in the beautiful town of Nice in southern France, the three boys made their plans to set sail for Genoa.

Next morning they astonished their parents by getting up early and eagerly helping their fathers to get off for the fishing. Of course, the sooner the men got off, the sooner the coast would be clear.

When the fishing fleet had gone off, the boys hurried down to the shore to the *Red Dragon*. There she was, a poor thing of a boat to grown-up eyes. She had only one sail, but on that sail there was a dragon painted in faded red. And the Mediterranean, which could be very stormy, was kind that morning. Not a cloud in the sky. There was a gentle breeze, enough to get them out of the harbor. As they reached the open sea, the breeze picked up, the sail filled out and grew big with the wind. It sometimes looked almost alive. The boys felt like masters as the *Red Dragon* flew over the water.

Soon they were all soaked with salt spray, but that felt fine in the warm sun. It made them hungry too. They looked with longing at their packages of food. First they nibbled at them and then, before they quite saw what was happening, they had eaten up all the sausage and olives. They managed to save the cheese and some bread for the next day. But it was not easy. Of course, they thought, when the food gave out, they could fish.

Carlo was the only one who was a little unsure as he watched the scudding sea and the flying shore. "When we do reach Genoa, how will we get to fight for Italy?" he asked. Giuseppe told him that his father had friends in Genoa, all good revolutionaries. "We will find them," he said with light-hearted assurance. And then his face grew solemn as he added, "This *Red Dragon* is carrying fear to the tyrants of Italy."

But the truth was that the only fear the *Red Dragon* brought was to the mothers of the three boys, especially when they found that the boat was missing. Quickly the mothers gathered on the beach and got in touch with the Coast Guard. The Coast Guard set out at once, taking Giuseppe's father aboard on the way. The boys had thought they were moving fast through the water, but their tub of a boat seemed to be standing still as the Coast Guard cutter raced up after them.

It was still only ten in the morning when at Monaco, the cutter caught up with the *Red Dragon*. The boys were still far from Italy. The mighty monster spread to his full length on the sail, but the Coast Guard boat had a number of sails that served it better than any dragon.

Giuseppe's father swung aboard the *Red Dragon* scowling. But his frowns of worry went away when he saw that the boys were safe. He told them he was glad they wanted to fight for Italy, but they would have to wait a few years. And as they set out for home, he gave them some good lessons in sailing that helped them all their lives.

But Captain Garibaldi learned something too that day. He knew now that Giuseppe was not the right boy to become a priest. Giuseppe's mother was disappointed, but she got over it because, in the long run, she thought everything her son did would turn out for the best.

Almost twenty years later, Giuseppe Garibaldi strode again on that beach at Nice. He was now a magnificent figure of a man with blond hair and a blond beard. His blue eyes shone out of his sunburned face. Around the eyes were the wrinkles that come from looking at the sun at sea. He had been in many places as sailor, mate, and captain. He had saved two men from drowning.

He had taken part in a Revolution in Italy. But his side had lost. Now, as he strode along the beach, he clenched an Italian newspaper in his hand. In it he read that he was condemned to death for his part in the Revolution. There was no safety for him even here in the home of his childhood. There were too many who might turn him over to the French police for a reward. He must get away.

But before he could do anything, the police grabbed him and put him in prison to wait for the Italian authorities. The prison didn't hold him long. He was like a cat on high places. He jumped from a window high above the ground. That night he signed up as mate on a ship going to Brazil in South America. South America then was a refuge for Italian patriots. Some day Garibaldi hoped to get them all together and go back to Italy. Right then Brazil was fighting for her own freedom from the King of Portugal. Garibaldi joined in the fight.

He was shipwrecked, he was shot, he was tortured. The Brazilian Revolution failed. But one night, standing on the deck of his poor little boat, Garibaldi saw a beautiful

girl on the shore. At first sight he fell in love with her. Her name was Anita Ribiero. Before the evening was over, he had asked her father for her hand. Dom Ribiero said no, and he locked his daughter away in her room. But a little thing like that would hardly stop a man like Garibaldi. The two eloped in the little ship. The Brazilian Navy came after them fast. A Navy shell knocked Anita onto a pile of dead men. But she was only stunned and soon came to. She was bandaging the wounded when the boat's only gunner was killed. Anita manned the gun. It was a strange honey moon.

Garibaldi's next fight for freedom took

place in Uruguay. Argentina, her next door neighbor, invaded the little country. Garibaldi got together a company of Italians. They fought there for five years until Uruguay was free. The enemy called Garibaldi's men the "Red Demons" because they wore red shirts.

At last the time came when Garibaldi and his Red Demons went back to Italy. There they managed to free the Italian island of Sardinia from the Austrians. "Where do we fight next?" asked Garibaldi.

"Rome," said the Italians.

Workmen, boys, old men, police, soldiers lined up behind Garibaldi, and they all marched to Rome. They fought and they died and again they lost. And again Garibaldi had a price on his head. Sixty-five thousand enemy soldiers were looking for him, but he escaped because the people of Italy sheltered him. And then Anita fell sick of malaria. She was too weak to ride or walk, so he carried her. And while he held her, he heard the sound of bloodhounds on their trail. Anita died in his arms.

And now the world thought that Italy had forever lost her freedom. But they forgot that Garibaldi never gave up.

This time Garibaldi escaped to the United States. He went to live in a cottage on Staten Island in New York Harbor where he could see and hear the ships he loved. There he worked as a candle-maker and only a few knew his hideout. He waited until at last word came again from Italy.

"Come home," the patriots begged. "We have a new young King, Emanuel II. He will protect you."

Italy was ready once more to fight for her freedom. But the enemies of Italian freedom were still strong and the new King gave Garibaldi only secret help. Garibaldi must raise his own army, get his own ships, all without money. Quietly he moved about. The men who lined up behind him wanted no money. There were only a thousand of them. They are still called "The Thousand" in Italy today. In their red shirts and their flaming anger they landed in Sicily.

In Sicily Garibaldi flew the green, white, and red flag that stood for Italian freedom. His men were only one thousand and they were faced suddenly with four thousand enemy troops. Garibaldi's own son fell. But Garibaldi said, "Here either we make Italy a free country or we die."

Garibaldi's men captured Sicily. Then more and more Italians joined them, fed them, armed them. Then they marched to Rome. Before them they drove an army of a hundred thousand men.

At last the whole of Italy was free. The Italian people worshiped Garibaldi. They wanted him to be King or President of Italy. But then he showed that he was great in peace as well as in war. He refused all honors, he refused a castle, he refused money. He went back to his little farm. Italy was free—that was his reward.

And in peace he grew old. We see him at the end sitting in a chair, an old man making a toy boat, perfect to the last detail, for his grandchild. As they sat there, two birds flew onto the window sill and started to peck at fruit in a bowl. The boy wanted to drive them away. "Don't," said Garibaldi in a near whisper. "I think they have come for me."

Perhaps they had. And on the stone that marked his grave were carved the words of a song he had taught his sons:

"Who dies for his country
Has lived enough."

The Narrow Escapes of a Chinese Patriot

SUN YAT-SEN

By Toby Bell

OVER and over again Dr. Sun Yat-sen, Chinese fighter for freedom, escaped death. Sometimes it was by a whisper in the night, sometimes by a minute of time, sometimes by a disguise. Year after year, in Hawaii, in New York, in San Francisco,

SUN YAT-SEN. Chinese statesman and revolutionary leader. Born near Macao, China, 1866. First graduate of new College of Medicine in Hong Kong, 1894. Forced to flee from China, 1895, because he championed democracy. In exile 1895–1911. Established a Republic, 1911, in spite of strong opposition from Chinese war lords. Died during conference of Chinese leaders in Peking, 1925.

secret agents followed him, tried to kidnap him, tried to kill him. Once, on a fashionable London street, they actually did kidnap him, and not one passerby so much as noticed! They wanted to kidnap him because he was trying to free China from her Manchu rulers. He wanted China to have a government like that of the United States.

He was only eleven years old when he made his first escape. This was from the backward school he went to where he learned nothing worth while. It was this way: The Sun family were tenants on a small farm near Canton in southern China. (The Chinese put family names first and given names last. Where we say Johnny Jones, they would put it Jones Johnny. So when they say Sun Yat-sen, they mean Yat-sen of the Sun family.)

The Canton farm brought the Suns almost no money. But one of their older boys, Ah-wei, had gone to Hawaii and was doing well. He sent money home so that his family could live in a good brick house. Yat-sen, who was born in 1866, was their youngest child. His name in Chinese means Free Spirit, and if there ever was a free spirit in the world, it was this boy. He was small for his age, but strong. He had a round face and black eyes.

People liked Yat-sen. But they could not understand why he should be so restless at school, though the school he went to began at seven in the morning and kept on till dark. Yat-sen didn't mind that. But during all those long hours the children did nothing but learn old books by heart. They were not taught a single thing that could be of use to a modern child.

When Yat-sen was ten years old, his brother Ah-wei came home for a visit. He said to his parents, "Let me take the boy back with me to Hawaii. I will send him to a school there where he will learn the things he needs and wants to know."

But Yat-sen's parents said they didn't want another son to go so far away.

Ah-wei was sorry for his little brother, and when he went back to Hawaii, he left the boy a little money. With that money Yat-sen ran away from home, stowed away on a ship, and escaped to Hawaii. There he went to a modern school. He learned English and history and geography and arithmetic. But above all else, he learned about the free government of the United States. That started a dream in his heart. If only China could be like that, he thought.

He stayed in Hawaii for five years, and then one day he said to Ah-wei, "My brother, I have been baptized. I am now a Christian."

"What!" exclaimed Ah-wei. "You have given up our ancient Chinese religion? What will our Chinese priests think? Now I cannot let you stay here. I shall have to send you home at once."

At home Yat-sen found his parents shocked too. They did not understand what Christianity was. When Yat-sen tried to explain, they would not listen.

Then Yat-sen did a foolish thing. He went to the Chinese temple and smashed the chief idol. That was not a very Christian act, and it certainly did not make the people in the village think any better of Christianity. They were angry and afraid of what the insulted idol might do as punishment. They set out to kill Yat-sen.

In his first escape from death his parents helped him. They smuggled him onto a boat bound for Hong Kong. Hong Kong at that time was ruled by the British.

In Hong Kong Yat-sen got a job as an orderly in an English hospital, and there a wonderful thing happened to him. The head surgeon at the hospital was Dr. James Cantlie, a Scotchman. Dr. Cantlie, seeing that Yat-sen was a bright and hard-working boy, guided him in the study of medicine. When he graduated from the medical school five years later as Dr. Sun, he was the first Chinese doctor of western medicine—that is, medicine as it was practised in the western world.

Most Chinese still believed in the same cures that they had used for thousands of years. And some of them were still good. But in Europe and America there had been great new discoveries in medicine that the Chinese knew nothing about. Because of this, Dr. Sun had trouble with some of his patients. When a young man was brought to him for an operation, his mother and father and various aunts and uncles and cousins came along with him.

Dr. Sun said, "I cannot work with all of you crowding around here. An operation needs all my attention. You must go away."

"Ho, ho!" said the relatives. "Do you think we will leave you alone with our young man so you can cut him up as you please?" And they crowded closer.

But Dr. Sun knew he had to operate at once to save the young man's life. He was afraid one of the watchers would nudge his elbow at a bad moment. By good luck, though, all went well for Dr. Sun. His patient got well.

But all did not go well with his beloved China. The Japanese started a war and the Manchus were too cowardly to fight. The Manchu ruler at that time was a woman. She was not only as cruel and greedy as the Manchu Emperors, but she was ignorant and did not know how to rule.

Japan won that war.

Dr. Sun knew that his people must get rid of the Manchus. Long back in the past before these conquerors came, the Chinese had been a wonderful people. They were the first in the world to use a printing press, the first to use coal for heating. They invented gunpowder, but they never used it for anything but fireworks.

China was bigger than the United States, yet ever since the Manchus had come three hundred years before, China had slipped steadily downhill. The Manchus were rich and had great armies. Dr. Sun Yat-sen was a poor man with no army and no arms. But he had friends who agreed with him when he said, "We want free education in China. We want schools where our children can learn useful trades. We want our young men to learn to use machinery. But, most of all, we must teach our farmers to grow better crops because there is never enough for the people to eat in China."

Dr. Sun went to Hong Kong, an island off the Chinese coast belonging to England. There he and his friends worked out a plan to smuggle arms to their people in China. They packed the arms in cases marked CEMENT. But customs officers of the Chinese Government examined the cases and seized the shipment. They raided Dr. Sun's headquarters, killed five of his friends, and arrested seventy. But they failed to find Dr. Sun himself. They searched every twisted lane and street and every house in the city. They offered a high reward for Dr. Sun dead or alive.

Once more the great Dr. Sun had escaped.

While all the searching was going on, three ragged men approached the wall of the city. It was two o'clock on a dark night. Two of the three were carrying a big basket. Police stopped them and looked into the basket. It was empty. "It is for the fish we are going to catch," said the men.

But at the wall, the smallest of the three, who was Dr. Sun, crept into the basket. The others fastened a strong rope to the basket and carefully lowered it over the wall. Soon they heard Dr. Sun whisper, "All right. I'm safe." And, after making sure there was no one around to see him, he stepped silently out of the basket. Ragged and dirty he walked and swam and sailed in boats until he reached Canton, the city of his birth.

But Dr. Sun knew that because there was a price on his head his family would be in danger. Whenever a man did anything the Manchus didn't like, they punished his family as well as himself. Dr. Sun realized he must get his family away. Once more Ah-wei came to the rescue. He sent money to his father so that the whole Sun family —except Yat-sen, of course—could slip away to Hawaii. When they got there, Ah-wei took them in.

Now Dr. Sun was an open enemy of the Manchus. He was in danger everywhere in China. He was nearly caught once on a river bank. Many Chinese women worked as rowers of boats. Dr. Sun and his friends managed to hire some of these boats. After they got far enough from shore, the men bribed the women to change clothes with them, and in the women's shabby clothes they got away.

But by now the danger was too great. To get out of China Dr. Sun disguised himself as a Japanese. First he cut off his pigtail. This was not only for disguise though. The Chinese pigtail stood for old obedience to the Manchus. Cutting it off was a sign of new independence. Dr. Sun then put on western clothes instead of the long Chinese robes, and slipped away to Japan. In Japan he lived in a poor room with little furniture but many books. There he went on with his secret work—writing letters to China and getting help from the Japanese to overthrow the Manchus.

Soon, though, he was no longer safe in Japan. So he set out on long years of travel all over the world. Wherever there were Chinese people, he met and spoke to them about what he was trying to do to free China. Those who had money gave him large sums. Poor laundrymen and other laborers who worked day and night gave what they could, and it was almost always more than they could afford.

Even in foreign countries Dr. Sun's meetings with Chinese people had to be secret. Detectives followed him everywhere. They would try to report back to China the names of any who helped him. And then their families back home would lose their property and sometimes even their lives. Dr. Sun was hunted like a criminal. One time on a ship crossing the Atlantic from the United States, a man burst into his cabin. The man was trembling though he carried a big knife in his hand. "Get down on your knees," he croaked. "I am going to chop off your head."

Dr. Sun looked at him in cool calm. "Why do you want to kill me?" he asked.

"For five thousand dollars. That is what I will get if I kill you. I need that money."

Dr. Sun talked quietly to the man, told him what he was trying to do for China. And before he was through, it was the would-be murderer who fell to his knees. He dropped his knife and, weeping, begged for forgiveness.

During these years of travel, Dr. Sun made millions of friends for his cause. Ten times he went back to China and tried to start a new rebellion. But each time the superior arms and vast amounts of the Manchus' money defeated him. Ten tries and ten defeats. Another man would have given up. But Dr. Sun went right on. It was a long, hard, slow build-up. But with each defeat he gained more friends in China.

Then, just when things seemed to be going well at last, the whole cause was nearly lost, and Dr. Sun's life with it. At this time Dr. Sun was working for the Revolution with the Chinese in London. Dr. Cantlie, now Sir James Cantlie, the great surgeon who had been Sun Yat-sen's medical teacher in Hong Kong, was now living in London. One evening Dr. Sun had dinner with Sir James and his wife. After dinner, though it was late, he decided to walk home. He always felt safer in London than anywhere else because the English are a law-abiding people. As he strolled along, another Chinese came up to him and said, "I have heard much of you, Dr. Sun. May I walk with you part of your way?"

Dr. Sun was used to this sort of thing and he said he would be pleased. After a little while another Chinese came up and greeted the first one. Now there was a man on each side of Dr. Sun. They kept smiling, but they held Dr. Sun's arms in a tight grip. Dr. Sun was strong and muscular, but these men were younger and there were two of them. And then he saw that they were leading him toward the Chinese Legation in London. When Dr. Sun tried to walk past it, the two men said, "Oh sir, you must come in and let us give you some refreshment."

In no time they were inside the door of the Legation. Two men with guns led Dr. Sun into a room. These armed guards backed out. The door clicked. Dr. Sun was a prisoner. He had been kidnaped. An officer came in the next morning and told him he had been arrested on orders from the Chinese government. He would be sent back there, a prisoner, to be tried for treason. That meant he would be beheaded.

Two guards always stood outside the door to his room. There was one window. It was high and barred, but Dr. Sun managed to pitch notes out of it. No one answered. Probably the people in the Legation were on guard and picked up the notes themselves.

Days passed. The only person Dr. Sun ever saw was a young man, an English servant who brought him his meals. His real name is not known. We'll call him Tompkins.

"Young man," said Dr. Sun one day to Tompkins, "do you know what they are waiting for, why they keep me here day after day? I should think they would put me aboard a ship."

Tompkins looked behind him at the closed door and then whispered, "They are trying to charter a special ship so that no other passenger will see you."

"So," thought Dr. Sun, "I will vanish and none of my friends will know what has happened to me."

Indeed, the Cantlies were already wondering why they had not heard from him.

Dr. Sun knew he had no time to lose. He must do something at once. But what? Perhaps Tompkins would help. At least it would be worth a trial. So the next time the man brought his dinner, Dr. Sun told him he had written a note. Would Tompkins take it to his friend the doctor, Sir James Cantlie?

Tompkins shook his head. "Sir, I cannot. I too am watched when I leave here. I don't know what they would do to me if they caught me slipping out a note for you."

Dr. Sun said, "Young man, are you a Christian?"

"Oh yes, sir," said Tompkins.

"As a Christian would you see me die

while you refuse to help?"

Without answering, the young man took up the tray and hurried out. But the next day he said, barely opening his lips, "This is my evening off. I can not take a note since I may be searched. Or I may be followed and watched. But tell me your message and I will see what I can do."

That evening, Tompkins told his wife what had happened. She burst out, "I could not sleep at night if our English people allowed such a shameful thing as this kidnaping of Dr. Sun. You go back to your job. I will do what I can to save Dr. Sun. I will get the message to Dr. Sun's friend."

Late that night Sir James Cantlie woke up suddenly. Yes, he was right; there was a tapping on the knocker of his door. He went to the window. On the steps he saw a woman with a shawl hiding her head. She looked up and put her finger to her lips. Then she made sure he saw her slip a piece of paper under the door. Before he could move, she vanished around the corner. He hurried down to read the note. It said: "Your friend is in prison. The Chinese agents have him. He will die unless you rescue him."

Sir James threw on his clothes, went at once to the police, and told them about Dr. Sun. But the Chief merely said, "This is nonsense. Why don't you mind your own business?"

Sir James was horrified. He wrote to the papers about what had happened. Not one of them printed it. He tried the courts. In vain. At last a popular newspaper published the story. And then it made a sensation in all of England. British newspaper men crowded into the Chinese Legation. Terrified, the officials thought of rushing Dr. Sun out on a regular passenger ship. But they were too late. England boiled with anger. So, quite forgetting their usual courtesy, the people at the Legation opened the locked doors and told Dr. Sun to get out at once.

He never forgot Tompkins and his wife. He knew it was nothing but their courage and daring that had stood between him and death. He saw to it that they were properly rewarded.

The newspaper stories about his kidnaping brought Dr. Sun new friends all over the world. In China itself millions of people rose in rebellion. They were not only the poor people but thousands of rich ones who knew that they too would be better off in a modern China.

Among these wealthy families were the Soongs, who believed in the American way of life. They gave money, advice, and help. In that family there were several sons and three beautiful daughters. The eldest daughter, Ai-lien, became Dr. Sun's secretary. Her beautiful sister, Ching-ling, became his wife. The youngest daughter, Mei-ling, married Generalissimo Chiang Kai-shek, making him Dr. Sun's brother-in-law.

In the year 1911, the revolution was won at last, and Dr. Sun Yat-sen was elected the first President of the Republic of China. The small man, true to his name of Free Spirit, had led the fight to get rid of the Manchus.

When Sun Yat-sen died, China wept. Today millions of Chinese revere his memory and love his spirit of freedom. But it is not only the Chinese who love him. He is one of the great heroes of the whole world.

India's Hero of Non-Violence

MOHANDAS GANDHI

By Rosemary Nicolais

M OHANDAS GANDHI, the boy who was later to be called Mahatma, the Great Soul, was married when he was only thirteen years old. He and his pretty little girl-wife, Kastourbai, lived in his father's house until they were old enough to have a house of their own. Child marriages were then the custom in Hindu families all over India.

One day Mohandas came home from school and Kastourbai could see that something was troubling him. Presently he told her the whole story.

The day before he had been in a great hurry to get home to the big house under the palms and banana trees because his father was ill.

"Oh, there you are!" his father had said. "I've been waiting for you to read to me." He pointed to a big heavy book written thousands of years ago by one of India's great poets. Mohandas had opened the book and begun to read aloud.

"I was supposed to go back to gymnasium in a little while," Mohandas explained to Kastourbai, "but I couldn't stop reading until my father told me to."

"You couldn't disobey your father, of course," agreed Kastourbai. Obedience to parents was considered the most important duty of a Hindu boy or girl. "Was your

MOHANDAS KARAMCHAND GANDHI. Hindu nationalist and spiritual leader. Born at Porbander in Western India, 1869. Preached and practised passive resistance against aggression. Shot by a Hindu fanatic in New Delhi, India, Jan. 30, 1948.

teacher very angry with you for missing the class?"

"He did not believe me," said Mohandas, miserably. "He knew I didn't like gymnasium and he thought I was lying."

The girl was almost in tears. "You! You, who hate lies so much! How shameful of him! But do not grieve, Mohandas. The truth always wins in the end." And the truth did win, for a day or two later the teacher told Mohandas, "You are a truthful boy. I was too hasty in accusing you. I believe now that you would not have made up such a story."

Young Mohandas was brought up strictly, but he was a happy child. He liked to play games like all boys of his age, and he had faults like all boys and girls too. He and his cousin once ate meat to see what it tasted like, even though they knew meat was forbidden to Hindus. Afterwards Mohandas told his cousin he would never again eat meat, and he never did.

Before Mohandas graduated from high school he learned what it was to be unhappy when his beloved father died. Kaba Gandhi, his father, had been Prime Minister to the Rajah of the Province in which the Gandhis lived. His friends were all learned men, and when they came to see him young Mohandas sat quietly in a corner and listened to what they were saying. He was especially impressed by one thing he learned from these wise men—that there is good in all religions, and that other people's faith must always be respected.

When the boy left school, his mother sent him to England to study law. This was a great adventure for a Hindu boy. He had to learn to live as the English lived. He had to give up the white knee-length trousers and tunic of the young Hindu and wear European clothes. He had to speak the English language. But he remained firm in his resolve not to eat meat or drink wine.

For four years Mohandas studied hard. He wanted to become a good lawyer. But that wasn't enough. Even then Mohandas Gandhi felt that some day he was going to help his own people and that he must prepare himself for that great work.

At last the day came for Mohandas to return to India. Kastourbai and their son, born just before he went away, were waiting for him.

Kastourbai's big brown eyes brimmed with happy tears. "Never leave us again," she begged him.

"Not if I can help it," he promised. "I must begin to earn some money, though, to support you and our son."

That was not easy in a country so full of poor people, and soon the little family had to be parted again. A rich merchant asked Gandhi to go to Pretoria, the capital city of South Africa, to settle a lawsuit for him, and there was nothing for the young man to do but go.

"It's only for a few months," he called out to Kastourbai who, with her little boy, stood on the pier waving goodbye.

The lawsuit was easily settled, for Gandhi was a good lawyer. And he was a good man too. He knew that the man who had lost the case was poor, so he said to the merchant, "Let me beg of you not to press this poor man now for all the money he owes you. He can pay you a little at a time. I will see that he does so."

But something far more important than this lawsuit came of Gandhi's visit to South Africa. Traveling from place to place to see his Hindu friends, he found that many of the laws passed by the British, who owned the country at that time, were unjust to his fellow-countrymen. Hindus had to ride in separate, uncomfortable cars on trains and in the back seats of street-cars. They were not allowed in hotels. They were paid next to nothing for the first five years they worked in the gold-mines, and they had to live outside the town in miserable hovels.

One new law was especially hard on the Hindus. Their taxes were heavy, and the law said that all Hindus who did not pay these taxes by a certain date would be shipped back to their own country. As these Hindus had left their homeland because it was already terribly overcrowded, going back there would mean that they and their families would starve.

Gandhi made up his mind he would persuade the British to get rid of this bad law. He began by uniting the Hindus and getting as many as he could to join in the struggle. Then he explained to them how he thought they should behave towards the Government if they wanted to win.

"Conquer the heart of the enemy with truth and love, not by violence," he said.

This idea, which came to be known as passive or peaceful resistance, was not new. The founders of India's great religions had taught men thousands of years ago that violent methods harmed those who used them. But unfortunately, people had grown accustomed to the violence of warfare. They said, "If you believe in something, you must fight for it." And Gandhi said, "Yes. But not with brute force. You will harm yourselves more than your enemy by being violent." And they came to see that there was something wonderful in this new-

old idea, and something wonderful too about the man who believed in it and based his life upon it. They began calling him Gandhiji. Adding *ji* to the end of a man's name is a Hindu way of showing great respect for him.

Gandhi saw that the work he had set himself to do was going to take a long time, so he went back to India to get his family and take them back with him to South Africa.

On his return he decided that the best way to tell the people of South Africa the truth about the unjust laws would be to write about them in the newspapers. But no South African newspapers would print what he wanted to write, so he started one of his own.

"We will live on a farm," he said to his followers. "We will call it Tolstoy Farm after the great Russian writer who taught men to live happily with few possessions. We will publish our newspaper at Tolstoy Farm. We will grow our own food there, and spin and weave the cloth for our clothes. And we shall do no harm to our friends or our enemies."

When a good many people live together there is bound to be some quarreling, and in the early days at Tolstoy Farm two Hindus began disputing the ownership of some little trifle and the dispute became violent. This grieved Gandhi, and he thought of a way to make them sorry they had behaved badly.

"It is my fault if you do wrong," he told them, "because I am your leader. So I will take the blame on myself."

And his way of taking the blame on himself was to go without food for several weeks. When the offenders saw him grow weak with fasting, they were ashamed and tried not to give him any more cause to take the blame for them.

During these years of struggle to help the oppressed Hindus in South Africa, Gandhi had to work hard and face many hardships. But he continued to preach "No violence!" until the idea no longer seemed strange to his friends. They saw that his way of resisting injustice had a great force behind it, though that force never became violent. And in the end they had a very practical reason for believing in his method, because before he left them the Government did wipe out the cruel tax law, and they knew they had won their victory by Gandhi's kind of passive resistance.

When Gandhi and his family went back to India at last, they spent some time looking for a place where they could build a settlement in the simple Tolstoy Farm style. Gandhi had decided to devote his life to his poor countrymen at home, to live among them, and to teach them to resist evil and oppression by peaceful methods, as he had taught his compatriots in South Africa.

The site he chose for his farm-settlement was outside the city of Ahmedabad, near the West Coast. He called it Ashram, or Place of Rest. He built a school where besides the usual subjects boys were taught carpentry and farming and girls were taught how to spin and weave cloth.

Gandhi himself did not stay at Ashram all the time. He traveled, sometimes on foot and sometimes by train, in third class cars with hard board seats, so crowded that passengers were always hanging on outside the doors and windows. His work was to be among the poor, and he felt he could understand them better if he lived as one of them. He never seemed to think there was any-

thing especially good or unselfish about this way of living. And everyone who met him talked of his gaiety and enjoyment of life. More and more, as people worked with him, though, they saw him as a Great Soul, a Mahatma.

The first big resistance movement Gandhi started in India was directed against one of his country's most ancient customs.

"What is the use of my teaching that all men are equal," he asked Kastourbai one day, "when all over the land millions of our people are considered 'Untouchables'?"

The Untouchables were Hindu families who lived by doing the necessary dirty work of the world. Gandhi called them "The people of God." He said "Their life is one of service, love, and sacrifice, because they keep the cities and villages clean." He shocked a great many Hindus, including many of his friends, by taking an Untouchable, a girl named Laxshmi, into his home. It was not long, though, before these same people began to follow his example.

Another injustice Gandhi resisted was the "Purdah" custom. By Purdah Hindus mean the custom of keeping women shut up at home and preventing them from being educated.

"Why should our women not walk out into the fresh air?" he asked. "What we are doing to our women and to the Untouchables is making us weak and helpless. Let us get rid of these foolish customs with one mighty effort."

On the flag Gandhi designed for India he drew a picture of a spinning-wheel. Many people wondered why he thought a spinning-wheel so important, so he explained what it stood for:

"The spinning-wheel is on our flag be-

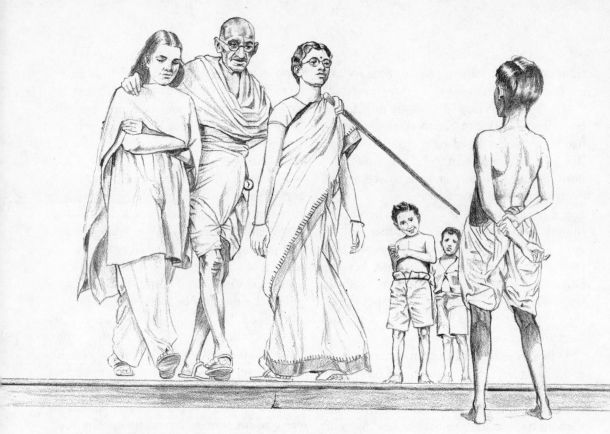

cause it is all the machinery India needs. Our country is different from Europe and America. There machines are all right. But here our people are dying of hunger. They must work to buy food—*now!* They cannot wait for the wonderful machines of the modern world."

India won her freedom from British rule during Gandhi's lifetime, but he was not happy about the way things turned out. Pakistan (meaning the Land of the Pure) in the North was made into a Moslem state, and the rest of India remained Hindu. So Gandhi's beloved India was now truly divided. All he would say about this separation was: "I have nothing to do with it." But he went from town to town and village to village—wherever he heard of violent outbreaks between Hindus and Moslems—and when he appeared men stopped fighting to listen to him.

"Wherever Gandhi is," said a foreign friend of India, "that becomes the capital of India."

Children were Gandhi's constant companions. They vied with each other in being his "walking-stick," because he liked to walk with a hand on the shoulder of some little boy or girl. His young grandson used to take hold of the end of the old man's cane and pull him along with it. People would laugh and say, "The leader is being led."

Mohandas Gandhi, the Mahatma, was mourned all over the world when he died. One winter evening in 1948 the news was broadcast that a Hindu enemy had shot and killed the great man, and Americans said in hushed voices, "Another Lincoln has been assassinated!"

But He *Did* Take All the Prizes

SIR WINSTON CHURCHILL

By Rosemary Nicolais

LADY RANDOLPH CHURCHILL, the cleverest and most beautiful woman in England, was unhappy. It was prize-giving day at Harrow, her son's school. She and her husband had started out early in their carriage from London, and on the way down she had told him, "Now Randolph, don't expect wonders. Winston will not take *all* the prizes." But she had not prepared him enough. She found that it upset him badly to see his twelve-year-old Winston stand at the foot of his class, carrying no prize at all.

"The boy isn't stupid," she said. "You'll see. He'll make a name for himself anyway."

"Precious little sign of it today," growled Lord Randolph.

Afterwards the boy explained. "You see, Mother," he said, "they never ask me the things I *can* tell them, only the things I *can't*."

Lady Churchill laughed. "Of course, dear," she said. "I remember when I was at school in America it was just the same."

Winston Churchill's American mother had known many sucessful men, and they had not all done well in school. She stuck to her belief in her son, and, as we know, he did not disappoint her. Winston Churchill's name became one of the most illustrious in modern history.

He began his career as a soldier.

A soldier's job, young Winston thought, was to fight. But there were no wars in Europe at that time. There happened to be one in Cuba, though. He would volunteer to fight the rebels there. He did, and won a medal for bravery under fire.

After the Cuban War was over he managed to get into some serious fighting in India, where the Northern hill tribes were making raids across their borders. Then the British were fighting the Arabs in Southern Egypt. Winston was late getting into that war, but he arrived in time to take part in the most important battle—the relief of Khartoum, the capital city.

An Army man has a great deal of time on his hands between wars. And that was Winston's opportunity to make up for all the time he had lost at school. He read and studied furiously. He began to write, too, for newspapers and magazines.

This is what he said about his writing:

"I was such a dunce at school that I was kept in the third form (fourth grade) for three years. This was luck. I had three years with the finest English teacher in the country. So I learned my own language thoroughly."

But that alone would not have made him the great writer and orator he became. He had, too, a special gift for using words in a vivid way, like all good writers.

During World War II, when he said,

WINSTON LEONARD SPENCER CHURCHILL. British statesman, writer, and military leader. Born in Oxfordshire, England, 1874. Educated for military career. Fought in Cuba, India, Egypt, South Africa and in World War I. Elected to Parliament, 1900. First Lord of the Admiralty, 1911. Prime Minister of England throughout World War II and again from 1951 to 1955 when he resigned. Author of monumental histories of both World Wars. Died in London, 1965.

speaking of the Soviet Union, "An Iron Curtain has descended across the continent," everybody knew in a flash what he meant. The term "Iron Curtain" became part of the language, though many who used it had no idea who had coined it.

He told the British people, during what he called their "darkest hour," "I promise you nothing but blood and sweat and toil and tears." His fellow-countrymen understood. He was saying he respected them, and knew they wanted the truth and could stand it, however cruel that truth might be.

Anyone might have said, "We will fight to the end." Winston Churchill, instead, painted a vivid picture. He said, "We will fight on the beaches, on the hills, in the streets . . ."

He praised the pilots of the Royal Air Force for their magnificent defense of Britain in words the world will never forget when he said, "Never in the field of human conflict have so many owed so much to so few."

After Winston Churchill had become a great statesman, he began to be known all over the world. People learned that he had served his country well not only in the Army but in the Navy too. He was First Lord of the Admiralty, and did his work there so well that when World War I broke out he was able to tell the King, "The Fleet is ready."

And with all that he found time to paint. The Royal Academy accepted his pictures as the work of a "Mr. Winter," the name Churchill used to sign his paintings. It was several years before he would acknowledge that he had painted them.

In spite of so much success Winston Churchill remained a modest, likeable man.

And perhaps the reason was that he knew a secret many people do not know—how to enjoy life. In fact sometimes in his youth his zest for life led him into rather reckless behavior.

He had an adventure during the Boer War in South Africa that made many of his countrymen indignant. They said he was foolhardy. Such behavior, they said, lowered British prestige abroad. Others smiled and secretly thought the young man a hero.

This is the story: The British and the Boers were fighting for the possession of the Transvaal, a large tract of South Africa north of the British possessions. Since those days, all South Africa has become part of the British Commonwealth of Nations. But in 1897 quarrels between the two peoples had to be fought out. (The word "Boer" is Dutch for farmer. But so many of the South African Dutch people were farmers that in time they all came to be called Boers.)

Winston Churchill had left the Army by 1897 and had become a newspaper man. He went to South Africa to report on the war.

The young man's troubles began when an armored train, that is, a train protected by thick iron plates to ward off bullets, was attacked by the Boers while it was on its way to the front in the Transvaal. The train was supposed to carry only armed troops, and Winston Churchill had no business to be on it. But he was. The Boers captured him with a number of British soldiers.

News traveled more slowly at that time than it does today, but in a few days the story of the armored train had spread all over the country. The Boers rejoiced at their luck in having in their hands the son of an English lord and grandson of a Duke. But their triumph did not last long. A week or so later they had to admit that the bird had flown. They offered a reward to anyone who could recapture him.

Churchill needed all his courage to escape from jail, for he knew nothing whatever of the Transvaal, where he found himself, except that it was in the hands of the enemy. He spent the first day following the railroad tracks eastward, as he knew he would reach neutral territory soonest in that direction. The distance was much too great for him to walk, but he hoped to find a freight train that would take him a good part of the way. He walked for two days, then the next night he managed to jump on a slow-moving freight car. He dared not risk discovery by remaining on the train during daylight.

The African sun was hot. He had had nothing to eat but a bar of chocolate since he left the jail, no water but what he found by chance in a ditch. After several more days of trudging alongside the tracks and hopping trains at night, he decided he would have to give himself up.

How he was going to do it, though, he had no idea, for there seemed to be no one to give himself up to. The desolate veldt (the Boer word for open country) stretched before him in all directions, an unbroken plain except for a few clumps of thorn-trees and one or two lonely hills. There wasn't a house of any kind in sight.

He dropped wearily to the ground, under an embankment, and fell asleep. When he woke up it was dark, and to his astonishment a light gleamed far off through the trees he had noticed earlier in the day. He made straight for it across the veldt.

The light came from the window of a

small bungalow that stood in the shelter of the trees, surrounded by a stone wall. Beyond the wall Churchill thought he made out the dark, bee-hive shapes of some native huts and a rambling, factory-like building. He ignored them and knocked boldly at the door of the lighted house.

"I may as well confess who I am," he announced to the man who opened the door, and he told him his name. To his surprise and immense relief the man motioned him inside, closed the door, and shook his hand warmly.

"You may thank your stars," his host said as he prepared a hasty meal on an oil-stove, "that you came to my house and no other.

I'm the only Englishman in these parts, the only man who wouldn't have either shot you at sight or escorted you back to jail."

Churchill's new friend was the manager of a coal mine, and it was in the pitch-dark coal mine that he hid the fugitive for nearly a week, until he could think of a safe way of getting him into neutral territory. He was able to persuade a friend, who was shipping a carload of wool through Portuguese East Africa to the coast, to hide Churchill among the bales. In this way the young man finally reached safety.

From the coast he sailed south to a town called Durban which was in British hands, where he was received with cheers and flags and band-playing. But Churchill was anxious to forget all about his escapade, and he wanted everyone else to forget it too. He joined the Army and served his country faithfully to the end of the war, without drawing any more attention to himself.

Back in England again, he ran for Parliament in 1901, and was elected. He married Clementine Hozier, daughter of a Scottish Colonel, soon afterwards, and, as he himself has said, they lived happily ever after.

During World War I Churchill was given command of the Admiralty because he understood how to handle the defense of island Britain against the enemy at sea. The British people had to get most of their food by sea from other countries. They would have starved if their Navy had not kept control of the seas. And Churchill saw to it that the British Navy did its job well. But he made one serious mistake. This was in the Eastern Mediterranean. British troops were being landed in Turkey when a Turkish force fell upon them and defeated them with heavy losses. As head of the Admiralty

Churchill was blamed and dismissed. For a while he dropped out of politics and fought with the Armies in France, but in 1916 the Government recalled him to take charge of the work of supplying ammunition to the fighting forces. Churchill speeded up the building of tanks and in this way hastened the ending of the war.

It was not until the outbreak of World War II that Churchill became head of the British Government as Prime Minister. Many people thought that if he had been in power during the Thirties it might have been impossible for Hitler to attack Western Europe. They thought Churchill had a better understanding of the dangerous ambitions of Hitler than any other British statesman of the times.

Throughout the war Churchill was the inspired leader not only of Britain but of all Western Europe. But by 1945, when the war was over, the people of England wanted to forget the war, and they voted Churchill out of office.

He was still active as leader of the out-of-office party in the House of Commons for six years. But he had more time on his hands than he had had as Prime Minister, and he spent much of this time writing his famous six-volume history of World War II. These books were widely read, and it was no surprise to his readers all over the world when in 1953 Winston Churchill was awarded the Nobel Prize for Literature. His reputation grew as people began to see that this great war leader was also a brilliant writer and historian. His wise and witty sayings became part of the English language.

Then, in 1951, the seventy-six-year old statesman was voted back into power again.

Later Queen Elizabeth made him a Knight of the Garter, the highest honor she could bestow. He had refused an earldom in 1945 and he spurned a dukedom in 1955 because men of such rank had to sit in the House of Lords. Churchill wanted to remain "a House of Commons man" where he could make laws, not just vote on them. On his eightieth birthday, when the world paid him homage, the prize he valued most was a book from the House of Commons signed by all its members and inscribed, in John Bunyan's words, ". . . so faithful, so loving, fought so stoutly for us."

After the end of the war in Europe, his countrymen repudiated him and his Conservative Party and gave the premiership to Labour's Clement Attlee. Bitter as it was for him, Churchill met this defeat with characteristic courage.

Fifty-seven years of happy marriage to his "darling Clementine" show still another side of this fighting man's nature—tenderness.

When the glorious statesman-soldier-historian died, at ninety, on January 24, 1965, one hundred and thirteen nations united to honor him. At his majestic funeral, even the Queen put herself in second place.

The panoply was for Churchill, the heroic Briton. But the United States, having made him her only honorary citizen, shared the mourning. At his own request, America's *Battle Hymn of the Republic* was sung for him at St. Paul's. All the world echoed its "Glory, glory, hallelujah."

Discoverers in Science and Invention

Thanks to Him, We All Have Books

JOHANN GUTENBERG

By Toby Bell

THE boy and girl were standing on a narrow street in Mainz, a small city in Germany, over five hundred years ago. They were staring at a shop with all its shutters closed.

"Come away, Reinhold," whispered the girl. "They say he's a wicked magician."

The boy laughed at her. He was a little scared himself, but he wasn't going to let his sister see it. Instead he gave one of her long blond braids a tug and crept closer to the shop, trying to peep in.

"Look! This Herr Gutenberg *must* be a magician," said the girl. "His is the only shop in town that hides behind shutters."

The little girl was frightened. In those days a magician was not a man doing tricks, but one who cast evil spells. "And you know," the girl went on, "this Herr Gutenberg is well-born; yet they say he works with his hands like a common man."

At that moment the door of the shop opened. The man who stepped out was frowning. He wore a rich velvet cape with a fur collar, but he was thinking so hard that he had forgotten to take off his leather apron. He did not notice the children. The

girl ran away. But Reinhold, the boy, stood his ground and spoke.

"Sir," he said, "are you really a magician?"

The man was half angry, half sad. "So!" he said. "Even the children talk this nonsense about me!" He looked down at the boy's eager face and suddenly smiled. "Would you like to see what I am doing in my shop? Silly people call this magic."

Reinhold gulped down his fear and his surprise, and in a small voice he said he would like it very much. At the door he turned and glanced down the twisted street to see his sister running wildly toward home.

Inside the shop Reinhold looked around for signs of the magician's art. He had heard about them often. There would be holy objects hanging upside down, maybe, or a cat that could talk, or a pannikin of blood, or a tiny dwarf. There were none of these here. But right in front of him stood a monstrous-looking wooden machine. Scattered about on tables were pieces of metal with strange marks on them. But when the boy noticed a beautiful crucifix on the wall, he was comforted. He knew the holy cross would not be found in a wicked place.

JOHANN GUTENBERG. Inventor of printing by movable type. Born in Mainz, Germany, about 1397. Suffered many misfortunes in trying to perfect his method of printing. Made first printed Bible, 1456. Died 1468.

He took off his flat cap, smoothed down his hair and crossed himself while the man watched with a half smile.

Herr Gutenberg now took off his fine cape and put on a leather jerkin. Leather was very good for turning aside the point of a sword; so workingmen, who had no swords, wore leather jerkins. But Reinhold thought, "This gentleman is a nobleman. He should not wear leather." And then the boy became even more confused when Gutenberg put back on his leather apron. Noblemen did not wear aprons of any kind.

But the man scattered the boy's thoughts by asking suddenly, "Would you like to be able to read?"

"Oh yes, sir," the boy replied. "But my father is not rich. We could never afford anything as expensive as a book. They say our Duke can read though."

"Why do you wish to read?" asked Gutenberg.

"Well, sir, my friend Paul who lives near to us—he can read. His father copies the Bible for the rich merchants, and he has taught Paul how to read. It would be wonderful if I could ever read all the stories he reads about saints and prophets and heroes."

"What are you going to be when you grow up, my boy?"

"I am to be apprenticed to a shoemaker. My father belongs to the Shoemakers' Guild."

Reinhold's future was all settled. He did not want to be a shoemaker, he told Gutenberg. But there were really only two ways he could get out of his father's trade. He could become a soldier. Or, if he could be properly introduced, he might become a priest or a monk. The monks were not sup-

posed to earn money. For the glory of God they copied the Bible by hand, and sometimes old Latin and Greek books.

Gutenberg thought to himself that perhaps he could take this bright boy to the monks and give him a chance to learn to read. But first he must know him a little better to make sure he was worthy of the special training. So he said, "Come, I will show you what I am working on. Watch now."

And he explained to the boy what a printing press and the invention of movable type could mean. Until then only the richest men could own a book.

Many of the books did not even look like a book of today. They were what we call scrolls, hand-copied manuscripts. These were wound around a wooden roller and were sometimes fifteen or more feet long. They had to be unrolled to be read, and that, of course, was a clumsy slow performance. The scrolls were full of Latin and Greek learning, instead of all the lively and varied things we read in books today.

Gutenberg took Reinhold to the monstrous-looking wooden machine the boy had noticed when he came in. "Why," said Reinhold, "it looks something like the press we use at home to make wine from our grapes."

Any modern boy who saw it would have known that it was a rough printing press. It was not as good as one that can be bought today at a modern toy store, and it was larger and clumsier.

"Now," said Gutenberg, "you take hold of this handle and turn it."

The boy did so and the upper part of the press rose. In the lower part Gutenberg laid a clean sheet of paper. It was not like the paper this story is printed on, but much heavier and very costly. In those days no one knew how to make cheap paper. Gutenberg then took up a frame with bits of metal set in it. It was a page of type. Today a printer would say Gutenberg had set it in a "form" and "locked" it.

Across the letters Gutenberg spread black ink. He put the ink-covered form in the press over the paper. "Take the handle again, son," he said. "But this time turn it the other way."

Out of the press Gutenberg picked the same sheet of paper, but this time it was covered with black letters.

Reinhold gasped. "Why, Mein Herr, it would take Paul's father a whole day to write a sheet like this! It took you only a few minutes. It is a miracle."

"It was more work than you think, Reinhold. It took me years to work this out."

Johann Gutenberg wondered at himself for explaining all this to a boy he had never seen before. But he was a lonely man. Besides, he had heard bad news this day about men he had trusted. And it helped him to talk to a bright boy who showed so much interest in what he was doing.

"But, Mein Herr," said Reinhold, "how did you happen to think of this wonderful thing?"

"When I was about your age," said Gutenberg, "I was very grateful to one of the monks who taught me. I wanted to write him a little poem. I thought I would carve the poem out of wood and then print it. It took me a long time. But when it was done, I was shocked to find that I had made two mistakes in Latin grammar. I was ashamed to give it to the holy man. And I began to think how wonderful it would be if I could

make the letters separately and move them around, as I wished. If I had movable letters, it would be so much easier to correct a mistake. So here, you see, we have the movable letters."

For hundreds of years before Gutenberg was born, Europe was a mass of fighting, cruelty, and ignorance. People lived in despair. The only safe spots were around the churches. There the people went for protection and for such little education as they could get.

But by Gutenberg's time—in the early 1400's—things were changing. Up to then, the only people who could read and write were priests and monks and a few noblemen. Now merchants began to get rich and they too wanted to learn to read. Also, they had to write each other letters. But writing was hard to learn.

Far away in China, centuries before, men had invented both paper and a kind of printing press. But in Europe they knew nothing of that. There was no way then for people to get news of far-off countries except when travelers returned from them and told tales about what they had seen and heard.

Paper was just coming into use in Europe around Gutenberg's time. But it was very expensive. A sheet of paper cost more than a whole book would cost today. Most people wrote on parchment, which was very beautiful, but it was stiff and heavy. It was made of goatskin or sheepskin. Or they wrote on vellum which they made from calfskin.

By this time the monks could not keep up with the demand for books; so many people wanted them. So there came into being a Copyists' Guild. Members of the Guild would copy anything: a letter, a page, or a whole book. It took both the monks and the

copyists years and years to make one copy of the Bible. Such books were as valuable as rubies and much more rare. Even with the monks and the copyists working steadily day after day, there were only a few books in all of Europe, because the only way to make a book was by this snail-like copying, letter by letter, page by page.

Most people never saw a book. Many believed that evil spirits lived inside them. They thought that if someone found a message in a book, devils were whispering to him from the pages.

And then came Gutenberg. He knew that seals were used to stamp important papers and that they were made out of metal, then covered with soft wax for stamping. And he knew that there were pictures and playing cards printed from carved blocks of wood. "Why not do this with letters too?" he thought. So he molded a letter. And next he thought, "Why not make the whole alphabet like this?" This too he did. And after that he made hundreds of each letter. It took him years to do this because he had to make each letter by hand. He made the letters in Latin because people in his day thought it was not polite to write in their own language, like Italian or French or German or English. Christians who could write, wrote in Latin. Jews wrote in Hebrew. Both sometimes used Greek.

When Gutenberg first began making his letters, he ran into all kinds of trouble. First he tried making the letters of wood. In the press those broke. Then he tried lead. The heat of the press made them too soft. Next he tried iron. That was too sharp and cut into the paper. Finally he put three metals together. They worked.

Then he had a hard time with the ink. A copyist, working by hand, used ink made of lampblack. He wrote slowly, with a goose-quill or a brush and it dried smoothly and neatly. But on a press this kind of ink smudged. Gutenberg tried many ways of making ink and at last he found the right mixture by adding linseed oil to the lampblack.

Gutenberg had had a sad disappointment on the day he told all this to Reinhold. His work, that we can read about so quickly here, had taken him years to make perfect. Nearly all parts of it were far more expensive than they would be today. The only part that was cheap was the lampblack, because it was easy to gather that from the rush lights and smoking oil cups that were used then instead of the bright clear lights we have today.

Gutenberg did not have nearly enough money; so he got two men to join him as partners. They paid for his supplies. But they wanted to make and sell books fast to make money. Gutenberg told them to be patient. He would not turn out hurried work that was smudged or imperfect. But his partners did not care about that. At last, out of patience with Gutenberg, they said that the whole place belonged to them because they had paid for it. So Gutenberg lost his printing press and all his letters and paper. All he was able to save for himself was his first printed book, a Latin grammar.

Gutenberg took the book to the monks. They were astonished and delighted with what he had done, and they bought the book from him. Gutenberg asked them whether they would be willing to teach Reinhold to read and write, and they promised they would.

But now Gutenberg was most unhappy

in Mainz. He wrapped up his clothes and rode in an oxcart to Strasbourg, a city where he had lived for years with his mother and father. In Strasbourg he went on with his work and produced a number of books. And he made his printing better and clearer.

He had spent five years in printing his greatest work. That was the Bible, and it was in two volumes. Forty-five copies still exist. One can be seen at the New York Public Library. That means it belongs to the people of the City of New York. It cannot be bought or sold, but it is worth a large fortune.

Gutenberg himself got little money for his great work. When it was finished he was still a poor man. He went back to Mainz, where he was born. There the monks and the learned men honored him. The Archbishop saw to it that he had a regular income, and for the first time in the long years since Gutenberg had begun his work on movable type, he did not have to worry about money. So, with a mind at peace, he got together a small printing shop and went on working to make his printing better.

But he was getting old and tired. And when greedy men tried to take his property away from him, he let it go. He was now rather grouchy with weariness and disappointment.

Before the time of Gutenberg, all the monks and all the copyists, though they worked as hard as they could, turned out only a few hundred copies a year. But a few years after Gutenberg gave the world movable type, and as paper became cheaper, millions of books were printed in Europe.

Books began to make the world a wholly different place. People began to read about men and women who lived far away, and they got to know strange lands. Because of what they read about the world, they went on great explorations. Fifty years later Columbus discovered America.

Today, because we can read all we want to, the average boy or girl can know more about the world than even the most learned scholars could in Gutenberg's time. Without his movable type, books would still be few and expensive today. And there would be no magazines, no newspapers, no comics.

When he was still a boy, Gutenberg began to dream of better ways of making books. But he would indeed be astonished if he could see a boy or a girl actually getting any number of books from school or borrowing them from libraries—all free. And if he could look over the shoulder of a child reading and enjoying a good book today he would smile and know that his years of work had been well repaid.

Little could he have dreamed that in the year 1955 the *New York Times* would print a news article headed "Gutenberg Bible Makes TV Debut."

The article reported a nation-wide television program featuring the highlights of modern civilization. One of the most important of these highlights was, of course, the invention of printing. The television people thought a good way to dramatize this great event would be to show the original Gutenberg Bible on the screen. They asked the Library officials whether they would consider lending them the book for the occasion. The Library officials agreed—on condition that their priceless treasure be given the utmost protection during transportation.

A few hours before the show was to go on the air, the Gutenberg Bible was carried out of the Library by the Curator of Rare Books, accompanied by a Library guard. Two policemen escorted them into a waiting automobile which drove them and their precious cargo, closely followed by a police patrol car, to the television studio just a little over a mile away. After its TV appearance, the Bible was returned, under the same guard, and put back into the vault where it is kept at the Library. For its brief trip from Library to studio and back, the precious book was insured for $500,000.

How it would have pleased poor old Gutenberg could he have known that five hundred years after he printed his Bible with so much labor and heartache, it would have been accorded so much worth and honor! What he would have made of its appearance, reverently mounted on a velvet-draped stand and exhibited to millions of viewers over such an undreamed-of invention as television, we cannot guess. But we can be grateful, as surely he would have been, that his Bible was actually seen by millions and millions of people. This was Democracy's tribute to Johann Gutenberg, the man who made reading—once the exclusive privilege of the wealthy few—a gift for all who care about the immeasurable riches in print today.

He Was Disgraced for Telling the Truth

GALILEO GALILEI

By Rhoda Power

THERE was once an Italian boy called Galileo Galilei, who liked to sit by himself in a corner and make toys which could be worked by wheels and pulleys.

His father was a clever man who enjoyed making experiments, but he was sorry his little boy showed such an interest in mechanical toys. "The child will be a mathematician when he grows up," sighed he, "and there's no money in that. I want him to be a merchant."

To be a merchant meant that Galileo must have a good education, so his father sent him to an excellent school where he worked hard for several years. As the boy's reports were so good, old Galilei decided that he would probably never be satisfied with buying and selling, and so he sent him to the university, hoping that he would become a doctor.

One day the young student happened to pass the cathedral and went in to say a prayer. It was beginning to grow dark, and

GALILEI GALILEO. Astronomer and physicist. Born in Pisa, Italy, 1564. Professor of Mathematics at Padua and Florence. Devised simple open-air thermometer and telescope. Published works confirming Copernicus' theory that the earth rotates around the sun. Was tried by Inquisition and forced to retract this belief. Died, blind and in disgrace, 1642.

as he rose from his knees, a man came in with a taper and lit a lamp which hung from the roof by a chain. He left it swinging to and fro and passed along with a glance of curiosity at the young student whose eyes were fixed with intense interest on the lamp.

Backwards and forwards swung the lamp, casting strange moving shadows on the walls. At first the swing was quite a long one; but as it began to die, the distance was shorter.

Galileo stared. It seemed to him that the lamp was taking the same length of time to swing a short distance as a long one. He swung it again, determined to make sure. But he had no watch with which to test it, and so he put his fingers on his pulse and counted the beats. He was right. When the lamp was nearly still it took as long to do its little swing as it had taken to do its big one.

Galileo had made a discovery. He had found that the length of time it takes a weight on a string to swing does not depend on the distance it swings, but on the length of its chain or cord. This was Galileo's first discovery and because of it people were able to make cuckoo clocks and grandfather clocks, both of which depend upon this kind of swing of the pendulum.

Soon after this Galileo made friends with an old teacher of mathematics. The subject fascinated him so much that he gave all his spare time to it. His father scolded him and warned him that he would never grow rich. But it was of no use. At the age of twenty-six, the young man became a professor of mathematics, and, instead of making the salary of a doctor, he earned hardly anything. But he was far more interested in knowledge than in money.

One day he found that a heavy weight and a light one would both fall to the ground at the same moment. When no one would believe him, he said, "Very well, I'll prove it. Meet me in the square by the Leaning Tower."

Eager young students, gray-bearded professors, and all sorts of people from the town came to the square, shrugging their shoulders and saying, "What nonsense. Well, it will do him good to make a fool of himself."

Galileo only smiled. He climbed the stairs of the famous Leaning Tower of Pisa and stood looking down at the crowd. On the edge of the tower he placed two cannon-balls. One weighed a hundred pounds and the other one pound.

"Pooh!" said the people. "The heavy one will fall a hundred times quicker than the light one." And they laughed. Just at that moment Galileo pushed the balls over the edge.

They struck the ground at the same moment. The old books, which the professors had believed without trying to prove, were quite wrong.

Meanwhile, Galileo had been thinking deeply. In his day most people believed that the earth was the middle of the universe with the sun moving around it. Galileo could not believe this. He had read about an old monk called Copernicus, who had lived many years earlier. Copernicus had watched the stars and planets and had seen that they were in different parts of the sky at different times. He came to the conclusion that the sun was the center of all this movement and not the earth. "The rising and setting of the sun," said he, "*is due to the spinning of the earth*. The earth is a planet like Jupiter or

Venus. It spins like a top for *day and night*, and at the same time it makes *the year* by slowly circling around the sun."

"Don't listen to that rubbish!" said the people. "The earth a planet, indeed! Why, it's dark. It doesn't shine. Just think of the solid earth with us and our houses and the trees and the hills and the seas spinning around and around like a top, and at the same time careering around the sun. What an idea! Ha, ha." And they continued to laugh for years at the ridiculous notion.

But Galileo did not laugh. He thought Copernicus was right and he wished he could examine the planets and find out more about them. "If only they were nearer!" he sighed.

While he was thinking about Copernicus and his ideas, Galileo began to make experiments with spectacle glasses. He had heard that a Dutch boy had been playing about in his master's workshop and had discovered that if he looked through two sorts of spectacle glasses at the same time, holding each at a different distance from his eye, he saw the church spire ever so much nearer and upside down. A General had made use of this discovery for finding out the movements of the enemy. "I'll make use of it," thought Galileo, "to find out the movements of the planets. It will bring them nearer and may help me to prove that Copernicus was right."

He set to work. But none of his experiments were of any use until, one day, he picked up a bit of old organ pipe and, pushing a bulgy spectacle glass into one end and a hollow one into the other, he looked through it. For a minute he said nothing; then his face lit up with a wonderful smile. His queer new instrument had made things look three times nearer and not upside down. Galileo had made the first telescope.

News of his wonderful invention flew all around Italy. Everyone wanted to look through Galileo's spy-glass. He became the hero of the hour.

His life was now more interesting than ever. He improved his instrument, making it stronger, and he began to explore the sky. He gazed at the Milky Way and found that this strange brightness was made by numbers of stars. He gazed at the moon and found that it was a world with mountains, valleys, craters, seas, and plains like his own country. This had never been known before, and now Galileo could *see* it. He found that the earth shone like the moon and that what a poet called "the old moon in the new moon's arms" was really earthshine.

"Rubbish," said the people who did not like new ideas.

"But Copernicus was right," said Galileo. "The earth is a planet."

One night in January, he made a marvellous discovery about the planet Jupiter. He found that, just as the earth has *one* moon, Jupiter had several moons. Yet, strange to say, there were still people who would not believe him even when they saw the moons through the telescope. Of course Galileo only laughed at them. He had many friends and there was no need to bother himself with folk who did not want to believe their own eyes. And so, for many years, he continued to make new discoveries, and to teach people about Copernicus. "The earth," said he, "moves around the sun," and he explained all the good reasons he had for believing this.

Unfortunately poor Galileo was living at a time when it was not always wise or safe to teach what other men did not believe. And now, when so many people were listening to Galileo, his enemies were alarmed and angry. "He teaches things which are not in the Bible," they said. "His ideas are wicked. The learned churchmen say the earth does not move around the sun."

Messages were sent to Rome saying that this man and his telescope were doing harm, and so hot and angry were the arguments that at last the Pope asked Galileo to come and explain his ideas. Away went Galileo, telescope and all. He was kindly received, and at first he thought his visit had been successful. But before long the trouble began again.

As time passed, Galileo's life became more and more difficult. He was growing old and weak and he knew that the people who did not want to believe the truth were working against him. In spite of this he wrote a book about the ideas of Copernicus, and numbers of people read it with eagerness.

When this book appeared, Galileo was once again summoned to Rome. He was accused of preaching something which was against the teaching of the Church. In vain did his friends plead that he was seventy years old and ill, that the roads were bad, and that there was a quarantine on account of the plague. It was of no use, Galileo was obliged to go to Rome and face the judges.

He was brought before a body of powerful churchmen, known as the *Inquisition*. They did not put him in prison but they questioned and threatened him until he was ill with weariness. They told him to deny all he had been teaching, to say the sun and planets went around the earth, and that the earth was the center of the universe.

For a long while Galileo would not give in, for he knew his ideas were right. But at last he could resist no longer. "I am in your hands," said he. "I will say what you wish."

In the presence of his judges he was made to kneel, clothed in the robe of a penitent, and to swear that what Copernicus had believed was untrue.

Legend tells us that, when he had sworn that the center of the universe was the earth which could not move, he rose from his knees whispering, "But it *does* move! It *does* move all the same!"

Utterly broken and disgraced, knowing that his enemies would rejoice at his downfall, Galileo went home.

He continued to make experiments and to use his telescope. But life had still to deal him one more blow. He wrote of it, some time later, in a letter to a friend. "Henceforth this heaven, this universe, which I had enlarged a hundred and a thousand times . . . is shrunk from me into the narrow space which I myself fill in it." Galileo had become blind.

When he died, no one was allowed to put up a monument to his name, but we, who live hundreds of years later, cannot forget him. We profit every day by the truth he discovered but was not allowed to teach.

The Man Who Could Make Anything

ELI WHITNEY

By Helen Woodward

Today a boy can go into a dime store and buy a whistle for only a nickel, and for that he can thank a man named Eli Whitney, who lived in Connecticut a long time ago. And a girl who can buy a baby doll for only a quarter, can thank Eli Whitney for that too. And if they own an automobile, the whole family can thank Eli Whitney—because Eli Whitney is the man who thought up what we now call the assembly line.

Before that, he made all kinds of things, even a fiddle for himself when he was a little boy. He mended everybody's watches just for fun. And when he was only twenty-eight years old, he invented the cotton gin—a machine that made cotton the cheapest fabric in the world instead of one that only rich people could afford.

One morning in the year 1793, some people sat eating breakfast at the house of Mrs. Nathanael Greene, in Georgia. They were all staying at the house because it was so hard to travel then that people didn't just drop in for an hour or an evening. They came riding up on horses and in carriages and stayed for a week or a month.

The ladies at the table were dressed in fine silk robes that they had ordered from London. The men wore tight black knee-length trousers and blue coats. The children were dressed like the grown-ups, only littler.

All of them were eating more than we would eat today at a dinner: grits, with molasses and milk thick as cream, eggs and wild ducks and cold ham and hot biscuits and corn pone rich with butter. Nearly all these things came from Mrs. Greene's plantation and didn't cost much.

Mrs. Greene was the widow of General Nathanael Greene of George Washington's army. Her little girl, who was about ten, sat as close as she could to a visitor, Eli Whitney, from New Haven, Connecticut. He had come to Georgia to earn money to pay his way through Yale College. It was by pure chance that he was staying at Mrs. Greene's house and he showed his gratitude by teaching the little girl French and arithmetic. He would have liked to teach her, also, how to use a hammer and saw, but in that day no lady was supposed to know anything about such things, not even how to hammer a nail.

In a break in the talk, the little girl whispered something. Boys and girls weren't allowed to cut into grown folks' talk then, but this little girl was bursting with her piece of news. "Mr. Whitney has made me a real doll house!" she exclaimed in delight.

"Mr. Whitney can make anything," Mrs. Greene said, smiling.

"I'm glad to hear it," said one of the men tucking a great linen napkin into his collar as was then the custom. "Because now, Mr.

ELI WHITNEY. American inventor. Born Westboro, Mass., 1765. Invented cotton gin, 1793, making for enormous increase in cotton production. Manufactured firearms, devised system of making interchangeable parts for guns. Operated factory near New Haven, Conn. Died in 1825. Elected to Hall of Fame, 1900.

Whitney, I wish you would make something that will take the seeds out of our cotton. Of course I'm joking; that would be a plain miracle. But those seeds are our big worry. The seeds in a cotton boll are as thick as the seeds in a cucumber. You know it takes a plantation hand a whole day to take the seeds out of one pound of cotton. You can't make anything much out of one pound of cotton."

"I know," said Eli. "We have a few small mills up North that could make much more cotton cloth if cotton wasn't so expensive."

The man with the big napkin nodded. "And all those English mills begging for more cotton!" he said. "All the ladies at home could weave more too if we could make it cheaper. Well, I suppose we'll just have to do the best we can by hand work. But if you find a way to get rid of the seeds we'll all become rich around here."

Eli did not answer. Indeed he did not say another word at that table, because the thought flashed through his mind that maybe he could run some kind of comb through the cotton.

He saw, in his mind, exactly how it could be done. But he said nothing because he wanted to try it first and be sure it would work.

After breakfast, he stood looking over the fields of cotton. They were very pretty; the plants were full of the cotton fruit, white as snow. Negroes were picking them and throwing them into great baskets, singing in rhythm as they worked.

Now by hand he made a rough cylinder and in it he put two wire brushes or combs. He set this on a wooden stand to hold it firm and he put on a handle. Then he turned the handle as fast as he could. The cotton came through but the seeds didn't. They were too big. It took twelve slaves to do by hand what Eli Whitney's first rough cotton gin could do when one man turned the handle. His cotton gin was so simple that it caught on like wildfire. Anybody could make it and everybody did. Eli Whitney made almost no money from his invention. There was no patent law in America then. He sued for money in court, but onlookers who came to hear the case walked out and made the cotton gin for themselves.

Cotton plantations spread through the South, and cotton mills through the North. Cotton became so cheap all over the world that even in far-off China and India, poor people could afford to wear cotton clothes.

But Eli Whitney was not a man to stay satisfied because he had done one big job. He went back to Connecticut and in time he graduated from Yale. But all the while he was there, he kept making things. And while his hands were busy, he dreamed of new ways of manufacturing better things and with less work. He remembered the doll house he had made for the little girl in Georgia and he thought of a way to make a thousand such doll houses at once for a thousand little girls. His chance to show his ability came some years later when the government of the United States ordered ten thousand muskets from him.

A Mr. Terry, who was a clockmaker, rode up one day to Eli's shop, and stopped for a clock wheel he had ordered. "Eli," he said, "I hear you've promised to make those ten thousand muskets in two years. You know you can't do that. There aren't enough gunsmiths around here to do the work in that time. Tell me, Eli, how long does it take you to make one musket?"

"Not this time," said Eli. "You wait and see."

What he did was this: He made one perfect musket. Then he took it apart again. Next he made a pattern for each piece. It was like the pattern for a woman's dress where you lay the pattern on the cloth and cut it out and you can cut a hundred or more like it if you wish. A pattern for metal is called a jig, which is a nice merry word for a hard-working piece of metal.

"A week," said Eli, "and that would be fast. But that's not how I'm going to do it."

"How else?" asked Terry. "When I make a clock, I make each piece just as perfect as I can. And then I take the pieces and put the clock together. And I never know till it's done if it's right. Isn't that the way you do with your muskets?"

Eli made a jig for each part of the musket and one for the wooden handle. Then he made a machine that could manufacture each of these jigs.

Then he put the metal and the wood in the jig machines and made ten thousand of each at once. He put each part in a separate box. And all a workman had to do was to pick a piece out of each box and put the pieces together. In other words, they *assembled* the muskets. That is what we mean when we speak of the assembly line today.

Of course, it made the manufacturing of muskets faster and cheaper. But it did more than that. A musket often got overheated or damaged in battle. Before Eli Whitney's day, when a part broke, a man would have to take the musket apart and make a new part by hand to take the place of the broken part. Sometimes it didn't fit and he had to do it over again. Now Eli, when he made the parts for the ten thousand muskets, made

a lot of extra parts, so when one broke down, Eli would supply a spare part so that it could be quickly mended.

Mr. Terry came and watched and began making his clocks on the assembly line. Now millions of people who had not been able to afford a clock or watch, and who had had to tell time by the sun were able to buy a clock because the new way made it cheap enough. And so today all kinds of things are manufactured on the assembly line—everything from a safety pin to a pre-fabricated house.

Eli Whitney was a shy and modest man. He never boasted about what he had done. But *we* can boast today about this man in old New Haven who changed our whole way of life.

It is an interesting thing that when Eli Whitney went to Yale, he went to study law. But he didn't like being a lawyer; so he went back to his beloved machinery. And aren't we all lucky that he did?

The Boy Who Loved Birds

JOHN JAMES AUDUBON

By Carolyn Sherwin Bailey

JOHN AUDUBON had a stepmother, not the kind of cross stepmother one reads about in fairy tales, but one who loved him very much. John's father was an American, but now the family was living in the small town of Nantes in the Loire Valley of France. John and his father had been travelers for nearly all of John's ten years. Santo Domingo, with its jungles, clipper ships, spices and coffee plantations; New Orleans with its beautiful gardens, soft-voiced Creole children, and tinkling guitars; sailing ships that crossed the Atlantic Ocean with cargoes of tea, indigo and silks; France in the period of 1790—the boy had seen all these because his father was a trader and later an officer in the American Navy. But when we see John first, he is in the breakfast room of the house in Nantes and with him is Mignonne, his pet parrot.

Mignonne was a wiser parrot than most. Perched on the back of John's chair she plumed her gold and green feathers and talked a stream of French. She always had her breakfast with the boy and that morning she ordered in her sharp voice, warm milk, a roll, and some sugar. John's good stepmother hurried in with the breakfast tray, but before she could set it down a flying ball of fur dropped from the top of a chest of drawers in the corner of the room. Before either the boy or his mother could do anything, John's pet monkey, who had also been waiting for breakfast, had caught poor Mignonne about the neck and choked her to death.

This is a sad way to begin a story, but Mignonne's death started a deep love of birds in John's heart. When his jealous little monkey killed Mignonne in a fit of temper because the parrot could ask for breakfast and the monkey could not, John Audubon made up his mind that no other bird should die if he could help it.

At this time Mr. Audubon, John's father, was away at sea. Before sailing he had entered John in a day school in Nantes, where he would be taught the lessons that were thought best for a boy in those days: drawing, arithmetic, geography, music, and fencing. John loved his drawing lessons and soon showed that he could paint and sketch better than any of his classmates. But he liked to escape from his hard school bench and go wandering into the forest and along the banks of the River Loire, looking for birds. John's stepmother understood his restlessness and knew how much the outdoors meant to him. When he wanted to spend a day in the woods watching the ways of birds and rabbits, his mother packed a large basket of lunch for him. Long days when he should have been in school were spent outdoors.

JOHN JAMES AUDUBON. American ornithologist and artist. Born in Haiti, 1785. Educated in France. Moved to U.S. 1803. Painted birds from life in Kentucky and along the Mississippi. Went to England to sell his work, 1826. Returned to America and settled on his estate in New York City, now known as Audubon Park. Died 1851.

WOODBRIDGE

Soon John's room looked like a museum. The walls were covered with paintings of birds, the shelves with birds' nests. All the drawers held birds' eggs, pressed flowers and pebbles, each one carefully labeled. John was teaching himelf to be a naturalist, but this helped him very little in his school work.

After a while his father came home from his sea trip. On his first evening at home, Mr. Audubon called John and his sister into the drawing-room to test them in their school work. The little girl played a piece on the piano without the music notes. She read some French stories, repeated the arithmetic tables, and danced all the figures of a minuet. But, alas, John failed very badly in everything that he should have been learning in school. His father did not scold him, but the next morning John's trunk was packed and his father took him in a carriage to the depot where horses for Paris were waiting. John James Audubon was sent to a boarding school, far away from the forests of Nantes.

The change, though, was for the better. The lessons John had at his new school helped him in his study of the outdoors. Geography taught him how climate controls the growth of plants and flowers, how it affects the habits of birds and animals. Painting was added to drawing. John made two hundred drawings and paintings of birds and animals before he was sixteen years old, and his school marks were so high that his father gave the boy a trip to America as a reward. That was Mr. Audubon's native land, although John had been born in Santo Domingo.

Mr. Audubon had a business friend in the United States, Miles Fisher, a Quaker. Mr. Fisher owned Mill-Grove Farm, not far from the city of Philadelphia, a place of wide fields, avenues of trees, thick orchards, an old mill, and a delightful cave in which the peewees built their nests and sang. There Mr. Audubon left John. Mill-Grove Farm was almost as pleasant a place as Nantes. Its only drawback in John's eyes was what Mr. Fisher made him do. The man let him have a short vacation, but then he sent the boy to school, had him work on the farm every day after school, and allowed him to spend only his spare time studying nature.

John thought of running away, but one day he met Lucy Bakewell, who lived on the next farm. Lucy was an outdoor girl and loved birds and flowers almost as dearly as John did. Together they skated in the winter and had picnics in the summer. John watched and listened to one bird every day, learning its song, its nesting ways, and its coloring. Lucy helped him with the school work that he disliked, and John taught Lucy how to paint and draw. When John's schooling was over he decided to go West where the plains were covered with different kinds of flowers, and there were strange birds and animals to study. Lucy Bakewell promised to take care of John's collection of birds' nests, eggs, and drawings, and to wait for his return.

That was the beginning of John James Audubon's adventurous life. He traveled through the entire United States, walking, riding horseback, following the rivers in a flatboat. After awhile he came back to Mill-Grove Farm and married Lucy. They went West and opened a general store in Louisville, Kentucky, where the blue-grass country was kind to the cardinal bird, and many other brightly colored birds nested too. But John found that standing behind a store counter was quite as tiresome as school had been. He made his way to the Mississippi Valley to study water birds. After that he found work in the new museum's collection of birds. Soon he traveled on again, always following bird and animal life and making wonderful paintings of them.

Several times John Audubon's paintings were destroyed. He had trouble finding a publisher who was willing to spend the money that would be needed to print his large collection of colored pictures of birds and the descriptions he had written about them. But he knew that he would be successful some time, and his wife, Lucy, helped him write, waited patiently for him to return from his nature-study trips, and had the same love of their little feathered brothers that he had.

He went back to France to study with the famous painter Jacques Louis David. Back in the United States again, he took up his beloved work of naturalist and woods-

man. There was hardly a forest of all the United States that did not feel the footsteps of this great naturalist. He wrote once in his diary:

"I never for a day gave up listening to the songs of birds or watching them or drawing them in the best way I could. During my deepest troubles, I often took myself away from the people around me and returned to some hidden part of the forest to listen to the wood thrush's melodies."

On the banks of the Hudson River in New York State there are some acres of land set apart and known as Audubon Park. It was there that Mr. Audubon had his last home. He lived in a roomy house with a wide porch on which all kinds of birds were at home. The grounds were alive with small wild creatures. Squirrels, rabbits, and chipmunks joined Mr. Audubon at his outdoor meals. A little river crossed by a rustic bridge ran through the grounds. A robin built her nest above the doorway.

In many states the birthday of John James Audubon is celebrated as Bird Day, and Arbor Day comes close to this date too. But Mr. Audubon liked every child to keep every day, winter and summer, autumn and spring, as a chance for watching and loving one bird, one small wild creature, or one flower. He was our great discoverer of birds. He taught us their beauty, their usefulness in helping the farmer, and their music. He was the greatest bird painter we have ever known. His pictures fill the many volumes of his work on *Birds of North America.*

Because of his story which began with Mignonne the parrot, boys and girls all over America, and in other countries too, have banded together to keep wild birds safe and happy.

How a Little Boy Entertained Company

LOUIS AGASSIZ

By Carrie Esther Hammil

LONG ago in Switzerland there lived a little boy who was one day to become a famous scientist. His name was Louis Agassiz. Louis' father was a minister of a small church in the little town of Motiers, and very often other ministers came to see him and to talk over their problems.

One day when Louis was helping his mother with the noonday dishes, they heard a sound out in front.

"Oh, dear!" Madame Agassiz said as she laid down the dish towel. "I hear a horse. Pastor Le Brun must be here. Papa is expecting him. But Papa isn't home yet."

"I'll go and see who it is, Mother," Louis offered as he dried his hands.

He was glad to have a chance to greet one of Papa's guests. He wanted to show how polite and helpful he could be.

As he opened the door, he recognized the tall man who was busy looping his horse's reins around the gate post.

"How do you do, Pastor Le Brun," Louis said. "Papa was called to see a sick man, but he will be back any moment. I will try to help him by talking to you until he comes."

"Well, Louis," the guest said, "you are growing up! You are going to be a good helper."

"Let us go into the house," Louis invited politely.

After the minister had spoken to Louis' mother, he and Louis and Auguste, the little brother, sat down in the parlor. Louis did want Auguste to behave. But he squirmed and squirmed.

"Would you like to see my pets?" Louis asked the minister, hoping he could keep Auguste busy and entertain his guest, too. Papa had said that a good host made sure his company was having a good time.

"Why, yes, Louis," Pastor Le Brun answered. "What kind of pets do you have—dogs or cats?"

"Wait and see," Louis replied, laughing. He turned to Auguste, who was glad to have an excuse for not sitting still. "Auguste, you may bring down the householder family and the hoppers. I'll show Pastor Le Brun the chorusers." He bowed to the minister. "Will you please come with me, sir?"

Pastor Le Brun followed the boy to a porch where there were many cages of birds, each trying to outchirp the other.

"Is there any kind of bird you don't have?" the minister asked.

"Oh, yes!" the boy replied seriously. "I have only a few kinds."

"What do you do with them?"

"I study them," replied Louis. "Some birds can crack seeds in their beaks." He pointed to different birds. "This one likes seeds, and that one doesn't."

"Louis!" Auguste's voice suddenly rang through the house.

Louis ran into the parlor. There, all over

LOUIS AGASSIZ. Naturalist. Born in Switzerland, 1807. Always interested in studying nature at first hand. Came to the U.S. in 1846 to lecture at Harvard. Made many explorations in the fields of plant and insect life. Wrote many important books on his findings. Died 1873.

the floor, were little turtles and big ones, brown ones and green ones. They were under Papa's desk and under the couch. One big brown fellow was heading for the fireplace, where the snapping flames no doubt sounded to him like another turtle.

Louis caught it when it was only a few inches from the hearth and thrust it into the startled pastor's hand.

"Please take him!" he cried. He turned to his little brother. "Oh, why did you let the householders get away!"

Just then the children's mother appeared at the door.

"What has happened?" she asked.

"The householders ran away, Mama," cried little Auguste.

"Well, be sure you catch them all," she said and disappeared.

"Why do you call them householders?" Pastor Le Brun asked.

"Because they own their own houses," Louis replied, backing out from under the table with a turtle in each hand.

He started to give them to the minister, who already held the big brown turtle in one hand and four small ones in the other. Two little heads peeked out of each pocket of his long-tailed coat.

Just then the door opened.

"Papa! Oh, Papa!" cried Louis, much ashamed that his efforts at being helpful had turned out so badly.

Papa Agassiz stood in the hallway with his tall silk hat in his hand. He bent forward in a courtly bow to his guest. He stared in astonishment.

"What is going on here?" he asked.

Then he and his guest burst into merry laughter.

"Welcome to your home, now taken over by the householders!" said Pastor Le Brun.

"Wait," said Louis' father as he started for the kitchen. "I'll get the clothes basket. Louis, this is the end! Out go those, those——"

And away he went, laughing and trying very hard to be a firm parent at the same time.

All his life Louis Agassiz collected creatures of different kinds. When he was in college, his roommate became as exasperated with him as his father had been.

In 1846 Louis Agassiz came to America. Later, at Harvard University, he began teaching classes in Nature Study.

One April Fool's Day a man thought it would be great fun to try to fool Agassiz. Very carefully he pasted together parts of various insects.

Handing this strange creature to Agassiz, he said, "Professor, would you please tell me the name of this fancy bug?"

Professor Agassiz gave it a quick glance. Then he looked up and with a very serious face replied, "Yes, humbug!"

Not long before his death, in 1873, Professor Agassiz established the first summer school of science on a small island off the coast of Massachusetts. There the students learned about nature not only from books but from direct contact with the growing things themselves.

Many claim that Louis Agassiz was America's greatest naturalist.

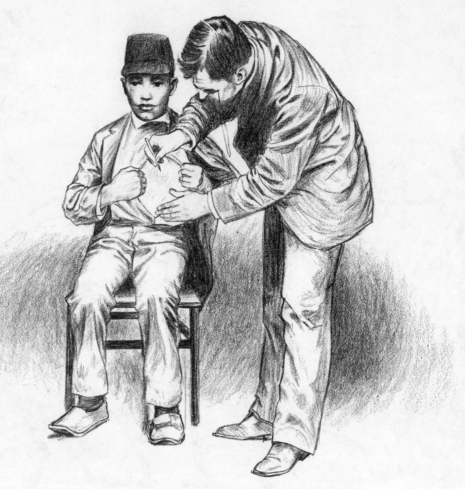

A Great Life-Saver

LOUIS PASTEUR

By Ariadne Gilbert

M<small>AD</small> dog! Mad dog!" That cry in any country, in any street, is terrifying even today. But how much worse was the cry "Mad wolf!" years ago in France through the nestling towns of the Jura Mountains! Very gravely Monsieur and Madame Pasteur cautioned small Louis and his own sisters to stay in the tannery-yard close to the house. Their fears were not groundless. Eight people in the neighborhood were bitten; and, for a long time, every one in the country around was in terror of

LOUIS PASTEUR. Chemist and bacteriologist. Born in France, 1822. Proved that fermentations are caused by minute organisms. Safeguarded milk and other foods by a method later named for him—*pasteurization*. Saved French silk industry by curing silkworm disease. Developed successful treatment of hydrophobia and rabies. Died 1895.

that mad wolf.

Louis Pasteur had been a Christmas present to his father and mother, for he was born, in 1822, only two days after Christmas, in the village of Dole in France.

Though the parents had little to give him but their love, the child soon found his own playthings in the bits of bark lying around his father's tannery-yard. Before long he began to feel proud of the good leather which his father made. The lessons of the tannery-yard were the beginnings of his training in science. They taught him to look for developments.

At school, the boy was so careful that people thought him slow. He slighted nothing. Only absolute sureness could satisfy him. "Dear Sisters," he wrote home, "When one is accustomed to work, it is impossible to do without it. Besides, everything in this world depends on that." In one of his letters he spoke of studying mathematics till he got a "pretty bad headache." But "those headaches never last long," he quickly added, not willing to worry anyone.

At nineteen he entered the Barbet boarding-school in Paris. He had grown tall and self-reliant, and he soon proved himself so capable that he was asked to help with the teaching. By this means, his schooling cost him only one-third of the usual price. Outside of study or teaching hours he had some good times. But Louis was always in danger of overworking.

In the Jura home, parents and sisters waited eagerly for Louis' thick letters. The hopes of the whole family were centered in the boy at school.

Pasteur carried his hunger for knowledge with him when he entered the Ecole Normale. Here, to save time, his chemistry class did not experiment to get phosphorus. They were merely told how to get it; and many were satisfied to go no further. Pasteur, however, worked it out for himself. He bought bones, burnt them to ashes, and then treated the ashes with sulphuric acid.

By a love for work that was almost a passion, Pasteur went on from questioning lifeless crystals to waging war for man. Whenever he found a need, he tried to meet that need with help. Crystals, acids, the ferments of milk and alcohol, the diseases of silkworms, hens, goats, pigs, and sheep—cholera, fevers, and hydrophobia—all these seized his eager attention. Scientific zeal, patriotism, and love for service goaded him on to further discoveries in conquering disease and healing the sick.

The tanner's son, through working and waiting, had grown very great, great enough to be known by the people everywhere. The vine-dressers, who tended their grapes on the sunny hills of France, they knew his name. Because Pasteur had found a way to keep vines healthy, they could sell their grape juice, and bring home shining coins to buy blue ribbons for Annette and stout shoes for Pierre. Pasteur had kept their hearts glad and their homes comfortable, and had saved one of the great industries of France.

By and by the shepherds, the goatherds, and the swineherds, even the poultry-men, heard his name. "Perhaps," one would say, "he would know what has got into our sheep." Twenty had died out of a hundred, beginning to droop only a few hours before.

"It may be Pasteur could cure my hens," a second would suggest, as he leaned over the poor staggering creatures that seemed to have fallen asleep while trying to walk.

How much the tanner's son could do who had begun life by "curing" leather! France was his own land, and the French his own people. In the sight of his eager patriotism, service done for the French was like service done for a big family.

Pasteur had never seen a silk-worm when, urged by the French government, he attacked the epidemic that had raged among the silk-worms for fifteen years. But the boy, Pasteur, had known how much depended on the making of leather and it was easy for the man, Pasteur, as he journeyed into southern France, to see that the hopes of hundreds of families depended on successful silk-worm culture. What other use had those groves of mulberry-trees? With no silk to spin what would become of the mill-workers? Three-year-old children understood that, whatever else happened, the fires that warmed the worms must not go out and everything that touched them must be perfectly clean. Silk-worms will not stay on dirty mulberry leaves. Pasteur, beginning with the tiny eggs, or "seeds" as they are called, used this sure method of protection: The moth, which dies anyway soon after her eggs are laid, was "crushed" in a mortar and mixed with a little water; the mixture was examined with the microscope—and, if a germ of the disease was found, the eggs, between 300 and 700 from each moth, were immediately destroyed with everything belonging to them. It was the old law of the survival of the fittest.

Only the eggs from healthy moths are used for hatching, for, as some one has said, "from healthy moths healthy eggs are sure to spring, from healthy eggs, healthy worms; from healthy worms, fine cocoons, and of course from the best cocoons the best silk."

Eggs are said to be "pasteurized" when they are the eggs of a perfectly healthy moth. The word "pasteurize" has worked into our dictionaries from Pasteur's great name and by it is meant that anything—milk, for instance—is pure, free from living germs. It is something for a man's name to stand in the dictionary, to the end of time, for safeguarding man's health.

In Pasteur's five years' work to save the silk-worms, he had the satisfaction of seeing disease conquered. He wanted no higher pay. Creeping from millions of "seeds" came millions of worms, so tiny that at first the mulberry leaf food had to be shredded. Soon, however, they were feeding away with a whispering noise, as if they were starved. Before long, from a moving mass of life, the separate worms showed themselves —great, grayish, velvety things as big as your little finger, fatter and fatter every day, and ravenously hungry. By and by they tried to stand on their tails in the feeding racks, and reared and stretched their necks as if asking to climb. Then it was time to bring bundles of brier brush—the silk-worm's ladders. And, at last, clinging to tiny branches, there "set to work millions of spinning worms that in their green shops weave the smooth-haired silk."

The "reels" spun by one worm are anywhere from a thousand feet to more than two miles long. In the light of Pasteur's cure, it is no wonder that, after years of failure, the silk-worm husking was a jubilee.

For Pasteur it was enough to have brought such joy to unnumbered homes.

Returned to his work of healing, as he entered the Zoological garden of the Institute, the children would run to him, throw their arms around him, and bless him with their

perfect trust. And silver coins slipped very naturally out of his pockets into theirs.

As his step was heard in the hospital, the heads on the pillows turned toward him and the faces lighted with smiles. It was worth the long hours spent in searching, the slow tests, the patient waiting; it was worth more than medals or degrees, this great love of thankful hearts. Pasteur had plenty of honors; but he counted them as merely words and ribbons. He was too great to think himself great.

He had a passion for scientific study and a great gift for teaching. His pupils came away filled with his love of truth, his unwillingness to state a fact unless proved and proved again. Pasteur would never rob a student of the joy of discovery. As a lad, it had meant much to him to make his own phosphorus. "Where will you find a young man," he would ask, "whose curiosity and interest will not immediately be awakened when you put into his hands a potato, when from that potato he may produce sugar, from that sugar he may produce alcohol, from that alcohol ether, and vinegar?"

At the root of all his teaching lay the principle of *usefulness*. "One man's life is useless if it is not useful to others," he said.

As he grew older and realized too fully that the years would not grant him time to solve all his problems, he looked to his pupils to carry on his work.

In Pasteur's life, the years 1885 and 1886 were marked by wonderful strides toward the conquest of hydrophobia. The terrible memory of the mad wolf of his childhood had never worn away. It came back to him in manhood with fresh horror when, one July morning, an Alsatian mother, poorly dressed and leading a nine-year-old boy by the hand, entered his laboratory. Little Joseph Meister could hardly walk, and his hands were fearfully bitten. Mrs. Meister begged Pasteur to save her child. "When the dog flew at him," she said, "he knew no more than to stand still and cover his face with his hands. A man, passing, beat off the beast with an iron bar. But there was my Joseph!"

"I am no doctor," answered the scientist humbly. "I am only trying to discover cures; but I shall do my best for little Joseph." As he spoke, he gently laid his hand on the child's head.

When Joseph found that the treatment was no more than a pin-prick, his eyes began to shine again. Out in the sunny garden, among the rabbits, chickens, and guinea-pigs, he was very happy, and he slept more peacefully than Pasteur, who tossed back and forth in the fear that his cure might not work and that the child would die.

But little Joseph got well. And in his long stay at the laboratory he grew to be such a friend of "Dear Monsieur Pasteur" that he would run in from the garden and climb into his lap.

Before long Pasteur's fame was world-wide. By means of a public subscription, four little Americans, children of poor laborers, were sent across the ocean to the wonderful healer. The mother of the youngest went with them. When her little boy, who was only five, felt the simple needle-prick, he asked, wonderingly, "Is this all we have come such a long journey for?" When, healthy and smiling, the four children came back to America, in answer to hundreds of questions about the "great man," they had no wonderful story. The treatment had been so easy!

But Pasteur had a story. On March 1, 1885, he could tell France that out of three hundred and fifty patients, only one had died.

If ever anyone was stimulated by obstacles it was Pasteur; but he removed obstacles for others. He made all healing free. No one was ever turned away. French, Belgians, Spanish, Portuguese, Russians, they came to him in daily crowds. Some came just out of curiosity—just to see Pasteur. He was always hard at work. Till within a few months of the very end, his energy went hand in hand with self-forgetfulness.

On September 28, 1895, he gave up his long battle. There was a great national funeral: a military band, infantry, marines, cavalry, artillery, and municipal guards, red-robed judges and members of University faculties in orange, red, and crimson robes. It was all more showy than the tanner's son would have asked. His simple grave-stone better commemorates his simple start in life. Though his name will always mean intense energetic action, that plain stone speaks of well-earned rest:

Here Lies Pasteur

In Insects He Saw a World of Beauty and Truth

JEAN HENRI FABRE

By Eleanor Doorly

No one would suppose that a man could win the title "great" by spending most of his life kneeling in the sand, or headfirst down a deep pit in his garden. But sometimes the world puts the label "great" on to the right man. It never dawned on Jean Henri Fabre that that was what the world was going to do to him.

He was born in the village of Saint Léons, high up in the barren mountains of France, where the snow sometimes lies in the village street till May. His father was so poor that his grandparents took the boy to their farm on the still higher and colder tableland of Malaval, so that there should be one less mouth to feed at Saint Léons. There, in a homespun pinafore trailing round his toes, his handkerchief tied to his belt with a piece of string because he lost it so often, Jean Henri made friends with the geese, the calves, and the sheep.

One morning, as he stood in the sunshine on the hillside, a thought came into his head: How did he see the sun? With his mouth or with his eyes? He opened his mouth wide and shut his eyes. The glory disappeared. He opened his eyes and shut his mouth. The glory appeared again. He did the experiment over and over again always with the same result. He had convinced himself that he saw the sun with his eyes. His grandparents laughed when he told them the tale in the evening, and some people think he must have been a very silly little boy. But the boy whom the great naturalist Darwin was to call "the incomparable observer" was practising observation.

One summer night he heard a strange singing in the bushes outside, a whirr, whirr . . . Night after night he went out in spite of being warned against the mountain wolves. He turned hither and thither to find out where the singing came from. At last he snatched at the sound and caught a grasshopper. He had learned by observation that grasshoppers sing.

When he was seven, he had to go home to Saint Léons because there was no school at Malaval. At Saint Léons the school was odd enough. There was only one room, which was schoolroom and kitchen, and it had the boarders' two beds neatly tucked in behind shutters in the yawning fireplace. The schoolmaster had many duties, such as ringing the church bell and acting as barber and getting in the harvest and clearing the Count's land of snails. The children, when they were not helping him, had to teach one another to read. They often interrupted lessons to steal a potato from the pot, or to play with the piglets or fluffy chickens that came tumbling into the classroom.

Jean Henri made very little progress except at studying the fine picture of a

JEAN HENRI FABRE. French naturalist. Born in St. León, France, 1823. Taught in South of France and Corsica. Retired to study habits of insects. Author of *Social Life in the Insect World* and other famous works on insect life. Died 1915.

pigeon on the *outside* of his A B C book. But one day his father bought him a card divided into squares, with the alphabet as initials for the names of animals: A for Ass, and so on. Then, because he loved animals, he soon learned to recognize the letters.

His father was growing poorer and poorer. To earn a few extra cents he set some duck eggs under a hen, and when Jean Henri saw them hatch out he was overjoyed. He took complete charge of the ducks. Every day he followed the yellow waddlers up the steep mountain path in search of a safe pond. He had a blistered heel, but he didn't bother too much about that. When the pond came in view, the ducks went head first into it and Jean Henri began to make a collection of wonders—a sky-blue beetle, a stone with a shell inside, sand that glittered like gold. Into his pockets went all the shining treasure, and when he followed his ducks down in the evening, his pockets bulged with fairy wealth. He never noticed that the pockets were torn. The young collector got a scolding at home, and his sky-blue beetle and glittering gold were thrown out as dirt.

Then his father, having failed in the village, took his family to town. There he failed again, though Jean Henri managed to go to a real school for a short time. He learned how to get honey out of narcissus, and how to play with other boys at hypnotizing turkeys, and other games that got them into trouble. But his family, by that time, was so poor that he had to tramp the roads to find odd jobs if he wanted to eat. But he spent his last cent buying a book of poetry, and he recited from it to quiet his hunger.

When Jean Henri came to the lovely town of Beaucaire on the Rhône, he worked as a laborer on the new railway to Nîmes. Afterwards he went to Avignon, where he won a free place in the training college for elementary teachers.

Next to his college was an old church which was used for teaching rich boys a subject which few people then knew much about. Even Jean Henri knew only its name —chemistry.

He longed to know what chemistry was. He climbed up to look through a window, but could see nothing but the "learned glass" being washed.

Then one day the elementary-school boys were promised that as a treat they could spend part of their next half-holiday seeing oxygen made. Jean Henri was so excited that he did not sleep all night. His first and only chemistry lesson ended in catastrophe, because the apparatus exploded before the oxygen appeared, and Jean Henri had to teach himself chemistry in the years that followed. He also taught himself mathematics because he wanted to get to the university to study. He became a mathematician and a chemist, but he never raised enough money to go to the university.

Instead, he found a way of studying insects different from anyone else's. To earn his living and support his family he taught in Carpentras, in Corsica and in Avignon. He was so interesting and he drew such crowds that the police had to come to control them.

The things he taught were then thought so surprising that even girls wished to break the rules which shut them out of science lessons, and longed to attend his lectures. He talked about such things as what water and air are made of, where the lightning and the thunder come from, why fire burns, and why we breathe.

But in those days, people thought such lessons were wicked, especially for girls, and Fabre was turned out of his post at Avignon. Heavy-hearted, he went to live at Orange and tried to feed his family by writing. But, though he wrote wonderful stories about nature that everyone now wants to read, in those days people scarcely bought his books.

He was very poor, but his poverty did not stop his work. Any day you might have seen him going out looking like a peasant herb-gatherer, with his trowel and his knapsack on his back and an odd collection of things slung around his shoulders: boxes, glass tubes, pincers, and a magnifying glass. In the heat of summer, he carried a big green umbrella for shade. The flies took shelter under it till the wasps found them and collected them as from a larder. Sometimes it was so hot under the scorching sun that Jean Henri would lie flat on his face to find shade, or put his head into a rabbit burrow. Once when he had sat in the sun all day watching the sand, some women, who had seen him there in the morning, noticed him still there in the evening, and exclaimed: "Poor thing, he is a little cracked; we must remember him in our prayers!"

Watching even one insect is not easy. Let anyone try it. Perhaps a moth or butterfly would fly through the air. Fabre had to run, stumbling through the stones of dry river beds, tearing his clothes and hands in clumps of bramble, often losing the thing altogether in the clear air. Perhaps some

creature laid its eggs at the bottom of a winding tunnel several feet deep. Fabre had to dig into the earth for the eggs without spoiling the tunnel. Perhaps the insect worked only in the dark. Fabre had to construct a house for it and make glass shutters that would close suddenly and imprison his insect. After Fabre had examined it he would open the shutters and let it go.

When Fabre wanted to know if bees flew straight home and how long they took, he had to catch them and mark them, and so gently that he didn't spoil their wings. But bees sting. And scorpions have to be treated with even more respect. These rewarded him and us for the trouble he took with them, by showing him night after night, in the glass he built for them, how they lived.

Careful watching helped Fabre solve many difficult problems. One day in a sunken sandy lane he discovered the carefully-made stony compartments which a certain bee makes to safeguard the grub that is to become the young bee. There was no entrance to the compartment and no exit and there were no holes in the wall; yet when Fabre broke through the stone he found a bee's grub eaten by a fly's grub! How had the enemy got in? For long days he followed the flies up and down the steep banks to see how they provided for their grubs. Patience and luck showed him one day that the fly's invisible egg hatches out not as a grub, but as a slim wriggling line, so slim that it can pass through stone as water seeps through an earthenware jug. In that form the fly's egg entered the bee's cell, changed into a grub inside the cell, and ate the bee's baby.

At last Fabre won one of the things he had longed for: a garden to which he could

OVER their tiny hills and cities bending,
An old man's face, kindly and comprehending,
Scans all the story of their little lives.

invite all kinds of insects and study them night and day. It was walled in to keep out disturbing people and lined with high pines, since insects don't want too much wind. It was crammed with bergamot and lavender, thyme and rosemary, lilacs and flowering cherries—all the plants and flowers that make luscious hiding places for shy insect creatures, and beauty for humans to enjoy.

In this garden Fabre could solve a thousand problems and see many strange sights. He wrote down all the stories of the beautiful, wonderful, unbelievable, fierce small creatures. He wrote charmingly in lovely French. He wrote only what he saw, but he saw more than anyone had seen before, and he introduced us all to a new world.

In his garden Fabre saw insects ugly and beautiful, insects with the worst and best of characters. There was the praying mantis who always ate her husbands. Then there was that little beetle that loved one wife all his life, though she was obliged to live at the bottom of a hole five feet deep and could never share his walks abroad. He gathered food for her to make loaves for his future children. He carried up day and night all the earth that came out of the five-foot hole. He ground the hard food and sent it down to her like flour and, as soon as their first child was provided for, he climbed out of the hole and died without reward.

We read Fabre's stories enchanted, as we read fairy tales. But scientists have learned his method of study and can use it now to save men and animals from being destroyed by insects. Fabre's work is deep in beauty and truth, and the world has given him the well-deserved title of "great."

How We Came to Have Telephones

ALEXANDER GRAHAM BELL

By Helen Woodward

Don and Debby Brown were sitting close together on the bottom step of the hall stairs listening to the thunderstorm that was raging outside. They were twins, ten years old, and they didn't like the noises the storm was making. The thunder rolled and banged; the wind howled and moaned. Debby whispered, "I wish Daddy was home." Don said in a clear, brave voice, "He 'phoned he'd be late."

Their mother called to them from the living room, "Come in here and see how beautiful it looks out of this window. The lightning makes the garden bright as day. We'll be able to see Daddy when he comes."

The twins ran in, eager to watch. But each of them did put an arm through their mother's. As the thunder came again, Debby said, "You know, Mother, it's the thunder I don't like. It's so loud."

Mrs. Brown said, "But Debby, the thunder doesn't do any harm. Thunder sounds like a growling dog, but it is the lightning that brings on the growling thunder. The lightning always comes before the thunder. By the time you hear the thunder, the lightning has gone."

"That's fine, Mother," Donald laughed. "Now when I hear thunder, I'll just say, 'Hi, Rover.'"

"That's right," smiled his mother, and added, "Did you ever stop to think how lucky you are to be able to hear, even if you don't like the sounds? There was once a Scotch boy named Aleck Bell who was so pleased with his own good hearing that he wanted to make it easier for other people to hear better. He began to think about it when he was quite young. His mother was growing deaf and he saw how hard it was for her to understand what people were trying to tell her. He did all he could to help her. And when he grew up, he thought how wonderful it would be if people could hear each other even when they were far apart. He thought about it so much that in time he invented the telephone."

"The telephone!" exclaimed Don. "Haven't people always had telephones?"

But before Mrs. Brown could reply, the lightning flashed again and lighted up the garden and the road outside.

Debby jumped up and down. "I see Daddy," she shouted, "I see Daddy."

After that they were so busy pulling off their father's wet things and spreading them out to dry that Mrs. Brown forgot to go on with the story of Aleck Bell and his invention. It wasn't until much later when Debby was in bed, half asleep, that she thought about the telephone again. "Aleck Bell," she said to herself, "that sounds nice." And she

ALEXANDER GRAHAM BELL. Scientist and inventor of the telephone. Born in Edinburgh, Scotland, 1847. Went to Canada, 1870. Worked on problems of deafness and speech defects, especially at Boston University, 1872. Founded American Association to Promote the Teaching of Speech to the Deaf. Became naturalized American, 1882. Died in Nova Scotia, 1922.

kept saying "Bell, Bell, tell, tell, telephone bell, hello, Bell" until she fell asleep.

Next morning the sun was shining and the twins came rushing downstairs. Both wanted to use the 'phone and each wanted it first.

But Mrs. Brown said, "Before either one of you can use it, I have to call up the market and give my order or we won't have any dinner to eat tonight." She went to the 'phone and lifted the receiver. But no sound came from it.

"The 'phone seems to be dead," she exclaimed, and remembering last night's storm, she said, "One of the poles must have fallen on the wires."

"Oh!" wailed Don, "then I won't be able to call Andy and tell him to come out with his skates."

"And I won't be able to call Ginny about our game," complained Debby. "Oh dear! What'll we do, Mother?"

"I wish I'd known the 'phone was out of order before your father left for the office," she said. "Now I suppose you children will have to walk down to the market and get what we need. I'll let you each take a shopping bag. You can stop in to see your friends on the way back. Their 'phones are probably out of order too. And the market man must be all upset if *his* 'phone isn't working," said Mrs. Brown.

"But, Mother," the twins grumbled, "it's such a long walk to the market. And Andy and Ginny will make other plans if we can't call them."

"Well," said their mother, "now you can see how it was in the days when there were no telephones."

"Why, Mother, how did people *manage* without a telephone? They've always had

them ever since *I* can remember," said Don.

"Yes, you've always had a 'phone," Mrs. Brown said, laughing because her children took it so for granted. "But when your grandmother was a little girl there were hardly any 'phones. Even Presidents didn't have any in the olden days. George Washington and Abraham Lincoln never even heard of a 'phone. Maybe if it hadn't been for Aleck Bell we wouldn't have one now."

"That's what I was trying to remember," Debby cried out. "Bell, Bell, tell, tell. You were going to tell us more about Aleck Bell. Tell us now."

"All right," said Mrs. Brown, glad to keep them from trying the 'phone every minute to see if it was working again. "This boy, Aleck, lived in Edinburgh. That's in Scotland. His name was Alexander, but everyone called him Aleck. His mother was getting deaf and Aleck and his father felt very sad about that. But she hadn't been born deaf. If she had, she might never have learned to talk. Children learn to talk by imitating the sounds they hear other people make. That's how you two learned—by imitating what you heard me and Daddy say."

The twins looked astonished. They had never thought of that. "Well," their mother went on, "Aleck's father taught children who had been born deaf how to speak. And Aleck helped with the smaller children, though he was only about your age when he began doing that."

"How did he do it, Mother?"

"He had many ways. One was this: Aleck would say a word while the deaf child put a hand on his lips to see and feel how they worked. Here, I'll show you. I'm going to say our name, Brown. You put your fingers

on my lips and see how it feels."

They did that, and Debby said, "It feels just like a little pop. What fun!'"

"Not so much fun," said Mrs. Brown, "when you have to do it for hours every single day just to find out how a sound is made. But Aleck Bell was very patient about understanding how deaf people felt. He had such extra-good hearing himself that he thought about hearing all the time. He even learned to play the piano just by listening to his mother who could play it and often did."

"Pretty wonderful; wasn't it?" said Debby.

"Indeed it was." And their mother went on, "One day Aleck's mother gave him a party to celebrate his tenth birthday. That was a little more than a hundred years ago. One of the little girls at the party said it would be nice if they could play 'Musical Chairs.' In that day there were no phonograph records and no radios."

"Didn't they have *anything* in those days?" interrupted Don.

"They had a great deal, but there were many things they didn't have. For one thing, they didn't have any way of making music unless they sang or played it themselves. And it just happened that none of the children at the party knew how to play the piano. There was some music on the rack, though, and Aleck went up and looked at it. He couldn't read a note of it, but he knew how it sounded and he had watched his mother's hands when she played. So he said, 'I'll play.'

"The other children laughed and said, 'You don't know how to play.'

"But he did. He played *Annie Laurie* and then he played *Home Sweet Home*. His mother hurried in and watched and his father came in and listened. They were certainly surprised and pleased."

"And then I suppose he took piano lessons," said Debby.

"He did, and he loved them. But he wasn't to become a musician. He had other things more on his mind even when he was a little boy."

"What things?" asked the twins.

"Well," said Mrs. Brown, "maybe this story about him will tell you. On that very birthday, his grandfather brought him a present. And what do you suppose it was?"

"An electric train," said Don.

"There were no electric trains then," said Mrs. Brown. "Things like that came much later, after Thomas Edison made his great inventions. No, his grandfather gave him a broken clock and said, 'Now you can play with this and put it together again.' "

"And did he?" asked Don.

"He did indeed." And there was something else about Aleck Bell and a clock that Mrs. Brown remembered. "It seems that in Aleck's school there was a tall clock in the hall. The clock had a booming chime that was supposed to strike on the hour but it never made a sound.

" 'You poor clock,' Aleck thought to himself. 'You want to ring your bell and tell us the time and no one will let you.'

"So one day when Aleck was in the hall alone, he climbed on a chair and went to work on the clock. And soon it struck one with a great and beautiful boom. The teacher came running out. He was very angry with Aleck. 'I told you not to touch that clock,' he said.

"Aleck was sorry, but the teacher punished him and he felt disgraced. What's more, the teacher stopped the clock's bell again because he said it made too much noise. But one day about a month later, Aleck noticed smoke coming out of a room

at the end of the hall. There were no fire alarms at that time, and there wasn't time to run through the school and cry 'Fire!' Quickly Aleck climbed on the chair, set the clock at twelve, and made it strike. Loud and clear came twelve strokes of the clock. The teacher came out, furious. But without a word Aleck pointed to the smoke. Everybody got out safely. And the teacher thanked Aleck before the whole school and said he had saved their lives."

"And then, Mother, did he invent the telephone?" asked Don.

"Not then," said Mrs. Brown. "He was still only a boy at that time. But years later when he and his family came to America to live, Aleck began to think that maybe he could find some way to send sounds over a wire. We had telegraphy then, but he wanted to make something better.

"You've seen the telegraph office," Mrs. Brown went on. "Words don't come over the wire."

"I know," said Don. "They change the words into a code, and then they send *long short, long short* over the wire. And it makes holes in a paper."

"Yes, that's right, Don. The *sound* doesn't come through the wire. Just the signals that we call the Morse Code.

"Aleck was living in New York at that time and teaching the deaf to speak. He was also showing children who could hear how to speak more clearly and not mumble their words the way some children I know do."

Mrs. Brown went on to tell them how Aleck spent every evening and holiday working on this idea he had of sending sounds over a wire. "But when you work on an invention like that," said Mrs. Brown,

"you have little models made to test it. And he hadn't money enough to pay a machine shop to make them.

"But one day Aleck had a great piece of luck. He met a mechanic named Thomas Watson. When Aleck told him what he was trying to do, Mr. Watson thought it was wonderful. He was a fine mechanic. After that Watson made the models and the two men worked together. But it took them years."

"I heard in school," said Don, "that some inventors just think of things and make them right away. Eli Whitney thought of the cotton gin and then went out and made it."

"Yes, he did," agreed Mrs. Brown. "But that doesn't happen often. Most inventors work hard for years before they can put their ideas to work."

"I've always thought I'd like to be an inventor," said Don.

"I hope you can," replied Mrs. Brown. "Maybe some day you'll invent something that will pick up clothes and put them in the closet."

The twins laughed.

Mrs. Brown told them that Aleck, about this time, fell in love with Mabel Hubbard, a very lovely girl who was deaf. They were engaged to be married. But Mabel's father didn't want his daughter to marry Aleck. He thought the young man was impractical and that he would never be able to support a wife, if he didn't stop having silly ideas about his invention. But Mabel believed in Aleck and said she would wait for him.

One day Aleck and Mr. Watson were sitting at opposite sides of a room, each with a little machine, trying to send sounds through it.

"Like a toy 'phone, Mother?" asked Debby.

"Well, no, not exactly. It had wires

wrapped around a spool. Each of the two men had a tuning fork and they would try to send the sound of the tuning fork across the wire to each other. One day they thought they had it, but to make sure Aleck went upstairs to another room. Suddenly, while he was up there, Aleck upset some chemical and his clothes caught fire. He called for help. He shouted, 'Mr. Watson, I need you!' And those words came to Mr. Watson over their wire. They were the first words ever heard over a wire. Mr. Watson rushed upstairs. 'We've got it!' he yelled. 'Not the tuning fork. Your actual words!' "

"But, Mother, how about Aleck's clothes that were burning?" asked Debby.

"I suppose they tore off his clothes and put out the fire. But do you know, neither of them said a word about that. All they could think of was the message over the wire.

"They showed their telephone to everybody, but most people thought of it as just a toy. Aleck and Mr. Watson were wondering what to do. But just about then there was a great fair in Philadelphia and Aleck went there to show his instrument. Nobody would look at it and he was getting ready to pack up and go home, when a tall handsome man walked into the room.

"Aleck was flabbergasted. 'That is the Emperor of Brazil,' he said excitely to an assistant. 'He won't remember me but he used to watch us when we taught the deaf. He wanted to learn how to do it.' "

"Mother, aren't you making a mistake?" asked Don. "Brazil has a President, not an Emperor."

"Yes, Donald, Brazil has a President, but this was long ago, in 1876, and at that time Brazil had an Emperor, Dom Pedro. He sud-denly saw Aleck and he came all the way down the long hall to shake hands with him. And he examined the telephone and he got other important people to look at it too, and they gave Aleck Bell the prize for the best invention at the fair. After that people believed in the telephone, even Mabel Hubbard's father. And Aleck married Mabel."

Mrs. Brown told the children how at first the telephone worked for just a little distance, but slowly Aleck made the words travel farther and farther. They didn't say "Hello" then. What people said when they answered the 'phone was "Ahoy."

"One day," Mrs. Brown went on, "a wire was connected between Washington, D.C., and the city of San Francisco in California. People all over the United States were agog to hear that they could now speak across such great distances over the telephone. President Wilson spoke into it from Washington to Aleck in San Francisco. And then Aleck spoke from San Francisco to Mr. Watson in New York. And the first words he said were 'Mr. Watson, come here, I need you.' "

"Oh, that was funny, wasn't it, Mother? Nice too!" said Debby.

"And now we have telephones all over the world; don't we?" said Don.

They all turned to look at their own 'phone and at that moment it rang. "It's all right again, thank goodness," said Mrs. Brown.

But the children were racing to get to it first. Suddenly they stopped with one motion. As often happened with them, the twins both had the same thought. Before they called up their friends, they said in solemn tones, "Ahoy, Mr. Aleck Bell! Thank you, thank you a lot!"

The Boy Who Wanted to Know

THOMAS A. EDISON

By Will Lane

Mr. SAMUEL EDISON came through the kitchen door and spoke to his wife. She was bending over the oven of her big black coal stove, sticking a straw into a cake to see if it was done.

"Nancy," said Mr. Edison, "I'm bothered about little Tommy. I don't think he has right good sense."

Nancy Edison stood up, hurt and annoyed, and answered, "Yes he has. He's a bright child."

"But listen," said Tommy's father, "do you know what he's doing now? He's squatting down on a nest of duck eggs. He expects them to hatch out. And it's mighty cold out there in the barn."

Nancy flung a shawl over her head and hurried out to the barn. There sat little Tommy, all scrunched up on a nest of eggs. His face was blue with cold, but when his mother made him leave the nest he cried with disappointment. He was only four.

"Why did you sit on those eggs, Tommy?" she asked as she hurried him indoors.

"I wanted to know," said Tommy. "I wanted to find out if I would do instead of the duck." He was saying what he was to say all the rest of his life, "I want to know."

The Edisons' kitchen was warm and pleasant. All their friends called it "a nice kitchen." It was, too, for a small town in Ohio in 1851. But to a boy or girl of today it would seem very old-fashioned. On a dresser to one side stood a row of kerosene lamps. Tommy watched his mother as she lighted two of the biggest. "Your father had a time cleaning these out this morning. The chimneys got all smoked up when you turned the wick too high last night just because you wanted to see what would happen. Now Tommy, you keep away from those lamps before you set us all on fire. Sit down now. Here's a good hot cup of cocoa to warm you up."

Tommy sat on a chair drinking the cocoa, but not thinking about it. He was a sturdy boy, strong and big for his age, but even so, his blond head seemed too big and his forehead too high. His face was a large round full moon. His bright blue eyes followed his mother as she worked over the big hot iron stove. She lifted a lid, looked at the fire, and said, worried, "I'm afraid the fire went down some. I hope that cake won't fall."

In a hurry she picked up some coal in a small shovel and poured it through the open lid of the stove. "Now my hands are all black," she groaned as she stood and watched the stove to make sure it reached the right heat. "Better turn up the damper now," she thought, pushing a lever on the chimney.

THOMAS ALVA EDISON. American inventor. Born in Milan, Ohio, 1847. Inventions include the phonograph, electric lamp, electric dynamo, electric motor, motion picture camera, receivers for radio sets, fluoroscope and improvements in telegraphy. Awarded gold medal by Congress, 1928. Died 1931.

"Mother," said Tommy suddenly, "why don't you have a longer handle on that coal shovel so you won't have to bend so much?"

Mrs. Edison was astonished. "Why, that *would* be a good idea," she smiled. "I wonder why I never thought of it."

She could not know that her little boy, with his wide-open blue eyes and his broad smiling face, would think of things, when he grew up, that would astonish a great many people. She could not dream that because of Tommy's ideas mothers would not have to shovel coal into cook stoves, that fathers would not have to spend hours cleaning and filling messy oil lamps. Nancy Edison could not look into the future when women would not have to carry great kettles of hot water from stove to washtub. She could not know that from the brain of that blond head would come electric lights and electric washing machines. And all because Tommy wanted to know, and asked questions, and then figured out a new and better way to do things.

When Tommy was seven, the Edison family moved to Huron, Michigan, where Tommy went to school for the first time. After two months his teacher sent for Mrs. Edison.

"This child is stupid," said the teacher. "He can't learn. He won't even try. He's not a bad boy, but he sits making drawings—not pretty drawings, but things that look like machines. Only they don't look like anything I ever saw."

Mrs. Edison was used to such remarks about her boy. But she knew better. She answered calmly, "He is not stupid. But you haven't any way here to teach him what he wants to know. You have a class full of children of all ages and many chores to do. I myself have six children all older than Tom. But I will find the time to teach him."

The teacher thought Mrs. Edison was one of those foolish mothers who spoil their children. "She'll find out," she said to herself as Mrs. Edison led her boy out of the school.

There was one special thing that bothered many a school teacher at that time. The children, like all children, liked to sing. Some schools had a little organ which the teacher would play. Sometimes the teacher led the singing. But most of the teachers could not play an organ or sing very well, and it was hard to teach music to the children. When he became a man this boy who was supposed to be stupid was going to invent the phonograph and phonograph records. Through them he would give everybody music everywhere and at any time. Today we are so used to the wonders of the phonograph that it's hard for us to think of a world without music whenever anybody wants to hear it.

After Tommy left that school he never went to another. But with his mother's teaching he learned fast. Besides, he was always learning on his own. He was so curious about everything that by the time he was ten he was reading exciting books about history and science. He was always busy. The cellar of the Edison house was crowded with jars and bottles and queer smells from his experiments. They didn't all turn out well. Once he set the cellar on fire and almost blew himself up. With all his learning he was not solemn. He laughed often, with a great roar of joy.

By the time Tom was twelve years old his experiments were beginning to cost a good deal of money and the Edisons had little to

spare. He made up his mind to earn the money he needed and he went to see the superintendent of the Grand Trunk Railroad that ran through his home town.

Tommy got a job as a candy and news "butcher." This didn't have anything to do with meat. It is what people called a boy who went through a train selling magazines and newspapers and candy. Tom did well with this "butcher" job and soon added fruit and vegetables he picked himself. And after awhile he got other boys to work for him. The boys liked to work for him. He never put on airs with them or acted like a boss and he gave them their fair share of what he got. They all had fun together

Two very bad things happened to Tom on the train. Once a brakeman, trying to help the boy get on a moving train, pulled him up by his ears. The wrench hurt the ears badly and Tom became partially deaf. He never got his hearing back. But he took his deafness well. He said it kept him from hearing things that didn't matter, and made it easy for him to keep his mind on his work.

The other bad thing was this. Tom had set up a laboratory in the baggage car where he tried out experiments while the train was running. One day a jar fell on the floor and broke, and fire flew about the car. The trainman said, "Good-bye Tom, you're fired," and that ended his life as a "butcher" boy on the trains.

But before that, something happened that set him out on his real career as an inventor. It was this way. The railroad telegraph operators were Tom's great friends. He gave them left-over magazines and candy. One day he was talking to Mr. Mackenzie who was a telegrapher at a place called Mt. Clemens. Suddenly Mr. Mackenzie's baby ran out on the track in front of a freight car that was coming down a hill. Instantly Tom Edison dashed out, grabbed the baby, threw him to safety, and then fell sprawling himself and almost lost a leg. Mr. Mackenzie was so grateful that he gave Tom the thing he wanted most at that time. He taught Tom how to be a telegraph operator.

That was wonderful. Tom was only sixteen but he studied day and night and got his first job as a telegraph operator on the Grand Trunk Railroad. He was earning $125 a month which was a good deal in his day. As always, he kept trying out new things. Samuel Morse had invented the telegraph, but there were more messages than the wires could take because each wire could send only one message at a time. The railroad men said Tom was wasting time on something that didn't make sense. But he

worked it out; he figured a way to send two messages one way and two messages the other way, all on one wire.

Tom Edison was now eighteen, but even after his great discovery about the telegraph messages, he had trouble getting people to believe in him. One reason was that he never cared how he looked. His coat was usually rumpled and shabby. His hair needed cutting and there were holes in his shoes where the torn stockings showed through. He went from place to place working a little while in each as a telegraph operator, always looking for someone to believe in him. He wound up in Boston.

Though he was partly deaf he could feel the vibrations coming over the wire. When he got a job in Boston as a telegraph operator, the other men were neat with their stiff high collars and paper cuffs to protect their sleeves. They looked at Edison's hair hanging over his eyes and the holes in his clothes and thought he couldn't be any good at the job. They set out to prove it by giving him the hardest work they could find, work they thought he wouldn't be able to do. They stood around grinning while the fastest operator on the line sent messages at his highest speed. For four hours, without a break, Tom Edison sat and took the messages and wrote them down without a mistake. But Tom liked a joke himself and at the end of the four hours he asked the champion sender if he couldn't go faster. Many a time people started by laughing at Tom Edison and ended in admiration and wonder.

Anyone who thinks up a new invention generally sends it to Washington and, if he pays the required fee, the United States government gives him what is called a patent on it. That means that the inventor can pick

out the people who will make and sell his invention. But Tom didn't have enough money to pay for a patent, and his invention on the telegraph was stolen from him. That was while he was in Boston. He got discouraged then and thought perhaps he would do better in New York.

When he got off the train in New York he didn't have a penny. He slept in a boiler room and walked the streets looking for a job. His clothes got worse and he had noth-

ing to eat except handouts from the engineer in the boiler room. But nothing could stop him. He repaired a broken machine and did it so well and so fast that he got a job as an engineer. The pay was $300 a month. But Tom felt that he could not really work out his own ideas unless he owned his own business.

From that time on, people paid Thomas Edison well for his ideas. But he still didn't understand much about money. He didn't know that when someone gave him a check he had to put his name on the back before he could cash it. He didn't understand that when you put money in a bank, the bank will pay you interest for using your money.

Thomas Edison still went about in shabby clothes and shaggy hair. Whatever he earned went into new experiments.

As the years went on wonders came fast from Thomas Edison. Alexander Graham Bell had invented a kind of telephone, but Edison thought it wasn't good enough. He worked hard on it for two years and made it work for everybody. Then came the phonograph. There was nothing like it in all the world before. It brought Edison fame and great wealth. From that time on, the whole world knew who Thomas Edison was. He was still shy and his dress was still careless, but no one cared any more. People liked his plain simple ways. When he wasn't shut away working on an invention he was friendly with everybody.

In those days, the streets were lighted with gas lamps at night. Men would come around with long poles and light the lamps one by one. In the morning they would come around again and turn them off. There was a sort of arc light but it wouldn't stay lighted and wasn't much use. Now Edison and his staff of men worked day and night for five years on his new idea. That was to make a kind of light that could be used in streets and houses and stay lighted for a long time.

One evening, after five years of effort on Edison's part, a whole section of the city of New York burst into light all at once. Thomas Edison had thrown a switch, that was all. And in the morning he threw another switch and all the lights went out at once.

Now almost everywhere people coming home after dark merely touch a switch at the door and the house lights up. But Edison remembered how, when he was a boy and came home to a dark house, someone had to go in ahead and find an oil lamp and light it with a match and carry it to the door so that the family could come in without falling over something. He was glad his invention would save people so much time and trouble. Everything he invented did that for people, and that was what made him happy.

He went on making even greater inventions. He invented the motion-picture camera. He set up a studio in New Jersey, where he directed and made the first silent movie. He was so fascinated by moving-picture making that for years he could think of little else and gave it his whole time. And because of him we have talking movies today. Indeed, what he did was to make the whole life of people today easier and pleasanter.

He became rich, but he always stayed modest and plain and friendly. And when people asked him what made him successful, he said, "Two per cent inspiration and ninety-eight per cent perspiration."

On the day Edison died, Herbert Hoover, who was then President of the United States, asked everyone to turn off electric lights for one hour as a tribute to the inventive genius of Thomas A. Edison. It is to him that our modern world owes so many of its comforts and conveniences.

The Man Who Created New Plants

LUTHER BURBANK

By Olive W. Burt

ONE day a young man named Luther Burbank was walking through his potato patch, examining the plants with his keen blue eyes. He saw something on a stalk which at first glance seemed to be a potato bug. It wasn't a bug at all, but a potato seed ball. As he had nothing else handy to mark the stalk, he immediately tore a strip off his shirttail and tied it around the stalk.

A seed ball is very unusual. Potatoes are generally planted from the eyes. These eyes are cut out of a good potato. Only once in a while does a potato develop a seed ball.

Luther ran to tell his mother about his discovery.

"As soon as it is ripe, Mother," he said, "I'll plant the seeds. I wonder what kind of potatoes will come from those seeds."

"You'll have to be patient," his mother said. "You won't be able to plant the seeds until next spring, and then you won't know what you'll have until you harvest them in the fall."

Every day Luther went to the potato patch to see how much the seed ball had ripened.

Then one day at dinnertime Luther didn't come in. His mother called and called him.

"The potato seed ball is gone," he cried, as he came in answer to her call. "I've looked everywhere for it!"

Indeed he had. Luther had started looking under every plant and feeling the ground for the seed ball from the moment he had discovered that it was missing.

"You can look tomorrow," said his mother. "Come in and eat, now. It is too dark to search for it any more tonight."

Early the next day Luther was in the potato patch, searching for the missing seed ball. He did not find it that day, but he kept looking and finally came upon it.

When the seed was ripe, he saved it very carefully, and the next spring he planted it. He was impatient at the delay. It would be a whole year before he would know what kind of potatoes came from it.

But fall came at last, and from that tiny seed ball Luther had twenty-three plants to harvest. He dug them up and studied the potatoes. There were twenty-three different kinds of potatoes!

Some were scrawny and ugly and full of eyes. Others were poorly shaped; others were soft. But among those twenty-three plants Luther found one on which the potatoes were fine and large, and when he cut into them, the meat was clear and white.

With high hopes Luther planted the eyes of the potato from this excellent vine, and when he harvested them the next fall, he found that he was right. These potatoes, too, were clear and white.

This potato brought the young man his first real fame. It won prizes at all the local

LUTHER BURBANK. American naturalist and plant-breeder. Born in Lancaster, Mass., 1849. Developed Burbank potato. Experimented in Santa Rosa, California, developed more and better varieties of plums, berries, lilies, roses, poppies, tomatoes, squash, corn, etc. Died 1926.

fairs. People came from miles around to look at it. Finally, one seed grower offered him one hundred and fifty dollars for all rights to the potato. Burbank sold the potatoes, keeping only ten for himself. The potato was named the "Burbank" and it has added millions of dollars to the income of farmers.

The money from this sale helped Luther begin the work he wanted to do—to create new plants and improve old plants. He said, "I shall be content if I can grow better fruits and fairer flowers."

This unusual man was born on a farm near the little town of Lancaster, Massachusetts, on March 7, 1849. His father's farm was situated in a bend of the Nashua River. There Luther found everything to delight a boy of nature: fields and flowers, orchards and gardens, swimming and skating, nutting and cranberry gathering.

Luther was not a big boy. He was slender, with fair hair and blue eyes. Though he looked frail, he was quite an athlete, especially good at racing and wrestling.

Luther was clever at drawing, as he was at many creative things. He was quite an inventor. When he was just a little boy he constructed a steam whistle from an old teapot; an outboard motor that would run a boat on water or a sled on ice; and a self-rocking cradle that saved him the trouble of rocking his baby sister to sleep.

Later, when he took a job in the Ames Plow Factory at Worcester, Massachusetts, to earn money for his schooling, this ability to invent cost him his job. Luther was employed to make little round pieces that went between the handles of a hand plow. He invented a device that made the rounds so fast that the other workers could not make plows fast enough to use them.

"You can make thousands of dollars as an inventor," Luther's uncle, the superintendent, told him. But the boy cared less for money than for doing the things he liked.

Luther's skill with instruments and his keen mind led his family to think that he should be a doctor. Luther thought so too for a while. He started to study medicine. But when his father died and he had to work to earn his living, Luther decided to be a farmer. He took the little money he had and bought a farm.

For the first time in his life Luther was completely happy. He had always loved growing things. As a child he preferred plants to animals. He treasured a potted cactus someone had given him more than toys or pets. He often amazed his father and mother with his eagerness to learn more about plants and to experiment with them.

Some of his plant experiments had not made his family too happy. There was the time when he planted field daisies, which were such a nuisance on the farm, in an attempt to raise bigger and prettier ones.

"If you have to raise bigger and better plants," his father scolded, "raise something useful."

But there were other experiments that had proved very sensible. Luther enlarged the cranberry bog by damming up a little creek. The Burbanks made a big profit on the cranberries that year.

Luther's older cousin, Levi Burbank, a professor of geology, had taken him on long walks through the pleasant fields around his home, teaching the boy many things about the lakes and creeks, the hundreds of little springs, and the plants, animals, and rocks. One week-end, he had brought Dr. Louis Agassiz with him from Cambridge and

Luther had learned much from his conversation with the great naturalist.

Though Luther had tried inventing, medicine, and plain everyday labor, he knew in his heart that he was most deeply interested in growing things. With his seventeen-acre farm he could do what he liked best and still earn his living.

Earning his living was important to the young man just starting out with a farm. He was competing with experienced, hard-headed Yankee farmers. It would be hard to break in on the market and make a place for himself. Luther began to wonder what he could do, since he was not very aggressive as a salesman and a bargainer. He thought his plants would help him.

He decided that if he could get his own corn to market earlier than the other farmers—and if it was very good corn—he could

not only demand a higher price for it, but he could show the public that he was really a farmer.

Luther decided to try something that never had been tried. While it was still too cold and wet to plant his corn in the field, he planted it in especially prepared beds inside the barn, and kept it wet. Very soon every grain of corn had sprouted.

When it was time to plant outdoors, and his neighbors were sowing their corn, Luther planted his sprouted corn and waited for the result. He didn't know whether every plant would die or grow.

It grew. It grew better than when planted outdoors first. Two weeks before any of his neighbors had corn ready for market, Luther had gorgeous big golden ears on sale. People were amazed. They said, "That Burbank boy has something!"

All this time Luther had followed a rather odd practice. At least it seemed odd to his friends and it was very annoying to his mother. In a field of corn, daisies, peas, or raspberries, whenever he found one plant that was extra large and healthy and handsome, he would mark it. When it went to seed, Luther would carefully keep that seed away from the common stock and plant it in a separate place. What made the habit annoying to his mother was that when Luther had no string in his pocket to tie around the plant, he would pull out his shirttail, tear off a strip and tie that on his chosen stalk.

This habit was the start of Luther's fame and fortune, for that is how he marked the potato seed ball which yielded the Burbank potato.

After the Burbank potato was successful, Luther sold his farm. He was too eager to see what he could do with new plants to wait a whole year for each crop, as he had to do in Massachusetts. He had heard that in California he could raise three crops in a year. So he bought a ticket to California, kissed his mother and sister goodby, and set out for the new land. He was twenty-six years old.

In California Luther looked about for a place to settle down and go to work. He had just ten dollars, ten potatoes, and the suit he was wearing when he arrived in Santa Rosa Valley, fifty miles north of San Francisco.

For some time the young man had to work at odd jobs in order to eat. He did carpentry work, ran errands, and even cleaned chicken coops. But he did not become discouraged. Finally, he found the kind of work that suited him best, helping in a greenhouse. Though the pay was very small, he saved all he could, economizing in every way, until he had enough money to buy himself a small plot of ground in Santa Rosa. He started his own nursery business. The first year he made a profit of only $15.20, but he was happy in his work.

Then a bit of luck came his way. A man named Dutton wanted twenty thousand prune trees within nine months, and no nursery in the vicinity could supply them. Burbank accepted the order. He then began to wonder how he would fill it. There must be some way, and he would find it!

At last he worked out a plan, based on his boyhood experiments in the grafting and budding of trees. He bought twenty thousand fine almonds and planted them, as he had once planted his corn. He knew that almond trees grow much faster than prune trees. When the almonds sprouted, he transplanted them into a special plot of ground. By the end of June, he had a miniature forest of almond seedlings.

Then Luther bought twenty thousand prune buds from a farmer whose prune trees were strong and healthy. He grafted these prune buds onto the almond seedlings. Then he partly broke off the almond tree tops so they would not grow any more and all the sap would go to the prune buds. When Mr. Dutton came for his twenty thousand prune trees that fall, Luther was ready to deliver them.

Dutton was amazed. He said Burbank was a wizard. This name stuck to him, though he did not particularly like it. But to the general public "wizard" seemed a good name for a man who, as the years went by, developed a thornless cactus, a white blackberry, an apple tree that bore five or more

different kinds of apples at one time, a perfumed calla lily, and thousands of other strange and wonderful plants.

For a while Luther was happy at his work in the nursery. People from all over the world were sending for his seeds and plants. He was becoming wealthy. But the nursery business took too much of his time. He wanted to breed new plants, not just raise seeds. So he sold the nursery and bought four acres of land where he started his real life-work.

There was so much he wanted to do that he arose early and went to bed late. Luther had help, of course, but no other person in the world could see with his eyes or feel with his fingers. Those eyes and fingers could tell from a seedling what the adult tree would be like and what kind of fruit it would bear. No one else had this power, so he had to do most of the work himself.

Sometimes his work was actually painful,

such as his experiments with the cactus. He started to wear gloves, but they slowed him down so much that he stripped them off and worked barehanded among the prickly plants. Sometimes his hands and arms and face would be torn and bleeding, his fingers burning with the pain of the cactus spikes. But he never let such things slow him down. He was trying to produce a thornless cactus, and he succeeded, although it took twenty years of hard work.

Another time a canner jokingly said that he would like to place an order for a variety of peas that would mature all at once, so that the whole crop could be harvested by machinery. He said, too, that he wanted each pod to contain the same number of peas, never dreaming that Luther Burbank could furnish him anything at all similar to these specifications. Within three years Burbank was able to supply the canner with a variety of small pea that met all his requirements. It was called the "Empson Pea."

Of his many experiments, Burbank liked best to work with flowers. One flower he wanted to develop, a big white daisy, was a continuation of work that he had started back on his farm in Massachusetts. For eight years Burbank grew hundreds of thousands of white daisies until at last he was satisfied. This new variety he named the Shasta.

After each experiment in which Burbank had used thousands of plants to reproduce one certain type of plant, the scientist would carefully protect the perfect specimen and tear out all the others and burn them. "Ten thousand dollar fires!" his neighbors would groan. "Why, we'd be glad to have his cast-offs."

But Burbank knew better. "I will do everything in my power," he said, "to prevent inferior plants from growing and producing seed." After a time this policy proved profitable, because people knew that whatever they bought from Luther Burbank was the very best, and so they did not hesitate to do business with him.

However, Burbank found it very expensive to keep up his experiments, and he was often short of money. When he had been in California thirty years the Carnegie Institute recognized the value of Burbank's work and gave him ten thousand dollars a year to carry on his work. They also wished to record his methods, so they assigned experts to follow him about and make notes. Burbank tried working this way for a while, but it so hindered his activity that he gave up the money. He preferred to work as he thought best, unhampered by explaining every step for someone to write down.

The school children of California loved him. He was never too busy to talk to them or take them into his gardens. In Burbank's honor, Arbor Day in California is called Burbank Day, and is observed on March 7, his birthday.

Burbank himself estimated that he had produced more than two thousand new species—not just variations of already existing plants, but absolutely new species never known before. Some of these, like the crimson California poppy and the great white Shasta daisy, merely added beauty to the world. Others, like the soft-shelled walnut, the plumcot, and the Satsuma plum, have added variety and richness to the world's food supply.

In April, 1926, he died at his Santa Rosa home. He was buried, as he had asked to be, under a favorite cedar tree near his home.

He Grew Riches from Peanuts

GEORGE WASHINGTON CARVER

By Mabelle E. Martin

Dark night had settled over the Carver plantation. In a tiny cabin back of the big house sat Mary, the Carvers' colored slave, rocking her sick baby boy. Suddenly she heard horses galloping down the road. She was terrified. It might be the night riders who stole slaves and took them down the river to sell to other plantation owners! "Hush, baby, hush," she whispered, as she started to run for her master's big house. But she was too late. The riders grabbed her and the baby and carried them off.

GEORGE WASHINGTON CARVER. American Negro botanist. Born in Missouri, 1864. Educated by owner of his slave parents. Directed Agricultural Research at Tuskegee Institute. Served in Bureau of Plant Industry, U.S. Department of Agriculture. Known especially for researches on industrial uses of the peanut. Died 1943.

The Carvers were angry and unhappy, for they were very fond of Mary and her baby. Mr. Carver offered a large reward for their return. Mary had already been sold, and they never saw her again, but the baby was finally found and brought back to them. He was very ill, and only Mrs. Carver's careful nursing kept him alive.

It was the custom in those days for a slave to take the family name of his master, so the little lad became known as George Washington Carver. He grew into a puny little fellow with pipe-stem legs, bony fingers, and a pinched little face. He was sick a great deal. His voice was high-pitched and cracked, and he stuttered. He was ten years old before he could talk so people could understand him. This made him shy and, when he was not working, he amused himself by wandering through the woods. He dug plants and brought them back for his own garden. He talked to the plants as he worked among them, and felt that they could understand him, even if people couldn't. He didn't know then that his interest in the soil and in growing things was later to make him famous.

George must have been about seven or eight when he began peeking in at the schoolhouse door. He couldn't understand or accept the fact that Negroes didn't go to school. Mrs. Carver gave him a spelling book, and he tried to teach himself, but it was too slow. There was so much to learn and anyway, spelling books didn't tell you "why" about everything. Gradually Mr. Carver came to realize that the young boy was really in earnest, and when George was eleven, Mr. Carver sent him to a distant town, where there was a school for Negro children. It took George all day to travel there on foot. When he arrived he had no place to stay, so he slept that night in a hayloft. The next day he went to school. The children laughed at his squeaky voice and funny clothes, but he was happy—until school was out. Then he went from house to house trying to find a place to work for room and board. Nobody seemed to want him, and he spent that winter attending school in the day and sleeping in the barn at night, half frozen, half starved.

Finally a colored woman, Aunt Mariah Watkins, took him into her home. She was a good mother to him. She taught him to wash and iron, cook and bake, sew and clean house. He had a natural talent for doing things with his hands and he soon learned how to crochet, hemstitch, and knit. For two years he lived with Aunt Mariah, helping at home and attending school. By then he had learned everything the school taught, and he had also learned that Negroes were supposed to do the kind of work that needed little or no education.

But George would not give up. He had heard of a high school in Kansas that taught both white and colored children. And so at the age of thirteen he left Missouri and traveled with a family moving to Kansas. Their wagon was so loaded with household goods that he had to walk most of the way. Once there, he had no trouble finding work, for Aunt Mariah had taught him well.

He did such excellent work in high school that, when he graduated, he was offered a scholarship at a university. But when he presented his letter at the university, he was told that they did not admit Negro students. In despair he turned to homesteading in western Kansas and tried to forget his thirst for knowledge. Then he heard of a little school in Iowa where he could go on with his studies. Once there, he set up a laundry in a woodshed and earned his way through school by caring for the other students' clothes. From there he went to the State Agricultural College at Ames, Iowa, where he did such brilliant and painstaking work that they put him in charge of the greenhouse when he graduated. At last he had exactly what he wanted! He could grow plants and study plant life. He had a good income and could live a good life.

But fate had other plans for the little slave boy. He received a letter from Booker T. Washington, head of the Negro school at Tuskegee, Alabama. "I cannot offer you money, position, or fame," wrote Mr. Washington. "The children, barefoot, come for miles over bad roads. They are thin and in rags. You would not understand such poverty. These people do not know how to plow or plant or harvest. I am not skilled at such things. I teach them how to read, to write, to make shoes and good bricks, and to build a wall. I cannot give them food, and so they starve."

But Mr. Washington was wrong. Carver did understand such poverty. Had he not suffered through it in his fight to become educated? And what good was his education if it could not help others like him? So he left his fine position and his fascinating work, and journeyed to Alabama.

Here he found problems, indeed. The southern farmers had grown cotton for so long that the soil was worn out. The crops were growing poorer each year. Carver advised them to grow peanuts to enrich the soil. "Peanuts!" exclaimed the farmers. "What would we do with peanuts?"

Carver answered that question, in time, by showing them that from peanuts they could make milk, cheese, butter, candy, ice-cream powder, pickles, mock oysters, and flour. In addition he showed them how to make more than 300 non-food products from peanuts, including plastics, paper, insulating boards, dye, ink, soap, shaving lotion, and linoleum. He did this by separating the chemicals in the peanuts and combining them in a new way to create new products. He was developing a new science —chemurgy. It has done a lot to change farming and increase the wealth of farmers, who now are raising the raw materials from which plastics and synthetic rubber are made.

Up to then most farm crops were intended as food for men and animals. But the farmers produced more food than was needed, and the surplus went to waste. Here was a way of using that wasted food, of turning it into money. Henry Ford, the automobile man, was one of the leaders in this movement. He and Carver became fast friends. Carver used soybeans to make a plastic which Ford used in his cars.

It is not surprising that, in 1940, George Washington Carver was chosen as the man of the year who had contributed most to science. He died in 1943 at about the age of eighty.

And so ends the story of the sickly little Negro slave, who strove for education against almost impossible odds, who arrived at a position of ease and importance, and then had the courage to give it up in order that he might be of service to his people. In so doing, he has been of service to the whole world—a countryman to be proud of!

Miracle Man of Electricity

CHARLES STEINMETZ

By Catherine Cate Coblentz

THERE was one word which Karl August Rudolph Steinmetz heard more frequently than most other children. The word was *No*.

"No, Karl, you cannot do that. No, for you it is impossible. No, do not put a lighted candle inside the tower of blocks. No, do not pour water over your water wheel in the house. No, do not try to play rough games the other children play."

And the children would cry, "No, no, go away. We can't be bothered with you." For Karl was little and weak, almost a dwarf in size. When he was young, he seemed old. But when he grew older, children were to love him and consider him one of themselves.

He must have grown very tired of hearing *No*. Then he discovered the land of books. Books never said *No*. They always welcomed him. He enjoyed all his studies, but he liked best the books about numbers. At seventeen Karl was graduated at the head of his school, and when he went to the university he still made an outstanding record. He continued to live at home, and he earned money by tutoring younger students, for his family was poor.

Karl August Rudolph Steinmetz was born and lived out his boyhood in Germany. His family heritage was both German and Polish.

The Germany of that day was not a very happy place to live in. There was discontent and rebellion, and the students were very much at the fore in rebelling. So, just as he was about to receive his degree, Karl was forced to flee into Switzerland to escape a prison term. Switzerland was not too happy to have him either, and he had to pay a weekly fine to remain there.

But in that land he met and became friends with a young Dane named Asmussen, who had lived in America and had an uncle there. From what Asmussen told him of America, Steinmetz decided it was a wonderful country. But as to going there—again there came the everlasting *No*. For he had very little money, and the Swiss officials were taking that away as fast as they could.

Then Asmussen suggested that, if they went steerage, he had enough money to take them both.

Steinmetz was delighted, and, on the way across the sea, he tried his best to learn English. But it is not a language to be learned in a few days. So, at Ellis Island in New York Harbor, where immigrants used to land in those days, Karl heard the same *No* to which he was so long accustomed. What? He spoke almost no English? He had no money in his pocket and no job waiting for him?

CHARLES PROTEUS STEINMETZ. American electrical engineer. Born in Breslau, Germany, 1865. Came to United States, 1889. Consulting Engineer for General Electric Co., 1893. Made valuable contributions to electrical science. Author of *Engineering Mathematics* and other technical works. Died 1923.

To make matters worse, he had caught a bad cold and one side of his face was swollen. Then there was his small stature, his hunched back. Enter America? *No!* He must return to Europe.

And then his friend Asmussen came to his rescue. Steinmetz would learn English quickly. And the money which Asmussen had, he declared, belonged to his friend as well. He would see that he was cared for if necessary. Besides, the country needed young Steinmetz. He was a very brilliant person.

So America reconsidered. "Yes," said the officials at Ellis Island, finally. "All right, come in."

Steinmetz remained with his friend for a week, trying to learn all the English he could. Then he went to the factory of Thomas A. Edison, of whom he had heard. But everyone was busy, and no one paid much attention to the strange-looking, ill-clad applicant. The answer was, "No, we have no job for you."

He went on, and at the next place he applied, a firm in Yonkers, New York, he was hired. "Yes, come at the end of the week. We need a draftsman. Twelve dollars." At last his luck had changed.

Steinmetz had come to a new land without a penny. Now, within two weeks he had a job. He could pay back his fare. He could support himself. America was treating the stranger well, far better than his own land had done.

He went straight to a courthouse and took out his first naturalization papers. He, Karl August Rudolph Steinmetz, was going to be an American citizen just as soon as he could.

True, his name didn't sound American. Once, when a fellow German watched him signing it, the German repeated the names one by one. For the first time Steinmetz seemed to realize that they didn't sound American. Very well, he would change his name. Instead of Karl, he wrote down Charles. That was better, he decided. But for a middle name?

Then he remembered the nickname which had been given him at the university. They had called him Proteus. The name was taken from Homer's *Odyssey*, and because he knew all the characters very well, the name had hurt Steinmetz. For Proteus was the wrinkled old hunchbacked man of the sea, who knew a million secrets. In its way the name said *No*, too. "No, you are not one of us," it said. "You are different."

Well, he was hunchbacked, and he knew secrets too, many of them. Determinedly he wrote his name, Charles Proteus Steinmetz.

He liked his work. He wanted nothing better than to work. Occasionally he went to meetings where the problems of electricity were discussed. For a long time, Steinmetz did not say anything; his English was not very good.

But the day came when he could keep quiet no longer. He knew secrets, secrets of electricity, secrets which dealt with figures, figures which meant laws. He began to speak about them. He began to write.

And then, just as he was nicely settled in his work, the concern was taken over by the General Electric Company. The change didn't matter very much to Steinmetz, as long as he could continue working with figures, discovering the secrets of electricity.

Because someone was careless, he worked for the company for weeks before he received a salary. He didn't even inquire about that. He just set himself to carrying on with what little he had saved. He was afraid to ask whether or not he was to receive a salary, whether he was to be allowed to remain with this important new company. He was still afraid of hearing that word, *No*.

But of course he didn't hear it any more. For the American scientist who had come from Germany knew more secrets, it seemed, than anyone else working with the new plaything of man—electricity.

He was soon known as the miracle man of electricity. He did about as he pleased. Whatever apparatus he wanted was his for the asking. He worked as long or as little as he liked. He was turning a plaything into man's servant. He was made head engineer of his company at a good salary.

And he was finding happiness. He built himself a laboratory, then a conservatory for his collections of cacti, ferns, and orchids. Last of all he built a home, and he invited a young engineer and his wife to live with him. They were soon calling him Dad. And their children in turn called him Grandfather. He had always delighted in having friends. Now he had a family.

America was shining from one end to the other with light. More and more, electricity was doing man's work. The country was very proud of Charles Proteus Steinmetz. Harvard University and Union College gave him degrees. The President of Harvard called Steinmetz "the foremost electrical engineer in the world." Edison, Marconi, Einstein came to his laboratory to see his work.

The newspapers were more than eager to print anything at all about him. He was honored in his profession. Children loved him. He had many friends. He had started life hearing the word, *No*. He ended it by hearing *Yes* on every hand.

Yes, Charles Proteus Steinmetz, America was and is proud of you!

They Discovered Radium for Humanity

MARIE AND PIERRE CURIE

By Toby Bell

FAR away from each other, in different countries, almost a century ago, there lived a boy and a girl. Marie Sklodovska, the girl, was Polish and lived in the city of Warsaw. Pierre Curie, the boy, was French and lived in Paris. Years later these two were to cross the distance between them. They were to fall in love, they were to be husband and wife. And together they were to discover radium in the black shining mineral, pitchblende.

No one, at that time, so much as guessed that there was such an element as radium. Marie, of course, had never heard of Pierre, and Pierre had never heard of her. Yet, little by little, although neither of them had any idea that such a thing was happening, their paths came closer.

In Warsaw Marie watched her scientist father as he worked in his laboratory. She was a pretty, plump little girl with a lovely complexion and blond hair that fluffed all over her head. She was lively and full of fun. But inside that fluffy blond head there was a fine brain. She was only sixteen when she finished her first two years at college. But that was as far as she could go in Poland. Marie knew that if she wanted to become a scientist she would have to go somewhere else to study.

She thought of trying to enter the Sorbonne in Paris. It was one of the world's great universities and Marie could speak French. She hated to leave home and she had almost no money. But she got a job as a governess and saved every cent she could. At last she had enough for a cheap ticket to Paris. It was the cheapest possible ticket. She rode in a car almost as bare as a freight train. There were wooden benches along the walls. These were all filled when Marie got on board. So she had to sit on a folding chair in the crowded aisle. On this shaky, uncomfortable seat Marie rode for three days and three nights. The train was cold and the food she had brought from home got dry and stale. At each station the passengers were given hot water to make tea, and that was the only hot food Marie had on the whole trip.

At last the train arrived in Paris. There, at the station, Marie was greeted by her sister who was married to a medical student and lived in Paris. Though they too were poor, they made room for Marie. But there was no room for her in the Sorbonne's School of Science. She did get a job, though, doing simple work in a laboratory. And then, not wanting to be a burden to her sister and brother-in-law, she found herself a place to live. It was a small cold attic room. There was no heat, no water, not even

PIERRE & MARIE CURIE. Pierre, a physicist, born in Paris, France, 1859. Marie, a chemist, born in Warsaw, Poland, 1867. Pierre was Marie's teacher at a Paris University. They married in 1895. They worked together, in desperate poverty, experimenting in radioactivity. Discovered radium, 1902. Awarded Nobel Prize in Physics, 1903. Marie awarded Nobel Prize in Chemistry, 1911. Pierre was run over and died in Paris, 1906; Marie died, acclaimed by the world, in 1934.

cold water, and it was up five flights of stairs.

Marie almost gave up eating. The small plump girl from Warsaw got so thin and frail that several times she fainted after she climbed the long flights of stairs to her room. Once she fainted in the laboratory. After that she paid more attention to her food because she knew that she had to eat to build up strength for the work she wanted to do.

At last she got into the Sorbonne as a student of physics and chemistry, the only girl in her class. She worked hard and got high marks.

All this time Pierre was in Paris too. But he had still never met or heard of Marie.

As a boy, Pierre had been serious and brilliant at mathematics. He had true scientific genius and he was still just a boy when he and his brother began to work out new ways to experiment. Unlike Marie, Pierre was able to go to the Sorbonne. There wasn't much money in his family either, but there was enough for that. He studied hard, did extremely well, and was still a very young man when he became a Sorbonne professor.

While he was teaching there, Marie was studying at the same place. But the Sorbonne is a huge institution with thousands of students; and at that time Pierre and Marie had still not met.

But one evening, after work, Marie went to visit one of her few friends who lived in the neighborhood. And there, at last, she met Pierre Curie. That very evening they found out that they both spent their days at the same university. Pierre was then a tall young man of thirty-five and Marie a frail young woman of twenty-seven. It took them no time at all to find out that they both cared above everything else for science.

New discoveries were their goal, not just old paths that others had followed.

They had plenty to talk about. They liked each other and fell in love. The quiet modest Pierre asked Marie to be his wife. In July of 1895, these two devoted people were married. Marie had no wedding dress. She wore a simple dark blue suit. But Pierre thought she was the most beautiful woman he had ever seen.

They lived in a cheap three-room apartment. Marie worked in Pierre's laboratory. And from that time on, they worked together on all their projects. To them their work seemed modest enough. But the day these two started to work together was also the beginning of the road that led to the discovery of radium. Work was not only their job; it was their pleasure and their life. They did love the country and on holidays they took long walks and rode bicycles over the lovely country roads near Paris. But even then they talked about their work.

That very year a German physicist named Roentgen had discovered the X ray. Scientists soon learned that it could do wonderful things but they did not know exactly how, or what it was. A French physicist named Becquerel was trying to find radium in the mineral uranium. When he got a little way along, he found that if he placed a piece of uranium on a photographic plate covered by black paper, the plate was affected as if by light. But he could go no farther.

The Curies were excited by the X ray and they made up their minds to work on it. But they had no money for the laboratory and equipment they would need. The Institute where Pierre taught offered them a miserable damp room that had been used only as a store-room. Piece by piece they got

their equipment, but the dampness in the room almost ruined it. They had to spend time protecting their instruments when they wanted to be working on experiments.

They got hold of some uranium and Marie began the hard work of trying this and trying that, and failing, and then perhaps getting a step ahead. Pierre had to keep on with his teaching to support them, but he worked with Marie nights and holidays.

They also tried thorium, another mineral. Thorium, like uranium, gives off radiation. But they did not succeed in finding what they were looking for.

The Curies had a baby girl by now and their money was short. But they were so sure they were on the track of a great discovery that they decided to take a risk. Pierre gave up his job at the Institute. And from that time on, they worked together day and night in the cold damp storeroom.

In 1898, three years after they were married, they were sure that the mysterious element was radium and that the best place to search for it was in a mineral called pitchblende. Pitchblende is dark brown or black and shiny.

The scientific world was excited. But

there was much work still to be done. They had to find out how to get the radium out of the pitchblende, free and pure by itself. They knew too that in a ton of pitchblende there was only a speck of radium.

The experiments went on day after day, night after night. They had to have tons and tons of pitchblende. And pitchblende was very expensive. But they were lucky. Glass manufacturers used great quantities of pitchblende. But they needed only part of it and they threw the rest away. The Curies were able to buy that thrown-away pitchblende for very little. But they had to have a larger place to work, and at last they found a shed they thought would do. It had no floor and its roof leaked. But it had a big rusty iron stove, and they needed a stove. So they took it.

Pierre had to go back to his job to earn some money for Marie and the baby, and while he was away Marie did all the heavy work of boiling the pitchblende. Ton after ton of it went into the great kettles, and painstakingly Marie Curie sought the speck of radium in each. Day after day she boiled and strained and stirred. The shed was icy cold in winter and hot in summer. She was a small woman and the work was back-breaking. When he saw how hard she worked Pierre lost heart. He helped all he could at night, but he felt the work was too heavy for his frail wife. Several times he wanted her to give up. But Marie had a soul and a will of steel. She drove herself on.

A few things helped. Once the Emperor of Austria sent them a ton of pitchblende. Others did a little here and there. But mostly the Curies just kept at it. They did not feel that their lives were hard. They were so excited by what they were doing that in spite of the hard work and discomfort, they said later that this had been the happiest time in their lives.

At last, in 1902, six years after they began their heavy work on pitchblende, their great day came. They found radium! In the laboratory radium was radiant with a blue light. And Pierre and Marie Curie were radiant too as they saw what they had discovered.

They had found, and pulled from its hiding place, radium, the magic mineral which lights in the dark, which heals the sick and saves lives.

The radium that is used on sick people is sometimes white like salt and sometimes grayish. It is two-and-a-half-million times as hot as coal. It is thousands of times as valuable as diamonds.

The Curies could have kept a patent on their discovery and grown rich on it. But they gave it freely to the whole world. They gave their first bit of radium to a hospital and that was the beginning of the many wonderful cures which radium has brought to the world.

Honors poured upon Pierre and Marie Curie. The whole world rejoiced with them. In 1903 they shared with Becquerel the Nobel Prize for physics which is the biggest prize a scientist can get in the world. Everything looked wonderful for them. They now had two attractive bright little girls.

Then, one day, Pierre stepped off the sidewalk in a Paris street and was hit by a heavy wagon. Two big horses ran over him. It was the end of a great life and a beautiful marriage.

It was a tragedy that Pierre Curie could not have lived to see the Institute of Radium

which the city of Paris built for Marie in 1909. He never saw the radium laboratory she planned for the place where she was born in Warsaw or the honors piled on her during her visit to the United States.

All these years after Pierre died, Marie was grief-stricken and ill. But she never stopped their work—the work they had started together.

The First World War broke out in 1914, and radium was ready to locate the hidden pieces of shell in the wounded. Marie worked for the wounded and taught scientists from all over the world how to use radium.

And then she paid the highest price. Radium can be as dangerous as it is a benefit. Marie became ill with radium poisoning. In July of 1934, a shadow of the bright girl from Poland, she died. She was buried, with the highest honors, beside her great husband.

This was one of the most wonderful marriages of all time. Perhaps neither alone would have discovered radium. But both the Curies were brilliant and self-sacrificing. Both were needed to bring radium to the world. And the whole world will remain forever in their debt.

Conquerors of the Air

ORVILLE AND WILBUR WRIGHT

By Carrie Esther Hammil

"COME on, Orv, there's Dad!" shouted eleven-year-old Wilbur Wright as he ran into the house. Orville, four years younger, came a close second.

Dad was a Bishop in the United Brethren Church in Dayton, Ohio. He had been away on a trip and the boys were happy to see him coming.

"Hello, boys," Dad said. "Here, catch!"

The toy he tossed into the air was most unusual. Instead of falling to the floor like any other toy, it started floating to the ceiling.

"Let's see that!'" Wil and Orv shouted, as they pounced on the toy when it landed.

"Here, here, boys!" said Dad holding the toy gently. "This toy is delicate. Don't grab it like that. I'll show you."

WILBUR AND ORVILLE WRIGHT. Pioneers in aviation. Wilbur born in 1867, Orville in 1871. Experimented with kites and gliders, 1896–1903. First successful flight in motor power plane at Kitty Hawk, N.C. Exhibition flights in France. Organized American Wright Company, 1909, to manufacture planes. Wilbur died 1912, Orville 1948.

He explained how the rubber band twisted around the propeller made it whir so that the air came up toward it and kept the toy in the air. "It's called a helicopter, a flying machine," he said.

Orville handled the machine carefully. "I'll make a bigger one," he said. "It will fly even longer, won't it?"

Wilbur and Orville Wright were always wanting to make things. Generally Orville was the one who thought of the idea, and Wilbur, the reader and thinker, helped Orville to make it into a reality.

One evening the family gathered together in their living room. Orville held an open book toward his father and asked, "What do you call this kind of picture, Dad?"

"That's a woodcut," said the Bishop.

"How is it made?" the boy asked.

"I don't exactly know," answered his father. "Let's see if we can find out in the encyclopedia."

After several days of studying the encyclopedia and reading a book from the library, Orville decided to try to make a woodcut. He made the proper kind of tool from a spring out of an old pocket-knife. The next Christmas Wilbur gave him a set of engraving tools. Bishop Wright had a little printing press for duplicating important letters, and Orville first tried printing his woodcuts on it. Orv found out that his old chum, Ed Sines, was just as interested in printing as he was. Orville traded a collection of magazines for a small printing press.

They started the firm of Sines and Wright, and they took in many jobs. Their biggest project was an eighth grade newspaper called *The Midget*. One day a man wanted to pay the boys in popcorn instead of money. That was all right, because they could sell the popcorn. Orville thought they should use the money to buy more type, but Ed simply wanted to eat the popcorn. They settled their problem when Orville gave Ed Sines his half of the popcorn in exchange for Ed's half of the business. Now it was simply called the Wright Printing Company.

"I need a larger press," Orville told Wilbur.

"How are you going to get it?" asked Wilbur.

"How did I get my first tool to make a woodcut?" Orville laughed. "I'm going to make it."

When the press was finished and running, a well-dressed stranger stepped into the shop and said, "Is this the press you boys made?" He took off his hat and scratched his head. "Queerest looking thing I ever saw! Does it run?"

Orville was just starting a job, so the stranger flopped down flat on his stomach to watch. He wanted to see the underside, where the machinery was. At last he stood up and started to wipe the grease off his trousers. "Well, it works," he admitted. "I don't see why it does, but it does."

"Say, Orv," said Wilbur, passing the newspaper to his brother one day, "here's something interesting. This German, Lilienthal, has been gliding down a hillside on a flying machine, just off the ground. His glider is just a set of wings on a frame. Remember our flying-machine toy?"

"Yes," said Orville. "Say! Wouldn't that be fun? Let's find out more."

The boys began to study all the material they could find on man's attempt to fly. Then one day they read that Lilienthal was dead. He had been killed when his glider crashed.

The boys determined to find out what was wrong with the Lilienthal glider. They would fix the fault, whatever it was. They would fly yet.

The biggest problem they had to solve was balance. At times, while in their bicycle shop, where they earned their living now, the brothers would hear a flock of birds whirring past. They would drop their work to rush to the window to watch them. Neighbors laughed if they came in and heard Wil and Orv arguing over what made a bird fly the way it did, but the brothers were determined to solve the problem of flight.

When one of them thought of something, he made a sketch. If they both thought it might work, they made a small model and tried it in the wind. Sometimes it worked; sometimes it didn't. They knew how to handle tools, so they were able to make what they needed.

"Wil, it seems to me that a man ought to have some way of changing the way the wings are lifted at the tips," Orv said. "We ought to figure out a way to lift a section at a time. Then if one wing needed more of a lift from the air under it than the other, that could be arranged." Orville made a sketch of his idea.

Wilbur looked at the drawing. "It looks right, Orv," he said. "You may have something there."

It was August of 1899 when they built a biplane kite and flew it in a little park at the edge of town. Attached to all the gadgets necessary to lift one part of a wing at a time were cords which could be operated from the ground. The men pulled or released these cords whenever help was needed to lift the kite. The kite flew. This test encour-aged Wil and Orv to go on experimenting.

By the summer of 1900 they decided the time had come for some real tests in actual flying and they planned to spend their vacation in trying out their glider. They applied to the Government Weather Bureau for a location where they could find hilly country with steady winds about eighteen miles an hour. From among the suggestions offered, the brothers chose Kitty Hawk, North Carolina. Wilbur went ahead to set up camp, and Orville came later.

All summer they worked, sending their glider into the air. At first they flew it as a kite so that they could observe it. Later they made glides from the top of a high sand dune called Kill Devil Hill. They were only two or three feet off the ground, but the important thing was that they *were* off the ground. The elevators, as they called the parts of the wing that they could raise to change the airflow, worked fine.

Back home again they made changes so that they could rise higher and stay up longer. Every time they thought of something new they had to study all the scientific facts to be sure that their idea was not contrary to the laws of nature. By the following summer they again had a glider to test. Although this glider was an improvement over the one they had made before, it was still not right. The boys decided to work out a new wing design.

Orville made a wind-tunnel out of an empty starch box and a weather vane. To his amazement he discovered that the Lilienthal calculations and those of other scientists that they had been following were wrong. No wonder the glider did not work as it should!

The brothers made a better wind-tunnel

with a motor-driven fan. They worked hard and prepared their own data from results they obtained in their experiments with the wind-tunnel. Finally, they knew exactly how their glider should perform in accordance with their calculations.

"Well, Orv," said Wilbur, straightening up from the columns of figures he had been working on, "do you want to go back to Kitty Hawk? I think we're ready."

Orville agreed, and at Kitty Hawk the brothers made more than a thousand glides in their new glider. Sometimes they went as far as six hundred feet before the glider came down. It began to look as though some day man would fly.

"What we need now is a motor," said Orville.

Wil agreed. "Yes, with a motor we wouldn't have to depend on the breeze to carry us along. The glider could furnish its own power. But it would have to be very light to stay up."

"We would need at least eight horsepower. We wouldn't want the motor to weigh more than twenty pounds per horsepower. About two hundred pounds, in all, would be right," Orville figured.

Wil wrote to motor makers and automobile companies. Each company wrote back that it was too busy to take on special jobs.

"You didn't tell them what it was for, did you?" Orville asked.

"Why no, of course not. But maybe they found out anyway," answered Wil.

Orville laughed. "I guess they're afraid they'd be laughed at if anyone found out they were making a motor for men to learn to fly!"

"What now?" asked Wilbur.

"Why, we'll make our own. It won't be the first time that we have made what we wanted, will it?" asked Orv.

When they finished the motor, it was even lighter and more powerful than they had hoped. They strengthened the wings of the glider and then started to work on the propeller.

Again they went to the library. They brought home stacks of books about the propellers that were used to make boats go. They thought that all they would have to do was to substitute air pressure for water pressure and they would have their propeller. Then they found out that boat propellers still were not perfect and frequently stopped. That could not happen with an airplane!

Months passed while Wil and Orv struggled. Finally, on September 23, 1903, the brothers left again for Kitty Hawk. When they inspected their propeller shafts they found that one of them was faulty and would have to go back to Dayton for repair. That meant two weeks of waiting. Meanwhile, they tried the motor indoors, and another shaft broke.

"This has happened too often," Wilbur decided. "We'll have to find the reason."

"I think I know why," Orville put in. "Hollow shafts just won't stand the strain. They don't spring right. We'll have to use solid steel."

"That will mean further delay," said Wilbur.

"I'll go myself," replied Orville, pulling out a suitcase. "The only way to get a thing made right is to make it yourself."

It was not until December 14, 1903, that Wilbur and Orville Wright were ready to make their test. They set out for Kill Devil Hill. There they ran up a little flag they had promised to fly so that the life-saving crew at the nearby weather station would know that they were planning to make a test. Five men came to help carry the machine and its take-off track to the starting point.

The brothers did not think of the importance of the occasion. They were interested only in flying.

Wilbur climbed aboard the light framework and stretched out on the lower wing. A strap went around his hips to keep him from rolling out. He gripped the control sticks in his hands. The motor rattled and chattered, and then settled into a steady roar.

Wilbur released the catch that held the restraining wire to the track and the curious-looking machine darted forward. It rose into the air! Then the cheers below turned into gasps. Wilbur had nosed the plane up too steeply, and it plunged to the ground only a hundred and fifty feet from its starting point.

"Some first flight!" Wil groaned in disappointment as he stepped out.

By the time the broken parts had been repaired, it was December 17. Wind swirled sand and sleet through the air. Orville shifted in the chair where he sat brooding.

"Oh, come on," he said, finally, "let's get the machine out. I'm not going to wait any longer."

Wilbur pulled on his coat. Up went the signal again. The men at the weather station gasped in surprise, but they came over anyway. The wind bit through warm coats and gloves, and even the flyers were driven indoors from time to time.

Wilbur turned to Orville and said, "It's your turn this time."

Just as Wil had done three days before, Orville stretched out in his place on the plane and grasped the sticks in his hands. He started the motor and let it warm up.

"Everything ready?" he shouted above the roar.

Wilbur nodded. Orville released the wire, and the plane moved forward. The wind was pushing against it, whirling and pitching to force the man-made bird to the ground, but the little plane stayed up. Then the force of the wind ended the flight.

Man had flown! The little plane had been up only twelve seconds, but it was the first time an airplane had risen from level ground on its own accord and had stayed up without losing speed.

Next it was Wilbur's turn, and again the plane flew, this time for thirteen seconds. Then Orville took another turn and flew the plane for fifteen seconds. Wilbur took the plane up again, and this fourth flight was the most successful of all. He stayed in the air for fifty-nine seconds and covered a distance of eight hundred and fifty-two feet.

The boys were as happy as they could be and rushed to the telegraph station to send a message to their father, telling him the good news and asking him to notify the press. The newspapers did not pay much attention to the feat. Other inventors had tried to fly and had failed. They were not going to be fooled again!

Orv and Wil returned to Dayton and quietly continued working on their plane. They offered to sell it to the United States Government, but the government was not interested. Another government offered the brothers a huge sum of money for the patent, but they said, "No, if it is worth that much to you, it is too valuable to take away

from our own country."

The United States Army began to be interested in planes a few years later, and in 1908 Orville demonstrated his airplane and won the contract to build planes for the Army.

About the same time Wilbur demonstrated his plane in Europe. The French people were especially enthusiastic about flying. France made the brothers members of the Legion of Honor, in recognition of their accomplishments. They received other honors and medals from many European countries.

Finally, the people in the United States began to appreciate the greatness of the two men. On their return to America they were received by President Taft in Washington. The Aero Club of New York presented

them with a gold medal.

Wilbur Wright died of typhoid fever just before the United States entered the First World War. Orville lived to see their machine perform its great service to mankind in helping to preserve the world of democracy in two great wars. He lived to see planes carry food and clothing and precious medicines to starving people in faraway places. He lived to see airplanes develop into huge, many-motored silver birds, soaring around the world in a matter of days. Orville Wright died on January 31, 1948.

At Kitty Hawk, North Carolina, stands a granite shaft, sixty feet high and equipped with a beacon. This monument was erected to commemorate the first successful flight of the Wright brothers, the two men who contributed so much to the world.

Scientific Genius of the Atomic Age

ALBERT EINSTEIN

By Bella Koral

ALBERT was late again. His father tapped on the table impatiently.

"Pauline," he said to his wife, "where is Albert and what is he doing? Why isn't he here for supper?"

Mrs. Einstein went out to call Albert. A few moments later a small boy, dark-haired, with large brown eyes, stood hesitating in the doorway.

"Albert," his father said sternly, "you are late again."

"I am sorry, Papa. I was at the end of the garden singing songs to myself. I forgot it was suppertime," he said.

Mr. Einstein drew out his heavy gold watch and held it toward his young son. "Come, see for yourself how late it is."

Albert was not at all interested in how late it was. But as he looked at his father's watch he became interested in the small gold charm dangling from the watch chain.

"What is that on your watch chain, Papa?" asked Albert.

"A compass," said Mr. Einstein. "It is very small, but it works just as accurately as the much bigger ones that are used to guide ships at sea."

"But what do those four little letters mean?" asked Albert.

"North, South, East and West," explained his father. "The black needle in the center points to North. Suppose you were lost in the woods. If you had a compass with you, you could find North right away and work out which direction to take."

"Does the needle always point North? Always?" the boy asked.

"Yes, always."

Mr. Einstein was pleased by Albert's interest in the compass.

"Why does the needle always turn North?" asked Albert.

"Because it is magnetized."

One question led to the next. Albert was so fascinated with the compass that in the end he fell asleep with it in his hand. The swinging needle had awakened in the small boy a great wonder about the mysterious force that made the needle move.

Albert had been born in the city of Ulm, in Germany, in 1879, but soon his parents moved to Munich, and there Albert spent his boyhood. He was shy and dreamy and would sit for hours listening to his mother play the piano. He would have liked to make friends at school, but his slow speech and shyness made the boys think he was stupid. While his schoolmates were busy at boisterous games in the playground, Albert would stand apart thinking his own thoughts. His idea of fun was to compose little songs and hymns on the piano and

ALBERT EINSTEIN. Physicist and mathematician. Born in Ulm, Germany, 1879. Professor at several European universities, 1909–14. Awarded Nobel Prize for Physics, 1921. Came to U.S. in 1933. Remained to be free of Nazi tyranny. Became a U.S. citizen, 1940. Became world-famous for his Theory of Relativity, 1905, and for the application of this theory later to the development of atomic energy. Author of *The Meaning of Relativity*, *Builders of the Universe*, and many other works. Died in Princeton, N.J., 1955.

hum them to himself.

At school his teachers, too, considered him a misfit. This was because the schools Albert went to were run like military academies as were all German schools at that time.

Albert liked to ask questions. But in those classrooms where strict discipline was the rule, questions were frowned upon. A pupil had to learn his lessons from his books and recite them word for word, whether he understood them or not. But Albert couldn't be satisfied with that. He *had* to ask "Why."

One day Albert heard the word "algebra." It was a curious word, so he asked his uncle, an engineer, what it meant. "Algebra," said his uncle, "is a lazy man's arithmetic. If you don't know a thing, call it X and act as if you do know it." That was enough for Albert. Before long, he had solved all the problems

in an algebra book his father gave him. And while his classmates were still grinding away at elementary arithmetic, Albert was studying advanced mathematics. "It's easy," said Albert. "Everything in geometry and calculus is so beautifully planned just like a Beethoven sonata."

When Albert was fifteen the Einstein family moved to Italy. Albert was sent to Switzerland to continue his schooling. At the school there Albert found that the teachers were not drillmasters as they were in Germany. Here they really tried to help boys and girls to think for themselves. And now he began to show amazing originality in mathematics and physics.

Albert decided he would become a teacher. He made a number of good friends among his fellow students. Many of them had come to Switzerland to escape tyranny and oppression in their own countries. Albert, listening to their stories, dreamed of freedom for all men.

After graduation young Einstein found several small teaching jobs. He married a young Yugoslav science student, Mileva Marec, and they had two sons. The family was poor and while Einstein was waiting for an appointment as a regular teacher he earned his living as a clerk in the Swiss Patent Office at Berne.

His job was to examine plans and models that inventors brought in. He had to say if he thought they would work and find out whether they had been copied or stolen. The work was not hard and it gave Einstein spare time to work on his own scientific studies.

In 1904, Albert Einstein, then twenty-five, could be seen every afternoon wheeling a baby carriage on the streets of Berne. Every now and then, the serious-faced young man, unmindful of the traffic around him, would stop to scribble down some mathematical notes in a notebook. He kept the notebook in the carriage with the baby.

Out of these scribbled notes in Einstein's notebook came some of the most startling ideas in man's age-old attempt to understand the riddle of the universe.

When he was twenty-six years old and still unknown to the scientific world, Einstein submitted an article on relativity to the most important physics magazine of that time. One of his startling new ideas might be made clear in this way:

Can you imagine an explosion of seven million tons of TNT? That would certainly be a terrific explosion, wouldn't it? Well, in Einstein's theory of relativity, he discovered that if a half-pound of any material were completely changed into energy, it would be just as powerful as such an explosion would be. Einstein expressed this in a formula that became the most famous formula in science. (For those of you who may want to know what that formula is, it is $E=mc^2$.)

As to the meaning of the word "relativity," as used in science, it means that what seems to be happening depends on who is observing it. For example, if you and your friend were seated opposite each other in a train moving at twenty miles an hour, your friend would seem to you not to be moving, since you would both be moving at the same rate of speed and his distance from you would not change. But to a man standing on the ground *outside* the train, it would seem that your friend was moving at twenty miles per hour. That is, in relation to you, your friend is not moving, but he *is* moving in relation to the man on the ground. This, of course, is only one very simple case of what Einstein called relativity. Only trained scientists and mathematicians can understand more difficult examples.

Though Einstein's theory completely changed man's ideas about the universe, few scientists at that time realized its tremendous importance.

But other scientists' experiments proved Einstein right, and soon he became world-famous. He was offered the position of professor at Zurich and later at Prague. Then, in 1913, a special position was created for him at Berlin, as director of the Kaiser Wilhelm Physical Institute, the highest scientific institution in Germany, which was then the most advanced country in the world in the study of science. And several

years later, in 1921, Einstein received the Nobel Prize for physics. Many other prizes and honorary degrees were bestowed on him too, by the most famous universities of the world.

When the dictator, Hitler, came to power in Germany in 1933, he took from the people their right of free speech and a free press. He compelled schools and universities to teach only those ideas that he approved. He turned Germany into a huge prison where everyone was watched by police or spied on by his neighbors. Those who showed the least sign of not liking Hitler's ways were arrested and thrown into jails and concentration camps, especially if they were Jews. Jewish scientists were dismissed from the universities even when no one could accuse them of anything wrong.

Now Einstein had for some time been interested in helping to establish a homeland in Palestine for Jews who were victims of hatred and prejudice in their own countries. When Hitler and his Nazis began at-tacking Jews in Germany, Einstein began actively to work against the injustice and cruelty of the Nazis.

He was in the United States on a lecture tour when Hitler came to power. Einstein's friends knew he would not be allowed to continue his work in Germany and they urged him not to return there.

Einstein became a special hate of the Nazis. His home was broken into. A bread knife was taken from the kitchen as proof that he was concealing dangerous weapons and was an enemy of the state! Finally the Nazis placed a price on his head of $4,500 as a reward for anyone who would "silence" him. Einstein smiled. "I didn't realize my head was worth so much," he said.

Einstein decided to remain in America and he accepted a position with the Institute for Advanced Study of Princeton, N.J.

In 1940, he became an American citizen. Now he was free to continue his studies in physics and mathematics, free to speak his mind on the political problems of the times, free even to oppose the policies and opinions of the leaders of the government if he wanted to. Einstein was happy he could live in this free country where he had already made so many warm friends.

Einstein himself never dreamed that his formula, $E = mc^2$, published in 1905, would some day be applied to the making of the atomic bomb. But in the late 1930's scientists learned that the Nazis were working all-out to develop such a bomb. These scientists knew it would take months for the United States government to set up the necessary laboratories and provide enough scientific workers to beat the Nazis to it. It would speed matters, they thought, to take the matter directly to President Roosevelt. Everything had to be kept absolutely secret.

The scientists appealed to Einstein. They urged him to write to President Roosevelt asking him to set up a great, secret project to work on the atomic bomb.

Albert Einstein, the gentlest of men, hesitated. He hated war and everything connected with it. He once said, "War seems to me to be a mean and contemptible thing. I would rather be hacked to pieces than take part in such abominable business." How could he then use his influence to urge the development of the most terrible weapon the world had ever known?

But he knew Germany would eventually develop the atomic bomb if given enough time. And he knew the Nazis would use it without hesitation.

Einstein bent over his desk and began writing one of the most important letters in American history. And not very long after, with the greatest possible secrecy,

the United States began work on the atomic bomb.

Hitler was defeated before the first atomic tests were made. But the United States was still fighting Japan. Einstein was among those who urged that the Japanese be warned of the new secret weapon. If representatives of the enemy saw what it could do, he thought, Japan would surrender immediately and there would be no more bloodshed.

But other scientists, as well as President Truman and his advisers, felt Japan's surrender would have to be forced by dropping a bomb on Hiroshima. An invasion of Japan, they argued, would cost the lives of many, many more Americans and Japanese.

Of course when Einstein first did his work on atomic energy, he had no idea it would be used to make bombs. He was simply trying to solve the mystery of the world around us. He said, "The discovery of nuclear chain reactions (atomic energy) need not bring about the destruction of mankind any more than the discovery of matches."

As a matter of fact, atomic energy is even now being used for many peaceful purposes. In medicine, it is being used to cure some diseases doctors used to consider incurable. And scientists predict that the use of atomic power can drive hunger and poverty from the earth and turn deserts into fertile gardens.

Einstein could never quite accept himself as a world-famous figure. He was happy at Princeton where his neighbors didn't consider it odd that he wore his flowing white hair long because he didn't want to bother with barbershops. And they didn't mind his

wearing old clothes that made him look odd but feel comfortable. The gentle-faced professor was a favorite with everyone, especially the children, for blocks around.

In 1945 Einstein retired from the Institute at Princeton. But he continued working there on his own. For the last thirty-five years of his life Einstein worked to try to discover laws that would apply to electricity, gravitation, and magnetism alike and that would show the connection between these three major physical forces. It will take scientists years to test his ideas.

Like many other great men, Einstein was shy and humble. Once when he walked into a meeting in Washington, everyone in the room burst into applause. Taken aback, he whispered to a friend, "I think they ought to wait to see what I say."

Einstein's final message to the world came several months after his death in April, 1955. In a statement released by his friend Bertrand Russell, the great British mathematician, Einstein was joined by other famous scientists in an appeal to mankind to abolish war. He hoped that the dreadful menace of the atomic bomb would lead the nations to find ways of living in peace. Another war, he felt, would wipe out civilization.

Not only for his discovery of the theory of relativity and for his important work on atoms, but also for his endeavors to bring peace to the world, will the name of Albert Einstein be forever remembered.

Writers of Stories Children Love

He Makes Us Laugh and Cry

CHARLES DICKENS

By Helen Woodward

As the boy walked through the dark streets late at night, he held his head high, but tears were running down his cheeks. Many years afterward, when he was the best-loved writer in the world, he told about these dark walks in his great novel, *David Copperfield:* "What I suffered in secret, no one ever knew. But for the mercy of God, I might easily have been a little robber or vagabond."

The author's name was Charles Dickens. He called the hero of his book David Copperfield. But Charles Dickens and David Copperfield were the same boy. Even their initials were the same, only turned around.

On those long walks each night the boy had good reason to cry, because he was going from a visit to his father in prison, to a wretched garret miles away.

Every morning Charles walked to the prison and every night he walked back to his own miserable little room, and as he walked he cried with loneliness, with hunger, and even with fear. The road was only half lighted and sometimes boys of his age were kidnaped and sent to ships at sea. Or they were robbed, and if they had nothing, they might be killed.

Until those sad nights, Charles had had a wonderfully good time. His father, John Dickens, had earned a good salary, and the family had lived in a nice house, where things were lively and jolly. John Dickens and his wife had all kinds of good times, and their children had fun with them. There was always something going on: magic lantern slides, games, jokes. Charles imitated everyone, and his sister Fannie sang and played the piano. Charles would write little plays and all of them, and their friends besides, would act them out. They did everything with might and main, so that the furniture was almost worn out.

But John Dickens and his wife were often foolish. They could not get it into their heads that if you owed money, you had to pay your debts. And so, in the middle of all the laughter and fun, there would come a knock at the door. And all of them would be afraid to answer because this might be someone asking to be paid. They tried to be pleasant so that the grocer and the landlord would trust them, and they were always astonished when these people got angry. Sometimes the Dickens family lived in beautiful places and had fine clothes,

CHARLES DICKENS. English novelist. Born in Portsmouth, England, 1812. Had little schooling. First published articles under name of Boz. Toured America, reading from his novels. Author of *Pickwick Papers, Oliver Twist, David Copperfield, A Christmas Carol*, and many other stories. Died 1870.

and sometimes they lived in poor places and were shabby and even hungry. But John Dickens laughed at it all. He always said things would come out all right.

The odd thing is that in the end everything *did* come out all right, but that was because when Charles grew up he earned enough money by his writing to make it so.

But when he was a boy, he was deeply ashamed of being sent to the pawnbroker with the spoons. And when he had to go to the grocer for a bit of tea or a piece of soap, and the grocer looked at him and said "Not until you pay what you owe me," he thought he would die of shame.

In some ways his mother was as foolish as his father. She would wash Charles from head to neck so he would look all right to go to church, but she didn't keep him really clean. To make up for this, when Charles grew up, he always wore clothes that were too fine, and he was too careful about how he looked. His mother did other foolish things too. Once she printed a lot of circulars saying she was opening a school. Then she rented a house for it. When the opening day came, there was not a single pupil. But that was just as well since Mrs. Dickens had forgotten to put any furniture into her school-house. There was no desk, no chair, not even a pencil. Everybody who has read *David Copperfield* can see that Mr. Micawber and his wife are just like Mr. and Mrs. Dickens. Though Charles loved his parents, he wanted to shake sense into them too.

One day, when Charles was twelve, the landlord came to the door again for his rent. But this time he did not go away. He brought an officer of the law, and John Dickens was taken off to Marshalsea prison.

In those days people who owed money were put in prison if they would not or could not pay. That seems to us a cruel idea because many a man owed money through no fault of his own. Besides, if a man was in prison, how could he earn enough money to pay his debt?

But do you think John Dickens worried about that? No indeed. He said it was such a comfort not to have the doorbell ringing all the time!

Of course the Marshalsea wasn't like the prisons of modern times. John Dickens was not in a cell, but in a fair-sized room. The prisoners could wander about inside the prison and visit each other. They could go anywhere as long as they stayed inside the prison walls. They played games like darts and skittles or chess or checkers. They formed a club called the Collegians. The members' sang and danced and put on little shows. In all this John Dickens shone, and he was popular with everybody.

Years before, the Dickens family had taken a young orphan girl out of an asylum for a servant. She loved them and stayed with them without pay when they were in trouble. Every day she came with Mrs. Dickens and the children to visit John Dickens in the prison. They stayed until night, and the orphan cooked their meals in the open fireplace in John's room. After awhile, when there was hardly any money left, Mr. Dickens could not afford to pay any rent for his family at all. So they moved into the prison and lived in the room with him. But there wasn't space there for Charles or for the orphan girl. They found a little room near by for the girl, but for Charles all they could get was a miserable cheap garret room miles away. So Charles walked

the weary miles and felt unloved and un-
wanted.

But one thing was even worse. Charles
had to leave school, and he was a boy who
wanted above all else to get an education.
There was no money for school and Charles
had to go to work. His uncles manufactured
shoe-blacking and they took Charles in to
wrap the pots of blacking. For this he got
twelve shillings a week. He was good at it,

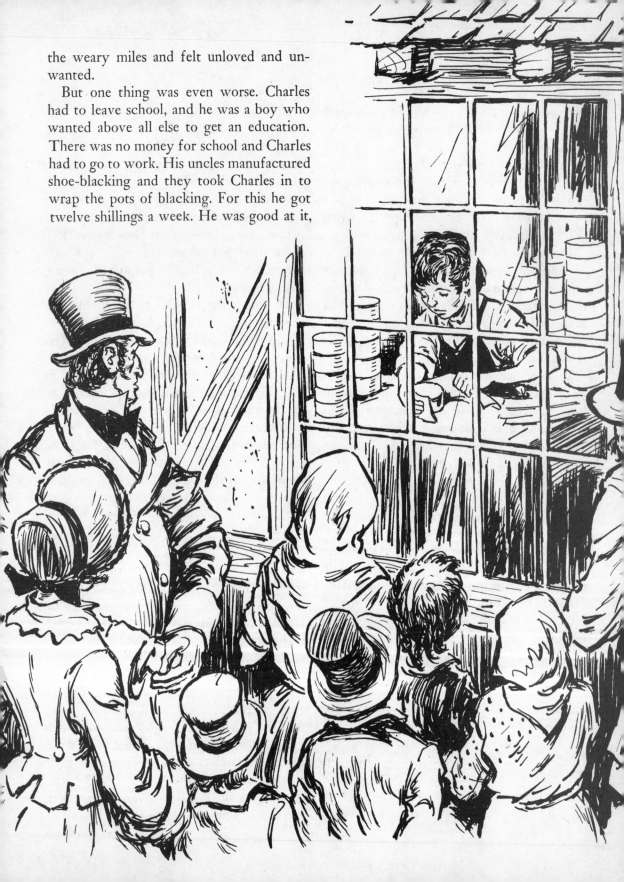

and he was a fine-looking boy with curly hair and blue eyes. So his uncles thought it would be a good advertisement to have Charles sit in a show window and pack the blacking. Charles' shame was beyond bearing. All he hoped for was to keep the whole thing a secret from his former school friends. But at the same time he didn't want the boys at the factory to find out how poor his people were.

The young men he worked with were Cockneys and spoke with a brogue. Charles spoke like an educated boy, and they thought he had a high and mighty air. They were good natured and did not tease him except to call him "the little gent."

One day Charles got very sick at work, and one of the young men offered to take him home. Charles was so ashamed of the place where he lived that he led the young man from place to place hoping he would get tired and leave. But he didn't. He was determined to see the boy home. So suddenly Charles walked up the steps of a fine house and rang the bell. He told the young man this was his home. He was so angry with that kind young man that, in a book he wrote years later, called *Oliver Twist*, he gave his name, Fagin, to the meanest character in all his novels.

You can see other signs of his experiences in his books too. For instance, the boots his fine people wear are always polished very bright with shoe-blacking. And when in *Pickwick Papers*, Mr. Pickwick first meets Sam Weller, the funniest and most lovable person in all the novels, Sam is polishing shoes in the courtyard of the inn.

But to get back to Charles' boyhood—after a few months, Mrs. Dickens' brothers paid her husband's debt, and he was allowed to leave Marshalsea Prison. The brothers could have paid the debt to begin with, but they thought their sister and her husband ought to be taught a lesson. This was no use. They never did learn, and over and over again they would get into trouble about owing money. Later on, when Charles grew rich and famous, he paid their debts and tried to straighten them out. This time when they came out of prison, they had to live in a poor little crowded place. But Charles was able to go back to school for a little while.

By the time he was sixteen, Charles made up his mind that he must do something to run his own life and not wait for things to happen. He was a good-looking young man. He was small, but he held himself straight so people would think him taller. Everyone who met him remembered him and people turned in the street to look at him. This was because his eyes were always ready to laugh and because he looked so eager and interested in everything.

He decided that the best way to get into the world he longed for was to study stenography. Most boys and girls first learning to read and write find it hard enough, even with a teacher. Stenography is much harder than ordinary reading and writing, and in Charles Dickens' day it was even harder than it is now. And Charles had no teacher. In *David Copperfield* Dickens lets David tell how the dot signs meant one thing when they were low down between the lines and another thing when they were high up, how there were circles and squiggles and things that looked like flies' legs and how the whole business of learning stenography was heartbreaking.

But Charles did learn and he became a perfect stenographer. This earned him his first real job. He was a reporter in the House of Commons for a newspaper. Tremendous debates went on and the reporters sat in a crowded little gallery making their careful notes. Charles said his knees got sore from being used as a desk. He became the best of all the reporters.

He loved the excitement of going out to the country to report a speech and then racing the other reporters back to London to get a scoop for his paper. Many a time he was stuck forty miles from London with a carriage buried in mud. In his novels he tells how he had been upset in every kind of carriage, four-wheeled, two-wheeled, gig, chaise. He told how he had transcribed his notes in pelting rain while two friends held a handkerchief over his paper to keep it dry, and how he wrote in shaking carriages with only the light of a flickering candle, riding through a wild rough stretch of road. Yet he never made a mistake.

He was never tired and he had so much energy left over that he began to write a story. He was thrilled when it appeared in print, though he got not a penny for it or for several other stories he wrote then.

And then came *Pickwick Papers*, and with that book Charles Dickens met his first great success. The book came out in instalments, and from the moment Mr. Jingle, one of the characters, appeared, people took *Pickwick Papers* to their hearts. And when Sam Weller gave his first impudent wise-crack answer, the whole of England was ablaze with delight over Charles Dickens. And soon the whole English-speaking world was waiting for the next instalment.

It was not easy work for Charles. In the beginning of each book he threw away as much as he wrote, as authors often do. But he loved writing more than anything else, and he worked hard. And from his pen came a stream of wonderful stories. He had David Copperfield say, "I never put my hand to anything on which I could not put my whole self," and David was Charles, of course.

In 1836, just before he wrote *Pickwick Papers*, he married Catherine Hogarth. They had nine children.

Dickens made several visits to the United States and made a great hit there although he had several amusingly unkind things to say about Americans.

Dickens never forgot anything that happened to him when he was a boy. And because he had seen so much misery, he never wrote a single book without trying in it to show up some of society's cruelties and making people ashamed of allowing them to go on. He was especially sympathetic with boys and girls who were ill treated or cruelly used.

In every corner of the world, people have found comfort in the warm tenderness and loving laughter in Dickens' lively pages. His books were written for grown-ups, but children too find in them rich stores of excitement and fun. They say they can't put a Dickens book down without knowing how the story ends. This is because Charles Dickens was a great weaver of plots, and there is always the wonder about how things are going to come out. How glad Dickens would be if he could know that boys and girls laugh and cry over the things that happened to him when he was a boy himself!

The Boy Who Liked Puppets

HANS CHRISTIAN ANDERSEN

By Carolyn Sherwin Bailey

MORE than a century ago, in Odense, a town of Denmark, there lived a shoemaker named Andersen, his wife, and his young son Hans. The family was very poor. The shoemaker had a great longing to make dancing shoes for princesses. In fact, he once

HANS CHRISTIAN ANDERSEN. Poet and story-writer. Born in Odense, Denmark, 1805. Son of a poor shoemaker. Published a book of stories before he ever went to school. King Frederick of Denmark had him educated, 1822–27. Wrote many plays and novels, but his Fairy Tales won him fame all over Europe. Died 1875.

made a pair from a bit of gold brocade, but no one bought them. The shoemaker and his family lived in only two rooms in a poor part of the town and no princesses ever came by that way. Yet they did not allow this to interfere with their happiness.

The shoemaker's bench filled most of the space in the small front room, but all the rest of the furniture, even Hans' little bed, had been carved by hand by the father. The walls had been made beautiful with pictures. Above the shoemaker's bench was a bookcase filled with well-worn books. The kitchen fairly glittered with its rows of shining brass and copper pots and pans. Someone was always singing, and on the roof of the small house, where Hans could reach it by climbing a ladder up from the kitchen, there was a garden. The street was paved with stones and the house had no land about it, but Hans' mother had carried earth up the ladder and filled boxes on the roof. In these boxes vegetables grew, and flowers blossomed. It was a gay and useful roof garden.

In the evening when the tap-tap of the shoemaker's hammer was stilled, young Hans began to have the best time of the whole day. All the leather, the tools, the nails and needles were cleared off the bench and his father made him toys. They already had a puppet theater built from an old box, with the curtain cut from cloth scraps. Little puppets made of paper, leather, and tinsel acted there in the light of a candle as the shoemaker told Hans stories. He also made scenery for the many plays they gave in the toy theater. He had made a magnifying glass too and a tin case in which to bring home the wild flowers they gathered on Sundays.

Oh, those happy Sundays! Hans would take his father's hand and they would start out for a long walk. There was very little green grass in the town, only stone-paved streets crowded, on Sunday, with workers, weavers, bakers, butchers, and builders. But at the end of the town there was a small bridge that crossed a stream and led straight to the moor. Flowering bushes, trees, and wild flowers grew there, and on summer evenings long-legged storks could be seen. Hans' father told him stories as they walked over the moor. They picked wild strawberries and strung them on long grasses. Hans made garlands of flowers to take home to his mother, and they brought also beautiful branches of greenery to fill the wide cracks of the little house through which the rain sometimes came in.

The puppet theater became quite famous in the neighborhood and Hans gave shows for the other children. He and his father made more scenery, churches, public buildings, and castles like those of the great nearby city of Copenhagen. They made and dressed many puppets, dancing princesses, soldiers in uniform, fairies, and other storybook characters. All these puppets needed clothing, from their tiny shoes to their crowns, caps, and cloaks. It was hard for the shoemaker to spare Hans even scraps, for they were a thrifty family; every bit of cloth and leather left from the shoes had to be used to patch their clothes. Still, the toy theater managed to costume its actors.

One day in the spring a splendid parade came down the narrow street where Hans lived. It was the annual spring parade of town workers. At the head marched a jester with bells. Then came the weavers. The bakers, the herders, the builders, and the candle-makers followed. Even the town butcher marched, driving before him a great white ox wearing a garland of flowers upon his horns. Up and down, and in and out of the streets of Odense, the parade went, and Hans followed. He lost one of his wooden shoes in the mud; but what did that matter? He had an idea, and in a few days he put it to work.

Not long after this, when the looms were clacking noisily in a cloth factory of Odense, the weavers were surprised to hear, above the din, a clear voice singing village songs sweetly. When the foreman looked to see who this singer was, there was Hans, the shoemaker's boy, going up and down among the weavers, singing as merrily as a bird. His music made the work go faster. Hans had been afraid when he entered the factory, but as he sang he lost his fear.

Hans wanted some scraps of silk, lace, tinsel, anything bright in which to dress the puppets for his toy theater. That was why he had formed this plan of singing in the factory. And the weavers gave him all the scraps of cloth he could carry home, to pay for his music. Hans returned and sang again and again for the weavers. Soon his puppets were better dressed than any others outside of Copenhagen, and his little theater was the delight of all who saw it.

Presently Hans began to earn money through his singing. He also began to write plays for puppets and for the real theater. When he had earned about thirteen dollars, he decided, although he was still young, to go to Copenhagen and try to earn his living. His father and mother still lacked comforts and Hans wanted to make their later years easier. So he packed his puppets and toy scenery, and said good-by to the shoe-maker's shop, the storks, and the town he loved so dearly.

It was not long until all Denmark was buzzing with talk about a new poet and writer of plays who had gained high fame in Copenhagen. His name was Hans Christian Andersen. Not only were his plays acted and his poems read widely, but he had become a much-loved story-teller. He had been invited to tell stories to the writer Charles Dickens, to the singer Jenny Lind, to the Queen of Denmark, the Queen of England, the King of Greece, and the Empress of Russia. The stories these great people liked best were *The Fir Tree*, *The Snow Queen*, *The Little Match Girl*, *The Red Shoes*, and *The Steadfast Tin Soldier*.

Hans Christian Andersen, who became such a famous story-teller, always carried about in one of his pockets a toy tin soldier which a little boy had given him. He did not seem to realize what a great man he had become, but when he entered a Court and began, "Once upon a time," troubled Kings, Queens, and Emperors forgot everything but the colors and scents of the moor flowers, the call of storks, and the dreams that dropped from the umbrella of *Ole-Luk-Oie*, as Mr. Andersen told his stories. Children came in hundreds to listen to these tales. As he told them, he cut out pictures to illustrate them. Before one's very eyes there grew paper shepherds, fields of flowers, dancers, and forests. So great became the fame of Hans Christian Andersen that his home town of Odense asked him to come back for a celebration in his honor.

His mother and father now lived in quite a grand house in Odense, which their son had bought for them. But Hans Christian

Andersen was still a very humble man. He was always at his ease when he was telling stories, but he disliked being made a fuss over. It is said that he had a very bad toothache when he returned to Odense for the celebration and tried to stay at home instead of appearing in the public square to review the parade in his honor, but his neighbors would not let him.

When at last he overcame his shyness, he discovered that his return to Odense as the town's most honored citizen was really the greatest event of his life. Schools were closed and the children marched before him and sang and danced. Flags flew. There was another parade of the workers, and in the evening a torchlight parade. A carriage was sent for Hans Christian Andersen, and his toothache disappeared with the coming of his happiness.

Hans Christian Andersen is known the world over as the author of such dearly loved fairy tales as *The Emperor's New Clothes, The Ugly Duckling, Thumbelina,* and all the other lovely fanciful stories that are favorites of children everywhere. No wonder Denmark is proud of being the land of his birth!

Barefoot Boy

MARK TWAIN

By Helen Woodward

RIGHT now, anywhere in the world, maybe in Arabia or Australia, there'll be a boy sitting, giggling over a book. And his father will come in and say, "What's so funny? What are you laughing about over there all by yourself?"

And the boy will chuckle and say, "I'm reading *Huckleberry Finn*."

"Oh, then I understand," the boy's father will answer. "That's the best book Mark Twain ever wrote. I remember how I used to laugh over it when I was your age. That boy Huck was a limb of Satan."

"What's a limb of Satan, father?"

"It's what Mark Twain called himself. It means he was full of tricks and nonsense. But his name was really Samuel Clemens. Mark Twain was his writing name."

The boy will want to know all about Mark Twain. And his father will tell him about this greatest of American writers and maybe get him a copy of *Tom Sawyer*, the other great book Mark Twain wrote about his boyhood.

He was born in 1835 and grew up in the little town of Hannibal, Missouri, which was then a frontier settlement where rough people fought and robbed. Sam once saw a man killed there, right before his eyes. But the thing that made Hannibal a place of adventure for a boy was the great Mississippi River that swept by. The Negroes called it Old Man River.

None of the boys in Hannibal ever thought of wearing shoes, except to go to church. Sam ran around barefoot like the rest. His badly-cut sandy hair stood out all over his head. His pants came halfway down to his ankles and were held up by suspenders. They had been cut down from a pair his big brother Orion had outgrown. His shirt was mended and patched. Nobody had much money and all the Hannibal boys dressed about the same.

One boy, named Tom Blankenship, looked much worse than the others. Sam's home, though small, was clean and in order. His mother and father worked hard to make it so. But Tom Blankenship had no mother and he slept wherever he could and often had only berries from the woods to eat. His hair stuck out through the holes in his straw hat. Sam Clemens envied Tom Blankenship because Tom didn't have to go to school and he didn't have to wash.

Sam had to go to school and he hated it. The little country school in Hannibal was not a good one, and they never taught Sam anything he wanted to know. So he'd play truant and wander about with Tom and his special crowd of children. From them he learned a lot of true things about animals and insects and plants. But they also taught him some wonderful things that weren't so, like how to work magic and how to cure warts.

MARK TWAIN. Pen-name of Samuel Langhorne Clemens. American writer and humorist, Mississippi River pilot, newspaper man. Born in town called Forida, Missouri, 1835. Prospected for gold in Nevada, 1861. Newspaper reporter, 1862. Author of *Huckleberry Finn, Tom Sawyer, Life on the Mississippi,* etc. Died in Redding, Conn., 1910.

One day Sam slipped out of the school yard during recess and ran as hard as he could to the edge of town where Holloway's Hill, a bluff, hung over Old Man River. Four other boys were there. One of them was Tom Blankenship. They yelled, "Hi Tom! Come on. We're going swimming."

They yelled not to make Sam hear because Sam was not far off; they just always yelled no matter how close they were to each other. The grown folks never could understand why they did it. Sam slowed up a bit. He was worried because he had almost drowned nine times trying to learn to swim. Tom had taught him how, but he just wasn't sure of himself yet.

"All right," Sam drawled now. "But just remember, a cat's got only nine lives. This'll be my tenth time."

"Cat!" they yelled. "Fraidy cat, you mean." Sam, red with shame, jumped into a flat rowboat with the others. They had found the boat deserted one day. It was their greatest treasure and they kept it hidden in a thick clump of reeds on the river bank. They rowed out to an island that was their next-to-favorite place. There they threw off their few clothes and all of them except Sam Clemens dived in. Sam stood a while and looked across the river to the banks of the opposite shore. "I wonder are there any runaway slaves now over there in those woods," he said to the boys splashing about in the water.

"Aw shucks," said Tom Blankenship, "that's Illinois, and anyway, they won't hurt us. Come on in."

"Wait till I finish my jawbreaker." Sam pointed to a lump in his cheek where a ball of molasses candy made him look as though he had mumps.

"Fraidy cat!" the boys yelled at him again. So Sam Clemens dived in. And this time he found that at last he could swim!

Sam was full of joy that day as he gathered driftwood and helped to build a fire on the island. They cooked fish and turtle eggs and roasted potatoes for supper and ate them all with relish. Afterward, when it got dark, they sat around their fire and watched a flatboat coming down the river. It had a round tent like an Indian wigwam in the middle. On the deck a bright fire burned and by its light they could see the dark figures of the boatmen moving around. The men were singing:

> Grasshopper sitting on a sweet
>   potato vine,
> Turkey came along and yanked
>   him from behind.

The boys joined in as loud as they could. "My," said Sam, "I'd like to go to New Orleans on one of those flatboats."

"Wouldn't we all," said the other boys.

The boat passed on and the river was dark and still. After awhile Sam noticed lights moving around their home place of Hannibal. "They're looking for us," he said. "Must be awful late. I reckon they think maybe we drowned."

At first the boys thought that was funny, but when they thought about how worried their parents must be, a pretty sad lot of boys rowed the boat back to shore. They knew there would be trouble for all of them, except for Tom Blankenship who didn't have a real home.

Sam's mother gave him a sharp tap on his head with her thimble. It hurt, but his father's shake of the head and sad look hurt more. Sam really tried to behave better after

that, but he just couldn't seem to manage it. He said it didn't come natural. So one day Sam played truant again. This time he went all alone to a cave he'd heard about. He went in carefully, but it was twisty-and-turny and dark, and bats flew over his head. There was a story about a slave running away who got lost in the cave and died.

"Maybe this is his ghost," thought Sam.

That very moment he heard footsteps behind him. They didn't sound right; they were too soft and slow. Sam tried to hurry, but there were so many turns, and it was all so dark, he didn't know which way to go. The footsteps kept on and Sam lost his head and began to run, anywhere, just so he could run. Then he heard a voice yelling. It was the familiar voice of Tom Blankenship. "You don't have to be afraid," called Tom. "That's only old Indian Joe. He won't hurt you."

Indian Joe was a poor little man who Tom said lived in the cave and didn't mind the bats. People said he even ate them.

The cave became the favorite place of the boys, even better than the island. Grown folks didn't know about it and many a time the boys hid there when the grown-ups were looking for them.

When Sam was twelve years old, his father died. The shock changed Sam and he was a different boy. He stopped his little-boy goings-on and thought of his mother's hard work and money worries. He wanted to help. He said, "You know, Mother, I'm not learning a thing at the school. Why, I know more about plants and birds and spiders than teacher does. She's scared of them. And the other things just don't sink in. I tell you, Mother, you let me go to work in Brother Orion's printing shop. I'll learn a lot there—spelling and writing and how to be a printer."

His mother sighed, but she gave in. Sam went to work in his brother Orion's printing shop. He learned a lot there. But the part he liked best was working on the newspaper that Orion published. It was here that Sam began to write stories.

But Orion's shop did not do well. Nobody around had much money and many people paid for their newspaper in vegetables, mostly turnips and cabbage. Sam got so fed up with them that he never would eat a turnip or cabbage again. He used to say that cauliflower was only cabbage with a college education and he wouldn't eat that either.

Once when Orion was away, Tom got a notion. He would try to amuse the readers with funny verses and stories in the newspaper. And sure enough everybody loved them. Sam was too shy to sign his own name; so he decided to make one up. The pilots on Old Man River dropped measuring lines into the water to see if it was deep enough for the boat to get through. Then they called out 'river pilots' words to tell the depth. One of their calls was "mark twain" which meant about four fathoms or twenty-four feet. Sam liked the sound of this, and from then on he signed the name Mark Twain to everything he wrote. And that's the name that boys and girls and kings and fathers and statesmen and presidents all over the world know him by to this day.

Sam's funny stories might have saved Orion's newspaper but Orion thought they weren't dignified enough; so he wouldn't have them. The paper made no money and Orion had to give it up. Sam was sorry, but it worked out all right for him because then he got his chance to carry out the dream of all the boys in Hannibal. To those boys the greatest heroes in the world were the pilots of the river boats. When the pilots blew their whistles everybody came running to the wharf. The boys looked up at the pilots sitting high in the wheelhouse, proud when they brought the boats safely to port through the restless waters of the mighty river.

Sam himself became a pilot when he was only sixteen, and from then on his life was rich with adventure. He saw the city of New Orleans where almost everybody spoke French. There he heard how men had discovered gold in California. And he set out for the West to find gold too and joined what we call the "Gold Rush." But that venture wasn't successful. If he discovered any gold, he lost it. He went back to working on a newspaper in the far West, and that was what he really loved. The West was dangerous country then, and Mark Twain wrote of the excitement he lived in. But always, no matter how dangerous, he could see something funny in it.

People in America began to read and like what he wrote, and soon his stories became popular all over the world.

He was famous and welcomed by important people everywhere. But his fame didn't keep him from being human. He worried about his mother back in Missouri. He remembered how hard she had worked when he was a boy, how she spun cotton and wove cloth for the family's clothes, how she sewed and cooked and baked, how she nursed them all, and how she helped to nurse neighbors when they were ill.

One time when he went home to see her, he said, "Mother, I want you to pick out a nice quiet place in the country where I can buy you a new house and you can have a good rest."

"I thank you, Sam," said his mother. "I'd like a comfortable house. But I don't want it to be in a quiet place in the country. I want to be on the busiest and noisiest street corner you can find because I want to watch people going by. When you are old, Sam, you want to see folks and lively doings. At least *I* do."

Mark Twain got his mother just the house she wanted and she sat at the window happily watching life go by.

Mark Twain's books were translated into every written language. Everywhere people begged him to come and talk to them. He went when he could, and with his white hair and the white suits he wore, he was a striking figure welcomed by grown-ups as well as children. He wrote many books on many subjects, but *Huckleberry Finn* and *Tom Sawyer*, the stories of his own boyhood, are still the favorites of boys and girls everywhere.

His own children adored him. When his daughter Susy was about ten years old, she wrote, "We are a very happy family. We consist of Papa, Mama, Jean, Clara, and me. Papa is a very good man and a very funny one. He *has* got a temper, but we all of us have in this family. And he is, oh, so absent-minded. He blows soap bubbles for us filled with tobacco smoke. There are eleven cats at the farm here now and our donkey Kiditchin. Papa's favorite is a little tortoise-shell kitten he has named Sour Mash.

"Papa rises about ½ past 7, writes, and plays tennis with Clara and me, and tries to make the donkey go. He started to ride Kiditchin to show us how, but Kiditchin threw him over her head. Papa thinks she didn't like the poem he wrote about her. Papa is known to the public as a humorist but he has much more in him that is earnest than that is humorous."

And so he had. But it is for his wonderfully humorous stories about boys that we remember him best.

He Had to Go to Bed by Day

ROBERT LOUIS STEVENSON

By Rosemary Nicolais

ROBERT LOUIS STEVENSON wrote stories and poems about children and for children all over the world. He was born in the beautiful city of Edinburgh in Scotland right in the middle of the last century. When he was a little boy, his mother and father called him Smoutie.

The word "smoutie" is Scottish for "little fish." Why little fish? Because that is what the Stevensons' little son looked like to them one day, squirming and wriggling to get upstairs in a great hurry at the age of only eight months.

His father was a famous builder of lighthouses. His mother came from a family of missionaries and merchants who were known for their brave deeds across the seas. On winter nights, red-faced bearded men of the sea visited the lighthouse-builder, Mr. Stevenson, at his house in Edinburgh. They filled the little parlor with pipe-smoke, and told tales of hair-raising adventure. They enchanted the little Smoutie—or Louis as he was called by this time. Sometimes when he lay in bed recovering from one of his many attacks of bronchitis, his mother would tell him about his wonderful uncles over the sea, or read about young David slaying the giant, or about the pilgrim, Christian, carrying his burden through the Slough of Despond up to the Gates of the Shining City.

And there was Cummy, his beloved nurse. Years later he dedicated to her his famous collection of poems, *The Child's Garden of Verses*, in which he wrote, remembering his pet childhood complaints:

> And does it not seem hard to you,
> When all the sky is clear and blue,
> And I should like so much to play,
> To have to go to bed by day?

Cummy was the best teller of tales of them all. Louis never forgot Cummy's stories. She made the old Scottish heroes come to life and fight again their fierce battles for freedom. She made the boy see the saints suffering again for their faith. Witches seemed to be hiding in the shadows of the room, fairies dancing in the woodlands.

Louis could be very brave even though his health was delicate. Once during a vacation with his parents he was climbing the rocks along a wild sea-coast. One of these rocks—the Black Rock—was very dangerous. Suddenly Louis noticed a boy smaller than himself caught on a slippery ledge halfway up the rock. He seemed unable to stand up or to climb either up or down. Without a moment's hesitation Louis made for the

ROBERT LOUIS STEVENSON. Writer of adventure stories and poems for children. Born in Edinburgh, Scotland, 1850. Traveled for his health in France and Belgium, 1876, 1879. Married Fanny Osbourne, 1880. Started on cruise from San Francisco to the South Seas, 1889. Settled in Samoan Islands. Wrote *Treasure Island, Kidnapped*, and other tales, and *A Child's Garden of Verses*. Died in Samoa, 1894.

opposite side of the rock and scrambled to the top. He threw himself on his face. The two boys could not even see each other

"Take hold of my hand," cried Louis, reaching one arm down as far as he could.

"I can't. I can't even stand up straight. There's no room for my feet."

"Yes, there is. Change your feet around. Put one foot where the other is."

The boy did what Louis told him and found he could stand firm. He raised his arm and grasped Louis' hand waiting for him.

"Now—you jump and I'll pull," said Louis. And the next moment the two boys stood together safe on top of Black Rock.

They became great friends during the rest of their vacation, and remained friends afterwards. Both grew up to be famous, Louis as a great writer and his friend as a judge.

As he grew older, Louis traveled a great deal and learned much about the various countries he visited. But he learned something deeper too—something he later expressed this way: "To travel hopefully is

a better thing than to arrive, and the true success is to labor."

He was now a tall graceful young man. He had big brown eyes and a quick smile. He liked to wear black velvet jackets and bright ties. He expected people to be friendly, so they were.

One evening at the end of a long day's canoeing on a river in France he tied up his boat and ran up a pathway to an inn where some friends of his were staying. Lightheartedly he jumped through the window to greet them. But the really important event of that night was the meeting between young Louis and Fanny Osbourne, the little dark-haired girl from America who was later to become his wife. What he thought of her we can see in the verse he wrote about her:

Trusty, dusky, vivid, true,
With eyes of gold and bramble-dew;
Steel-true and blade-straight
The great Artificer
Made my mate.

Without Fanny's loving care Louis would probably never have lived to write *Treasure Island*, the story about Long John Silver and Jim Hawkins, or the poem about the "little shadow that goes in and out with me." For he had to struggle all his life against attacks first of bronchitis and later of a more serious weakness of the chest. Fanny saw how the cold winds and mist and rain of Scotland made him cough, and as often as she could she hurried him away to the Alps or to the sunny coasts of the Mediterranean. The wonder was that he could still be gay, ill as he often was. He loved the world that was "so full of a number of things." And he was certainly a good deal happier than most kings. A friend once said of him that he "seemed to skip upon the hills of life," and all those who knew him agreed.

Treasure Island came to be written in a rather roundabout way. It started not as a story but as a map. Fanny's young son, Lloyd Osbourne, liked to draw and paint, and one rainy day in Scotland Louis drew a map to keep the boy amused. He told Lloyd to paint it.

"What shall we call it?" Lloyd asked when it was finished.

Louis suggested "Treasure Island."

They talked so much about this island that did not exist except in their own minds, that it began to be a real place to them, a place where real things might happen. And soon Louis was writing the story, a chapter a day. Fanny and Lloyd and Louis' parents would gather around after the supper table was cleared away, eager to hear what new exciting things had happened to the strange characters who had grown so familiar to them. That villain, Bill Bony—what was he so scared of? Who was the terrible blind beggar? And the one-legged man? What was in the oil-skin packet Jim Hawkins found in the sea-chest? "Sail!" says he. "We sail tomorrow!" Now they would hear where their friends sailed to—Squire Trelawny, the good doctor, and Jim, the cabin-boy.

Treasure Island was a great success. So was *Kidnapped* which he wrote soon afterwards, and *A Child's Garden of Verses*. His books were read in America even more than in England, and when Louis' father died he and Fanny decided to go to America to live, and to take Lloyd and Louis' mother with them.

What a welcome the little party received when the steamer *Ludgate Hill* arrived in New York Harbor. Louis had, as usual, to go to bed as soon as he reached the hotel, but that made no difference to his admirers. They swarmed up the stairs into his room —people who had read his books, people who wrote about them, newspapermen and ordinary people curious to see what the great Scottish writer looked like. And there he lay, propped up by pillows, laughing at the enthusiasm of his visitors and at himself for enjoying it all so much.

They stayed in America a year among their new friends. Then Louis became restless. He was always dreaming of finding life more wonderful just over the hill.

Fanny could read his thoughts. The sea was calling him, she knew. He was forever talking about sailing a boat over the blue seas under a blue sky and finding some beautiful island where they could live and be happy, where he would find health and write all the exciting stories that buzzed around in his head.

Fanny didn't like the sea. She sent him off to visit his friend Mark Twain, hoping he would forget about the sea. She said she would go to San Francisco for a while and look up some of her cousins there. It wasn't long before Fanny found herself wandering along the San Francisco Bay looking at the boats for sale. One day she wired Louis:

"Have found just the boat for a cruise to the South Seas. Shall I hire it?"

Louis wired back immediately "Yes" and hurried across the continent in a fever to see the wonderful boat Fanny had found.

The *Casco* was as beautiful as a bird. Its

new owners had to wait for a few repairs to be made to the masts and to engage a captain and crew. But the moment all was ready off they sailed into the Pacific, headed for the Marquesas Islands.

The voyage delighted Louis. He wrote to a friend in England, "Life is far better fun than people dream who fall asleep among chimney-pots and telegraph wires."

On their arrival at the Marquesas, the Island Queen paid them a visit and brought them gifts. At Tahiti, where they went next, a native Queen insisted upon herself nursing Louis through an illness.

They voyaged on among the islands delighted with the warm tropical skies and the long idle days on deck, enchanted by the courteous manners and strange customs of the natives. Captain Otis, master of the ship, overheard a Tahitian lady praying that her friends, the Stevensons, might have a safe voyage and "that the *masts* would be strong." This made him wonder whether the masts *were* strong. He inspected them and found them so rotted at the bottom that they could not have lasted through a storm. The lady's prayer had actually saved the *Casco* from shipwreck.

Their last voyage brought them to Samoa. And there in the little village called Apia they settled down. Everything about the place pleased them—the little straw huts like bee-hives, the golden sands, the palm trees, the beautiful distant mountain, Vaea, against the blue sky.

They built a fine house and painted it green and peacock blue. They made a garden and flew both the British flag and the American flag on their lawn. They found five streams close by and named their home Vailima, which in Samoan means *five waters*.

Soon the Stevensons had friends all over the island. And once more Louis was given a nickname. The Samoans called him "Tusitala" which meant *teller of tales*. He was more pleased by this new name than by any he had been called before.

The Stevensons lived in their South Sea Island for many happy useful years. Louis' dearest wish was to write always more truly and with greater understanding. He worked hard at it and succeeded; the last books he wrote were his best. He always wanted to see kindness and friendship and love triumph over hatred and envy and cruelty. He felt that he personally could not do much to make this possible; yet wherever he went across the world, kindness, friendship and love did seem to blossom and to make the world a little better place to live in.

We know that a simple Samoan native comforted himself as he lay suffering in a hospital by repeating over and over again the words, "I belong to Tusitala."

On the top of Mt. Vaea, within sound of the sea, a stone marks Louis' grave. His Samoan name, Tusitala, is carved on one side, and these characteristically courageous and serene words of his own are on the other:

Under the wide and starry sky,
Dig the grave and let me lie;
Glad did I live and gladly die,
And I laid me down with a will.

This be the verse you grave for me:
"Here he lies where he longed to be,
Home is the sailor, home from sea,
And the hunter home from the hill."